SOCIAL WRITING: PUBLICS, PRESENTATIONS, AND PEDAGOGIES

PERSPECTIVES ON WRITING
Series Editors, Susan H. McLeod and Rich Rice

The Perspectives on Writing series addresses writing studies in a broad sense. Consistent with the wide ranging approaches characteristic of teaching and scholarship in writing across the curriculum, the series presents works that take divergent perspectives on working as a writer, teaching writing, administering writing programs, and studying writing in its various forms.

The WAC Clearinghouse, Colorado State University Open Press, and University Press of Colorado are collaborating so that these books will be widely available through free digital distribution and low-cost print editions. The publishers and the Series editors are committed to the principle that knowledge should freely circulate. We see the opportunities that new technologies have for further democratizing knowledge. And we see that to share the power of writing is to share the means for all to articulate their needs, interest, and learning into the great experiment of literacy.

Recent Books in the Series

Laura R. Micciche, *Acknowledging Writing Partners* (2017)

Susan H. McLeod, Dave Stock, and Bradley T. Hughes, *Two WPA Pioneers: Ednah Shepherd Thomas and Joyce Steward* (2017)

Seth Kahn, William B. Lalicker, and Amy Lynch-Biniek (Eds.), *Contingency, Exploitation, and Solidarity: Labor and Action in English Composition* (2017)

Barbara J. D'Angelo, Sandra Jamieson, Barry Maid, and Janice R. Walker (Eds.), *Information Literacy: Research and Collaboration across Disciplines* (2017)

Justin Everett and Cristina Hanganu-Bresch (Eds.), *A Minefield of Dreams: Triumphs and Travails of Independent Writing Programs* (2016)

Chris M. Anson and Jessie L. Moore (Eds.), *Critical Transitions: Writing and the Questions of Transfer* (2016)

Joanne Addison and Sharon James McGee, *Writing and School Reform: Writing Instruction in the Age of Common Core and Standardized Testing* (2016)

Lisa Emerson, *The Forgotten Tribe: Scientists as Writers* (2016)

Jacob S. Blumner and Pamela B. Childers, *WAC Partnerships Between Secondary and Postsecondary Institutions* (2015)

Nathan Shepley, *Placing the History of College Writing: Stories from the Incomplete Archive* (2015)

Asao B. Inoue, *Antiracist Writing Assessment Ecologies: An Approach to Teaching and Assessing Writing for a Socially Just Future* (2015)

SOCIAL WRITING/SOCIAL MEDIA: PUBLICS, PRESENTATIONS, AND PEDAGOGIES

Edited by Douglas M. Walls and Stephanie Vie

The WAC Clearinghouse
wac.colostate.edu
Fort Collins, Colorado

University Press of Colorado
upcolorado.com
Louisville, Colorado

The WAC Clearinghouse, Fort Collins, Colorado 80523–1040

Printed for the WAC Clearinghouse by University Press of Colorado, Louisville, Colorado 80027

ISBN 978-1-64215-006-3 (PDF) | 978-1-64215-007-0 (ePub) | 978-1-60732-861-2 (pbk.)

Printed in the United States of America

Library of Congress Cataloging-in-Publication Data

Names: Walls, Douglas M., 1973– editor. | Vie, Stephanie, editor.
Title: Social writing/social media : publics, presentations, and pedagogies /
edited by Douglas M. Walls and Stephanie Vie.
Description: Fort Collins, Colorado : The WAC Clearinghouse, [2018]
Series: Perspectives on writing | Includes bibliographical references.
Identifiers: LCCN 2017059424| ISBN 9781607328612 (pbk.) | ISBN 9781642150070 (epub)
Subjects: LCSH: Social media—Authorship. | Social media—Psychological aspects.
| Authorship—Study and teaching (Higher) | Social media in education.
Classification: LCC PN4557 .S63 2018 | DDC 306.44—dc23 LC record available at
https://lccn.loc.gov/2017059424

Copyeditor: Don Donahue
Designer: Mike Palmquist
Series Editors: Susan H. McLeod and Rich Rice

This book is printed on acid-free paper.

The WAC Clearinghouse supports teachers of writing across the disciplines. Hosted by Colorado State University, and supported by the Colorado State Univeristy Open Press, it brings together scholarly journals and book series as well as resources for teachers who use writing in their courses. This book is available in digital formats for free download at wac.colostate.edu.

Founded in 1965, the University Press of Colorado is a nonprofit cooperative publishing enterprise supported, in part, by Adams State University, Colorado State University, Fort Lewis College, Metropolitan State University of Denver, Regis University, University of Colorado, University of Northern Colorado, Utah State University, and Western State Colorado University. For more information, visit upcolorado.com. The Press partners with the Clearinghouse to make its books available in print.

CONTENTS

PART 3: PEDAGOGY

ACKNOWLEDGMENTS

I would like to thank our contributors for their ideas, work, and patience. I have met many new friends and colleagues through this project and I am better for it. Thanks also to Stephanie Vie for working on the project with me. She will always have a better eye for details than I. I would also like to thank the support of the University of North Carolina and my colleagues in the Masters of Science in Technical Communication program. I could not ask for better support professionally. I would like to especially thank my wife, Leslie Wolcott, who has always encouraged me to take more risks professionally than I am inclined to. Her support and understanding are the intentional "stuff" of all the work I do.

—Douglas M. Walls

Thank you to all of the contributors for their support of this project and their excellent scholarship, which we are proud to see collected here. Thanks also to Douglas Walls for his dedication and commitment to this project. I appreciate the excellent copy editing skills of Rachel Molko, Heather Vazquez, and Jennifer Roth Miller, who all helped shape this project in numerous ways. And of course, no major writing project is possible without institutional and professional support. The Department of Writing and Rhetoric and College of Arts and Humanities at the University of Central Florida have always been so supportive of my scholarship in social media, and I appreciate it immensely. And to my husband Jeff Stockberger—thank you as always for understanding the often wacky aspects of being an academic, including working tirelessly into the night instead of heeding the siren song of Netflix and the comfy couch. Without your unwavering support, this book would not exist.

—Stephanie Vie

FOREWORD

AVAILABILITY MATTERS (AND SO DOES THIS BOOK)

William Hart-Davidson
Michigan State University

WRITING IS A TIME MACHINE

Writing is a time machine. It has always been a way to alter the constraints of space and time such that we humans might make available, to others and ourselves, ideas and the means to interact with these ideas: recall, view, edit or otherwise change, use, re-use, or share them. Texts afford that impressive list of interactions. This is writing as a technology, a thing invented by people.

The act of writing, then, is a deliberate move to engage the affordances of our time machine. This is true of the simple act of making a list of items for oneself to pick up at the grocery store, tagging a subway car with graffiti, or building a dictionary of definitions and their etymologies. It is true, too, of inscribing a thank-you card with a bon mot and penning a novel of genre fiction. We do each of these things to extend our ability to interact with others in time and space, to make something of ourselves available beyond the immediate moment and beyond the physical limits of human contact defined by an immediate moment.

This idea—availability—may be the least obsessed-over term by rhetoric scholars in Aristotle's famous definition of rhetoric from his treatise *On Rhetoric*: "the faculty of observing in any given case the available means of persuasion." And yet, if we consider it carefully for just a moment, in that one word lies much of the nuance of other essential terms of contemporary rhetorical thought that are not present in the definition: *context*, *situatedness*, *culture*, and even *power*. After all, what is and especially what is not available in a given time and place to one person is of tremendous import in any analysis of rhetorical activity. We may analyze these conditions in instrumental terms— "do you mean this place doesn't have Wi-Fi?"—or in socio-economic ones—"the fact that public meetings were held in a location without easy access to public transit limited the means by which affected citizens could voice opposition to the proposal." For Aristotle's place-based conception of rhetoric, availability can act like gravity or inertia, as a physical but invisible law that limits who can speak (no slaves or women allowed!) how, when, and where.

Availability matters. And, today, as an issue of rhetorical theory and rhetorical theorists, it might matter most of all. The reason is that we have a (relatively) new technology on the scene: network writing.

NETWORK WRITING IS A QUANTUM LEAP

Network writing (Jones, 2015) dramatically changes the foundations on which the act of writing is predicated. And it does so by scaling up and out—in a manner difficult to overstate—what it means to make ourselves and our texts become available to others, over time, across vast distances, (almost) instantaneously.

If writing is a time machine, we have for the most part in our theory and pedagogy of writing offered strategies for availability with a fairly linear and very slow understanding of time. Network writing introduces a quantum shift in how we must think about availability in the moment of composing, both in terms of the available means of persuasion (as Aristotle would have them) and the availability of others to whom we might connect to achieve our rhetorical aims. This latter group includes not only those people who we understand as our audience(s), but also those who we might count on to spread our message (willingly or not, consciously or not) and those we might enroll to help create it in the first place. In these space/time dynamics, we begin to see the import of availability for a wide variety of phenomena that, if not new, are suddenly much more matters of concern due to network writing, from trolling to trigger warnings.

But in writing studies, we are still wrapping our heads around what all of this might mean. And this is why I am so very grateful for the work Vie and Walls have assembled in this important collection. The pieces here help rhetorical scholars engage in an informed dialogue about the material conditions of network writing where they are most readily observable: in social networks. This is a timely collection.

Let me offer an example that shows how our sense of the affordances of time-travel—teaching students to use the time machine functions of writing—have been more H. G. Wells than Kurt Vonnegut in *Slaughterhouse-Five*. A few years ago now, the Writing in Digital Environments Research Center sponsored a national survey that captured a large, representative sample of the 2010 enrollment class in the United States. Nearly 3,000 students from all over the country and from different types of institutions of higher education responded to the survey. Demographically, our sample looked like the U.S. college student population in 2010. It was mostly young women. It was mostly white, but reflected a growing population of Hispanic and African American women. We asked this group of students questions about their writing lives, in particular what kinds of things they routinely wrote and what technologies they used to write.

We learned some fascinating things from this survey, but perhaps no single thing surprised our colleagues more than the most common writing instrument was their mobile phone. More often than they picked up a pencil or a pen, they would reach for their phone to do the kinds of writing they did the most: short, informal genres to connect with other people in their lives. But they also use them for every other kind of text they reported writing, from screenplays to reports. They weren't just sending LOLs to one another.

So it bears consideration: What does a mobile phone have that a pencil and paper do not? The answer: Mobile phones have dramatically improved affordances for making writing resources available. Mobile phones offer easier access to reference material as well as the previous writing students have done. And they make trustworthy, knowledgeable people easy to contact for advice and feedback. All of these are important things that speak to the quantum shift of network writing.

We still see teachers of writing banning mobile phones in classrooms. Why? Perhaps they fail to see how the mobile phone is not a tool for fooling around; instead, it represents the ability to compose with a vast array of human knowledge resources at one's fingertips and with other knowledgeable and trustworthy people at one's immediate disposal simply by hailing them. It represents that chance to engage invention as the thoroughly social act that we have been saying it is for decades now in composition studies. Sure, it also means that I can reply to a friend with just the right animated gif of Nicolas Cage saying a line from a campy film because OF COURSE that gif exists and I can send it from my phone to hers with just a few long presses of the screen. But the dramatic change here is that this clip is available to me. And that friends are available to one another, even if she is four time zones away in a sales meeting and I am at home on my couch.

WHAT MAKES DIGITAL OBJECTS AVAILABLE? OR WHY YOUR PHONE IS BETTER THAN A PENCIL

Because writing is spread out in time as we live it—laminated chronotopically as Paul Prior and Jody Shipka (2003) have said—phones are much, much more useful for writing than pencils are.

Everything you write with your phone is going to stand a chance of being found again. Everything can quickly and easily—even instantly—be moved to another composing space. It can be shared with others. It can be combined with another thing you wrote earlier without standing apart as two distinct texts . . .

that is, your phone can accommodate the relationships among texts that represent the larger things you are writing.

Another way to think about this is to say that everything we write with our phones has more of the features that make the resulting text "available" than anything we write with a pencil. So, you might ask, what makes a text more available? A text is more available if it is . . .

a. Digital, by which I mean numerically encoded. Why? Because we can perform computing operations to transform it and move it across disparate forms of networks: coaxial and fiberoptic and social.

b. Highly addressable (Witmore, 2010), by which I mean that rather than consisting of inscrutable wholes, texts are understood and represented as consisting of an array of pieces, each of which may be useful in combination or in isolation.

c. Well-indexed, by which I mean that each of those small pieces of text that may need to be available has a known, communicable location. Text messages are better indexed by these criteria than photos are, because we have stable, relative location information for every character (this is why you can highlight and select a passage by using copy/paste).

d. Easily reiterable, by which I mean that they exist in a format and a space that allows them to be copied, preferably in a non-destructive way (that is, in a way that leaves the prior version intact).

Network writing creates texts that are more available than non-networked. Sometimes vastly more available. And this has important, sometimes devastating and sometimes liberatory consequences. Availability matters.

MAKING OURSELVES AVAILABLE TO ONE ANOTHER

The primary focus of my work has been to explore the possibilities and the implications of increased availability for textual objects that result from network writing. The list of four features above is an attempt at a tidy synthesis of that work. I have written about what network writing does to teaching and learning writing, how it changes the work of writing (knowledge work), and how it changes the status of those who write in the knowledge economy. Many others have written about how network writing makes for new experiences of reading and composing. Indeed, the field of computers and writing has made this a central topic; Gail Hawisher et al. (1995) traced the origins of this conversation. And there is no doubt much more to come.

But I believe the most disruptive effects of network writing lie in the ways it permits humans to be available to one another when they are engaged in writing. If you have ever had your pulse quicken when you posted an emotionally charged comment on someone's Facebook wall with whom you disagree, you have a sense (or a sense memory) of what I am talking about.

With social networks in particular, we can be present with, to, and for one another in ways that are only just beginning to resolve for us as a cultural phenomenon. And yet in these spaces we are writing. Together. My colleague Jeff Grabill (2014) has called Facebook "possibly the biggest, most significant collaborative writing project in human history."

I have seen him say this to crowds of people and the reaction is a wave of emotion: bemusement at first, then something like fear both signaled by nervous laughter, then something like quiet assent or agreement signaled by the proverbial smattering of applause. In a few cases where writing teachers and researchers have made up a majority of the audience, there is a second reaction that comes later when the implications of this claim hit home. What if we took it seriously? What if we understood Facebook for what it empirically is: a huge, collaboratively authored, multi-modal ruckus of a text, reaching billions (with a B) of people every day? What if we took social media writing seriously?

And what if we don't?

William Hart-Davidson
Michigan State University
September 2015

REFERENCES

Aristotle. (350 BCE). *Rhetoric* (W. Rhys Roberts, Trans). Cambridge, MA: The Internet Classics Archive, MIT. Retrieved from http://classics.mit.edu/Aristotle/rhetoric.html.

Grabill, J. (2014). Texting is good for us or why we write more now than at any time in human history. *TEDx Lansing 2015*. Retrieved from http://wkar.org/post/watch -now-tedx-lansinged-2014#stream/0 .

Grabill, J., Hart-Davidson, W., Pigg, S., McLeod, M., Curran, P., Moore, J. & Brunk-Chavez, B. (2010). Revisualizing composition: Mapping the writing lives of first-year college students [White paper]. Retrieved from the WIDE Research Center.

Hawisher, G. E., LeBlanc, P., Moran, C. & Selfe, C. L. (1995). *Computers and the teaching of writing in American higher education, 1979–1994: A history.* Mahwah, NJ: Greenwood.

Jones, J. (2015). Network* writing. *Kairos: A Journal of Rhetoric, Technology, and Pedagogy, 20*(1). Retrieved from http://kairos.technorhetoric.net/20.1/topoi/jones /index.html.

Prior, P. & Shipka, J. (2003). Chronotopic lamination: Tracing the contours of literate activity. In C. Bazerman & D. R. Russell (Eds.), *Writing selves, writing societies: Research from activity perspectives* (pp. 180–238). Fort Collins, CO: The WAC

Clearinghouse and University Press of Colorado. Retrieved from https://wac.colo state.edu/books/selves_societies/ .

Witmore, M. (2010). Text: A massively addressable object. *Wine Dark Sea*. Retrieved from http://winedarksea.org/?p=926.

SOCIAL WRITING/SOCIAL MEDIA: PUBLICS, PRESENTATIONS, AND PEDAGOGIES

SOCIAL WRITING AND SOCIAL MEDIA: AN INTRODUCTION

Douglas M. Walls
North Carolina State University

Stephanie Vie
University of Central Florida

Worldwide, social media use has grown substantially since the initial days of these technologies in the late 1990s and early 2000s. Early sites like Classmates .com (originating in 1995) and SixDegrees.com (originating in 1997) had membership levels in the low millions—Classmates.com had 55 million members in 2002 (Perez, 2012), for example, and SixDegrees.com had over a million members in its early years (Barker, Barker, Bormann & Neher, 2012, p. 197). Once hugely popular, Friendster.com—which was founded in 2002 and released to the public in 2003—was copied by multiple other social media platforms hoping to capitalize on its popularity. At the time of its acquisition by MOL Global, Friendster had 115 million members (Fiegerman, 2014). In the early landscape of social media technologies, most sites served niche markets and struggled to keep users' attention. These tools had not yet been incorporated into our society as substantially as they have today.

Today, popular social media technologies measure their populations in the high millions to the low billions. Facebook, for instance, captured 1.79 billion monthly active users as of September 2016 (Facebook, 2016). Twitter has 313 million monthly active users who tweet 500 million times per day (Twitter, 2016). Even newer sites like Instagram, launched in late 2010, boast similar numbers: 500 million monthly active users, more than 95 million images and videos shared per day, and 4.2 billion likes on photos daily (Instagram, 2016). Social media technologies have become nearly ubiquitous in our culture, with the ability to tweet an online news link or send a funny picture to someone on Facebook simply a click away. Websites embed buttons to share and like information via Facebook, LinkedIn, Twitter, Pinterest and other social media sites; trending hashtags make their way into global news. People consult Yelp for new restaurant suggestions, post pictures of their food and pets to Instagram, curate dream boards for weddings and share household tips and recipes on Pinterest. The Associated Press even circulated a short glossary of Twitter terms in 2013 and offered Twitter chats with guest experts monthly that were then archived using another social media tool, Storify. In short, social media can be found nearly everywhere.

That is, social media use is not simply a phenomenon popular among teenagers; this stereotypical view of these technologies may have been true in their early days, but today, adults are also part of the social media landscape, with usage growing among all sectors, even those aged 65 and older. The Pew Research Center (2014) has noted that 74 percent of online adults use social networking sites as of January 2014. Most of these adults visit Facebook, which social media researcher Nicole Ellison has described as "a daily practice for many people . . . the default social site" (as cited in Weise, 2015). Teenagers, who go online almost constantly thanks to the ease of access that smartphones and tablets provide, participate in social media technologies nearly as often as adults. Teens aged 13–17 use a variety of sites, like Facebook (71%), Instagram (52%), Snapchat (41%), Twitter and Google+ (both 33%), Vine (24%), and Tumblr (14%) (Lenhart, 2015). And newcomers to the social media landscape are emerging all the time, with new apps and sites arising daily.

Participants in social media technologies enact a variety of literacy practices: Writing and composing more broadly through practices like hashtagging, captioning, constructing personal profiles, and other ways of writing oneself into being comprise a large amount of users' time in a social media site. Stacey Pigg et al. (2014) described these kinds of composing practices as reflecting the "rhetorical complexity of our social lives as they have become increasingly mediated by writing technologies" (p. 92). Through the writing activities they perform in social media technologies, students actively create literacy ecologies and thereby shape their social and personal lives (Pigg et al., 2014, p. 93). Thus we see Classmates.com and SixDegrees.com's millions of users giving way to the widespread and pervasive use of social media among billions of users worldwide today.

STUDYING SOCIAL MEDIA

The near-ubiquity of social media on a global scale allows scholars studying the impact of these technologies a fascinating glimpse at emergent composing practices. There are a myriad of composing activities taking place in social media and a rich variety of genres, audiences, stylistic choices, and pedagogical possibilities represented. Thus in this collection, we call for increased scholarly attention to the intersections of writing and social media platforms and tools in higher education. As Andrea Lunsford (2010) compellingly argued in an op-ed piece, "Our Semi-Literate Youth? Not So Fast," "these changes alter the very grounds of literacy as the definition, nature, and scope of writing are all shifting away from the consumption of discourse to its production." Because of this constantly changing landscape of social media, scholars in the field of writing studies are afforded rich sites for analysis, sites that offer us compelling questions, too, about the role of research and ethics in digital technologies such as these, the potential place of social media technologies in our pedagogy, and the future of activism and community-based efforts connected to social media.

But while recent scholarship abounds on multimodal and digital composition broadly (Ball & Kalmbach, 2010; Delagrange, 2011; Journet, Ball & Trauman, 2012; Palmeri, 2012), scholarship on social media is still developing within the field of writing studies. In this respect, our collection, *Social Writing/Social Media: Publics, Presentations, and Pedagogies*, builds on previous work articulating the role of multimodality in composition studies by extending ongoing conversations that have asked readers to expand notions of networked literacy in the twenty-first century. Our collection also offers something new to the field. It offers a more narrowly defined focus on social media and its platforms by examining the impact of social media on three writing-related themes: publics and audiences, presentation of self and groups, and pedagogy at various levels of higher education. The sixteen chapters in this collection pay attention to an undertheorized aspect of writing online—that is, the acts of composing that occur specifically in social media spaces—an aspect of writing that is both timely and compelling.

There are many ways that social media have impacted societies at a global level, but one of the more compelling moments in 2016 stands as an example of why examining social media composing is crucial moving forward. The 2016 U.S. presidential election was not the first time a presidential candidate leveraged the power of social media in his or her campaign—after all, Barack Obama was nicknamed the first "social media president" for his strategic use of social media technologies in his 2008 campaign (Schulman, 2016). However, the 2016 presidential election showcased social media's role in political campaigns today, illustrating that candidates today can tap into the networks of Twitter, Reddit, Facebook, and other social media technologies in ways that can upset traditional approaches to understanding political campaigning. President-elect Donald Trump continued his use of social media in the days leading up to his inauguration in ways previously unseen—to attack the press, to trumpet his achievements, and to air grievances. The 2016 presidential election placed social media front and center as a key player in the ability of a political candidate to garner votes. Within this context, Lunsford's discussion of social media's impact on literacy as a series of changes is even more compelling:

> If we look beyond the hand-wringing about young people and literacy today . . . we will see that the changes brought about by the digital revolution are just that: changes. [They occur] across a wide range of genre and media, away from individual "authors" to participatory and collaborative partners-in-production; away from a single static standard of correctness to a situated understanding of audience and context and purpose for writing.

The 2016 U.S. presidential election was just one moment that pointed to the need to pay further attention to social media and how composing in these technologies has the power to impact our world. Whether one's reaction to the election was shock, surprise, disgust, or joy, it is clear that social media composing—like it or not—is here to stay and has real, demonstrable influence on society in multiple and powerful ways.

ORGANIZATION OF THE COLLECTION

Social Writing/Social Media: Publics, Presentations, and Pedagogies is organized around three sections: social media and public audiences, social media and presentation, and social media and pedagogy. The sixteen chapters in this collection offer exciting and productive reflections on the roles of social media in public, professional, and pedagogical arenas. Here we have included a broad range of scholars, from graduate students to full professors, who themselves interact with social media in their personal and professional lives. Our hope is that this collection will open a space for continued research on social media and literacy in the twenty-first century, and that it will have a wide range of appeal for academics in rhetoric, composition, writing studies, and communication on an international level.

PART 1: PUBLICS AND AUDIENCES

The first section, social media and public audiences, focuses on the ways that social media are being used to develop and sustain writing-related efforts. Every social media technology has the potential attention of a broad public audience. Authors who use social media tools to compose have the reach of these tools to their advantage: With the billions of active daily and monthly users in popular social media technologies like Facebook, Twitter, Instagram, and others, composers can address a massive group of listeners—very rapidly at that—and, if desired, attempt to rouse them to action of some kind.

Indeed, it is social media's ability to reach broad audiences and rouse potential action that is at the heart of Section I of this collection. Since the beginning of

Western society, texts have organized and supported social activity. Too, rhetoric has been a foundational element of how citizens have discussed problems. The fact that social media and writing platforms continue that tradition, while at the same time altering it, should not come as a surprise to us (again, consider Lunsford's assertion that changes wrought by digital composing tools are just that—changes). As well, it is no surprise that as rhetoric and compositionists recommit themselves to the "public turn" (Mathieu, 2005; Sheridan, Ridolfo & Michel, 2012) that social media platforms, the dominant form of delivery that the public uses to discuss issues of activism and public trust, should take on greater importance in terms of writing studies research. After all, the role of rhetoric in digital contexts has, for some time, been a focus of the field (Eyman, 2015; Sullivan & Porter, 1997; Warnick, 2007), with scholars attending particularly to digital technologies and tools and their impact on writing and writing pedagogy.

Public authors today frequently use digital tools to seek to address social problems. As a result, scholars attend to the ways public authors engage in and across networked social writing platforms to achieve their goals. These examinations take on new urgency as writing, technological, and social networks influence and alter larger societal discourses and meanings. The nature of that alteration is still relatively new as network writing platforms like social media become part of activists' projects. Contrary to the popular cynical dismissal of hashtag activism as "slacktivism" (Gladwell, 2010), social writing platforms have played key roles in contemporary social movements of our time such as the Occupy movement (DeLuca, Lawson & Sun, 2012; Penney & Dadas, 2014), the #blacklivesmatter protests, #yesallwomen and other feminist projects (Dixon, 2014), and the Arab Spring of 2011 (Harlow & Johnson, 2011). Rather than dismissing this work as mere slacktivism, we counter that the composing practices that happen in social media can instead be forms of digital activism (Vie, 2014, 2015). This is but one example of how public authors and public audiences interact in social media technologies in ways that attract the interest of writing and rhetoric scholars, but as the chapters in this section illustrate, there are many other examples that are of interest.

Chapters in this section span various writing-related efforts in local, national, and global communities, from online activism to ethnographic research to fan service. Given our field's sustained interest in community-based learning and research, service learning pedagogies, and community and critical literacy efforts, this section draws from these theoretical areas to articulate methodologies, literacy practices, and other elements pertinent to rhetorical action in public social writing and activist projects. In "Hashtag Activism: The Promise and Risk of 'Attention,'" Caroline Dadas examines the ability of social media to call attention to challenging political issues that affect and coordinate global publics. Estee Beck

7

combines discussions of digital literacy and surveillance studies in "Sustaining Critical Literacies in an Age of Digital Surveillance" to tackle the role of literacy in the wake of the National Security Agency and big data collection. Tabetha Adkins uses her chapter, "Social Spill: Ethnographic Data Collection When Facebook is a Site of Activism," to examine public engagement on Facebook when corporations make the wrong rhetorical moves in engaging the public. Crystal Broch Colombini and Lindsay Hall address social writing, media attention, and collective problem-solving as forum publics responded to the housing crises and Great Recession of 2008 in "Networking Hardship: From Sharing Stress to 'Paying Forward' Success in LoanSafe Forum Interactions." Cory Bullinger and Stephanie Vie's "After a Decade of Social Media" looks broadly at the landscape of social media, examining two frequently forgotten groups: social media abstainers and ex-users. Finally, we close this section with Liza Potts writing about fan cultures' ability to generate and maintain publics through combined uses of both strategies and tactics. These chapters demonstrate the different ways that composers in social media use strategic rhetorical communication techniques to reach out to various publics, and in turn they examine the effects of those choices. In Section II, authors move away from a focus on the relationships between public-facing authors and the public audiences for which they compose, instead concentrating on the choices both individuals and groups make in social media technologies that affect how they are perceived by others. That is, Section II attends to the performance of identity in social media, looking at how writing plays a part in how we are able to represent our selves in these tools.

PART 2: PRESENTATION OF SELF, GROUPS, AND DATA

The second section is most concerned with discussions of how individuals and groups use writing to create, maintain, and reshape their presentations in social media spaces. Authors in this section examine how people use text specifically and multimodal composition more broadly to represent themselves to various audiences and for various purposes in composing profiles, News Feed posts, "likes," microblogs, pins, hashtags, and other writing in spaces like Facebook, Twitter, and Pinterest. This section examines specific aspects of performance (such as gender, sexual identity, race and ethnicity, group affiliation, and so on) within specific online and offline rhetorical situations. Authors in this section interrogate how individuals or groups use writing in social media to create, maintain, and reshape their identities in relation to others, and how data plays a role in such performances of identity.

Performance is the focus of the second section, and these chapters are particularly interested in interrogating the relationship between the performance of identity and the discursive tools offered in social media technologies. Today, robot vacuums (@SelfAwareROOMBA) have their own Twitter accounts. Pets have their own Facebook pages. At the same time, drag performers have been removed from some social media sites because of "real name" policies that require them to use the name assigned at birth rather than the name used by the performer. Native Americans who used their native language or alphabet, such as Cherokee, for their names have been accused of using fake names (Bogado, 2015). What these stories illustrate is that identity performances in social media spaces are intrinsically linked to both the structure of the tools themselves as well as other discursive forms of performance available in the sites. When robot vacuums have their own Twitter accounts, it is the performance of identity that supersedes any static sense of self.

And so authors in this section attend to "performances" rather than identities to displace the focus on individuals' subjectivities and instead embrace discussions of the nonhuman and the collective as well as the individual subject. That discussion begins with Bronwyn T. Williams' conversation about presentations across multiple mobile media formats in "Having a Feel for What Works: Polymedia, Emotion, and Literacy Practices with Mobile Technologies." In "Visualizing Boutique Data in Egocentric Networks," Douglas M. Walls finds new ways to present rhetorical activity in social network platforms around individuals. Amber Buck examines the presentation of professionalism for graduate students in "Grad School 2.0: Performing Professionalism on Social Media" by examining the construction of audience on the part of graduate students. Les Hutchinson engages issues of collective and nonhuman performances through queer and feminist rhetorical acts of inquiry in "Writing to Have No Face: The Orientation of Anonymity in Twitter." Kristin L. Arola asks a very different performance question in "Indigenous Interfaces" about what Facebook's interface might look like if it were designed with American Indian epistemological understandings in mind. Finally, Kara Poe Alexander and Leslie A. Hahner use their chapter to discuss "The Intimate Screen: Rewriting Understandings of Down Syndrome through Digital Activism on Instagram" as a personal yet public way to use images and social networks to direct a certain kind of action.

PART 3: PEDAGOGY

Finally, the third section questions how social media spaces are shaping and being shaped by educational issues related to writing studies. We have selected chapters that engage pedagogy at various educational levels, ranging from first-year composition to graduate courses to writing programs more generally and including distance education. This is the most overtly pedagogical section, but we have selected chapters that marry pedagogy and data-driven research (such as case study and survey-based approaches). Thus, this section is one that draws from educational research, classroom studies, and other theoretically based pedagogical discussions of the impact of social media on the field of writing studies.

Perhaps inevitably given rhetoric and composition's educational mandate at many institutions, much of the preliminary work in the field on social networks has focused on the impact social media discourses and technologies have had on traditional literacy education in the classroom. Early work forecasted the rise of network writing technologies. Along with the work of researchers like Gail Hawisher, Cynthia Selfe, Gunther Kress, and Charles Moran, authors like Sullivan and Porter (1997) were already asking questions such as, "Why have there been so few studies of wide-area network interaction, of cross-class interaction, or network interaction within the corporation?" (p. 57). Such education-centered questions point to the largest impact of network writing technologies on the classroom: the fact that "the classroom," as a contained writing ecosystem, soon would not be a self-contained writing ecology, if it ever was. To borrow a turn of phrase from contemporary information system discourse, extra-classroom writing technology disrupted the power dynamics, content, and traditional model of the writing classroom. Today, in the face of the ubiquitous writing technology that is social media, we must ask how writing teachers should address it. For good (we think) or for ill, social media is a part of every writing classroom, whether sanctioned or not.

Thus, this section features scholars who attend specifically to the incorporation of social media into pedagogy. The first chapter, "A Pedagogy of Distraction: The Impact of Media Use on the Writing Process," from Patricia Portanova tackles the omnipresent question of distraction in the writing classroom, asking how digital distractions impact the writing process and product. Her analysis provides compelling evidence that teachers should not shy away from incorporating digital technologies into their teaching simply for fear of distracting students or pushing them to multitask to the detriment of their writing. In Lilian W. Mina's chapter, "Social Media in the FYC Class: The New Digital Divide," readers are provided a specific focus on first-year writing through a mixed-method study of social media in this context. Arguing for the informed and critical use of social media in writing classes, Mina asserts that social media use in first-year composition is one way to fight against digital divide issues. Like Mina, Michael J. Faris also offers a data-driven study of social media, this time in an upper-division writing class. His chapter, "Contextualizing Students' Media Ideologies and Practices: An Empirical Study of Social Media Use in a Writing Class," provides an analysis of literacy practices and understandings of those practices that complicates our understandings of students' uses of social media in meaningful ways. Finally, Chris M. Anson's chapter, "Intellectual, Argumentative, and Informational Affordances of Social Media: Bridging Public Forum Posts and Academic Learning," attends to the field's interest in studying students' extracurricular composing practices through a descriptive study of public forum posts in sites like YouTube and Reddit. Separating students' extracurricular composing practices from the writing occurring in the classroom may prevent us from seeing exciting opportunities for developing different dimensions of students' literacies.

CONCLUDING THOUGHTS

It is our hope that readers will find in this collection a series of essays that ask the kinds of critical questions needed at this juncture. That is, social media have been (for quite some time now) part of the fabric of our lives. But as with many new technologies, it often takes a while for us to be able to step back, assess the tool's impact, and consider what's next. This collection offers one of the first sets of scholarly work in our field that responds to social media's influence on both popular and extra-curricular writing as well as scholarly communication. Too frequently, social media is dismissed as non-academic, unworthy of sustained attention by researchers. The authors featured here present compelling reasons why this oft-neglected form of writing deserves—and demands—continued academic response.

REFERENCES

Ball, C. E. & Kalmbach, J. (Eds.). (2010). *RAW (Reading and writing) new media.* Cresskill, NJ: Hampton Press.

Barker, M. S., Barker, D. I., Bormann, N. F. & Neher, K. E. (2012). *Social media marketing: A strategic approach.* Mason, OH: South-West/Cengage.

Bogado, A. (2015). Native Americans say Facebook is accusing them of using fake names. Retrieved from https://www.colorlines.com/articles/native-americans-say -facebook-accusing-them-using-fake-names.

Delagrange, S. (2011). *Technologies of wonder: Rhetorical practice in a digital world.* Logan, UT: Computers and Composition Digital Press/Utah State University Press.

DeLuca, K. M., Lawson, S. & Sun, Y. (2012). Occupy Wall Street on the public screens of social media: The many framings of the birth of a protest movement. *Communication, Culture & Critique, 5*(4), 483–509.

Dixon, K. (2014). Feminist online identity: Analyzing the presence of hashtag feminism. *Journal of Arts and Humanities, 3*(7), 34–40.

Eyman, D. (2015). *Digital rhetoric: Theory, method, practice.* Ann Arbor, MI: University of Michigan Press.

Facebook. (2016). Company info. Retrieved from http://newsroom.fb.com/company-info/.

Fiegerman, S. (2014, February 3). Friendster founder tells his side of the story, 10 years after Facebook. Retrieved from http://mashable.com/2014/02/03/jonathan-abrams -friendster-facebook/#FznuWRQ7Riql.

Gladwell, M. (2010, October 4). Small change: Why the revolution will not be tweeted. *The New Yorker*. Retrieved from http://www.newyorker.com/magazine /2010/10/04/small-change-malcolm-gladwell.

Harlow, S. & Johnson, T. (2011). Overthrowing the protest paradigm? How *The New York Times*, Global Voices and Twitter covered the Egyptian revolution. *International Journal of Communication, 5*, 1359–1374.

Instagram. (2016). Press news. Retrieved from https://www.instagram.com/ press/?hl=en.

Journet, D., Ball, C. & Trauman, R. (2012). *The new work of composing*. Logan, UT: Computers and Composition Digital Press/Utah State University Press.

Lenhart, A. (2015, April 19). Teens, social media, and technology overview 2015. *Pew Research Center*. Retrieved from http://www.pewinternet.org/2015/04/09/teens -social-media-technology-2015/.

Lunsford, A. (2010). Our semi-literate youth? Not so fast. *Stanford study of writing*. Retrieved from https://ssw.stanford.edu/sites/default/files/OPED_Our_Semi -Literate_Youth.pdf.

Mathieu, P. (2005). *Tactics of hope: The public turn in English composition*. Portsmouth, NH: Boynton/Cook.

Palmeri, J. (2012). *Remixing composition: A history of multimodal writing pedagogy*. Carbondale, IL: Southern Illinois University Press.

Penney, J. & Dadas, C. (2014). (Re)Tweeting in the service of protest: Digital composition and circulation in the Occupy Wall Street movement. *New Media & Society, 16*(1), 74–90.

Perez, S. (2012, June 11). Classmates.com parent United Online acquires school-focused friend finder SchoolFeed. Retrieved from http://techcrunch.com/2012/06 /11/classmates-com-parent-united-online-acquires-school-focusedfriend-finder -schoolfeed/.

Pew Research Center. (2014). Social networking fact sheet. Retrieved from http:// www.pewinternet.org/fact-sheets/social-networking-fact-sheet/.

Pigg, S., Grabill, J. T., Brunk-Chavez, B., Moore, J. L., Rosinski, P. & Curran, P. G. (2014). Ubiquitous writing, technologies, and the social practice of literacies of coordination. *Written Communication, 31*(1), 91–117.

Ridolfo, J. & DeVoss, D. (2009). Composing for recomposition: Rhetorical velocity and delivery. *Kairos: A Journal of Rhetoric, Technology, and Pedagogy, 13*(2). Retrieved from http://kairos.technorhetoric.net/13.2/topoi/ridolfo_devoss/index.html.

Schulman, K. (2016). The digital transition: How the presidential transition works in the social media age. Retrieved from https://www.whitehouse.gov/blog/2016 /10/31/digital-transition-how-presidential-transition-works-social-media-age.

Sheridan, D. M., Ridolfo, J. & Michel, A. J. (2012). *The available means of persuasion: Mapping a theory and pedagogy of multimodal public rhetoric*. Anderson, SC: Parlor Press.

Sullivan, P. & Porter, J. (1997). *Opening spaces: Writing technologies and critical research practices*. Westport, CT: Ablex.

Twitter. (2016). It's what's happening. Retrieved from https://about.twitter.com /company.

Vie, S. (2008). Digital divide 2.0: "Generation M" and online social networking sites in the composition classroom. *Computers and Composition, 25*(1), 9–23.

Vie, S. (2014). In defense of "slacktivism": The Human Rights Campaign Facebook logo as digital activism. *First Monday, 19*(4). Retrieved from http://firstmonday.org /ojs/index.php/fm/article/view/4961/3868.

Vie, S. (2015, March). *The Human Rights Campaign Facebook logo*. Retrieved from http://civicmediaproject.org/works/civic-media-project/thehumanrightscampaign facebooklogo.

Warnick, B. (2007). *Rhetoric online: Persuasion and politics on the World Wide Web*. New York, NY: Peter Lang.

Weise, E. (2015, January 19). Your mom and 58% of Americans are on Facebook. *USA Today*. Retrieved from http://www.usatoday.com/story/tech/2015/01/09/pew -survey-social-media-facebook-linkedin-twitter-instagram-pinterest/21461381/.

PART 1: PUBLICS AND AUDIENCES

CHAPTER 1

HASHTAG ACTIVISM: THE PROMISE AND RISK OF "ATTENTION"

Caroline Dadas

Montclair State University

On May 24, 2014, the hashtag #yesallwomen emerged on Twitter in response to a killing spree in Isla Vista, California. The gunman left behind a video, widely circulated on social media, in which he claimed that his hatred of women spurred his rampage. The day after the killing spree, people took to Twitter to engage in what has come to be known as hashtag activism: the attempt to use Twitter's hashtags to incite social change. Through its rapid circulation, the resulting hashtag #yesallwomen sought to call attention to the misogynist roots of the Isla Vista tragedy, emphasizing that yes, all women suffer from a culture that rewards men's aggressive behavior toward them. By using the hashtag, Twitter users enacted a desire to redirect media coverage toward the systemic misogyny that allegedly inspired this rampage.

#Yesallwomen stands as only one example within a broader movement to use hashtags for directing attention to social and political causes. Beginning with the Occupy Wall Street movement (during which "hashtag activism" came into popular use), hashtags such as #kony2012, #justicefortrayvon, #bringbackourgirls, and #notyourasiansidekick have sought to bring attention to race, class, and gender-based injustices, often garnering mainstream media coverage. Regardless, critics have charged that simply bringing attention to a cause remains a vague and ineffective political goal; as David Carr (2012) put it, "Another week, another hashtag, and with it, a question about what is actually being accomplished." In the case of the #kony2012 campaign, for example, concerns arose about outsider Americans presuming that they know how to best address events in another country. In response, this chapter focuses on attention as the motivating force behind several instances of hashtag activism. I have limited my scope to Twitter because the hashtags that I discuss originated on that platform. While other social media platforms such as Facebook and Instagram have hashtag capabilities, Twitter is the source of the particular hashtags that I examine.

Using Sara Ahmed's (2006) work on orientation toward objects, I position hashtag activism as an effort that simultaneously draws attention to a cause and obscures important facets of the cause such as historical background or socio-political context. I am deviating from Ahmed's application by using this framework to study non-objects (e.g., socio-political environments, constructions of gender); doing so, I believe, highlights the flexibility of Ahmed's insight that attention inevitably also implies concealment. While #bringbackourgirls and #kony2012, in particular, have been credited with bringing media and governmental attention to injustices that had been largely ignored, these same instances of hashtag activism exemplify how "some things are relegated to the background in order to sustain a certain direction; in other words, in order to keep attention on what is faced" (Ahmed, 2006, p. 31). The "things relegated to the background" in these cases include the complex socio-political environments in Nigeria and Uganda, respectively, of which many hashtag users had only a cursory knowledge. While little debate emerged about whether the kidnapped girls in Nigeria should be returned home or that guerilla leader Joseph Kony should be brought to justice for war crimes, critics have argued that hashtags in general tend to oversimplify the contexts of the injustices they describe (Gay, 2013; Goldberg, 2014; Murphy, 2013). In short, the complex politics, histories, and economics that led to these injustices cannot be reduced to a hashtag. In this chapter, I employ Ahmed's concept of attention as a framework for considering the repercussions of backgrounding important context when we use hashtags to bring publicity to a social cause. I then provide an overview of Twitter as a network that enables both broad and fast circulation among actors. After analyzing the cultural and political contexts surrounding both #bringbackourgirls and #yesallwomen, I offer suggestions for engaging in hashtag activism in ways that take advantage of the affordances of Twitter while also negotiating the constraints of this approach to activism. Ultimately, I argue that those engaging in hashtag activism need an understanding of the political and historical context of the issue(s) they are describing; an awareness of how rhetorical velocity and remix might affect their tweets; and a willingness to include links to reputable news stories in their tweets, in addition to other factors.

TWITTER AS A NETWORKED, CIRCULATORY PLATFORM

During the past few years, scholars have interrogated the purposes for which people have used Twitter. Recent scholarly texts have explored Twitter as a method for circulating information during a disaster (Bowdon, 2014; Potts, 2013), as a way for companies to market their services (Ferro & Zachry, 2014), as a space for community building (Wolff, 2015), and as a site of activist gestures (Dixon, 2014; Loken, 2014; Loza, 2014). Twitter users represented in this literature range from Toni Ferro and Mark Zachry (2014), who detailed how companies utilize the platform in their marketing campaigns, to William Wolff (2015), who catalogued an in-depth corpus of Bruce Springsteen fans' Twitter activity related to a particular concert. More central to the focus of this chapter, Kitsy Dixon (2014), Meredith Loken (2014), and Susana Loza (2014) all identified the uses of hashtags (particularly #bringbackourgirls and #solidarityisforwhitewomen) for activist purposes to alert Twitter users to instances of misogyny and racism. This chapter builds on this foundational scholarship regarding hashtag activism while also drawing on frameworks established by rhetoric and composition scholars such as Liza Potts (2013), who detailed how Twitter served as a critical platform for communicating in the immediate aftermath of the 2008 Mumbai attacks. In her study of social media and disasters, Potts offered four stages of how social media participants create knowledge: problematization, interessement, enrollment, and mobilization. The first two terms refer to the lead actors' defining of the event and their efforts at encouraging more participants to accept their definition(s) via consistent hashtags (or "immutable mobiles"). The network becomes further stabilized during enrollment, when actors accept the definition of the space by contributing additional content, and finally through mobilization, when knowledge is effectively and efficiently disseminated. Potts' study offers a useful framework for understanding the rapid circulation of knowledge on social networks—particularly in critical moments such as disasters, when accuracy is paramount. Potts' study only references hashtags as organizational devices, however; she cites examples such as #mumbai, #eqnz (for the 2011 New Zealand earthquake) and #Japan (for the 2011 tsunami) to illustrate the capacity of Twitter to efficiently catalogue information. Aside from using hashtags as organizational devices, Twitter users may also harness them to advocate for causes. While Potts' framework proves useful in describing how a particular hashtag becomes stable, we in writing studies and technical communication need to further account for the particularities of hashtag use as an activist gesture (see also Kara Poe Alexander and Leslie Hahner's chapter in this collection).

The capacity for a hashtag's broad reach stems from the way Twitter is structured. In their work on networks, Lee Rainie and Barry Wellman (2012) have articulated how our personal networks—the direct and indirect relationships we maintain via social media—organize how we engage with information. Their description of how information circulates on Twitter emphasized the speed and ease with which people can advocate for a cause:

> The many bridges between Twitter clusters means that chains of information from one Twitter follower to a follower of that follower and so on encompass about 83 percent of all Twitter users within five steps of interconnection. On average, about half of the people on Twitter are only four links away from each other. Of course, not all followers retweet each message—or even look at them—but the news spreads quickly. While messages usually get read and retweeted by those who speak the same language, they cross substantial distances, a mean of about 1,540 kilometers (955 miles). (p. 55)

In particular, the notion that "83 percent of all Twitter users [are] within five steps of interconnection" illustrates how a topic can reach a broad audience, considering the potential for retweets. The speed at which a concept (such as a hashtag) can circulate among various audiences eclipses face-to-face networks that require more time and personal connection between actors. Today's social media networks are more dispersed, fluid, and informal, thereby generating great potential for a message to circulate broadly, thereby finding a sizable audience.

While the connection between actors represents one aspect of networked communication, the movement of information between those actors remains equally important. David Sheridan, Jim Ridolfo, and Anthony Michel (2012) have emphasized the importance of circulation in public rhetoric, arguing that composers must give issues of circulation equal consideration as other rhetorical features. In fact, they equate an understanding of circulation with success as a rhetor:

> Our contention is that *all* successful public rhetoric is successful only if it effectively negotiates the material-cultural challenges of circulation . . . composers' decisions *anticipate* future considerations of distribution. Processes of circulation inform both the material and the symbolic considerations of composing. The moment of circulation inhabits the moment of composition. (pp. 63–64)

In order for a hashtag to gain traction on Twitter, composers must consider an issue such as brevity; the hashtag must be short enough so that future participants will have plenty of space to add their own messages within the 140-character limit (p. 85). Conversely, failure to consider how the hashtag might be employed in future use could hamper its circulation. In his study of tweets about President Obama's healthcare reform, John Jones (2014) detailed how using multiple hashtags in a tweet allows users to connect multiple networks, also called "switching." Doing so illustrates the power of placing various networks into contact with each other. An understanding of how networks function via hashtags, how tweets might be recontextualized by others, and how a writer must be able to utilize brevity to her advantage are all tactics that savvy Twitter users must learn to implement.

Twitter remains unique in its emphasis on concision, thereby increasing the circulatory potential of its messages (tweets). In addition to the brevity of tweets, the retweet function also encourages the rapid spread of information. In this sense, Twitter appears well designed for the project of garnering attention to a cause. The retweet function illustrates Jim Ridolfo and Danielle DeVoss' (2009) concept of rhetorical velocity, which they described as "the strategic theorizing for how a text might be recomposed (and why it might be recomposed) by third parties, and how this recomposing may be useful or not to the short- or long-term rhetorical objectives of the rhetorician." Retweeting allows for another party to repurpose the original tweet, including additional information or altering its context; users may also simply retweet a message in its original form without altering it in any way. As Liza Potts and Dave Jones (2011) have argued, the retweeting function holds considerable value because it allows writers to spread their message beyond their immediate network:

> Retweeting can mean that some participants might see the same message multiple times if they are following both the tweet's originator and the person retweeting. It also means that the message may reach other participants who do not follow the tweet's originator. (p. 343)

By retweeting a message, a Twitter user can spur a tweet's velocity by circulating it beyond the author's visible network (people s/he is following or is followed by). In this sense, the rhetorical velocity of a tweet can ensure broad readership in a short amount of time. The ability to embed short URLs enables Twitter users to encourage their followers to read further about the context of a hashtag or brief argument—all while staying within the constraints and generic expectations of the platform. Knowing when and how to include articles about a topic constitutes a kind of social media literacy that helps protect against uninformed tweeting.

The two hashtags that I focus on in this chapter, #bringbackourgirls and #yesallwomen, both illustrate how a keen understanding of social media's functionality can yield thousands of participants in a short period of time. I chose these two hashtags not only because of the high number of times they have been used on Twitter, but also because they both gained mainstream media attention (which speaks to gaining attention for a cause). While I touch on the hashtags' effectiveness—whether they accomplished their stated goals—I primarily focus on how their broad circulation brought attention to particular aspects of the respective issues they represented. I also trace some of the unintended results of such attention, in addition to the important contextual elements that became backgrounded as these hashtags logged thousands of tweets.

#BRINGBACKOURGIRLS: A WORTHY AND OVERSIMPLIFIED CAUSE

One of the more compelling examples of using a hashtag for activist purposes, #bringbackourgirls emerged in response to the April 14, 2014, abduction of 276 girls from a school in Nigeria. The perpetrators, a militant group named Boko Haram, object to the education of women, their name literally meaning "Western education is a sin" in the Hausa language. In July 2014, 63 of the girls escaped captivity; the rest have never been heard from again. In the immediate aftermath of the abduction, few outlets in the mainstream media even mentioned the tragedy. In early May 2014, *Salon*'s Mary Elizabeth Williams publicly wondered, "Why is the media ignoring 200 missing girls?" (as cited in Taylor, 2014). On April 25, 2014, Ramaa Mosley, a film director in Los Angeles, first tweeted the hashtag #bringbackourgirls to bring attention to the event (Dixon, 2014). By April 30, 200,000 tweets per day contained this hashtag (Taylor, 2014).

Figure 1.1. Pope Francis participates in #bringbackourgirls.

Because the hashtag sought to publicize the girls' abduction, the effort reached beyond Twitter to other social media platforms such as Facebook, where people could be seen holding a sign with the hashtag written on it. Mainstream media coverage soon followed—some focusing on the abduction itself and others on the resulting social media phenomenon. In his May 6, 2014, *Washington Post* article, Adam Taylor bemoaned the incident's initial lack of media attention. He then explained,

> In the past few days, however, the situation appears to be
> different. Not only is the story a major news item, but, on

Tuesday, the United States pledged to send a team, including military personnel, intelligence and hostage negotiators, to help find the girls. So what changed? Although there are no doubt many other factors in the visibility of the Nigerian girls' story, one factor does stand out: the remarkable rise of #BringBackOurGirls.

As Taylor indicated, the United States soon offered military assistance to Nigeria to aid in the recovery of the schoolgirls. What remains unclear is whether the #bringbackourgirls publicity contributed to the government's decision. The "you" implied in the declarative sentence #bringbackourgirls could include both the United States and the Nigerian governments. According to *Time*, Nigerian President Jonathan "waited two weeks before speaking publicly about the attack. He also rebuffed immediate offers of help from the U.S. and U.K." (Walt, 2014). Indeed, many people who participated in the hashtag appeared motivated by the hope that they might shame government officials into taking more decisive actions toward a rescue. Regardless of whether the hashtag inspired them to search more aggressively for the schoolgirls, it was likely that Nigerian government officials at some point learned of the hashtag and of its participants' collective outrage.

From the perspective of effective circulation, the #bringbackourgirls hashtag achieved a stunning amount of publicity. The ability for participants to coordinate with each other—to tweet about the event in a concentrated period of time, building on each other's insights—also likely factored into the significant media attention. If the purpose of the hashtag was to bring attention to a cause, the hashtag's participants were successful. But to what end? As a July 7, 2014, *Time* headline read, "#Bringbackourgirls still hasn't brought them back." The fact that the majority of the kidnapped girls remain to be found stands as a stark reminder that attention does not necessarily lead to action. Or, perhaps, that action does not necessarily bring about the desired result. Although #bringbackourgirls offered an opportunity for many people to learn about the tragedy in Nigeria, it simultaneously backgrounded the broader context of why this incident happened—and why it has been so difficult to find the missing girls and bring their captors to justice. While it is impossible to know how many hashtag participants knew of the current political and economic state in Nigeria, the hashtag encouraged Twitter users to distill the situation's broader context into a pithy command. In her work on orientations toward objects, Ahmed (2006) addressed the capacity of technology to shape experience: "Technology (or techne) becomes instead the process of 'bringing forth' . . . The object is an effect of 'bringing forth,' where the 'bringing forth' is a question of the determination of form: the object itself has been shaped for something, *which means it takes the shape of what it is for*" (italics original; p. 46). If we consider the hashtag as an object, it was "brought forth" in particular ways via Twitter: as concise, decontextualized, urgent. The tragedy ultimately took the shape of something that must have "attention brought to," not something that must be carefully researched. Considering that many uses of the hashtag included little more than the phrase itself, participants in these cases were not encouraged (via a link to a news story, for example) to research the situation in any depth. Gaining a fuller understanding of the incident would require moving beyond the ways in which the incident was being brought forth to audiences on Twitter.

Additionally, the phrasing of the hashtag positioned the missing girls in problematic ways. According to Meredith Loken (2014),

> While laudable in effort, scope, and reach, #BringBackOurGirls reproduces the problematic narratives of women as rights-deserving only through their capacity to be claimed. In one circulated image, a protest sign reads, "#BringBackOurGirls, our sisters and daughters deserve better." . . . This dualistic construction of women as worthy of political recognition due to their relationship to a more privileged agent works power-fully in the age of hashtag activism through its ability to draw emotional response . . . however, this imagination also risks infantilization and positions women as full political and social actors only through their potential as property. (p. 1100)

The phrasing of the hashtag exemplifies Ahmed's claim that objects takes the shape of what they are for—in this case, locating the girls. Simultaneously, this phrasing conceals the missing girls' capacity to be seen as fully-realized, independent people who deserve their freedom irrespective of how they are related to others. Thus, the hashtag bears traces of imperialism and paternalism.

While our actions as social media participants are never determined (Feenberg, 1991), the case of #bringbackourgirls shows how easy it can become to support the cause of bringing attention to an unjust scenario while never delving deeper into the economic and political complexities that gave birth to it. In circulating the hashtag, many participants assumed that increased attention in itself was productive. But some participants failed to consider the full range of repercussions that might result from an increased media focus. According to Nigerian American author Teju Cole, "'Part of the horror was that the girls were ignored,' Cole wrote. 'An opposite problem now is CNN's heavy sensationalist interest'" (as cited in Taylor, 2014). Sensationalism carries nota-ble repercussions for Nigerians, who have long experienced a corrupt military and a low standard of living. The process of bringing attention often proceeds without acknowledging factors such as these. For example, on May 5, 2014, traders in Lagos shut down several major markets in protest over the missing girls; following the economic losses, Patience Jonathan—the president's wife—ordered the arrest of the lead protesters and claimed that the kidnappings were a fabrication meant to diminish her husband's power. Though impossible to say whether publicity from the hashtag contributed to these events, leaders in the government have experienced considerable pressure from within and outside of the country—and have reacted in ways intended to bolster the power of the government above all.

While it is not possible to make a pronouncement about whether #bringbackourgirls did more harm than good, we must remain cautious when using the considerable reach and speed of social media merely to bring attention to a cause. Yes, the schoolgirls' kidnapping needed to be publicized more quickly and widely than it was in those first weeks after the incident. But simply circulating #bringbackourgirls without acknowledging the socio-economic complexities of Nigeria results in backgrounding critical information (information that also might help explain why the girls have not yet been rescued). It remains important to be aware of "the background" because, as Ahmed (2006) claimed, the background is often made so for a reason:

> We can think, in other words, of the background not simply in terms of what is around what we face, as the "dimly perceived," but as produced by acts of relegation: some things are relegated to the background in order to sustain a certain direction; in other words, to keep our attention on what is faced. (p. 31)

If bringing attention to the incident required brevity and decontextualization, then it is easy to see how more comprehensive details about the kidnappings would be omitted. But in offering an oversimplified version of events, we might unwittingly create additional turmoil.

#YESALLWOMEN: CONSCIOUSNESS-RAISING AND ITS REPERCUSSIONS

Only a month after the #bringbackourgirls hashtag found broad circulation, another widely-publicized hashtag emerged: #yesallwomen. As with #bringbackourgirls, this hashtag found its exigence in a specific event. Unlike the more time-sensitive goal of locating the kidnapped schoolgirls, #yesallwomen advocated for the elimination of structural and systematic misogyny. Spurred by the previously mentioned Isla Vista shooting, #yesallwomen argued that all women have experienced misogynist treatment by men. Sasha Weiss (2014), among many others, argued in the popular press that everyday instances of misogyny contribute to an environment in which some men find violence an appropriate reaction to rejection by women:

> Perhaps more subtly, [#yesallwomen] suggests that [the killer] was influenced by a predominant cultural ethos that rewards sexual aggression, power, and wealth, and that reinforces traditional alpha masculinity and submissive femininity. (This line of thought is not intended in any way to make excuses for Rodger's murderousness, but to try to imagine him as part of the same social world we all live in and not as simply a monster).

Weiss, along with others who used the hashtag, interpreted the Isla Vista shootings as a kairotic moment to address socially-sanctioned aggression toward women. Four days after the hashtag was first used, participants tweeted #yesallwomen over 1.2 million times (Grinberg, 2014), arguably making it more successful—from a circulation standpoint—than #bringbackourgirls.

Although past instances of online activism have often targeted fellow women as a community-building effort, participants in #yesallwomen sought to broaden their audience base in sophisticated ways. According to Emanuella Grinberg (2014), the hashtag accomplished the rare feat of espousing feminist perspectives while achieving mainstream appeal: "While most feminist-driven Twitter campaigns preach to the choir, #YesAllWomen has succeeded in drawing the mainstream—including men—into the conversation . . . More unique is the conversation's focus on misogyny and its negative impact on women and men." At the same time, a feminist reading would critique the notion that women's concerns only achieve validation when they affect men. In terms of circulation, however, offering a connection to men's well-being enabled the hashtag to be tweeted on a broad scale. For some participants, doing so meant pointing out that four of the shooter's victims were men. Others made the argument that fathers should be concerned about the repercussions of misogyny for both their daughters and sons. By perceiving men as core audience members for this message, the hashtag exceeded the reach of previous online feminist activism.

While some men participated in the hashtag, tweeting their own thoughts about the treatment of women, others resented the call to action. Within days of #yesallwomen's circulation, the hashtag #notallmen made the argument that men were being unfairly targeted as a homogenous group of women-haters. Those who participated in the #notallmen hashtag argued that because they personally had not committed violence against women, they should not be implicated in a male culture that mistreats women. Additionally, some men claimed that they objected to being associated in any way with the Isla Vista shooter. Such arguments were met with tweets and responses in the popular press that critiqued the denial of personal responsibility (see Figures 1.2 and 1.4). Participant Karin Robinson composed one of the more widely circulated tweets in response to #notallmen (see Figure 1.3), pointing out that even though not all men mistreat women, all women still have to live with the constant threat of violence:

Figure 1.2. One example of how #yesallwomen supporters reacted to #notallmen.

Figure 1.3. #yesallwomen participant @karinjr (2014)
pointing out the flawed logic of #notallmen.

Figure 1.4. A male #yesallwomen participant defends the hashtag.

The #notallmen hashtag played into arguments that have been used against feminists for decades: that sexism is largely a fiction forwarded by a feminist agenda; that calling attention to misogynist behavior constitutes "reverse sexism";

and that only a small minority of men mistreat women, making misogyny an issue of personal responsibility instead of a structural, historical pattern of behavior. Those who objected to the #notallmen hashtag cited these arguments and others to point out how women's concerns often become purposefully derailed.

In fact, the appropriation of hashtags frequently occurs for purposes counter to the hashtag's original intent. Cultural critics, among others, have pointed out the tendency for hashtags that critique racial and gender-based inequalities to be quickly co-opted. Trudy, whose blog addresses black women, art, media, social media, socio-politics, and culture, makes a similar argument:

> The constant pilfering of Black culture and ideas in social media . . . has become a behavior so common and pathetic that even as Black people are participating in a hashtag on any given day, we already expect the content to be exploited and stripped of context within minutes or hours, not days. (Gradient Lair, 2014, para. 6)

In the case of #yesallwomen, a hashtag designed to speak back to patriarchal notions about women became used as fodder in long-standing arguments about alleged men-hating women and the damage that they inflict.

Soon after the hashtag was established, debates about #yesallwomen moved beyond Twitter, finding their way onto a #yesallwomen Wikipedia page. Numerous contributors to the page charged that the descriptive history of the hashtag amounted to "misandry" and subsequently edited the page to say so. According to Kate Dries' (2014) account,

> In some instances, Wiki contributors have made edits to the page to give it a more "neutral point of view," noting that despite edits, "It's still kind of a giant pile of feminist propaganda." Others have made changes because they allege that the page contains/ed lots of "misandry."

The above charge of neutrality positions a male perspective as the default perspective. Additional perspectives are marked as Other, detailing imagined plights and unreasonable demands. In other words, because the hashtag itself alleged misogyny, it was not being neutral (as if neutrality was ever a desired outcome of activism). Rather than attending to the concerns raised by the hashtag, some of the Wikipedia authors sought to situate it as "feminist propaganda." A sizable number of people have shared this opinion, considering that a current Google search for #yesallwomen yields the phrase "#yesallwomen is bullshit" as the fifth most-searched option. While the hashtag in itself does feminist work, the urge to rewrite the history of the hashtag represents a recent example of how activism for women's rights continues to be pushed to the margins, as has histor- ically been the case (Ritchie & Ronald, 2001). In this respect, some users seem to be using Wikipedia as a platform for silencing women's voices, particularly when those voices point out misogynistic behavior. As the page undergoes con- stant revisions—even years after its establishment, indicating sustained attention on the part of some contributors—a look at the revision history reveals how articulations of women's concerns undergo frequent contestation, their mere articulation threatening to some.

Both the #notallmen hashtag and the charges of misandry on Wikipedia reflect an attempt to relegate women's concerns to the background in order to keep attention focused on issues considered more important (by some). In the case of #notallmen, those who participated in the hashtag objected to the idea that violence toward women—often positioned as a marginal issue that only concerns a minority of women and men—was no longer being relegated to the background, as it so often is. The increased attention, via the Twitter hashtag, posed a potential threat to supposedly more important issues that involve the populace at large. Such a perspective, however, not only underestimates the per- vasiveness of violence against women (and its negative implications for men) but also assumes that the public's attention exists in finite quantities: If we spend too much time talking about #yesallwomen, then other issues will lose out. Richard Lanham (2007) has addressed our recent cultural shift from an econ- omy of goods to an economy of information, arguing that because we are inun- dated with information, the ability to garner attention holds significant value. While Lanham positions style as the new currency in this information economy, Twitter—a platform on which a thousand followers is not unusual—demon- strates how attention is increasingly perceived in quantitative terms. For some, the attention that #yesallwomen received, measured in tweets and retweets, became a threatening commodity.

While the criticism of hashtags as slacktivism have been well rehearsed in the popular press, feminist-oriented hashtags such as #yesallwomen have gen- erated a significant amount of interest both within the feminist community and from audiences who do not identify as such. Perhaps the most notable example of social-media-based debates among feminists occurred when Twitter users critiqued a 2013 report entitled *Feminist Futures*, authored by Vanessa Valenti and Courtney Martin, by tweeting under the hashtags #FemFuture and #SolidarityisforWhiteWomen (Loza, 2014). At issue was the perception by some that the report privileged the role of white feminists at the expense of women of color. The ensuing debate illustrates the dialogue that can happen (not all of it positive) when voices that have been silenced for decades within the feminist movement—those of women of color, genderqueer individuals, working-class women, and those who identify as having a disability—find a platform to speak candidly. Adam Banks (2006), for example, has written about "the ways cyberspace can serve as a cultural underground that counters the surveillance and censorship that always seem to accompany the presence of African Americans speaking, writing, and designing in more public spaces" (p. 69). While Banks made this observation in the same year that Twitter was founded, more recently others in the popular press have written about the role of black Twitter as a vibrant and valued cultural space for often-marginalized voices (McDonald, 2014). Similarly, when challenges such as #notallmen surface, communities can find the experience of speaking back to the hashtag helpful in terms of coalition-building and intra-community dialogue. In her examination of the #yesallwomen hashtag, Kitsy Dixon (2014) argued, "What's important to understand in the online discussion community of Twitter and other social media formats is the grounding of community being formed through identity as a 'feminist' and emotions shared with the collective group." From this perspective, counter-arguments—as offensive as they can be—can serve to refine the purpose and (re) direct the attention of a loosely-organized group. The strong reactions that the #yesallwomen hashtag generated suggest that consciousness-raising does carry considerable consequences.

Perhaps the evidence of people feeling threatened indicates a capacity for hashtag activism to effect change. As the examples in this chapter show, establishing causality between a hashtag and significant, timely change remains difficult. But the strong reactions of people opposed to a hashtag such as #yesallwomen signals that attention may have value in itself. Activist Suey Park, the woman behind the #notyourasiansidekick and #cancelcolbert hashtags, has argued that before change occurs, a significant number of people must become aware of the injustice at hand:

> I was struck realizing how a shift in historical consciousness
> was necessary before any large social movement. For me,
> hashtags are a way to use a tool created for corporate brand-
> ing and use it for base building and consciousness raising. (as
> cited in Yandoli, 2014)

Here, Park alludes to the subversive nature of hashtag activism: Repurposing a corporate advertising technique by using hashtags to critique social inequalities. She also makes a distinction between the hashtag as the activist moment and the hashtag as a tool that can help bring about the activist moment. In other words, a hashtag does not (and cannot) comprise the entirety of a movement. While Park's hashtag #notyourasiansidekick garnered 50,000 tweets from over sixty countries, she responded to questions about the hashtag's material consequences by tweeting, "This is not a trend, this is a movement. Everybody calm down and buckle down for the long haul, please" (Loza, 2014). In the years since her hashtag trended globally, Park has joined 18 Million Rising, a grassroots Asian American advocacy group (Loza, 2014). Park's actions demonstrate how one of the most well-known hashtag activists in recent years acknowledges that even effective uses of online advocacy should be used in conjunction with a grassroots component.

MAXIMIZING THE PROMISE OF ATTENTION

As both #yesallwomen and #bringbackourgirls have shown, hashtags can prove a valuable resource through their ability to bring attention to a cause; at the same time, they also run the risk of oversimplification by backgrounding important contextual information. The risks of this activism should not dissuade participants from using hashtags to bring publicity to their cause, however. Like any form of public activist work, hashtags require a critical awareness of audience, context, and purpose. In particular, Ahmed's work on attention reminds us that what comprises the background has been placed there in order to keep attention focused elsewhere; backgrounding is an active process of exclusion. With that in mind, we as hashtag participants (and social media users in general) need to be cognizant of what is being concealed when we advocate for increased attention to a cause. The costs of not doing so can significantly temper any good that increased attention might bring.

Being more aware of the background also means developing a more critical, well-rounded socio-political perspective. For example, in the case of #bringbackourgirls, some participants used the hashtag as an opportunity to comment on United States foreign policy, complicating the argument that the United States should intervene in Nigeria based on the horrific nature of the kidnappings. When Michelle Obama posed with #bringbackourgirls written on a sign, users remixed the image by altering the writing on the sign (see Poe Alexander and Hahner's chapter in this section on the use of photographic-based argument and hashtags on Instagram). In one striking example, the new text read, "My husband has killed more Muslim girls than Boko Haram ever could." The designer of this remix made the point that while #bringbackourgirls directed many U.S. citizens' attention to violence committed against girls in Nigeria, we have largely excused our own president's use of violence via his drone attacks. This critique implicated the many users who forwarded the unaltered Michelle Obama photo, suggesting that they need to think more critically about the circumstances in which people across the globe become victims of violence. While comparisons between Boko Haram and Barack Obama require more detailed justifications than the image could provide, calling attention to the number of lives that each has allegedly ended represents an incisive rhetorical strategy. Drawing on Ridolfo and DeVoss' theory, the representatives of the Obama administration responsible for this photo failed to account for rhetorical velocity. The remixed #bringbackourgirls sign undermined Michelle Obama's attempt at boosting the hashtag's underlying message in addition to causing #bringbackourgirls to lose some traction. Whoever in the White House's communication office authorized this image of Obama made her (and President Obama, by implication) vulnerable to the remixing efforts of anyone with photo-editing capabilities. This incident remains representative of both the complex nature of navigating social media networks and also the ability for social media users to call attention to previously backgrounded contexts.

Hashtag participants, then, need to compose with an anticipation of rhetorical velocity, keeping in mind that future participants will add their own content to a hashtag and perhaps even remix it. When online memes and other forms of communication are remixed, they often spread more widely than if they remain the same throughout their circulation due to their identification with multiple audiences (Vie, 2014). In seeking to advance an argument, writers also need to consider who/what might be excluded by a hashtag that advocates a particular course of action. While most would argue that #bringbackourgirls voiced a noble cause, participants varied dramatically in their opinions about how that goal should be accomplished. What struck one participant as a straightforward rationale for rescuing the kidnapped girls struck another participant as a conflicted perspective in light of current U.S. policy. In Stephanie Vie's (2014) examination of online memes, she argued that users should investigate the original intent of a meme before they spread/remix it; that argument can be extended to claim that hashtag participants should be aware of the origins of their particular hashtag, as well as its multiple iterations. Doing so reflects a technological literacy that acknowledges the practices of remix and rhetorical velocity: an understanding that online arguments can be repurposed quite rapidly. Vie acknowledged that because memes—and similarly, hashtags—must circulate quickly in order to be effective, "a tension will likely remain between the swift transmission and rapid peak of Internet memes spreading and the careful attention required to critically assess political campaigns, companies, and causes before supporting them." While this tension will likely persist, gaining a broader awareness of the historicity of a hashtag and all its variations can offer hashtags activists a broader, more nuanced perspective than they might otherwise have.

In the present fractured media landscape, social media users need to be proactive in not only seeking out opinions different than their own, but also in gathering the contextual information that often gets ignored. As mentioned earlier, linking to a reliable news story represents one way of encouraging other participants in a hashtag to develop a deeper understanding of an issue. Other social media platforms such as Facebook may be more well-suited in this respect, as users have more space on that interface to provide details about a story. The capability to embed concise URLs means that even on Twitter, however, a participant can incorporate a link in addition to a hashtag and her own brief message in one tweet. With a link, audiences have the option of reading the longer news story after their attention has been attracted by the hashtag. This kind of composition requires an anticipation of how misunderstandings might occur on a platform such as Twitter, which privileges brevity. For example, in 2014 *The Colbert Report* tweeted a racially insensitive remark without indicating that the comment was part of that night's satiric take on racially insensitive remarks. Having included a link to clips from the show may have provided important contextual information to readers and averted some of the outrage. Dan Zarrella's (2012) findings complicate this scenario; however, as he found, "there is no correlation between retweets and clicks. In fact, 16.12 percent of the link-containing tweets I analyzed generated more retweets than clicks, meaning many people will retweet a tweet with a link without even clicking on that link." The pressure to compose quickly in a social media environment means that some people do not read all of the content that they circulate. Zarrella suggested that users counter this tendency by composing concise tweets (between 120 and 130 characters), trying different link placement in tweets, and experimenting with timing, word choice, and other factors. In short, a good deal of strategy factors into the effective, responsible circulation of content on social media platforms. While the use of activist hashtags can focus readers' attention, we should also seek to acknowledge that which falls beyond the field of attention: politics, historical context, competing arguments.

The cases of #bringbackourgirls and #yesallwomen demonstrate that increased attention to a cause via a social network may carry significant repercussions. In light of these and other recent examples, those of us who use Twitter for activist purposes need to consider Twitter more seriously as a platform for composition. Doing so means thinking more carefully about who is excluded and how misunderstanding might occur. While the platform itself encourages speed and brevity, we can still compose in such a way as to include information that will make our activism more meaningful. Additionally, we should address effective techniques for circulating messages on Twitter in our classes, particularly in professional writing courses. Whether in activist or workplace contexts, students should be aware of the tactics needed to use social media for purposes other than socializing. Finally, scholars in rhetoric and composition need to continue to theorize how composition on social media represents a rich site of rhetorical activity in a variety of contexts. Only through continued study will we gain a better sense of how massive grassroots efforts such as #blacklivesmatter seek to address deep-seated structural inequities through, among other methods, a social media campaign.

REFERENCES

Ahmed, S. (2006). *Queer phenomenology: Orientations, objects, others*. Durham, NC: Duke University Press.

Banks, A. J. (2006). *Race, rhetoric, and technology: Searching for higher ground*. Mahwah, NJ: Lawrence Erlbaum.

Bowdon, M. A. (2014). Tweeting an ethos: Emergency messaging, social media, and teaching technical communication. *Technical Communication Quarterly, 23*(1), 35–54.

Carr, D. (2012). Hashtag activism, and its limits. *The New York Times*. Retrieved from http://www.nytimes.com/2012/03/26/business/media/hashtag-activism-and-its -limits.html?pagewanted=all&_r=0.

Cho, E. [EugeneCho]. (2014, May 26). Don't hate the #yesallwomen hashtag. Hate that it has to even exist. Hate the injustice of gender inequality. Hate violence against women. [Tweet]. Retrieved from https://twitter.com/EugeneCho/status /470954496823398400.

Dixon, K. (2014). Feminist online identity: Analyzing the presence of hashtag feminism. *Journal of Arts and Humanities, 3*(7). Retrieved from http://theartsjournal.org /index.php/site/article/view/509/286.

Dries, K. (2014). There's a battle going on over the Wikipedia page for #yesallwomen. Retrieved from http://jezebel.com/theres-a-battle-going-on-over-the-wikipedia -page-for-y-1586704111.

Feenberg, A. (1991). *Critical theory of technology*. New York, NY: Oxford University Press.

Ferro, T. & Zachry, M. (2014). Technical communication unbound: Knowledge work, social media, and emergent communicative practices. *Technical Communication Quarterly, 23*(1), 6–21.

Francis, P. [Pontifex]. (2014, May 10). Let us all join in prayer for the immediate release of the schoolgirls kidnapped in Nigeria. #BringBackOurGirls. [Tweet]. Retrieved from https://twitter.com/Pontifex/status/465189535672832000.

Gay, R. (2013). Looking for a better feminism. Retrieved from http://www.npr.org /blogs/codeswitch/2013/08/22/214525023/twitter-sparks-a-serious-discussion -about-race-and-feminism.

Goldberg, M. (2014). Feminism's toxic Twitter wars. *The Nation*. Retrieved from http://www.thenation.com/article/178140/feminisms-toxic-twitter-wars.

Gradient Lair. (2014, April 20). Buzzfeed's cultural appropriation and infantilization of Black colloquialisms. Retrieved from http://www.gradientlair.com/post/83350005 053/fuck-buzzfeed-fuck-whites-who-appropriate-black-culture.

Grinberg, E. (2014). Why #yesallwomen took off on Twitter. Retrieved from http://www.cnn.com/2014/05/27/living/california-killer-hashtag-yesallwomen/.

Jones, J. (2014). Switching in Twitter's hashtagged exchanges. *Journal of Business and Technical Communication, 28*(1), 83–108.

Lanham, R. (2007). *The economics of attention: Style and substance in the age of information.* Chicago, IL: University of Chicago Press.

Loken, M. (2014). #BringBackOurGirls and the invisibility of imperialism. *Feminist Media Studies, 14*(6), 1100–1101.

Loza, S. (2014). Hashtag feminism, #solidarityisforwhitewomen, and the other #femfuture. *Ada: A journal of gender, new media, and technology.* Retrieved from http://adanewmedia.org/2014/07/issue5-loza/?utm_source=rss&utm_medium=rss&utm_campaign=issue5-loza.

McDonald, S. S. N. (2014). Black Twitter: A virtual community ready to hashtag out a response to cultural issues. *The Washington Post.* Retrieved from http://www.washingtonpost.com/lifestyle/style/black-twitter-a-virtual-community-ready-to-hashtag-out-a-response-to-cultural-issues/2014/01/20/41ddacf6-7ec5-11e3-9556-4a4bf7bcbd84_story.html.

Murphy, M. (2013). The trouble with twitter feminism. from http://feministcurrent.com/8403/the-trouble-with-twitter-feminism/.

Plait, P. (2014). #YesAllWomen. *Slate.* Retrieved from http://www.slate.com/blogs/bad_astronomy/2014/05/27/not_all_men_how_discussing_women_s_issues_gets_derailed.html.

Potts, L. & Jones, D. (2011). Contextualizing experiences: Tracing the relationships between people and technologies in the social web. *Journal of Business and Technical Communication, 25*(3), 338–358.

Potts, L. (2013). *Social media in disaster response.* New York, NY: Routledge.

Rainie, L. & Wellman, B. (2012). *Networked: The new social operating system.* Cambridge, MA: Massachusetts Institute of Technology Press.

Ridolfo, J. & DeVoss, D. (2009). Composing for recomposition: Rhetorical velocity and delivery. *Kairos: A Journal of Rhetoric, Technology, and Pedagogy, 13*(2). Retrieved from http://kairos.technorhetoric.net/13.2/topoi/ridolfo_devoss/intro.html.

Ritchie, J. & Ronald, K. (Eds.). (2001). *Available means: An anthology of women's rhetoric(s).* Pittsburgh, PA: University of Pittsburgh Press.

Robinson, K. [karinjr]. (2014, May 25). No, #NotAllMen are violent against women, but #YesAllWomen have to navigate a world where those who are look the same as those who aren't. [Tweet]. Retrieved from https://twitter.com/karinjr/status/470523930353352704.

Sheridan, D. M., Ridolfo, J & Michel, A. J. (2012). *The available means of persuasion: Mapping a theory and pedagogy of multimodal public rhetoric.* Anderson, SC: Parlor Press.

Taylor, A. (2014). Is #bringbackourgirls helping? *Washington Post.* Retrieved from https://www.washingtonpost.com/news/worldviews/wp/2014/05/06/is-bringbackourgirls-helping/?utm_term=.b874b62d5a2b.

Vie, S. (2014). In defense of "slacktivism": The Human Rights Campaign Facebook logo as digital activism. *First Monday, 19*(4). Retrieved from http://firstmonday.org /ojs/index.php/fm/article/view/4961/3868.

Walt, V. (2014). Nigerians critical of government's slow kidnappings response. *Time*. Retrieved from http://time.com/95558/nigeria-kidnappings-government/.

Weiss, S. (2014). The power of #yesallwomen. *The New Yorker*. Retrieved from http:// www.newyorker.com/culture/culture-desk/the-power-of-yesallwomen.

Wolff, W. I. (2015). Baby, we were born to tweet: Springsteen fans, the writing practices of *in situ* tweeting, and the research possibilities for Twitter. *Kairos: A Journal of Rhetoric, Technology, and Pedagogy, 19*(3). Retrieved from http://kairos.technor-hetoric.net/19.3/topoi/wolff/index.html.

Yandoli, K. L. (2014). Do hashtags count as activism? Retrieved from http://www .buzzfeed.com/krystieyandoli/do-hashtags-count-as-activism.

Zarrella, D. (2012). New data indicates Twitter users don't always click the links they retweet. *Where marketers go to grow*. Retrieved from http://blog.hubspot.com/blog /tabid/6307/bid/33815/New-Data-Indicates-Twitter-Users-Don-t-Always-Click-the -Links-They-Retweet-INFOGRAPHIC.aspx.

CHAPTER 2

SUSTAINING CRITICAL LITERACIES IN THE DIGITAL INFORMATION AGE: THE RHETORIC OF SHARING, PROSUMERISM, AND DIGITAL ALGORITHMIC SURVEILLANCE

Estee Beck

The University of Texas at Arlington

What does *sharing* mean in social media? Is the sharing of thoughts, videos, music, and other such digital compositions the sole purpose of sites like Facebook, Twitter, and SnapChat? Does sharing content with others imply a type of digital self or identity? Do social media companies also share in user-generated content by providing a space for people while at the same time taking and collecting metadata about their online activities? And, if this is the case, how do these companies share user metadata with advertisers and other third parties, like governments and large corporations? What is the role social media companies have in sharing how they benefit from user-generated data? Are these sites helping to sustain divisions in face-to-face relations because people reach for a screen during uncomfortable moments? Or, might it be true that these social media websites bring people closer together since people broadcast their lives to others on a regular basis?

Granted, social media encourages people to share information, to be digital citizens who comment on cultural, social, and political concerns in global and local communities. At the same time, many social media websites mine individuals' log data and web histories (albeit designed as a "personalized" experience) for billions of advertising revenue. On the surface, the opt-in rhetoric of *sharing*—connecting, networking, and supporting others—encourages people to engage with the proprietary and template-driven design to bring people together, not drive them apart. In many ways, the relationships people and social media sites forge rests upon a prosumer model of interaction. As people produce and consume content in Web 2.0 spaces, they also become the users and products of social media because of the range of data tracking and surveillance technologies monitoring and recording user actions. The larger issue at stake with *sharing* in social media arises from contrary models of sharing from a prosumer perspective and the opaque, but oftentimes invisible, hand of capitalism. Sharing—built on ownership and control—allows for reciprocity, trust, and at its best, altruism. Yet, despite the best intentions of Silcon Valley's attempt to capitalize on the rhetoric of sharing, a dark side reveals itself through capitalistic exploits of unpaid labor of its users and digital algorithmic surveillance to persuade people to certain actions and beliefs both online and off.

By examining the convergence of prosumerism as a response to shifts from the industrial era to the information era, and by briefly considering how rhetoric and composition scholars and the ideology of the open-source movement contend with prosumerism as a model without financial gain, I suggest that market-driven prosumerism will continue to thrive in the digital information age. However, I argue that it is up to educators, especially writing teachers, to sustain critical literacies in their classrooms in service of connecting, and possibly subverting, the market-driven prosumerism for an exchange benefiting humankind without financial incentive. Why do I make this argument? I believe the connection is important for writing teachers to make as oftentimes writing courses provide students with the means to consider possibilities for positive change to policy, procedure, and values—all with the power to enact such change through writing. One way we might facilitate such an opportunity is through a civic education by asking students to closely attend to the ideological freight in our online lives and spaces. However, it is first helpful to dive into historical considerations of prosumerism, then move to how such a model plays out on social media spaces with digital algorithmic surveillance—or how companies use mathematical formulas to track what people do online—to understand the larger role of writing teachers may play with critical literacy and civic education.

PROSUMERISM FROM THE INDUSTRIAL TO INFORMATION ERA

Prosumerism developed in the 1980s through American writer Alvin Toffler's 1980 work *The Third Wave,* wherein he described civilization's development in three waves: the agricultural revolution (first wave), the industrial revolution (second wave), and the information age (third wave). Each wave advanced and expanded as distinct political, economic, and social apparatuses to increase the social order, organization of activities for the common public, and sustainability of labor. For example, in the first wave, "land was the basis of economy, life, culture, family structure, and politics" (p. 21) with clear divisions of labor among the various classes in societies, and with many people assuming the role of a jack-of-all-trades. The second wave expanded on the foundation of the common public by introducing mass industrialization and consumption, introducing skilled laborers, and centralizing governments and economies. The third wave synthesized the labor practices of the first and second waves with consumers performing the tasks of specialized laborers (e.g., a grocery self-checkout lane places the labor of scanning and bagging groceries upon the buyer instead of relying upon the skilled labor and knowledge of a grocery store checkout clerk). Additionally, the function of labor in the third wave assumes a do-it-yourself ethos based on the notion that people can fulfill many of their everyday tasks as empowered individuals. Consequently, corporations, businesses, and non-profits outsource labor to consumers with the hype of self-reliance, adaptation to changes, and educational resilience for learning how to make and create products without compensation for labor. Thus, the prosumer is a person who produces labor to consume goods and services that are also available in the marketplace. IKEA's build-your-own furniture, self-service gas pumps, automated teller machines (ATMs), store-purchased medical kits (diabetes, pregnancy, etc.) are just a handful of examples of prosumerism. While many of Toffler's ideas are rooted in the historical and cultural mechanisms of his day (e.g., he makes mention of refrigerators with 1-800 numbers for people to call to repair their products on their own), much of what he forecasted has become commonplace in the information age. Currently, millions of people in high-technology cultures live in the third wave and are prosumer citizens.

With the development of the do-it-yourself culture in the 1980s, and the evolution of the World Wide Web turned Internet in the 1990s, prosumerism has expanded in scope from Toffler's early contributions. In straddling the shift from the industrial revolution to the information age during the 1980s, prosumerism congregated around the labor practices of products and services from the industrial era before moving into online spaces. With the rapid development of old media (telephones, televisions, and their corresponding networks), information distribution began a de-centralization process during this period. This development fostered the spread of DIY culture through various communication channels, periodicals, radios, telephones, and televisions through paid advertisements. The first home pregnancy test advertisement appeared in *Mademoiselle* magazine in 1978 (National Institute of Health, n.d., p. 7). And, Service Star Hardware aired a 30-second spot in 1982 promoting their do-it-yourself discounted items available in their stores (Service Star, n.d.). Gradually advertisements featured products and services promoting consumer labor as a way to save time and money. In the case of do-it-yourself culture, self-help books and information saturated bookshelves during the 1980s and 1990s, and big-box retailers promoted ways for consumers to build and create at home instead of relying on craftsperson labor. When the World Wide Web came into existence in 1994, the infancy of the network allowed people to create static websites using HTML; however, subscription-based companies like CompuServe, Prodigy, and America Online helped popularize the Web for people. From 1994 to 1999, the Web experienced rapid growth; companies, governments, and organizations latched onto online spaces and began commercializing websites with advertisements. Most of the early adopters of online advertising, especially for websites without a subscription, made claims that the advertising helped pay for server space and other overhead costs. But, the practice of marketing to people online became institutionalized, and in order for advertisers and programmers to understand how people interacted with marketing content (and websites in general), tracking technologies developed to monitor user actions. The prosumer model evolved from its origins; Internet companies relied upon the unpaid labor of people clicking around online to generate revenue.

Despite the fact that Toffler's prosumerism is grounded in the shifts of socioeconomic customs from agriculture and industrialization to the information economy, ultimately prosumerism is a sharing culture. Boundaries blur among production and consumption with the production of goods and services among specialists and non-specialists. Yet, it is worth considering Toffler's theory to articulate the gap between what he thought prosumption would be and what it has become in the digital information age. For Toffler, prosumerism was the rise of transferring activity upon consumers in an act of displacing labor from producers. While this model is active in the digital information age, there is also another form of prosumerism where the exchange of ideas, goods, and services benefit humankind instead of corporate financial interests.

OPEN SOURCE AND COMMODITY PROSUMERISMS IN WEB 2.0 SPACES

With the prosumer model's institutionalization within Internet cultures, by the time Web 2.0 took off during 2002–2004, the do-it-yourself culture did not disappear. On the contrary, the rhetoric of sharing positioned prosumerism as a viable economic model for digital commerce. One early social media space, Friendster, encouraged its users to connect through a friend network and share content and media within that chain of connections. While Friendster experienced financial and technological issues from 2004–2006 (Fiegerman, 2014) and nearly left the social media landscape in the United States, the social media upstart developed technological processes that were later approved for U.S. patents. One such patent (Lunt et al., 2009), "Method for sharing relationship information stored in a social network database with third party databases," allowed for third-party databases to access content in Friendster's databases through an identification token to better target information to particular users. In this particular case, Friendster invented a method for third parties to access primary database content with the help of an intermediary ID tag. I speculate here that this invention arguably transformed how social media providers viewed sharing of information with others—a means for a revenue stream.

By the time social media became significantly popular in 2004, prosumerism had long been an economic concept promoted as a method of empowerment and individualization. Why pay or wait for a specialist when Jane Doe can perform the labor and feel a sense of reward in the process? In many ways, the tectonic shift from specialized work to individual endeavors represented a decentering of separation and elitism. People in various social classes—who also had access—could control the creation of products and services through DIY culture and participatory culture (Jenkins, 2006). Within rhetoric and composition, Daniel Anderson (2003) suggested prosumerism empowers students to be creators in digitally mediated spaces. This statement, born out of a historical transition from alphabetic to multimodal content in the discipline, echoes much of the rich disciplinary discourse around new media literacies (Hawisher & Selfe, 1999, 2000; Selfe, 1999a, 1999b) and later multimodality (DeVoss, Cushman & Grabill, 2005; WIDE Research Collective, 2005; Wysocki et al., 2008) and multiliteracy (Selber, 2004). These situated discussions developed in response to the changing landscape of composition practices, with considerable advocacy of educating students and colleagues on how to write for various audiences using multiple digital tools (e.g., audio, video, animation, and text). For example, within this edited collection, Liza Potts chronicled how fans of media content co-produce material fan-fiction and distribute such work in various networks, and in some cases, as Potts mentioned, create new content.

It is here I also want to tease out a fine distinction between the prosumerism I see happening in the discipline of rhetoric and composition, especially within computers and writing, and the prosumerism I view as a market-driven practice. The type of prosumer practice that has been developed and encouraged by scholars and teachers in rhetoric and composition represents, in my mind, a rhetorically based process that is also divergent from prosumerism in most social media spaces. Within rhetoric and composition, I view prosumerism as a type of open-source practice. By open source, I do not mean the traditional associations of universal access and free licenses of software, but the ideological banner driving open-source work: interactive and dynamic sharing of content that benefits and improves systems, processes, individuals, and societies as the *currency* for the exchange of information. Content creators assume responsibility for the creativity and labor of a project or service for educational purposes and/or for open distribution, not necessarily for third-party revenue (unless the creator builds this into the design model). In the global and economic workplace, I view the type of prosumerism happening in social media spaces as a commodification of human activity and engagement with goods and services. Unlike open-source prosumerism, where content creators develop material for inquiry and information, commodity prosumerism tends to rely upon exploitation. Such exploitation in this prosumer model results from the establishment of an unpaid labor system. In the example of social media, tracking technologies monitor user movement and activities, collect such data, and use the data for various reasons including analytics and site usage, but also for revenue—all without passing such profit on to the users in the form of payment for their time on the site.

To understand the seductive lure of commodity prosumerism, it is necessary to comment upon how the capitalist fantasy of controlling resources engenders desire and control of economic wealth. Sociologists George Ritzer and Nathan Jurgenson (2010) argued that prosumer capitalism benefits companies and people who originate products and services to amass capital in the marketplace. In their definition, Ritzer and Jurgenson pointed to production (Marx) and consumption (Baudrillard) as a co-dependent method for the everyday person to both create and consume. Taken further, Baurdrillard's notion of consumption relies upon the annexation of production by producers to create desire and need in consumers. Essentially, producers create the products, market the demand, and seduce consumers into needing the product to fulfill their desires. Seen this way, producers develop goods and services and then create demand, thereby conditioning consumers to need the products. Taken one step further, producers market goods and services under the ethos of do-it-yourself to shift the expense of labor onto consumers. In turn, producers control not only the fantasy of desire and wealth, but also the distribution of labor in a free-market economy. By controlling labor, producers deepen their commitment to the prosumer model since such practices yield cost savings and maximize profits.

Such concepts are consistent with approaches in political economy practices. In his work on prosumption and surveillance, critical media theorist Christian Fuchs (2011) critiqued the problems with capitalist behaviors in Web 2.0 spaces. He argued that traditional capitalist models of economic exchange between the public and the owners, left over from the industrial revolution, provided a need of supply and demand of resources and goods. But in Web 2.0 spaces, prosumption distorts the traditional capitalist model because social media producers deliver content based on algorithmic calculations, personalized for user categories, and for the purposes of creating demand for advertisers' products and services. The more people engage with sites like Facebook, Google, Twitter, and even Amazon and Netflix, the more these companies collect consumer information data for billions in advertising revenue. This model is a problem for the public because of the time and energy people place into using these products with little to no compensation. Facing the facts of living and working in a capitalist society means people contend with unfair labor practices. For the corporate owners, there is great incentive to use computer algorithms to monitor, classify, and track people online. Such a model provides an exceedingly healthy revenue stream in the digital information age. Otherwise put, prosumers under this model are really the products of a social and cultural advertising delivery system designed to stimulate desire and create need.

It then becomes far easier to overlook these practices as people attend to daily habits and responsibilities. Why actively question or resist multi-trillion dollar methods of collecting consumer data when we can just settle for the latest hot product or app to show off to family and friends? Put another way, when we fail to consider the inherent problems with this model, our energies to resist, subvert, or develop alternative models of interaction recede into our collective backgrounds. As writing teachers, we also miss opportunities to engage in civic education to consider the highly complex methods and methodologies of interrogating macro systems of power. If we are committed to teaching students digital critical literacies, then we also need to attend to the systems that bind us to a rhetoric of sharing for a market-driven prosumer economy.

DIGITAL ALGORITHMIC SURVEILLANCE

Social media spaces deploy commodity prosumerism through digital algorithmic surveillance. Digital algorithmic surveillance, a term originally introduced by sociologists Clive Norris and Gary Armstrong (1999), describes how surveillance technologies store, categorize, and sift through complex datasets through step-by-step procedures for specific results. Many of the algorithms social media sites use, including the now retired Facebook PageRank algorithm, categorize people based how they interact (e.g., clicking, pressing, and talking with the sites through their screen technologies). In addition, algorithmic surveillance takes form through tracking technologies like cookies and web beacons that are in a sense identifying tags associated with websites and people's web browsers and computing machines. In an age of digital algorithmic surveillance, it is normative for Internet companies, especially social media sites, to personalize information for people.

In his research on Facebook, activist Eli Pariser (2011) claimed the company filtered content on people's screens through data collected using digital algorithmic surveillance. This "filter bubble," as Pariser called this occurrence, works by using algorithms to rank characteristics like how many times a person clicks on information or interacts with another person on the site, and even calculates this data over a period of time. The danger of this practice, as Pariser argued, arises when the personalized filtering systems—driven by algorithms—change people's cognitive frameworks—or, in rhetorical terms, persuade people. Filtering systems do so by presenting content that reinforces people's existing values and beliefs from data harvested from their machines, which also limits their access to contrary information. Filtering content through surveillance techniques consequently limits the public's engagement with political, economic, social, and cultural events and ideas, but also hides how personalization works underneath the interface:

> While the Internet has the potential to decentralize knowledge and control, in practice it's concentrating control over what we see and what opportunities we're offered in the hands of fewer people than ever before. . . . What's troubling about this shift toward personalization is that it's largely invisible to users and, as a result, out of our control. (p. 218)

Pariser does not explicitly discuss prosumerism within the filter bubble, but instead comments upon the division and replacement of human labor with algorithms. Indeed, the algorithms tend to perform the labor of sorting through large quantities of information in replacement of human labor. Arguably, the quick computational processes algorithms offer frees up time, labor, and energy for people in their everyday lives when working with digital technologies. From a civic standpoint, I argue commodity prosumerism forms the basis for many of the algorithmic processes in social media sites. The underlying ideological assumption of digital algorithmic surveillance is not one of agnostic values of learning how people interact with site content (such content includes advertising, friend and page/group suggestions, and recommendations for products and services), but for social media producers to classify and categorize people into distinct classes in order to deliver content relevant for people in that social and cultural class. Ultimately, the filter bubble—while a concern for online democracy and civic interaction—is an important model for businesses to rake in revenue. By relying on a commodity prosumer model for personalization in social media sites, questions about humanistic practices of agency, decency, and respect of the common good become paramount concerns for the public.

Social media users have already seen the effects of digital algorithmic surveillance from the alteration of Facebook algorithms in a research experiment conducted by Adam Kramer, Jamie Guillory, and Jeffrey Hancock (2014). In their study, "Experimental Evidence of Massive-Scale Emotional Contagion through Social Networks," the three researchers altered Facebook algorithms for approximately 700,000 Facebook users in a controlled study to learn if people experienced emotional reactions to experiencing more positive or negative content through their screens. (See Tabetha Adkins' chapter in this collection for further discussion of Kramer, Guillory, and Hancock's study and its ethical implications.) The altered algorithms either limited or increased positive posts in the control group's Facebook newsfeed. As a result of this experiment, the researchers determined people did respond to the limitation or increase in positivity in the feed. Those who experienced fewer positive posts posted less frequently in Facebook and did not contribute as many positive posts, and vice versa. Of course, social media and Internet companies altering content is not a new invention as danah boyd (2014) elsewhere reported, but all too often, algorithmic alterations in social media spaces persuade people to certain actions, thoughts, and feelings—as the emotional contagion experiment suggests. In an age of sharing content online, social media producers have, in a sense, conditioned consumers. People share content to connect with loved ones, colleagues, and acquaintances, all the while as algorithms categorize people into social and cultural classes from data harvested from computing machine data. In turn, algorithms provide content to people reflecting a composited digital self.

American culture and media theorist John Cheney-Lippold (2011) argued this is a form of "algorithmic identity" in which algorithms categorize people from "use-patterns online" resulting in social sorting, which is consistent with what I call the "invisible digital identity," or the identity computer algorithms create about us (as cited in Beck, 2015). These classifications cause people to have unequal and uneven experiences online, which hint at implications of discrimination and censorship (Guzik, 2009; Introna & Wood, 2004). The relationship between prosumerism and digital algorithmic surveillance helps people better understand the shifting models of sharing, capitalism, and participatory action in social media spaces.

This is all not to argue that digital algorithmic surveillance as a force in social media leaves users with little agency, lest this become a discussion skirting around technological determinism. In many ways, the politics and economics of social media leave the power to control information exchange to the owners of these sites where digital algorithmic surveillance is concerned, since users of these sites do not have access to create or modify these algorithms. However, individuals do have a visible agency in social media. By visible, I mean the type of agency where people share content for other people to engage with online. Within this edited collection, Tabetha Adkins discusses how West Virginians used Tide's Loads of Hope Facebook public page to denounce Tide's decision to not send Loads of Hope into the regions of West Virginia affected by Freedom Industries' toxic dump of 4-methylcyclohexanemethanol (MCHM) in the Elk River, which left approximately 300,000 individuals without access to clean water. As Adkins suggested, the influx of comments on the Facebook page represents a type of social activism where people can rally for production action for the common good. Additionally, Les Hutchinson wrote in this collection about her decisions to choose anonymity in Twitter as an act of agency in order to play with a dynamic and fluctuating identity online.

Although individuals have some say in how to engage in social media spaces, I maintain that in the case of commodity prosumerism and digital algorithmic surveillance, there's an edge of hard determinism at play. It is difficult for me to get past the notion that the invisible and opaque processes that order online spaces also regulate social and cultural interactions. This is especially at play with commodity prosumerism and digital algorithmic surveillance when sorting and classifying individuals results in people experiencing specific advertisements, recommendations, friend suggestions, and content delivery. This is not to say that people do not have the agency to disrupt, subvert, or challenge these coded processes under the interface. Quite the contrary, under a soft determinist stance, people do have the opportunity to participate in ways that offer productive decisions in the moment and in the long term. Through the lens of Judy Wajcman (2015) in her book *Pressed for Time*, she mentioned how scholars in science and technology studies have expressed consideration for soft determinism because technology does have social effects. Admittedly, I struggle with my own relationship with social media technologies, at times participating in issues of social justice and activism, but also knowing my actions in spaces like Twitter and Facebook become commodities for these companies. This is also why I wrestle with hard and soft determinist stances toward technology.

At times, it is difficult to assess similarities and differences in the open-source and commodity prosumerisms at play in social media spaces. For example, when a student or teacher shares open-source prosumer projects like a 30-second public service announcement video created in class by a student (or students) on a social media network, I value the contribution as an educator deeply vested in training people to become rhetorically savvy writers of media content. I also know that the video will become a commodity in that social media space. However, introducing open-source prosumption in social media spaces also means reconceptualizing the civic force of such spaces. Essentially, by introducing such projects in spaces that ultimately constrain remuneration or fair compensation of labor, this leaves open individual and collective agency to develop social media spaces that pay people to post content. Such a social media space, at the time of writing this chapter, already exists: tsū. This social media application works by paying its users money for posting content and growing its network—money taken from advertisers, but money also returned to users for their labor on their network.

SUSTAINING CRITICAL LITERACIES IN SOCIAL MEDIA SPACES

When individuals participate in any social media site, they are active prosumers; they give their data—their unpaid labor—away to social media companies under the appeal of *sharing* content with others online. Social media sites using commodity prosumerism also make it difficult for people to understand how companies profit from user data. However, since educators, researchers, and students in high-technology cultures often use social media, it is crucial to sustain critical literacies as a mode for civic education.

Critical literacy approaches to the teaching of digital technologies within rhetoric and composition has often involved examining the ideological freight embedded in the architecture and code of such systems within our field. As rhetoric and composition specialist Joseph Janangelo (1991) reminded us, power inequities thrive in online spaces because of abuses of surveillance systems. For Cynthia Selfe and Richard Selfe (1994), interfaces mark sites of contact zones where raced and classed boundaries exist and oppress marginalized populations. Drawing attention to student participation in computer-mediated environments, Kristine Blair (1998) and Donna LeCourt (1998) examined sites of conflict and discourse practices among diverse student populations to illustrate how ideologies inform participation in virtual spaces. Of course, these contributions provide relief from the ideological forces that assert control over others by modeling participatory methods of critical literacy engagement with students. In some instances, students critiqued technologies in ways that reinforced their own worldviews, which is a common practice critical pedagogues routinely experience in classrooms. However, the takeaway from these scholarly contributions give meaning to rethinking perspectives about our own beliefs and the ones embedded in our screens. As educators discussing critical technology literacies, we've focused on teaching students as a primary audience for critical education. However, it is also crucial that readers of this chapter turn toward the public, to consumers in general, to educate people both online and offline about prosumerism and digital algorithmic surveillance, along with how critical literacies help people make informed decisions about participation in social media.

Computer algorithms have enormous potential to inspire and shape discourse activities of people, but these algorithms do so at the expense of cultivating economic, political, and social scripts designed to persuade citizens toward certain pathways of thinking and action. An example occurred during the collective

47

reporting of citizen activists around the August 2014 police shooting of 18-year-old Michael Brown in Ferguson, Missouri. Taking to Twitter, millions of people expressed opinions about the shooting and the later real-time events of the police militarization of the city in the greater St. Louis area. Many tweeters reported that the Ferguson hashtag (#Ferguson) dominated their Twitter streams, while news on Facebook focused on the ALS Ice Bucket Challenge, a media campaign event whereby participants dumped ice water on their heads and bodies for donations to ALS research. Because Twitter uses real-time tweets, the events in #Ferguson on Twitter helped keep the spotlight on racial inequity and use of police force on peaceful demonstrators in town. However, because Facebook uses complex algorithms to curate news items on newsfeeds, many tweeters reported that Ferguson received hardly any attention within Facebook and pointed out that the ALS ice bucket challenge dominated their newsfeeds. The political and social outpouring on Twitter since the shooting of Michael Brown illustrates algorithmic manipulation. Journalist John McDermott (2014) argued that the implications of this algorithmic disparity between Facebook and Twitter are considerable given the reliance of the sites to provide information to millions, as he argued:

> The implications of this disconnect are huge for readers and publishers considering Facebook's recent emergence as a major traffic referrer. Namely, relying too heavily on Facebook's algorithmic content streams can result in de facto censorship. Readers are deprived a say in what they get to see, whereas anything goes on Twitter. (2014, para. 3)

Not only is censorship a concern for all that use Facebook, but the algorithmic practices of the social media space also affect people's attention toward certain social and political issues over others at the expense of cultivating civic responsibility and action. If end users are unaware of this type of algorithmic persuasion occurrence in Facebook and in other websites, information literacies efforts led by librarians, for example, become hindered because people are unable to access, evaluate, and use diverse knowledge bases to form a more democratic digital and real-life society. Therefore, taking civic action helps loosen some of the scripts and allows citizens to assert control in less democratizing spaces online.

An example of civic action occurs in the work of communications and gender scholar Safiya Umoja Noble. In 2012, Noble reported in *Bitch* magazine the results of a Google search for "black girls." Instead of results showcasing positive websites that embraced black identity and provided role models for young black girls, the top result in Google was SugaryBlackPussy.com. While she may not consider herself a critical pedagogue, Noble brought these search results to her students to show the power structure of search processes in Google. By bringing this example into the classroom, she called attention to the values Google replicated in its search results and discussed how to subvert those values to promote more equitable and diverse results for black girls and women. This is not to say that Noble's work changed the way Google's search results operated, since such results are based on any number of signals such as geographic location, IP address, web search history, and so forth. However, in examining and making space for dialogue about the practices inscribed by Google in the classroom and in a national feminist magazine, Noble's pursuit for political and social justice yielded positive results and an excellent example of critical pedagogy in action by analyzing algorithmic features in search engine spaces and sharing such information in a national and public publication.

Thus, it is here that educating our students, as part of a civic position, about the many-layered definitions of *sharing* in social media, open-source and commodity prosumerism, and digital algorithmic surveillance leads people (both producers and prosumers) to make productive changes in participatory Internet cultures. The manner in which people may address such topics develops through sustaining critical literacy. Drawing upon Stuart Selber's (2004) work in *Mulitliteracies for a Digital Age*, civic engagements may include the following:

- Educating individuals about prosumerism in national publications, not just academic journals: What might well-placed articles in publications in both liberal and conservative periodicals do for promoting awareness and encouraging people to advocate and challenge commodity prosumerism in social media sites?
- Volunteering or contributing funds to national non-profit organizations like the American Civil Liberties Union (ACLU), Electronic Frontier Foundation (EFF), and FreePress to support efforts to curb digital algorithmic surveillance online.
- Raising awareness by writing in local newspapers, either by contributing columns or by writing letters to the editor about unpaid labor in social media, but also addressing how people may conceptualize and critique the power structures in social media and understand the myriad institutional forces that profit from such sites.
- In local communities, talking to neighbors, community members, and acquaintances about why and how commodity prosumerism is designed to persuade people to need and desire products and service in social media.

Taking time to advocate and educate community members and the public about the implications of consumer prosumerism and digital algorithmic surveillance must be at the forefront of civic engagement. As educators, we have a responsibility to inform the public about these issues while honoring our field's history of encouraging open-source prosumerism. It is no longer enough for writing educators to discuss these concerns in scholarly journals and venues. Instead, scholars and educators must expand into public spaces and help individuals develop and acquire the literacies necessary to subvert digital algorithmic surveillance and make productive decisions about sharing content on sites that use commodity prosumerism. We must also cast a critical eye toward technologies that may use individuals' labor without compensation or attribution. Learning how commodity prosumerism and digital algorithmic surveillance shapes content, persuades people to actions and beliefs, and redirects cognitive frameworks will become increasingly important in the next decade as more advanced technologies develop with algorithmic processes.

New media literacies, whether they focus on developing search literacies, visual literacies, or Web 2.0 literacies, involve a host of political, social, technological, and cultural conditions across several domains of life. The acquisition and sustainment of theoretical and process-oriented social literacies support larger societal goals of democracy and freedom from oppression. Certainly learning how to identify, analyze, and possibly subvert structures of power can enable critical consciousness, and sustaining critical literacies in digital spaces is further needed as computer programmers and engineers continue to find ways to build a sharing web. Educators play important roles in teaching students and the public about such literacies through national, regional, and local outreach about necessary skills for the general population in today's digitally driven information environment.

On the whole, making educational inroads with students and the public regarding such critical literacies and civic education brings about the potential to change the rhetoric of sharing and the market-driven prosumer culture into a diversified sharing digital information age. Not that open-source prosumerism becomes the de facto model for exchanging information, experiences, and emotions, but it instead gains prominence in mainstream networked cultures. By attending to the student ventures that bring change, we can indeed create a sharing web for the benefit of humankind.

REFERENCES

National Institute of Health. (n.d.). A thin blue line. Retrieved from https://history.nih.gov/exhibits/thinblueline/index.html.

Anderson, D. (2003). Prosumer approaches to new media composition: Consumption and production in continuum. *Kairos: A Journal of Rhetoric, Technology, and Peda-*

gogy, 8(1). Retrieved from http://kairos.technorhetoric.net/8.1/coverweb/anderson /story.html.

Beck, E. (2015). The invisible digital identity: Assemblages of digital networks. *Computers and Composition, 35*, 125–140.

Blair, K. (1998). Literacy, dialogue, and difference in the "electronic contact zone." *Computers and Composition, 15*(3), 317–329.

boyd, d. (2014). What does the Facebook experiment teach us? Growing anxiety about data manipulation. Retrieved from https://medium.com/message/what-does-the -facebook-experiment-teach-us-c858c08e287f.

Cheney-Lippold, J. (2011). A new algorithmic identity: Soft biopolitics and the modulation of control. *Theory, Society & Culture, 28*, 164–181.

DeVoss, D. N., Cushman, E. & Grabill, J. T. (2005). Infrastructure and composing: The *when* of new-media writing. *College Composition and Communication, 57*(1), 14–44.

Fiegerman, S. (2014). Friendster founder tells his side of the story, 10 years after Facebook. Retrieved from http://mashable.com/2014/02/03/jonathan-abrams-friendster -facebook/.

Fuchs, C. (2011). Web 2.0, prosumption, and surveillance. *Surveillance & Society, 8*(3), 288–309.

Guzik, K. (2009). Discrimination by design: Data mining in the United States' "war on terrorism." *Surveillance & Society, 7*(1), 1–17.

Hawisher, G. E. & Selfe, C. L. (2000). *Global literacies and the world-wide web*. New York, NY: Routledge.

Hawisher, G. E. & Selfe, C. L. (Eds.). (1999). *Passions, pedagogies and 21st century technologies*. Urbana, IL: National Council of Teachers of English.

Introna, L. D. & Wood, D. (2004). Picturing algorithmic surveillance: The politics of facial recognition software programs. *Surveillance & Society, 2*(2/3), 177–198.

Janangelo, J. (1991). Technopower and technoppression: Some abuses of power and control in computer-assisted writing environments. *Computers and Composition, 9*(1), 47–64.

Jenkins, H. (2006). *Convergence culture: Where old and new media collide*. New York, NY: New York University Press.

Kramer, A. D. I., Guillory, J. E. & Hancock, J. T. (2014). Experimental evidence of massive-scale emotional contagion through social networks. *PNAS, 111*(24), 8788–8790.

LeCourt, D. (1998). Critical pedagogy in the computer classroom: Politicizing the writing space. *Computers and Composition, 15*, 275–295.

Lunt, C. & N. Galbreath. (2009). *U.S. Patent No. 7,478,078*. Washington, DC: U.S. Patent and Trademark Office.

McDermott, J. (2014). Why Facebook is for ice buckets, Twitter is for Ferguson. Retrieved from http://digiday.com/platforms/facbeook-twitter-ferguson/.

Mirani, L. (2015, February 9). Millions of Facebook users have no idea they're using the internet. *Quartz*. Retrieved from http://qz.com/333313/millions-of-facebook -users-have-no-idea-theyre-using-the-internet/.

Noble, S. U. (2012). Missed connections: What search engines say about women. *Bitch, 54*, 37–41.

Norris, C. & Armstrong, G. (1999). *The maximum surveillance society: The rise of CCTV.* Oxford, England: Berg.

Pariser, E. (2011). *The filter bubble: What the Internet is hiding from you.* New York, NY: Penguin Press.

Ritzer, G. & Jurgenson, N. (2010). Production, consumption, presumption: The nature of capitalism in the age of the digital "prosumer." *Journal of Consumer Culture, 10*(1), 13–36.

Selber, S. (2004). *Multiliteracies for a digital age.* Carbondale, IL: Southern Illinois University Press.

Selfe, C. L. (1999a). Technology and literacy: A story about the perils of not paying attention. *College Composition and Communication, 50*(3), 411–436.

Selfe, C. L. (1999b). *Technology and literacy in the twenty-first century: The importance of paying attention.* Carbondale, IL: Southern Illinois University Press.

Selfe, C. L. & Selfe, R. J., Jr. (1994). The politics of the interface: Power and its exercise in electronic contact zones. *College Composition and Communication, 45*(4), 480–504.

Service Star. (n.d.). Service star. Retrieved from http://retromercials.hostoi.com /Commercial%20-%20Service%20Star%20Hardware%20-%201982.mp3.

Toffler, A. (1980). *The third wave.* New York, NY: Morrow.

Wajcman, J. (2015). *Pressed for time: The acceleration of life in digital capitalism.* Chicago, IL: University of Chicago Press.

Writing in Digital Environments (WIDE) Research Center Collective. (2005). Why teach digital writing. *Kairos: A Journal of Rhetoric, Technology, and Pedagogy, 10*(1). Retrieved from http://kairos.technorhetoric.net/10.1/coverweb/wide/.

Wysocki, A. F., Johnson-Eilola, J., Selfe, C. & Sirc, G. (2004). *Writing new media: Theory and applications for expanding the teaching of composition.* Logan, UT: Utah State University Press.

CHAPTER 3

SOCIAL SPILL: A CASE-BASED ANALYSIS OF SOCIAL MEDIA RESEARCH

Tabetha Adkins

Texas A&M University-Commerce

Following the January 9, 2014, spill of an estimated 10,000 gallons of toxic crude 4-methylcyclohexanemethanol (MCHM) into the Elk River, which serves as a water supply for 300,000 West Virginians, the Tide Loads of Hope Program received many requests to bring their services to the area.[1] Tide Loads of Hope, according to their website, is a "mobile Laundromat" that travels to disaster zones in times of need. On January 12, three days after the accident, Tide posted the following message to their public Facebook Page:

> Thanks for all the interest in Tide Loads of Hope for Charleston, West Virginia. Our hearts go out to all those affected by this unfortunate event. We are investigating whether it's possible for Loads of Hope to help. Please stay tuned to our status updates for any announcements.

Two days later, water use restrictions were slowly lifted, zone by zone. Tide posted on Facebook: "We're pleased to learn there has been progress in lifting some of the water restrictions to the Charleston, WV area. At this time, we have decided not to send Loads of Hope since the time it takes to arrive and set up operations will likely be longer than the water ban." Tide's Facebook page was flooded with approximately 1,400 posts related to these two announcements, and the announcements were shared or posted on individuals' own Facebook pages a combined 1,434 times.

As a scholar interested in literacy and social justice, I was intrigued by the enormous response Tide received following the announcement. I was fascinated not only by this immense response but also by the format of the response. Social

---

1   Full disclosure: I am a native West Virginian who grew up in the region affected by this accident. My mom and stepdad could not use the water in their home for a week. We still doubt the safety of their water and use bottled water for drinking and cooking. My personal investment in this story led me to follow multiple details of the story closely.

media websites like Twitter, Facebook, and Tumblr have enabled writers to communicate with audiences immediately, therefore changing social activism dramatically. This effect of social media on movements like Occupy Wall Street and the Arab Spring was well documented by scholars like Summer Harlow and Thomas J. Johnson (2011), but there is an additional appeal to what Malcolm Gladwell (2010) referred to as "slacktivism" and Tony Scott and Nancy Welch (2014) called "clicktivism" (p. 565). Christina Neumayer and Judith Schoßböck (2011) wrote that slacktivism "can be defined as having done something good for society without actively engaging in politics, protest, or civil disobedience, or spending or raising money." While some scholars like Gladwell despairingly wrote that slacktivists "do the things that people do when they are not motivated enough to make a real sacrifice," Stephanie Vie (2014a) argued that there are positive effects of slacktivism. She wrote that "in a world where microaggressions of all kinds are very real, the virtual support shown in one's community through sharing images of goodwill and support can in fact make a difference" and memes commonly utilized by slacktivists "help draw attention to societal issues and problems and can result in increased feelings of support for marginalized groups." This concept is closely related to what Caroline Dadas called "hashtag activism" in this collection.

While the immediacy of online publishing is certainly attractive, scholars like Welch (2008) helped us understand that "a post-September 11th development" has been the reduction of "public programs, rights, and geographic space" (p. 6). In light of the decline in opportunity and increase in risk for public protest, sites like Facebook have become an alternative for would-be protestors. Indeed, social media outlets have become what Elenore Long (2008) called a "local public," which she defined as "where it is that ordinary people most often go public" (p. 5). Brian Jackson and Jon Wallin (2009) argued that while we should not buy into the "rhetoric of inevitability" or the myth that the web will lead to a more democratic society, there is "little doubt that the Web has made possible democratic activity, even radical democratic activity, in ways unimaginable ten or more years ago" (p. W384). This activity, they argued, has changed not only public discourse but also commercial behaviors (p. W384).

But these forms of protest and activity create a conundrum for scholars who want to study this new kind of activism: How does one collect data for an ethnographic study of activism when this activism is conducted online? What ethical considerations must one make when researching a digital artifact or text? What familiar methodologies can we model in this new frontier? How do scholars address the challenge of connecting online action with actual impact?

In this chapter, my focus is on social media research, but I use my own study of social media responses to Tide to illustrate my points. I begin the chapter with a discussion of important methodological and ethical issues to consider in research design, data collection, and reporting of results of social media research. I introduce two concepts, *consistent associations* and *remote associations,* terms that have helped guide my own research decisions. Next, using my own research to illustrate my points, I show how social media data acts differently than other data. I then move on to a discussion of my coding and results to illustrate how social media can come together, and I conclude with some recommendations for scholars interested in ethical practices for social media scholarship.

METHODOLOGY AND ETHICS OF SOCIAL MEDIA RESEARCH: CONSISTENT AND REMOTE ASSOCIATIONS

Many scholars (Banks & Eble, 2006; DePew, 2007; McKee & Porter, 2009, 2012; Sidler, 2007) have taken up the problems of ethical Internet research. Heidi McKee and James Porter (2009), for example, took up the important questions surrounding the citation of Internet posts. They showed that while researchers often want to keep users' identities anonymous, a simple Google search of "a fragment of a quotation" from a research study revealed the "entire post and then the original thread from 1994 where participants often used their first and last names from their offline world" in "0.34 seconds" (p. 107). Issues of informed consent are complicated in Internet research. Some argue that consent is not necessary because the information is easily accessible. Janne C. H. Bromseth (2006) did not accept this argument and saw the issue as much more complicated. Indeed, McKee and Porter (2012) urged social media scholars to realize that "notions of privacy are shifting" (p. 79). While some scholars may be tempted to think of all Internet data like "broadcast media" that should be treated like a text to be quoted rather than the content of a subject to be protected, this issue is much more complex.

I argue that one element that must be considered when making ethical decisions about research design and reporting is to consider the community in which the users are creating the texts, whether they are alphabetic or visual. This consideration aligns closely with what Julia Romberger (2007) called an ecofeminist methodology. This methodology aims to "reorient technology toward humanity" and requires scholars to "be aware of context and its complexity" in research (p. 250). Romberger argued that this "context is critical to rhetorical analysis because 'individuals . . . belong to discourse communities'" (p. 285). It is when users are operating strictly within these discourse communities—especially with long-term connections—that they must be most closely protected in research design and reporting. Consider online locations such as support groups, chat groups, and affinity group meeting spaces and it is easy to think of examples of groups that maintain long-term connections, or connections I have come to think of as *con-*

sistent associations. Consistent associations require longevity, repeated participation from individuals, and an archive of discussion.[2] Consistent associations may occur in various kinds of web spaces including social media, journaling and blogging, chat rooms, games, etc. During my research of the responses to Tide Loads of Hope, however, I found that these posts were the result of an altogether different kind of relationship between users I call *remote associations*. While the majority of these individuals were linked in that they were affected by the same industrial accident, there was not a long-term context to consider, nor was there a long-term event to study. These individuals may never interact online again.

As scholars have shown, Internet research is complex and context-dependent. McKee and Porter (2012) provide an excellent set of seven questions to consider for Internet research (pp. 246–253). Table 3.1 lists McKee and Porter's questions, how I answered each question for my research, and an example of how this question might be answered for a different kind of study.

Table 3.1: McKee and Porter's (2012) questions for Internet research

McKee and Porter's question	In my study . . .	A different study might find . . .
1. Are you studying texts or persons or both?	Because I determined these were remote associations, I felt I was studying text, not people.	An Internet chat group with consistent associations would likely include the study of people.
2. Do you view the Internet as a place or a space?	Privacy was not expected, so this was a space.	If privacy is expected, it is a place.
3. What are "public" and "private" online?	I drew an analogy to off-line research. Listening to public speech is public (a protest, for example).	Listening to private speech is private (placing an audio recorder under a park bench, for example).
4. Is informed consent necessary?	Consider the purpose of the speech act. (Many users who posted about the WV water crisis urged other users to share this information.) Also, consider risk.	Someone posting about marital abuse in a chat group likely does not want that information shared. Sharing that information not only violates the trust of the user but could also place them in danger.

---

2   I'm including the archive as a requirement for consistent relations, though I acknowledge that websites like 4chan prohibit archival and may still host consistent relationships.

Table 3.1—*continued*

McKee and Porter's question	In my study . . .	A different study might find . . .
5. What is the degree of interaction of researcher with online participants?	My presence on the Tide page did not change the conversation. Posters did not assume their posts were only being read by a select group.	As I detail below, Facebook researchers recently found themselves in trouble when their interaction crossed over into manipulation.
6. What is the sensitivity of the material being used?	Consider intention: the posts on Tide's page were supposed to be public.	Content is sensitive when it is something the user may not utter to his or her own family, friends, or coworkers.
7. What is the vulnerability of the material being used?	Users who posted to Tide's page wanted to bring attention to this issue.	A group of users in an online support group might suffer from the attention brought to them or their online space by a published research study.

I want to emphasize that scholars must consider these questions on a case-by-case basis. And as McKee and Porter (2012) pointed out, "it is particularly important not to think individualistically but also collectively" (p. 252). In other words, while researchers are often juggling pressure from editors, deadlines, granting institutions, and pressures from both institutions and the public, social media scholars must think of how the attention their work may receive could negatively affect their research subjects.

Further, McKee and Porter argued that "if online data . . . is deemed to be public, then no consent is needed to study and quote from the materials (although copyright permissions may be needed)" (p. 250). However, this definition is more complicated than it seems. Consider the recent trouble Facebook found itself in (also discussed in Estee Beck's chapter in this collection). In March 2014, researchers at Facebook published the results of a study conducted in 2012 on nearly 700,000 users (approximately 0.04 percent of Facebook's users) to determine if the mood of posts in users' newsfeeds would affect users' moods. Facebook's scholars conducted this study without receiving informed consent from participants. To conduct the study, Facebook manipulated the items in users' newsfeeds to determine if the post they made after reading their newsfeed would reflect the same mood of posts in their feeds. The study argued that consent was unnecessary because it was implied in the terms of use each user must agree to upon creating an account. According to a Facebook post written on June 29, 2014, by the principal scholar on the study, Adam D. I.

Kramer, the scholars involved felt the study was minimally invasive. Kramer (2013) explained, "Nobody's posts were 'hidden,' they just didn't show up on some loads of Feed. Those posts were always visible on friends' timelines, and could have shown up on subsequent News Feed loads." He wrote that in his view, the benefits of the study outweighed the risks:

> The reason we did this research is because we care about the emotional impact of Facebook and the people that use our product. We felt that it was important to investigate the common worry that seeing friends post positive content leads to people feeling negative or left out. At the same time, we were concerned that exposure to friends' negativity might lead people to avoid visiting Facebook. We didn't clearly state our motivations in the paper.

Many people are understandably upset about this study. In an interview for *The Guardian*, scholar Max Masnick explained the outrage:

> As a researcher, you don't get an ethical free pass because a user checked a box next to a link to a website's terms of use. The researcher is responsible for making sure all participants are properly consented. In many cases, study staff will verbally go through lengthy consent forms with potential participants, point by point. Researchers will even quiz participants after presenting the informed consent information to make sure they really understand. (as cited in Arthur, 2014)

As Vie (2014b) showed, the terms of service question is even more problematized by the fact that most media users are not rhetorically aware of the implications of privacy and usage policies. In fact, while "terms of service documents are couched in legalese, difficult to read and understand for the average user," she cited a 2008 study by McDonald and Cranor that estimated "the average user would have to spend approximately forty minutes per day reading through the privacy policies" each time that user visited a new website (p. 175). And in a blog entry quoted in *The Guardian*, James Grimmelmann (2014), Professor of Law at the University of Maryland, clarified that this study did in fact do harm because human emotions were manipulated, and he drew parallels, much as I have in this chapter, to face-to-face research examples. He explained:

> The unwitting participants in the Facebook study were told (seemingly by their friends) for a week either that the world was a dark and cheerless place or that it was a saccharine para-

dise. That's psychological manipulation, even when it's carried out automatically. (para. 10)

As scholars have shown, social media research has opened up a host of new questions about research methodologies and ethics that must be considered case-by-case and with an eye toward the rights of social media users. I will illustrate in the next section that the mechanics of research, data collection, and data storage pose specific challenges to social media researchers, as well.

SOCIAL MEDIA DATA

Social media texts are exciting and compelling for scholars who study writing because these artifacts are user-generated, published immediately, unfiltered by a proprietary third party, and (generally) uncensored. A social media text can grow, change, or even shrink by the minute. Studying social media texts helps scholars understand the exigent, current reactions from average people. For example, as I write this chapter, I am reading not only the United States Supreme Court's decision on *Burwell v. Hobby Lobby Stores* (2014) and *Conestoga Wood Specialties v. Burwell* (2014)—cases that challenged the Affordable Health Care Act's mandate for employers to provide no-cost birth control to female employees—but also a torrent of responses on Facebook and Twitter. Within minutes of the announcement that the U.S. Supreme Court had decided on a 5–4 margin that the Affordable Health Care Act's mandate violates the 1993 Religious Freedom Restoration Act, graphics and memes appeared in social media spaces explaining the court's decision and the potential impact of that decision. My understanding of the Supreme Court's ruling is enhanced because I also understand how friends, acquaintances, and strangers are reacting to the decision on their Tumblr pages. This context created by social media lends a deeper awareness to the impact of the decision, but because these social media texts move and transform so quickly, studying these texts can be especially complicated.

Similarly, in wake of the toxic industrial accident in the Elk River, I turned to social media sources to learn about how locals were reacting. As I became more interested in the Facebook users' responses to Tide Loads of Hope, I noticed that the number of comments on each post changed. For example, when I started this research on January 29, 2014, seventeen days after the second announcement, the initial post announcing the investigation received 423 posts, and the post announcing the decision against bringing the program to West Virginia received 956 posts. As I write this chapter in June 2014, the initial post has 421 replies (two fewer than before), and the second announcement remained steady at 956 comments. This decrease in comments on the initial post could be attributed to deleted comments or deactivated Facebook accounts. Facebook users commented on the story steadily until January 24. Given that social media users can delete their comments or deactivate their accounts at any given moment, social media data is vulnerable and timeliness is important. As Stuart Blythe (2007) reminded us, web research is unstable (p. 204).

Since web research is unstable and data shifts, scholars studying social media texts must create archives of their research. While Internet programs like the Wayback Machine can provide users with archived webpages, these programs do not currently function with some social media websites and, specifically in my case, not with Facebook because, according to their Automated Data Collection Terms (2010), Facebook requires written permission for web crawlers to index their websites.[3] Facebook most likely instituted this policy to protect user data. Similarly, Twitter has terms of use for developers (2014) looking to utilize "Twitter's ecosystem of applications, services, and content" and all social media sites like Tumblr, Academia.edu, Reddit, Instagram, Vine, Livejournal, Craigslist, and Google+ contain privacy policies that regulate how users and developers utilize their services. (Though Vie [2014b] showed that users do not generally read these policies.) To create my own archive, I initially used screen shots. In total, I created 409 screen shots. I quickly realized, however, that these screen shots would not be searchable, so I also used copy and paste commands to create repositories in a Microsoft Word document. This strategy generated 185 pages of searchable data I could edit, highlight, and use Microsoft's "insert comment" function to tag. Decoding is very slow, however, as is transferring webpage code into Microsoft Word code, so this process was slightly tedious. I hope that in the future, tools will be developed that allow researchers to archive, tag, search, share, and sample their data, though I acknowledge that such tools may raise privacy concerns. Until these tools are developed, however, researchers will have to rely on traditional means of collecting and coding data. In the next section, I discuss the themes that emerged in my research to demonstrate the kinds of findings social media research can produce.

RESPONSES TO TIDE: CODING AND FINDINGS

Blythe (2007) wrote that:

> Coding requires researchers to identify a set of artifacts . . . to define a unit worth analyzing within them, to create codes for classifying instances of that unit, in many cases to test the re-

---

3   Every social media scholar should be lucky enough to be married to a software engineer who can explain bots and web crawlers. Thanks, Bill Shato, for the clarification.

liability of that work, and to make these decisions and actions public. (p. 204)

However, "digital artifacts present new challenges because they are less stable than printed artifacts, alter relations between creator and audience, and can incorporate multiple media" (p. 204). In other words, the very aspects of digital or multimodal media that attract both users and researchers are the same elements that complicate the coding of these texts. But as Blythe reminded us, coding is simply about defining a set of texts and selecting a sample from that text. I used dates to narrow my own analysis because the relevance of the event expires after a certain period of time. This approach narrowed my analysis down to the 667 posts made during the most active period of the incident. Blythe also outlined different ways in which units of analysis can be defined, including verbal units (in which he includes words, phrases, and clauses; t-units; exchanges; and rhetorical units) and nonverbal units (pp. 209–211). For my own coding, I focused on rhetorical units, which Blythe defined as "a segment that can be classified as one type of rhetorical move—a move with the same author, intended audience, and purpose" (p. 210). This unit of analysis seemed most appropriate for my coding because I looked at posts made almost entirely for the purpose of appealing to Tide. This methodological decision to focus on rhetorical units also echoes McKee and Porter's (2009) call to depend on rhetoric and casuistry to address problems in research ethics (p. 13). This unit of analysis led me to four code categories: appeals to Tide to change their position; expressions of anger with Tide for their decision; information exchange; and, finally, declarations of West Virginian identity. In this section, I briefly detail the subcategories of these codes and show what other social media scholars can learn from my codes.

The first theme that became relevant in my coding was appeals to Tide to change their decision. This strategy was the most often used of all the strategies for which I coded: 55.6 percent (or 371) posts used this appeal. These appeals utilized different rhetorical strategies, including descriptions of West Virginians who were affected by the accident as deserving of help, or an appeal utilizing ethos. For example, Rita Morrison posted, "I do not live there but those that do deserve your respect. ☺." The use of the emoji here points to the importance of looking at text rhetorically since this unit of analysis allows researchers to consider audience, author, tone, and purpose while other units of analysis might limit a scholar to text alone. Susan Hilligloss and Sean Williams (2007) argued that "the visual, far from being an adjunct to the verbal expression, instead merges with it to form a coherent argument or perspective on the topic being addressed" (p. 238). For more about visual activism, especially on Instagram, see Kara Poe Alexander and Leslie Hahner's chapter in this collection.

A second subcategory that emerged from this theme was users presenting the facts of the situation (logos) in an effort to convince Tide of the need of their services. This appeal was used in 36.4 percent of posts—243 posts. One user who utilized this strategy, Megan Lowry, said:

> Still thousands of people without water that won't have it for quite a while. They've lifted very few zones and have tons to go. And even the ones who zones were lifted some are still having significant water problems. The least they could do is setup where the water is safely working and help out the ones who won't have water for a while. (2014, January 15)

The final category that emerged in this theme was the trend of presenting details of the situation that might appeal to the readers' sympathies (pathos). Angela Messenger-Rishel (2014, January 13) wrote:

> Please reconsider! I am not affected, however, I have very dear friends that are. They have driven 2 hours to their family's house to bathe and do their laundry . . . they have 3 small children. Many people do not have the resources to get to an area to do this and for most people it's not even an option, especially if they don't have any family or friends out of that area. These people need your help! It's almost been a week that they haven't been able to use their water. Think of how that would affect you and how much laundry you would have.

That these appeals can be labeled so clearly with rhetorical terminology should be of no surprise. Long (2008) argued that local publics are communities constructed by people "around distinct rhetorical agendas" (p. 15).

The second theme that emerged from my coding was expressions of anger with Tide's decision. Anger was expressed in two ways: First, there were many calls for boycotts. Some users created memes to encourage others to boycott, while others simply declared their intention to never purchase Tide products again. Thirty-seven percent of the posts (247) declared a boycott. One Facebook user registered as Chris n Hollie Workman, whose comment resembles many other comments, urged readers to "dump your Tide down the toilet! They actually don't wanna come because it's not enough publicity!" (2014, January 13). Another strategy for expressing anger I found in this theme was to portray Tide representatives as not as tough or resilient as West Virginians affected by the accident. Twenty-three posts (3.4%) used this strategy. As an example, Mike Wilson commented, "You stupid city slickers wouldn't have lasted one day . . .

ONE DAY! and would have been throwing a fit" (2014, January 13). If we accept that Facebook and other social media outlets are the new spaces for public protest in a privatized world, it is important for social media scholars to properly categorize and characterize expressions of anger in social media outlets. This particular strategy was closely related to the next theme I found.

The third category that emerged from my coding was declarations of West Virginian, Appalachian, or "hillbilly" identity. One hundred and twenty-three posts (18.4%) relied on this strategy. The effects of these posts were either to help create a sense of support and unity among the affected West Virginians or declare independence from outsiders and corporations. The importance of showing support to others online cannot be overemphasized. In this collection, Crystal Broch Columbini and Lindsey Hall underscore the significant role "lateral and supportive networks" played for homeowners struggling to renegotiate the terms of their mortgages in light of the 2008 housing crisis. One example of a post encouraging unity among West Virginians came from Brittni Woods and read, "We are mountaineers. We are strong and we love our neighbors and each other. We will stay strong and prevail once this is over" (2014, January 13). This post references both the state motto, *montani semper liberi* (mountaineers are always free) and the Bible's command to love thy neighbor. An example of a post declaring independence from outsiders, in addition to the post referencing city slickers already mentioned, is "A country boy will survive!!!! And country girls too! We don't need you so good luck when your sales go down TREMENDOUSLY!!!!!" (Clark-McCallister, 2014). This post references a well-known country song "Country Boys Can Survive" by Hank Williams, Jr.—a song with the lyrics "we come from the West Virginia coal mines" and a video that could have been shot on the Elk River itself.

Expressions of West Virginian, Appalachian, or "hillbilly" identity are complicated by the fact that these expressions are often imbedded in what Blythe (2007) called "latent content" (p. 215). As opposed to "manifest units," which are "observable phenomena in a text," "latent content, on the other hand, 'shifts the focus to the meaning underlying the elements on the surface of a message'" (p. 215). In other words, because I lived in West Virginia for twenty-three years, I recognize these expressions of identity that are intended for insiders to understand. A scholar who lacks this insider status may not correctly interpret or even detect latent content. This emphasizes the need for interviews with participants or a code reviewer who has insider status. One exemplar model that comes to mind here is McKee's interviews with researcher Yukari Seko in order to understand the methodological choices Seko made in her 2006 study of posts disclosing suicide in Internet chat groups (McKee & Porter, 2009, p. 104).

The final category I identified in my analysis was the use of this space as an information exchange. Two hundred and eighty-five posts (42.72%) utilized this space to share or obtain information. The sharing of information—both disseminating and gathering—reflects what Jackson and Wallin (2009) called the "back-and-forthness" of online exchanges, or what Barbara Warnick (2007) called "interactivity." Information changed hands in the comments section of Tide's posts between people affected by the accident giving "real facts" of the situation, people affected by the accident attempting to gather "real facts" of the situation, and people outside not affected by the accident attempting to gather "real facts" of the situation. Liza Potts (2014) showed that "victims (of disasters) use the web to reach out to loved ones, find friends and family, or simply find help from the Red Cross or other emergency relief organizations. In essence, they have adapted the older practice of using media to 'reach out and touch someone'" (p. 10).

Further, she drew on more regulated systems in the wake of disasters like CNN's Katrina Safe List, which was unusable and incomplete (pp. 40–58). I can imagine that if the storm happened today, survivors would create a better system utilizing a twitter hashtag like #katrinasafelist or #KSL to locate loved ones. This trend of using social media to obtain and disseminate information rather than relying on regulated or established sources of news reflects a distrust for news media and public officials that not only pervaded the West Virginia area during the aftermath of the Freedom Industries accident, but also permeates through society. In fact, a recent study released by the Pew Research Center (2014a) found that only 19 percent of adults in the age range of 18–32 (the group known as millennials) say most people can be trusted. Take into account another Pew Research Center study that found that 90 percent of American millennials use social media (2014b) and we can see why distrust was a common theme among these posts. And, in fairness, this group of people had just lost faith in representatives who were supposed to protect them from problems like toxic chemicals in their water supply. Their distrust was justified.

In this section, I discussed what my codes showed about the data I researched. I conclude this chapter with some final recommendations for other social media scholars.

FINAL RECOMMENDATIONS

Methodological decisions, issues of informed consent, and other ethical decisions should not, as McKee and Porter (2009) showed, "be regarded so much as a binary with two unambiguously clear meanings at either end but rather as an interrelated continuum" (p. 77). Rather, social media scholars must consider context, location, and the processes that are appropriate and ethical for each social media artifact. Some final guidelines I urge social media scholars to consider include:

1. Scholars should be familiar with how sites function before studying them. By function, I do not only mean how the technology works (e.g., what links to click to get to specific e-locations), but I also mean how the social media artifact functions in people's lives. Is this a public space? Do these users consider this a place rather than a space? Is this content sensitive? Are the users posting content that makes them vulnerable? Is attention to this text desirable?

2. Determine whether the interactions that occur in an e-location are consistent associations or remote associations. This distinction helps answer many ethical questions.

3. When in doubt about how to proceed in an e-location, draw a parallel between that location and a comparable face-to-face location. For example, in my study, I compared the Tide boycott posts to a protest march. Creating these comparisons to non-virtual spaces helps determine how to advance in virtual locations. In another example, I often use Twitter to communicate with corporate officials (e.g., I tweet to American Airlines to complain that my parents are stranded in Atlanta due to a plane's mechanical failure or I tweet to Haverty's thanking them for rescheduling the delivery of my new bed). These kinds of social media posts might be thought of like letters to the editor in a newspaper or private letters to corporate officials depending on the context. A blogging site like LiveJournal, WordPress, or Tumblr, on the other hand, poses a more complicated rhetorical situation for researchers. Individual texts must be considered on a case-by-case basis since some blog entries function like published texts and others are thought of as personal diaries.

McKee and Porter (2012) urged scholars to develop a "flexible process" for conducting Internet research, and this is especially true of social media texts, given the importance these spaces and places play in modern life. Similarly, Potts (2014) argued for understanding these systems "as participatory ecosystems that must allow for flexibility and responsiveness" (p. 2), which has become more crucial for scholars to "experience activities in ways similar to how participants experience them" (p. 9). As I found with my study of protest posts on Tide's Facebook page, social media has created a new space for writers to be heard and seen. Social media scholars must be cautious and methodical when determining how to study and represent their findings because the relationship between life on and off the web is complex and complicated.

REFERENCES

Arthur, C. (2014, June 30). Facebook emotion study breached ethical guidelines, researchers say. *The Guardian*. Retrieved from http://www.theguardian.com/technology/2014/jun/30/facebook-emotion-study-breached-ethical-guidelines-researchers-say.

Banks, W. & Eble, M. (2006). Digital writing research: Technologies, methodologies, and ethical issues. In D. DeVoss & H. McKee (Eds.), *Digital writing research* (pp. 27–47). Cresskill, NJ: Hampton Press.

Blythe, S. (2007). Coding digital texts and multimedia. In H. A. McKee & D. N. DeVoss (Eds.), *Digital writing research: Technologies, methodologies, and ethical issues* (pp. 203–227). Cresskill, NJ: Hampton.

Bromseth, J. (2006). *Genre trouble and the body that mattered: Negotiations of gender, sexuality and identity in a Scandinavian mailing list community for lesbian and bisexual women* (Unpublished doctoral dissertation). Norwegian University of Science and Technology: Trondheim, Norway.

Clark-McCallister, T. (2014, January 14). A country boy will survive!!!! And country girls too! We don't need you so good luck when your sales go down TREMENDOUSLY!!!!! [Facebook comment]. Retrieved from https://www.facebook.com/Tide/posts/10151871476253231

DePew, K. E. (2007). Through the eyes of researchers, rhetors and audiences: Triangulating data from the digital writing situation. In H. A. McKee & D. N. DeVoss (Eds.), *Digital writing research: Technologies, methodologies, and ethical issues* (pp. 49–69). Cresskill, NJ: Hampton Press.

Facebook. (2010). Automated Data Collection Terms. Retrieved from https://www.facebook.com/apps/site_scraping_tos_terms.php.

Gladwell, M. (2010, October). Small change: Why the revolution will not be tweeted. *The New Yorker*. Retrieved from http://www.newyorker.com/magazine/2010/10/04/small-change-malcolm-gladwell.

Grimmelmann, J. (2014, June 28). *As flies to wanton boys*. Retrieved from http://laboratorium.net/archive/2014/06/28/as_flies_to_wanton_boys.

Harlow, S. & Johnson, T. (2011). Overthrowing the protest paradigm? How *The New York Times*, Global Voices and Twitter covered the Egyptian revolution. *International Journal of Communication, 5*, 1359–1374.

Hilligoss, S. & Williams, S. (2007). Composition meets visual communication: New research questions. In H. A. McKee & D. N. DeVoss (Eds.), *Digital writing research: Technologies, methodologies, and ethical issues* (pp. 203–227). Cresskill, NJ: Hampton.

Jackson, B. & Wallin, J. (2009). Rediscovering the "back-and-forthness" of rhetoric in the age of YouTube. *College Composition and Communication, 61*(2), W374-W396.

Kramer, A. D. I. (2013, June 29). OK so. A lot of people have asked me about my and Jamie and Jeff's recent study published in PNAS, and I wanted to give a brief public explanation. The reason we did this research is because we care about [Facebook update]. Retrieved from https://www.facebook.com/akramer/posts/10152987150867796 .

Kramer, A. D. I., Gullory, J. E. & Hancock, J. T. (2014). Experimental evidence of massive-scale emotional contagion through social networks. *Proceedings of the National Academy of Sciences of the United States of America, 111*(24), 8788–8790. doi: 10.1073/pnas.1320040111

Long, E. (2008). *Community literacy and the rhetoric of local publics.* Fort Collins, CO: The WAC Clearinghouse and Parlor Press. Retrieved from https://wac.colostate.edu/books/long_community/.

Lowry, M. (2014, January 15). Won't be purchasing tide no more this is bs still thousands of people without water that won't have it for quite a while they've lifted very few zones and have tons to go. And even the ones who zones were [Facebook comment]. Retrieved from https://www.facebook.com/Tide/posts/10151871476 253231.

McKee, H. A. & Porter, J. E. (2009). *The ethics of Internet research: A rhetorical case-based process.* New York, NY: Peter Lang.

McKee, H. A. & Porter, J. E. (2012). The ethics of conducing writing research on the Internet: How heuristics help. In L. Nickoson & M. P. Sheridan (Eds.), *Writing studies in practice: Methods and methodologies* (pp. 245–260). Carbondale, IL: Southern Illinois University Press.

Messenger-Rishel, A. (2014, January 13). Please reconsider! I am not affected, however, I have very dear friends that are. They have driven 2 hours to their family's house to bathe and do their laundry . . . they have 3 small children. Many people do not have the resources [Facebook comment]. Retrieved from https://www.facebook.com/Tide/posts/10151871476253231.

Morrison, R. (2014, January 13). Do you have clean clothes? I do not live their but those that do, deserve your respect. Help them :-) [Facebook comment]. Retrieved from https://www.facebook.com/Tide/posts/10151871476253231.

Neumayer, C. & Schoßböck, J. (2011). Political lurkers? Young people in Australia and their political life worlds online. In P. Parycek, M. J. Kripss & N. Edelmann (Eds.), *Proceedings of the International Conference for E-Democracy and Open Government,* 131–143. Retrieved from http://www.donau-uni.ac.at/imperia/md/content/department/gpa/zeg/bilder/cedem/cedem11_final_version.pdf.

Pew Research Center. (2014a). Millennials in adulthood: Detached from institutions, networked with friends. Retrieved from http://www.pewsocialtrends.org/2014/03/07/millennials-in-adulthood/.

Pew Research Center. (2014b). Social networking fact sheet. Retrieved from http://www.pewinternet.org/fact-sheets/social-networking-fact-sheet/.

Potts, L. (2014). *Social media in disaster response: How experience architects can build for participation.* New York, NY: Routledge.

Romberger, J. E. (2007). An ecofeminist methodology: Studying the ecological dimensions of the digital environment. In H. A. McKee & D. N. DeVoss (Eds.), *Digital writing research: Technologies, methodologies, and ethical issues* (pp. 203–227). Cresskill, NJ: Hampton.

Sidler, M. (2007). Playing scavenger and gazer with scientific discourse: Opportunities and ethics for online research. In H. A. McKee & D. N. DeVoss (Eds.), *Digital writing research: Technologies, methodologies, and ethical issues* (pp. 71–88). Cresskill, NJ: Hampton.

Scott, T. & Welch, N. (2014) One train can hide another: Critical materials for public composition. *College English, 76*(6), 562–579.

Twitter. (2014). Developer policy. Retrieved from https://dev.twitter.com/overview /terms/policy#3._Respect_Users%E2%80%99_Control_and_Privacy.

Vie, S. (2014a). In defense of "slacktivism": The Human Rights Campaign Facebook logo as digital activism. *First Monday, 19*(4). Retrieved from http://firstmonday.org /ojs/index.php/fm/article/view/4961.

Vie, S. (2014b). You are how you play: Privacy policies and data mining in social networking games. In J. deWinter & R. M. Moeller (Eds.), *Computer games and technical communication: Critical methods & applications at the intersection* (pp. 131–187). Burlington, VT: Ashgate.

Warnick, B. (2007). *Rhetoric online: Persuasion and politics on the World Wide Web.* New York, NY: Peter Lang.

Welch, N. (2008). *Living room: Teaching public writing in a privatized world.* Portsmouth, NH: Boynton/Cook.

Williams, H., Jr. (1982). A country boy can survive. On *The pressure is on* [record]. Nashville, TN: Elektra.

Wilson, M. (2014, January 13). You're an idiot. You stupid city slickers wouldn't have lasted one day . . . ONE DAY! and would have been throwing a fit. [Facebook comment]. Retrieved from https://www.facebook.com/Tide/posts/10151871476253231.

Woods, B. (2014, January 14). So disappointed in Tide. How can such a huge company pass up the chance to help thousands of people in need! Charleston has been without water since last Thursday and they choose to make a decision about whether or not [Facebook comment]. Retrieved from https://www.facebook.com /Tide/posts/10151871476253231.

Workman, C. & Workman, H. (2014, January 13). This is stupid 300,000 still don't have clean water and only 4 zones have been named to start flushing. Me and my family of 4 including 2 small children have mountains of laundry! This could have helped so many! Ask [Facebook comment]. Retrieved from https://www.facebook .com/Tide/posts/10151871476253231.

CHAPTER 4

AFTER A DECADE OF SOCIAL MEDIA: ABSTAINERS AND EX-USERS

Cory Bullinger
FIS

Stephanie Vie
University of Central Florida

Early research on social media in rhetoric and composition frequently focused on analyses of particular social media technologies, such as Facebook and MySpace (Balzhiser et al., 2011; Maranto & Barton, 2010). Similarly, small-scale studies offered detailed case studies of social media users (A. Buck, 2012; DePew, 2011). Fewer studies gathered quantitative and qualitative data about social media use and impact at a larger level; while some early exceptions exist (e.g., Vie, 2007, 2008), the field's push toward more data-driven research on social media at a national level has intensified only recently (Jones, 2014; Mina, 2014; Pigg et al., 2014; Potts & Jones, 2011; Shepherd, 2015; Wolff, 2015). Indeed, several of the authors in this collection, such as Michael J. Faris and Lilian W. Mina, continue this emphasis on data-driven social media research in rhetoric and composition.

What is apparent from this literature is that our field seems to have reached a turning point in its awareness of social media, one that reflects larger turning points in the United States regarding social media. That is, social media use has reached a critical mass in this country such that those who do not use these technologies may feel left out, unable to share in certain moments common to social media users. This near-ubiquity of social media use illustrates that being a part of social media technologies like Facebook, Twitter, Pinterest, Instagram, and others is fast becoming a given for American adults. Indeed, other chapters in this collection explore the ways that social media have quickly become embedded into our lives. As a result, greater numbers of faculty are either already incorporating social media into their personal, professional, and pedagogical lives or are feeling the pressure to do so. But as recent research results show, faculty remain divided about how to incorporate social media into their teaching and for what purposes (Seaman & Tinti-Kane, 2013; Vie, 2015). Similarly, individuals speak of the tensions between personal and private use of social media (see Les Hutchinson's chapter in this collection for an exploration of reasons why anonymity in social media is deeply necessary today as a result of these tensions).

Because early research has painted detailed pictures of social media users and their literacy practices, it is important that we also step back, so to speak, and examine the larger landscape surrounding social media use in our field. As well, it is important to balance pedagogical research about social media in rhetoric and composition (Bowdon, 2014; E. Buck, 2015; DePew, 2011; Williams, 2009) with scholarship that addresses non-academic uses of social media. Indeed, it may be even more important to attend to scholarship that addresses non-use of social media entirely. Social media abstainers and social media ex-users (those who began using such technologies and then stopped, not having returned) are important groups to study. In this chapter, then, we offer a content analysis of recent popular press pieces to analyze how the media depicts abstainers and ex-users.

IMPETUS FOR THE STUDY

The landscape of social media use is constantly changing: Sites rise and fall in popularity, services and features evolve, and users shape new practices like hashtagging and viral memes. This constant change affects research on social media too: Research on social media frequently demonstrates a "pro-innovation bias" (Rogers, 1995, p. 100). The pro-innovation bias occurs in research on technologies when scholars imply that an innovative technology should be diffused and adopted rapidly by all members of society. Indeed, Everett M. Rogers (1995) recommended that researchers should work against this pro-innovation bias by examining the broader context in which innovations diffuse, which "helps illuminate the broader system in which the diffusion process occurs . . . and increase our understanding of the motivations for adopting an innovation" (p. 110).

The study that we report on in this chapter attempts to address the pro-innovation bias that is easy to fall prey to in social media research. In other words, given how social media has diffused throughout American society (and indeed throughout the world), it is tempting to argue that—for example—rhetoric and composition faculty should adopt social media technologies for the classroom because of their ubiquity. And we want to be careful to point out that our aim here is not to argue against the value of social media; as Vie (2007, 2008, 2015) has argued elsewhere, social media technologies can offer significant advantages for the rhetoric and composition classroom, especially given the rhetorical and compositional elements at play in such technologies. Instead, we offer here a discussion of some of the broader context within which the innovations of social media technologies have diffused in our field; this context allows readers to see the complex landscape surrounding social media use—personally, professionally, and pedagogically—in the field of rhetoric and composition at this moment. As a result, readers are afforded as well a glimpse into the spaces in between, the spaces where non-users and social media abstainers can be found. Current research in rhetoric and composition and beyond does an excellent job of paying attention to social media, exploring its benefits (both personal and professional) and critiquing various elements of its spread. However, this scholarly research tends to default to a focus on social media users, examining topics such as user personalities (Correa et al., 2010) and motivations for using specific networking sites (Guadagno, Okdie & Eno, 2008; Hargittai & Hsieh, 2010; Hughes et al., 2012; Joinson, 2008; Nadkarni & Hofmann, 2012). What the current research in rhetoric and composition lacks is attention to those who choose not to use social media.

THE UBIQUITY OF SOCIAL MEDIA

Social media is now ubiquitous in our "always on" culture. According to a 2013 Pew Research report, 73 percent of online adults use at least one social networking site and 42 percent use multiple sites (Duggan & Smith). In the past decade, social networking sites have exploded in popularity. Facebook grew to over 1.3 billion monthly active users since its inception in 2004. In 2015, Twitter users sent 500 million tweets a day, an impressive increase from 20,000 a day when launched in 2006. Social media now permeate American culture, with the Pew Internet Research Center estimating that 74 percent of online adults use social networking sites. However, this is not just an American phenomenon: Fast-growing social networks like WeChat, Weibo, and Qzone dominate Asia, while India records remarkable social networking growth and was projected to have the world's largest Facebook population by 2016.

Like other pervasive technologies such as the telephone, the television, and the car, participation in social media has permeated our collective culture so deeply that it is now considered de rigueur for today's global citizen. Indeed, it is often assumed and even taken for granted that someone else is a social media user. Much like having a cell phone (and today, even having a smartphone) is taken for granted, having a social media presence is taken for granted as well. But as Alice Marwick (2011) has asserted, "Cellphones have gone from luxury product to necessary object in a decade" (para. 5). Not owning a cell phone "puts one at a serious disadvantage," so much so that programs like SafeLink offer cell phones to those without them for safety reasons (Marwick, 2011). Similarly, social media have moved from niche product to necessary technological tool for participation in today's global marketplace. This perspective—that social media is necessary and participation is expected—then raises the question, what about the non-users and those who choose not to participate in these technologies? As researchers like Cynthia L. Selfe (1999) and Dennis Baron (2009) have argued, the pervasiveness of technologies renders them invisible; we would argue here that the ubiquity of social media now renders non-users nearly invisible as well.

Specifically, non-use or refusal of social media technologies requires scholarly attention. Social media non-use has consequences in today's society. Non-users may feel a sense of disconnect from friends and family; they may miss out on updates, family photos, and invitations to social events. Pavica Sheldon (2012) argued that non-users are frequently "significantly older and score higher on shyness and loneliness, [are] less socially active, and [are] less prone to sensation seeking activities" (p. 1960). Because of the significant impacts on non-users' and abstainers' social lives and even mental health, it is important to examine the discourse surrounding social media non-use—either those who have never adopted (abstainers) or those who have quit using social media (ex-users)—in order to assess larger trends surrounding social media use and preferences. A better understanding of the nuanced spectrum of motivations surrounding non-use could help developers create better social media tools and users think more carefully about the inclusion of social media into their personal, professional, and pedagogical lives.

USERS, ABSTAINERS, AND NON-USERS

When rejecters of technology are considered, they are frequently considered "anti-users," merely the opposite of users of social media. In other words, a binary emerges: Individuals are either users or non-users of social media, and there is little opportunity to expand beyond that simple dichotomy. However, assessing the discursive trends that frame a dichotomous conception of individuals as users or non-users has important rhetorical implications for social and cultural frameworks. Much of the current research regarding social media use has maintained this binary—studies are concerned with the factors that mark and distinguish users from non-users or are predictive of use/non-use (Choudrie et al., 2013; Hargittai, 2008; Lampe, Vitak & Ellison, 2013; Ljepava, Orr, Locke & Ross, 2013; Ryan & Xenos, 2011; Sheldon, 2012; Steiger, Burger, Bohn & Voracek, 2013). Indeed, in an early landmark study, Hargittai (2008) specifically posed this binary as what she termed the "significant antecedent question . . . that has been largely ignored: Are there systematic differences between who is and who is not a SNS user?" (p. 276).

However, further research is needed to step beyond a simplistic view of user/ non-user and instead expand our understanding of social media interaction into a more nuanced continuum. Such a continuum might include a variety of positions individuals could take, from people who rapidly switch among multiple social media and platforms (see Bronwyn T. Williams' chapter in this collection for examples of interviews with such users), to those who tend to stick to the same one or two social media tools because their friends are there, to those who used certain social media tools but quit using them or abandoned their accounts, to those who never adopted social media technologies at all. This continuum can also include those whose level of technological access prevents them from participation in social media technologies.

Emergent research has begun to track users' experiences as they quit social media entirely or otherwise leave certain social media platforms (Azarbakht, 2014; Baker & White, 2011; Baumer et al., 2013; Bobkowski & Smith, 2013), including exploring reasons why they quit (Turan, Tinmaz & Goktas, 2013). Rivka Ribak and Michele Rosenthal (2011) have argued that "if carrying a Blackberry or iPhone has certain cultural connotations, then not owning one is equally meaningful," especially so if this rejection "requires conscious effort" (p. 2). Studying social media refusal, rejection, or lapses can offer glimpses into users' reasoning behind such rejection, particularly when—as Ribak and Rosenthal have noted—to not participate requires conscious effort. For instance, an individual who doesn't participate in social media may have to deliberately reach out to friends and family through alternative means of communication, such as the telephone or email, and may have to put forth particular effort to keep these lines of communication open. Comparatively, an individual who is already tapped in to his or her networks of friends and family in a social media site like Facebook would be offered an experience curated by the site to maintain connections among users. Prompts like, "It's Bob's birthday today! Why don't you say happy birthday?" are automatic reminders of friendship connections that the technological interface of a social media site provides to keep users connected.

METHODS

This chapter examines how social media non-users (both abstainers and ex-users) are referred to and discussed in general discourse, or what Laura Portwood-Stacer (2013) referred to as "everyday conversation, journalistic coverage (newspapers, magazines, blogs), and conversation within social media platforms themselves" (p. 3). Thus, this chapter analyzes current discourse within the popular media surrounding social media non-users and users and the possible rhetorical implications of such a narrative. Specific research questions are as follows:

RQ1: How do users rhetorically frame non-users in popular discourse?

RQ2: How do non-users rhetorically frame themselves?

RQ3: What are the specific reasons given for not using social media, if any?

This analysis ultimately seeks to reveal how non-users are rhetorically constructed by themselves and by others within the current societal and cultural narrative surrounding social media technology. Identifying and analyzing common rhetorical constructions and motivations across current social media discourse is important to better understand how technology refusal, and more specifically social media refusal, is framed within larger cultural narratives. By revealing the language that circulates around social media non-use and abstention, we can reveal more about those users along the continuum that we often forget.

This study was comprised of a content analysis of current online media regarding social media non-use (as opposed to social media use). While technological access and digital divide issues remain of concern in global Internet and social media use, we paid attention particularly to discourse around voluntary non-use rather than non-use related to lack of technological access. In order to attend to popular conceptions of social media non-use, our search results were limited to online news and general media, including blogs, online magazines, and other social media sites.

To ensure that the search results were relevant, publication years were limited (i.e., published on or after 2010), though of course even limiting to a current date range at the time of research may still produce dated results given the constant change associated with social media research and the slow academic publishing cycle. The results were limited to online posts or articles concerning social media non-use in any of its forms: quitting, abstaining, taking a hiatus, detoxing, etc. Also included were discussions framed from individual non-use as well as business or corporate non-use (so long as the content did not devolve into social marketing advice).

An initial literature search of "social media AND refus*" was conducted using the University of Central Florida (UCF) Library's OneSearch function. This search produced several applicable results and helped reveal additional relevant search terminology. Search terms included social media, social network*, SNS, Facebook, Twitter, LinkedIn, Tumblr, Pinterest, non*use, refus*, resist*, reject*, avoid, abandon*, delet*, quit*, drop+out*, non*adopt*. Various combinations of these terms were used to search LexisNexis, Google (not Google Scholar), and specific news media sites (*The New Yorker, The New York Times, The*

Atlantic, Newsweek, Time, and *NPR*). Applicable media were then reviewed for citations or links to other potentially applicable media.

After applying the inclusion criteria, 73 articles (including blog and forum posts as well as online newspaper and magazine articles) were deemed applicable and reviewed for coding themes. Six major themes were identified and used to code the reviewed literature: (1) *quitting/fatigue*, (2) *non-use* (individual or business), (3) *cons of social media*, (4) *ubiquity of social media*, (5) *costs of non-use*, and (6) *social media and professional writers*. These themes helped provide a framework for the analysis as well as guide the discussion of the findings in the following section.

FINDINGS

SOCIAL MEDIA: INEVITABLE, UBIQUITOUS, AND ADDICTIVE

One consistent theme across the corpus of results was the perception that social media, in whatever form it may take, is fully entrenched in our society and culture. In other words, social media use is normalized, and non-use is consistently framed as abnormal. As commenter Michael Quinlain put it, "it bugs the sh*t out of me when people assume that EVERYONE has an account on Twitter or Facebook, and when they find out you don't they look at you *like you have two heads*" (as cited in Martin, 2013, emphasis ours). Conversely, users repeatedly describe interactions with non-users as "awkward" because users are forced to find common ground outside social media: e.g., "You have to try to find a way to converse with the non-Facebooker" (Wind, 2012). Despite the knowledge that social media is still optional in society, users may "still look at a person like they are speaking some sort of indiscernible language when they [say] that they don't use Facebook" (Wind, 2012). Another author succinctly summarized the disconnect between users and non-users in terms of collective experience: "The social media abstainer does not . . . share in the Facebook eye of [her] social collaborators" (Davis, 2012, March 6, para. 10).

Repeatedly across these articles and posts was an acknowledgement (tacit or explicitly stated) that social media is everywhere, it is overwhelming, and it is inescapable, whether one is a user or a non-user. As one author put it, "even if you unfriend everybody on Facebook, and you never join Twitter, and you don't have a LinkedIn profile or an About.me page or much else in the way of online presence, you're still going to end up being mapped and charted and slotted in to your rightful place in the global social network that is life" (Salmon, 2013). Such a perception gives individuals a feeling of inevitability, making them feel as though it is impossible to truly quit or abstain from participating in social media. This perception also notes the nature of social media in allowing individuals in today's society to make decisions about others—determining hierarchies, connections, and relationships based on social cues and markers found in social media technologies. In the absence of these cues and markers, individuals must then do the more difficult work of reaching out to learn more about a person through targeted face-to-face interactions.

Perhaps unsurprisingly, despite the fact that many users recognize the less desirable nature of certain social networking practices and norms (e.g., its always-on nature, its promotion of self-centered posts and updates, its ability to categorize and hierarchize users), social media use is still perceived as "inevitable" (Zhang, De Choudury & Grudin, 2014, p. 1). The following excerpts from the corpus of literature gathered help illustrate this point:

> We have allowed [social media] to change us, such that *there's no going back.* Even the people who resign in style generally find their way back sooner or later. They may switch from Twitter to Facebook, but *it's hard to live without social media nowadays.* (Lu, 2013, emphasis ours)

> I salute these quitters and dream of a world in which I could also drop off the grid and return to a time when my phone didn't feel like an extra appendage. . . . *But is quitting the digital world a realistic option? No way.* (McGuire, 2013, emphasis ours)

> That's why I wonder if I can get away from social media. . . . Nobody really escapes social media. . . . I feel no different than the five-year-old who threatens to "run away from home" and doesn't get any further than three houses down the street. (Comm, 2014)

> You can't get away from it. It's everything. It's everywhere. . . . The moment we're in now is about trying to deal with all this technology rather than rejecting it, because obviously *we can't reject it entirely.* (Timberg, 2012, emphasis ours)

> Social media's efficacy could hold the seeds of something quite dark, a tipping point where an individual feels it is less an option and more an obligation to be present on a social media platform. Could it effectively become compulsory—if not in law then in civic and practical terms—to join in the "conversation"? (Avocado Sweet, 2013)

These excerpts underscore the "point-of-no-return" metaphor with use of terms like "there's no going back" and "tipping point." (This theme was further reinforced by the repeated references to The Eagles' song "Hotel California" and joking reminders that "you can check out but you can't ever leave.")

Moreover, the literature gathered repeatedly discussed the issue of addiction; that is, social media (Facebook in particular) was discussed as especially addictive. Social media was described as "mental junk food" that lacks the nutrition provided by other, healthier communication modes as well as metaphors likening social media use to a drug addiction: "Facebook [is] the gateway drug to hyper-connection" (Hoium, 2012). Again, depictions in the popular media of social media as an inevitable and addictive element reflects not only the ubiquity of these technologies in the day-to-day lives of many worldwide, but also how seamlessly they have been incorporated into activities related to building and maintaining relationships between people.

THE ABSTAINERS AND DISENCHANTED EX-USERS

The two non-user typologies gleaned from this study were those (1) completely abstaining from social media and (2) those quitting social media (some of whom described their "social media fatigue")—the abstainers and the ex-users. These two typologies emerged throughout various online genres, including rants about just having quit (or an intention to do so), reflections on lessons learned from having quit, essays on the high costs of quitting and/or not using social media, and posts about being jealous of those who never used or were able to stop using social media. Several motivations for non-use were repeatedly cited across the literature that support findings in previous research (Azarbakht, 2014; Baumer et al., 2013). Baumer et al. (2013) codified these according to the following six "interpretive themes": privacy, data use and misuse, banality, productivity, addiction, and external pressures.

Non-use in general (whether an abstainer or ex-user) was often met with negativity or disappointment on behalf of users. More specifically, non-users were often referred to in terms of simply not existing to users: "If you're not on Facebook, it's possible you don't exist" (Hill, 2012). Moreover, this user-based discourse generally reinforced an oversimplified view of non-users. For instance, one blog post posited only two possible motivations to stop using social media: either due to inaccessibility or voluntary shunning of "the orthodoxy of society" (Avocado Sweet, 2013). Additionally, in the instances of users discussing social media non-use, users typically framed discussions according to the costs associated with non-use. These costs include the perception of non-use as "suspicious" or somehow indicative of deviance (Hill, 2012) and the "missed opportunities for self-expression, personal growth, learning, support, and civic exchange" (Hartzog & Selinger, 2013).

Abstainers: The Social Media Holdouts

The abstainers (also known as the non-users, the resisters, or "refuseniks") were typically discussed from a third-party point of view, such as stories documenting why individuals or certain professions have not (yet) adopted social media. That is, unlike the many posts written by social media quitters, there were few posts or articles written from a non-user's perspective (see Rollheiser, 2013, for an example of a non-user perspective). This may be the result of the focus on digital tools within this study—non-users may be less likely to use blogs or forums, whereas quitters might simply be using other online services. Indeed, many authors documenting their abandonment of social media were often explicit that they were only quitting one tool but would continue to use other social media services (e.g., quitting Facebook but not Twitter or their blog).

Quitters: The Tired, the Proud

Articles and posts regarding quitting social media were generally separable into either those discussing (a) completely deleting one's account and quitting social media or a specific service or (b) taking a prolonged hiatus due to social media fatigue. The latter often described being tired of tedious activities associated with social media (i.e., account upkeep, or what Zeynep Tufekci (2008) referred to as online "social grooming" activities) or simply having grown tired of social media altogether. Quitters often cited social media (specifically Facebook) as an unnecessary waste of time, tying back to the earlier theme of addiction—some individuals described reaching a breaking point of addiction that then led to a reflective examination of what really mattered to them in their daily use of time, leading to the eventual choice to quit altogether rather than meter out their social media use differently.

Analysis of the literature gathered revealed that, overall, posts and articles by ex-users about their quitting largely supported existing research on the performative aspect of media refusal (see Portwood-Stacer, 2012, 2013). Many were celebratory essays to validate the now ex-user's decision to buck the trend of social media; some were pragmatic cost-benefit analyses; several provided readers links to "virtual suicide" sites and campaigns such as QuitFacebookDay.com and SuicideMachine.org that would "kill off" one's Facebook or other social media tools. Additionally, many quitters made a point to assert that their opting out of social media (or a specific social media site) did not mean a complete rejection of technology: "Opting out of social networks that are noisy and offer marginal benefits is not the same as opting out of technology" (Shawghnessy, 2012); "Facebook is a website; it's NOT the web" (mmilan,

2010); "disconnecting is not the same thing as being disconnected" (Majewski, 2012).

As noted by Portwood-Stacer (2012), social media quitters are often seen by users as "elitists" who "perceive themselves to be somehow better" than their user counterparts. Within the literature analyzed, several authors explicitly countered this perception in an attempt to preclude such a reading. For instance, one author included the disclaimer: "Please know that I am not placing judgment on anyone who likes or loves social media or blogging or any of the benefits of them. If it's something you enjoy, that's great! It just wasn't a good fit for me" (Mason, 2014). Another clarified to readers that her "intent was not to break up with the social media site to assert some 'I'm too cool to even be on the grid' hipster mentality" (Weaver, 2014). By contrast, one ex-user *did* embrace this elitist perception, noting that she went so far as quitting her job at Facebook and moving to a small town far away from the constant connectivity of bigger cities. She described the constant performative aspect of social media as a tiring activity despite non-use; in other words, she found that even though she had quit using social media, she was nonetheless a performer within it: "Social media makes all the world a stage" (as cited in Timberg, 2012).

IMPLICATIONS FOR PROFESSIONALS

Only a few articles and posts were concerned with non-use among professionals. Of those that were deemed applicable for inclusion in this study, several articles discussed non-use within a professional context (e.g., medicine, law). Barriers for professionals revolved around the ethical aspects of social media use. For instance, doctors have largely been discouraged from participating in social media for fear of patient privacy issues, though private social media services are available specifically for doctors. Similarly, pharmaceutical companies and banks have avoided social media given concerns over regulatory compliance and privacy. Even some academics have grown wary after widely publicized cases like that of Steven Salaita. Additionally, there are known costs to non-use: namely, missing out on all of the online interactions. "Society exists where people interact" (Baribeau, 2011) and now those interactions occur ever more frequently online in sites like Facebook and Twitter.

Others specifically discussed social media use and costs associated with non-use for professional writers and communicators. Overall, for professional communicators, social media was deemed necessary to accomplish career goals. Even those professional communicators who were writing about quitting social media acknowledged the importance of these technologies on their field and careers (though some did warn readers not to use them at the expense of other non-online/digital tools). However, most of the articles that discussed the implications of social media non-use on professional writing framed it from the perspective that social media was unavoidable; these articles assumed that *some* social media would be used, but one's choice of site would vary according to his or her specific needs. Several articles were personal accounts of professional communicators and even some social media consultants quitting social media; these were largely accounts of quitting one specific site (usually Facebook). One author noted that Facebook lacked the control over information that she needed as a professional journalist (Angwin, 2013), illustrating again that social media non-use and abstention is much more complex than simply seeing users as rejecting all social media. Instead, certain technologies and platforms might be refused given an individual's career goals or location (see Hutchinson's chapter in this volume for a discussion of how her previous university set up a chilling social media policy.)

ACROSS THE YEARS, ACROSS THE SITES

After sorting by year, certain trends emerged. Namely, specific topics surfaced at key points, typically in reaction to factors related to social media. For instance, a substantial amount was written in 2013 concerning the supposed "exodus" of teenagers from Facebook (Saul, 2014). Many articles about quitting in 2011 were in reaction to changes made to Facebook's privacy policies, whereas many articles about quitting in 2014 were about personal decisions to stop using the site. These specific acts of refusal in response to particular issues or concerns (e.g., site policy changes) are essentially users' form of protest. This further reinforces existing research concerning the performative aspect of the act of quitting. In the content reviewed in this analysis, such protests were more often framed by (ex-)users as the final recourse in response to being unhappy or otherwise dissatisfied with a site's service. Indeed, one *New York Times* blog post author conveyed the seriousness of what is essentially a protest by almost immediately distinguishing "this [current] round of complaining [about Facebook] from the 'I-don't-care-what-you're-eating-for-breakfast' camp," noting that the reported wave of Facebook quitters "see themselves as *taking a principled stand* on how their data is used even if it means sacrificing an easy way to see a sister's baby photos" (Brustein, 2010). Thus, these users felt the need to push back against social media because they found that the benefits of social media, specifically Facebook, did not outweigh the costs, and these costs were comprising these users' external values, specifically regarding data ownership and privacy (Morrison & Gomez, 2014).

Additionally, although the literature was not formally coded in any way according to social media site, the prevalence of only a few sites and the small scope of this analysis allowed themes concerning specific sites to emerge none-theless. For instance, it became evident that many users ascribe different charac-teristics to different sites. Twitter was consistently described as "different" insofar as it did not induce the same negative behaviors associated with other social media, especially Facebook: "Twitter doesn't enter my mental space like the [other social media sites] do" (Milnor, 2014). Thus, quitters often mentioned keeping their Twitter account despite having deleted their Facebook, Instagram, Pinterest, or other accounts. For example, one author noted that she would remain active on Twitter, asserting that Twitter "is the one social media platform I've always used responsibly—and one that doesn't give me angsty, FOUL [Fear Of an Unfulfilled Life]-like feelings" (Turgeon, 2014). These findings about the importance of the specific social media platform reinforce Guo et al.'s (2012) assertion that social media preference plays an important part in the use of a site, which supports a more nuanced approach towards categorizing non-users' motivations. Thus, there are difficulties with making generalizations across social media sites, as each has its own strengths and weaknesses and its perceived use-fulness depends largely on a user's individual needs. Some participants may leave Twitter but stay in Facebook; others may lurk in Twitter and Instagram but never bother to join Facebook. Again, the data gathered for this study illustrates that social media use is more complex than simply a binary state of use or non-use.

DISCUSSION

RQ1: How do users rhetorically frame non-users in popular discourse?

The literature written *by* users *about* non-users (including non-adopters or ex-users) largely discussed the costs of non-use. That is, social media users writing about non-use framed their discussions according to the missed opportunities and the perceived liability of not participating in social media spheres. Moreover, non-users were framed as abnormal, suspicious, or deviant. Such a rhetorical framing is not surprising given that social media was almost unanimously per-ceived as ubiquitous and inescapable. Thus, popular discourse frames non-use as representative of dissent against the now-normalized and institutionalized modes of social-media-based communication and participation. The major exception to this framing was articles or posts about teenagers leaving Facebook, which was a popular topic among general web-based discourse. In these instances, the non-users (the teenagers) were discussed in terms of the impact of their absence on Facebook rather than on the liabilities incurred due to their non-use.

RQ2: How do non-users rhetorically frame themselves?

Non-users, including ex-users and abstainers, consistently framed themselves as single individuals with legitimate motivations for their specific instance of non-use. Many felt the need to thoroughly explain their decision, and others even included disclaimers and caveats to their confessions so as to anticipate possible rebuttals from users (i.e., the need to justify their deviance). In general, the non-user-authored discourse reinforced the assertion that non-use includes a wide spectrum of individuals and varying motivations. That is, non-users framed themselves differently according to their specific situation: some framed themselves as active dissenters with a deliberately political stance, whereas others were simply individuals making a personal decision to stop using social media. Thus, this analysis further supports the assertion that non-users cannot be as neatly categorized as previously assumed.

RQ3: What are the specific reasons given for not using social media, if any?

Specific reasons given for non-use largely followed previous research findings (Baumer et al., 2013; Morrison & Gomez, 2014). These included, but were not limited to, privacy and safety concerns, perceived lack of control over data, context collapse, self-presentation and identity management issues, time constraints, poor quality of online interactions and friendships, dislike of the service and/or site itself, dissonance of values with a specific site's practices, feeling overwhelmed, and addiction concerns. Much of the literature, including that written by users, acknowledged these as undesirable but unavoidable consequences associated with social media use, and most presented their own cost-benefit analysis to justify their decision regarding social media use. For instance, some users noted these concerns but argued that they were not enough to outweigh continued use; on the other hand, non-users found these concerns to outweigh the benefits of use and thus presented these reasons as justification for quitting. Overall, this discourse analysis supported previous findings regarding non-users' motivations for not using or stopping use of social media (Azarbakht, 2014; Baker & White, 2011; Baumer et al., 2013; Bobkowski & Smith, 2013; Turan, Tinmaz & Goktas, 2013).

CONCLUSION

The current literature on technology refusal asserts that it is vital to assess and understand individual-level rejection because "the reasons why these individual users may reject a technology must also be part of the discourse on sociology of technology" (Murthy & Mani, 2013, p. 4). Thus, research on non-users is important to provide the nuanced motivations that drive non-use decisions. Given the ubiquity of social media as a normalized social tool, it is unsurprising to hear non-users likened to "an outsider, hearing nothing, not being heard" (Avocado Sweet, 2013). However, ensuring that non-users are heard despite this general perception is vital. The goal of this chapter was to explore the larger cultural perceptions of social media non-users and better understand the rhetoric framing these perceptions—that is, to better understand the implications of this constructed cultural and social narrative surrounding social media technology.

This information adds to the existing body of literature by offering a more nuanced discussion of social media consumption and perceptions within general media discourse. Given the tendency to privilege users and marginalize non-users through omission, this research provides valuable data and context to the overall debate surrounding non-use. Based on the findings presented, non-users are a nuanced group deserving of further scholarly attention. Better understanding the legitimate motivations driving non-use is crucial to ensuring non-users are not marginalized or left behind in the coming decades.

REFERENCES

Angwin, J. (2013). Why I'm unfriending you on Facebook. Retrieved from http://juliaangwin.com/why-im-unfriending-you-on-facebook/.

Avocado Sweet. (2013). Social media: The party invitation you can't refuse. Retrieved from http://www.avocadosweet.com/social-media-the-party-invitation-you-cant-refuse/.

Azarbakht, A. (2014). Abandonment of social networks: Shift from use to non-use and experiences of technology non-use. *Proceedings of the SIGCHI Conference on Human Factors in Computing Systems, 28 April–1 May, 2014, Toronto, Canada.* New York, NY: ACM.

Baker, R. K. & White, K. M. (2011). In their own words: Why teenagers don't use social networking sites. *Cyberpsychology, Behavior, and Social Networking, 14*(6), 395–398.

Balzhiser, D., Polk, J. D., Grover, M., Lauer, E., McNeely, S. & Zmikly, J. (2011). The Facebook papers. *Kairos: A Journal of Rhetoric, Technology, and Pedagogy, 16*(1). Retrieved from http://kairos.technorhetoric.net/16.1/praxis/balzhiser-et-al/.

Baribeau, P. (2011, August 31). Can people and businesses succeed if they reject social software? *TribeHR*. Retrieved from https://humancapitalleague.com/can-people-and-businesses-succeed-if-they-reject-social-software/.

Baron, D. (2009). *A better pencil: Readers, writers, and the digital revolution.* New York, NY: Oxford University Press.

Baumer, E. P. S., Adams, P., Khovanskaya, V. D., Liao, T. C., Smith, M. E., Schwanda Sosik, V. & Williams, K. (2013). Limiting, leaving, and (re)lapsing: An exploration of Facebook non-use practices and experiences. *Proceedings of the SIGCHI Conference on Human Factors in Computing Systems, 27 April–2 May, 2013, Paris, France.* New York, NY: ACM. 3257–3266.

Bobkowski, P. & Smith, J. (2013). Social media divide: Characteristics of emerging adults who do not use social network websites. *Media, Culture & Society, 35*(6), 771–781.

Bowdon, M. A. (2014). Tweeting an ethos: Emergency messaging, social media, and teaching technical communication. *Technical Communication Quarterly, 23,* 35–54.

boyd, d. & Ellison, N. (2007). Social networking sites: Definition, history, and scholarship. *Journal of Computer-Mediated Communication, 13*(1), 210–230.

Brustein, J. (2010, May 12). Is there life after Facebook? *The New York Times.* Retrieved from http://bits.blogs.nytimes.com/2010/05/12/is-there-life-after-facebook/?_r=0.

Buck, A. (2012). Examining digital literacy practices on social network sites. *Research in the Teaching of English, 47*(1), 9–38.

Buck, E. (2015). Facebook, Instagram, and Twitter, oh my: Assessing the efficacy of the rhetorical composing situation with FYC students as advanced social media practitioners. *Kairos: A Journal of Rhetoric, Technology, and Pedagogy, 19*(2). Retrieved from http://technorhetoric.net/19.3/praxis/buck/.

Choudrie, J., Vyas, A., Voros, T. & Tsitsianis, N. (2013). Comparing the adopters and non-adopters of online social networks: A UK perspective. *46th Hawaii International Conference on System Sciences (HICSS), 7–10 January 2013, Maui, HI.* New York, NY: IEEE. 2823–2832.

Comm, J. (2014, March 24). *I am leaving social media.* [LinkedIn post]. Retrieved from https://www.linkedin.com/pulse/20140324190941-3561889-i-am-leaving -social-media.

Correa, T., Hinsley, A. W. & de Zúñiga, H. G. (2010). Who interacts on the Web?: The intersection of users' personality and social media use. *Computers in Human Behavior, 26,* 247–253.

Davis, J. (2012, March 6). The high cost of abstention. Retrieved from https://thesoci etypages.org/cyborgology/2012/03/06/the-high-cost-of-abstention/.

Davis, J. (2012, April). *Diagnosing (digital-social) technological ambivalence.* Presented at Theorizing the Web 2012: Logging Off and Disconnection, College Park, MD.

DePew, K. E. (2011). Social media at academia's periphery: Studying multilingual developmental writers' Facebook composing strategies. *The Reading Matrix, 11*(1), 54–75.

Duggan, M. & Smith, A. (2013, December 30). Social media update 2013. *Pew Research Internet Project.* Retrieved from http://www.pewinternet.org/2013/12/30 /social-media-update-2013/.

Guadagno, R. E., Okdie, B. M. & Eno, C. (2008). Who blogs? Personality predictors of blogging. *Computers in Human Behavior, 24*(5), 1993–2004.

Guo, Y., Goh, D. H.-L., Ilangovan, K., Jiao, S. & Yang, X. (2012). Investigating factors influencing non-use and abandonment of microblogging services. *Journal of Digital Information Management, 10*(6), 421–429.

Hargittai, E. (2008). Whose space? Differences among users and non-users of social network sites. *Journal of Computer-Mediated Communication, 13*(1), 276–297.

Hargittai, E. & Hsieh, Y.-L. P. (2010). Predictors and consequences of differentiated practices on social network sites. *Information, Communication & Society, 13*(4), 515–536.

Hartzog, W. & Selinger, E. (2013, February 15). Quitters never win: The costs of leaving social media. *The Atlantic*. Retrieved from http://www.theatlantic.com/technology/archive/2013/02/quitters-never-win-the-costs-of-leaving-social-media /273139/.

Hill, K. (2012). Beware, tech abandoners. People without Facebook accounts are "suspicious." *Forbes*. Retrieved from http://www.forbes.com/sites/kashmirhill/2012 /08/06/beware-tech-abandoners-people-without-facebook-accounts-are-suspicious /#5a64c9f18456

Hogan, B. & Quan-Haase, A. (2010). Persistence and change in social media. *Bulletin of Science, Technology & Society, 30*, 309–315.

Hoium, T. (2012, January 21). The perils of social media connectivity: You just can't quit. *Daily Finance*. Retrieved from http://www.scoop.it/t/social-kat-nips/p /1023624099/2012/01/22/the-perils-of-social-media-connectivity-you-just-can-t -quit-dailyfinance.

Hughes, D. J., Rowe, M., Bately, M. & Lee, A. (2012). A tale of two sites: Twitter vs. Facebook and the personality predictors of social media usage. *Computers in Human Behavior, 28*(2), 561–569.

Joinson, A. N. (2008). Looking at, looking up or keeping up with people?: Motives and use of Facebook. *Proceedings of the ACM Conference on Human Factors in Computing Systems, 5–10 April 2008, Florence, Italy*. New York, NY: ACM. 1027–1036.

Jones, J. (2014). Programming in network exchanges. *Computers and Composition, 34*, 23–38.

Lampe, C., Vitak, J. & Ellison, N. (2013). Users and nonusers: Interactions between levels of Facebook adoption and social capital. *Proceedings of the 2013 Conference on Computer-Supported Cooperative Work, 23–27 February 2013, San Antonio, TX*, pp. 809–819. New York, NY: ACM.

Ljepava, N., Orr, R. R., Locke, S. & Ross, C. (2013). Personality and social characteristics of Facebook non-users and frequent users. *Computers in Human Behavior, 29*, 1602–1607.

Lu, R. (2013, November 22). Facebook etiquette: Why quitting social media is a losing proposition. *The Federalist*. Retrieved from http://thefederalist.com/2013/11/22 /facebook-etiquette-quitting-social-media-losing-proposition/.

Majewski, M. (2012, August 15). Goodbye, social media; I'm leaving you. Retrieved from http://lockergnome.com/2012/08/15/goodbye-social-media-im-leaving-you/.

Maranto, G. & Barton, M. (2010). Paradox and promise: MySpace, Facebook, and the sociopolitics of the writing classroom. *Computers and Composition, 27*, 36–47.

Martin, T. (2013, December 19). Is there a future for smartphone users who reject social media? Retrieved from http://pocketnow.com/2013/12/19/social-media -requirements.

Marwick, A. (2011, August). "If you don't like it, don't use it. It's that simple." ORLY? [Blog entry]. *Social Media Collective Research Blog*. Retrieved from http://socialmediacollective.org/2011/08/11/if-you-dont-like-it-dont-use-it-its-that-simple-orly/.

Mason, T. (2014, March 24). Why I quit social media and why it matters to you. *Living the Story*. WordPress.com.

McGuire, M. (2013, October 4). You can't quit social networks. Get used to it. *PandoDaily*. Retrieved from https://pando.com/2013/10/04/you-cant-quit-social-networks-get-used-to-it/.

Milnor, D. (2014, January 2). Why I deleted my social media accounts. Retrieved from http://www.smogranch.com/2014/01/02/why-i-deleted-my-social-media-accounts/.

Mina, L. (2014). *First-year composition teachers' uses of new media technologies in the composition class* (Unpublished doctoral dissertation). Indiana University of Pennsylvania, Indiana, PA.

mmilan. (2010, May 8). Why I'm leaving Facebook. *Feynman's Radio*. Retrieved from http://mmilan.tumblr.com/post/581710593/why-im-leaving-facebook.

Morrison, S. & Gomez, R. (2014). Pushback: Expressions of resistance to the "ever-time" of constant online connectivity. *First Monday, 19*(8). Retrieved from http://firstmonday.org/ojs/index.php/fm/article/view/4902.

Murthy, S. R. & Mani, M. (2013). Discerning rejection of technology. *SAGE Open, 3*(2), 1–10.

Nadkarni, A. & Hofmann, S. G. (2012). Why do people use Facebook? *Personality and Individual Differences, 52*, 243–249.

Pigg, S., Grabill, J. T., Brunk-Chavez, B., Moore, J. L., Rosinski, P. & Curran, P. G. (2014). Ubiquitous writing, technologies, and the social practice of literacies of coordination. *Written Communication, 31*(1), 91–117.

Portwood-Stacer, L. (2012). Media refusal and conspicuous non-consumption: The performative and political dimensions of Facebook absention. *New Media & Society, 15*(7), 1041–1057.

Portwood-Stacer, L. (2013). How we talk about media refusal: Popular frames for understanding resistance to social media platforms in everyday life [PowerPoint presentation]. Retrieved from http://www.lauraportwoodstacer.com/wp-content/uploads/2013/03/ttw13-slides.pdf.

Potts, L. & Jones, D. (2011). Contextualizing experiences: Tracing the relationships between people and technologies in the social web. *Journal of Business and Technical Communication, 23*(3), 338–358.

Rey, P. J. (2012, May 10). Social media: You can log off but you can't opt out. Retrieved from https://thesocietypages.org/cyborgology/2012/05/10/social-media-you-can-log-off-but-you-cant-opt-out/.

Ribak, R. & Rosenthal, M. (2011, May). *Rethinking marginality: Media ambivalence and resistance in an age of convergence and ubiquity*. Paper presented at the annual meeting of the International Communication Association at Boston, MA.

Rogers, E. M. (1995). *The diffusion of innovations* (4th ed.) New York, NY: The Free Press.

Rollheiser, H. (2013, June 5). Social media: Abandon all hope, ye who log in here. The Cascade. Retrieved from http://ufvcascade.ca/social-media-abandon-all-hope-ye-who-log-in-here/.

Ryan, T. & Xenos, S. (2011). Who uses Facebook? An investigation into the relationship between the big five, shyness, narcissism, loneliness, and Facebook usage. Computers in Human Behavior, 27, 1658–1664.

Salmon, F. (2013, February 12). The social network you can't opt out of. Retrieved from http://blogs.reuters.com/felix-salmon/2013/02/12/the-social-network-you-cant-opt-out-of/.

Saul, D. J. (2014, January 15). 3 million teens leave Facebook in 3 years: The 2014 Facebook demographic report. iStrategyLabs. Retrieved from https://isl.co/2014/01/3-million-teens-leave-facebook-in-3-years-the-2014-facebook-demographic-report/.

Seaman, J. & Tinti-Kane, H. (2013, September). Social media for teaching and learning. Retrieved from http://www.pearsonlearningsolutions.com/higher-education/social-media-survey.php.

Selfe, C. L. (1999). Technology and literacy in the twenty-first century: The importance of paying attention. Carbondale, IL: Southern Illinois University Press.

Shawghnessy, H. (2012, August 7). Downgrading Facebook. Tech abandoner? Or rational lifestyle choice? Forbes. Retrieved from http://www.forbes.com/sites/haydnshaughnessy/2012/08/07/downgrading-facebook-tech-abandoner-or-rational-lifestyle-choice/#4c8b442d1494.

Sheldon, P. (2012). Profiling the non-users: Examination of life-position indicators, sensation seeking, shyness, and loneliness among users and non-users of social network sites. Computers in Human Behavior, 28, 1960–1965.

Sheppard, J. (2009). The rhetorical work of multimedia production practices: It's more than just technical skill. Computers and Composition, 26(2), 122–131.

Steiger, S., Burger, C. Bohn, M. & Voracek, M. (2013). Who commits virtual identity suicide? Differences in privacy concerns, Internet addiction, and personality between Facebook users and quitters. Cyberpyschology, Behavior, and Social Networking, 16(9), 629–634.

Timberg, C. (2012, August 3). Refugee from Facebook questions the social media life. The Washington Post. Retrieved from https://www.washingtonpost.com/business/economy/fugitive-from-facebook-questions-the-social-media-life/2012/08/03/5e4f855c-d0f3-11e1-adf2-d56eb210cdcd_story.html.

Tsatsou, P. (2011). Digital divides revisited: What is new about divides and their research. Media, Culture & Society, 33(2), 317–331.

Tufekci, Z. (2008). Grooming, gossip, Facebook and MySpace: What can we learn about these sites from those who won't assimilate? Information, Communication & Society, 11(4), 544–564.

Turan, Z., Tinmaz, H. & Goktas, Y. (2013). The reasons for non-use of social networking websites by university students. Comunicar, 21(41), 137–145.

Turgeon, J. K. (2014, February 10). I quit social media for 30 days . . . now what? The Retrieved from http://www.huffingtonpost.com/jordan-turgeon/quit-social-media_b_4756214.html.

Vie, S. (2007). *Engaging others in online social networking sites: Rhetorical practices in MySpace and Facebook* (Unpublished doctoral dissertation). The University of Arizona, Tucson, AZ.

Vie, S. (2008). Digital divide 2.0: "Generation M" and online social networking sites in the composition classroom. *Computers and Composition, 25*(1), 9–23.

Vie, S. (2015). What's going on: Challenges and opportunities for social media use in the writing classroom. *The Journal of Faculty Development, 29*(2), 33–44.

Weaver, S. (2014, January 10). How I resolved to quit Facebook and rediscovered the world. Retrieved from http://www.phillymag.com/news/2014/01/10/resolved-quit -facebook-rediscovered-world/.

Williams, B. T. (2009). *Shimmering literacies: Popular culture and reading and writing online.* New York, NY: Peter Lang.

Wind, J. (2012, October 24). Social media causes the fall of community. *The Cascade.* Retrieved from http://ufvcascade.ca/social-media-causes-the-fall-of-community/.

Wolff, W. (2015). Baby, we were born to tweet: Springsteen fans, the writing practices of *in situ* tweeting, and the research possibilities for Twitter. *Kairos: A Journal of Rhetoric, Technology, and Pedagogy, 19*(3). Retrieved from http://technorhetoric.net /19.3/topoi/wolff/.

Zhang, H., De Choudhury, M. & Grudin, J. (2014). Creepy but inevitable? The evolution of social networking. In *Proceedings of the 17th ACM Conference on Computer-Supported Cooperative Work and Social Computing, 15–19 February 2014, Baltimore, MD.* New York, NY: ACM.

CHAPTER 5

NETWORKING HARDSHIP: SOCIAL COMPOSING AS INVENTIVE RHETORICAL ACTION

Crystal Broch Colombini
University of Texas at San Antonio

Lindsey Hall
University of Texas at San Antonio

Beginning around 2006, the collapse of the American financial system and the subsequent economic downturn brought hardship to the lives of countless citizens. As catchy media sobriquets like "the mortgage mess" commemorate, American homeowners were the iconic victims of the crisis. Trapped in bad loans, strapped by job and income loss, unable to refinance or sell due to plummeting real estate values, homeowners were forced into default (and ultimately bankruptcy and foreclosure) at rates exceeded only by those of the Great Depression. From the early days of the housing market downturn, many individuals found their challenges exacerbated by financial institutions that took a "tough love" stance against defaulting mortgagees. As a result, struggling individuals who reached out to their banks to request loan modifications or other accommodations were likely to encounter, if not outright denial, then convoluted, vexing, and often degrading processes that rarely led to agreeable resolutions.

The conceit of the merciless lender acquired a human likeness in May 2008, when an untoward communication from the CEO of lending giant Countrywide Financial, Angelo Mozilo, gained the attention of the news media. The incident began when a struggling Countrywide client named Daniel Bailey, deeply in default and in danger of losing his home of sixteen years, reached out by mass email to a number of the firm's executives, Mozilo included. Describing his dire circumstances and pleading that Countrywide alter his loan terms in order to lower his payments, the message was Bailey's version of the hardship letter, a narrative document required with most short sale and loan modification requests. Mozilo's response—intended for a colleague, but received by Bailey due to the inadvertent selection of reply rather than forward—was unsympathetic, though interestingly his complaint was not Bailey's delinquency per se. Apparently irate at what he saw as a formulaic missive, Mozilo (2008) wrote: "This is unbeliev-able. Most of these letters now have the same wording. Obviously they are being counseled by some other person or by the internet. Disgusting."

Though not amiable, Mozilo was perspicacious: Bailey had indeed found aid from an Internet community, a fact that would have further implications for both men. Prior to broadcasting his hardship plea, Bailey had been attempt-ing to negotiate a loan modification unsuccessfully for some months, and his frustration had led him to LoanSafe.org, a then-new site dedicated to helping individuals fight foreclosure. Compiling various resources for struggling home-owners, LoanSafe also hosted well-traveled discussion forums wherein modera-tors and members shared stories and exchanged guidance, including on hardship narratives. Thus while Bailey's (2008) details were his own, his letter was shaped with the help of the community, and some language—including declarations that he wished to "make amends" and "get this settled so we all can move on"— was taken from its templates. His strategy for reaching upper management was also inspired. Frustrated by futile interactions with overworked loss mitigation employees, LoanSafe users had begun compiling contact information for influ-ential bank personnel under the premise that "all it takes is 1 person to re-code your file" (Freedomwon, 2011). Yet ultimately, Bailey received aid beyond coun-seling: When he despairingly shared Mozilo's missive with the LoanSafe com-munity, the site's charismatic and controversial founder, Maurice "Moe" Bedard, was quick to alert the news media. The ensuing negative press attention spurred growing public outrage for corporate intransigence—and apparently prompted Countrywide to address Bailey's case (Reckard, 2013).

We begin by recounting this event because it points to a number of dynam-ics we see as relevant to this collection's exploration of networked interaction and social writing. Certainly it illustrates the friction between individuals and financial institutions at this historical moment—what the Wall Street Journal called "a rare instance when candid comments from a powerful C.E.O. entered the public realm" (Morgenson, 2008). Mozilo's incivility appeared to confirm that banks were actively, even cruelly, disregarding the needs of the same people from whom they had profited richly during the housing boom. However, it also calls attention to the presence and influence of lateral networks among citizens. As the crisis spread, so did the sense of disenfranchisement among struggling homeowners, giving rise to the need for new collectives defined and motivated by shared experiences of financial hardship and mortgage institutional alien-ation. The Internet answered this exigency succinctly. Demonstrating the spon-taneous, need-based organization that Clay Spinuzzi (2007) called typical of today's networked culture, online social platforms emerged as spaces wherein citizens in diverse geographical locations could seek reassurance, share insights, and cultivate an empowered rhetorical agency. In particular, sites like LoanSafe emphasized a participatory form of knowledge creation by inviting members to pool successes and failures in order to curate a body of collective practical wisdom—what in rhetorical terms we call phronesis.

Rhetorical studies have increasingly sought to illuminate the multivalent roles that online social interaction plays in mobilizing issue publics, with recent research from Barbara Warnick (2007), Warnick and David S. Heineman (2012), and many others exploring the public rhetorical potential of networked discourses. Highlighting the outrageous excesses of financial institutions and the dire consequences of speculative capitalism, the mortgage crisis sparked a vehement outcry, with Occupy Wall Street and other social movements facilitated in key ways by social media (DeLuca, Lawson & Sun, 2012; Penney & Dadas, 2014). Without diminishing the import of these highly visible protest rhetorics, this chapter seeks to discern the ways that social interaction in online networks also has implications in more localized rhetorical domains. As the Mozilo incident suggests, Online Communities (OCs) like LoanSafe are capable of instantiating rhetoric to sway opinion in the public sphere. Yet the site's primary project was to support individual action with and against financial institutions, and thus we must seek to understand its rhetorical production accordingly. In keeping with the focus of this collection, we are most interested in understanding LoanSafe as a site of social writing. Framing the fight against foreclosure as rhetorical action raises questions: How do online collectives focused on that action define and produce the rhetorical knowledge to accomplish it? How do participants harness that knowledge as symbolic and persuasive communication?

While other chapters in this collection consider how social writing engenders change—Liza Potts' chapter, for instance, shows how members of fan culture alter power structures through networked collaboration—we examine social writing as a means of *collaboratively and interactively making* the rhetoric to achieve change. Specifically, we argue that online interactions in LoanSafe mediate the experience of hardship through interwoven practices of social writing and what we call *social composing*. As users establish themselves within the community, their interchanges coincide with and are motivated by purposeful efforts to craft appeals that will compel an external audience of lending personnel. Yet what constitutes persuasion in the notoriously oblique processes of default and foreclosure is often unclear, necessitating a recursive relationship between the "back and forthness" (Jackson & Wallin, 2009) of community interactions and the experiences of individual members. As Jeffrey T. Grabill and Stacey Pigg (2012) pointed out, analyzing rhetorical activity in open forums is "messy": Interaction is non-linear, membership transitory, and discourse fragmented. To cultivate a specific focus on the interactive integration of ideas over time, we borrow Samer Faraj, Sirkka Jarvenpaa, and Ann Majchrzak's (2011) orga-nizational concept of knowledge collaboration. Taking examples from specific LoanSafe members, we suggest that as users progress from the initial sharing of hardship particulars and reception of advice to the posting of success stories and the coaching of others, they not only socialize into a networked discourse but shape practices and processes for socially composing. In doing, they *socialize* hardship itself, cultivating a communal knowledge with both positive and nega-tive public rhetorical potential.

KNOWLEDGE COLLABORATION IN ONLINE COMMUNITIES

As technological affordances become more varied and diverse, so do opportu-nities to examine new discourses and consider new implications for rhetorical action. From Gail E. Hawisher and Cynthia L. Selfe (1998) onward, writing and rhetorical studies have looked to networked discourses to discern their potential for classroom teaching and learning. Yet in accordance with what Paula Mathieu (2005) and others called the field's public turn—which prompts us to consider classroom work in terms of real-world situations while also orienting to the forms and purposes of composing beyond the academy—we have increasingly sought to understand how the "profoundly social" (Alexander, 2006, p. 33) technolo-gies of Web 2.0 engage people with social and political problems. Warnick and Heineman (2012) pointed out that what they call interactivity aids users in learning about and taking stances on issues relevant to private and public aspects of their lives, mobilizing them to participate in individual and collective resolu-tion. In what they described as an "admittedly utopian vision," David Sheridan, Jim Ridolfo, and Anthony Michel (2012) depicted the public sphere as "a space where nonspecialists self-reflexively engage in an extended 'conversation' char-acterized by the rhetorically effective integration of words, images, sounds, and other semiotic elements" (p. 805). With their accessibility and broad, circu-latory reach, social network sites (SNSs) proffer grassroots means of swaying public sentiment—e.g., Caroline Dadas' description (this collection) of the use of Twitter hashtags to influence media coverage and incite social change.

Problem-solving efforts prompt a range of interactivity, with different plat-forms serving specific communicative needs and enabling specific kinds of aid at critical moments. Some exigencies are dire, immediate, and uniquely addressed by broad public networks, such as the use of Twitter to access and distribute information after natural and manmade disasters (Potts, 2014). Others are acute but ongoing and, because they concern obscure, private, or stigmatized matters, are taken up in the relatively more close-knit realm of the Online Community (OC). Often sharing some but not all recognizable technical features of SNSs (boyd, 2007), OCs enable users to forge social connections with strangers who share specified interests, problems, or concerns. Sources of relationships that structure how users engage with information (Rainie & Wellman, 2012), OCs are, like many other social networks, sites of knowledge creation linked to the potential for rhetorical action.

While scholars have long expressed interest in how individuals make use of OCs to navigate medical hardship (see for example White & Dorman, 2001), less has been said about their role in mediating financial hardship. Our research suggests at least two functions: Most obviously, OCs like LoanSafe provided what Marsha White and Steve M. Dorman (2001) called "online social support" (p. 693), enabling participants to commiserate regarding mortgage-related financial difficulties in a protected space. Certainly open online spaces are never entirely safe, with trolling and other forms of abuse being well-documented phenomena (Buckels, Trapbell & Palhaus, 2014). Still, the potential for judgment-free dialogue on hardship, debt, and default is meaningful given the longstanding associations of these topics with silence and shame. Some suggested these associations are weaker than they were: David B. Gross and Nicholas S. Souleles (2002) and Scott Fay, Erik Hurst, and Michelle J. White (2002) found the opprobrium of bankruptcy fading well before the mortgage crisis, while Luigi Guiso, Paolo Sapienza, and Luigi Zingales (2013) were among those who perceived the crisis to have drastically diminished the stigma of foreclosure, prompting many homeowners to default "strategically"—e.g., by choice, not necessity. Given the bleak situations many have faced, we ourselves are cautious of making reductive distinctions. Moreover, we perceive that online social collectives founded on principles of empathy responded to powerful public discourse of shame and blame. The American Dialect Society's (2007) selection of subprime as the 2007 "Word of the Year," for instance, recalls the rhetorical culture characterized by hyper-attentive criticism to the plight of the homeowner.

Yet while social support was critical, it does not circumscribe the value of the OC in the fight against foreclosure. Users sought not only solidarity but solutions—and these were difficult to find. Among other consequences, the crisis animated the emergent risks of *securitization*, the practice of bundling and selling loans as mortgage-backed securities. Dispersing the risk of creative loans made on overpriced homes in hot markets, securitization saw mortgages moved from originating firms to nebulous investor pools. As loans were bundled and bundles were sold and sold again, the authority to make decisions about them also became indeterminate. Consequently, citizens seeking to renegotiate their loan terms—especially before Obama-administration initiatives like the Home Affordable Modification Program (HAMP) introduced some consistency— often encountered chaos, with even bank personnel unsure as to how or by whose approval such decisions could be made. With processes differing from bank to bank, the political and economic situation in constant flux, and the rise of predatory loan modification scams, among other problems, struggling home-owners lacked clear sources of guidance.

If the crisis highlighted a gap in available, authoritative knowledge, OCs reme-diated that gap by offering a networked means of cultivating *phronesis*, understood by rhetoricians as practical wisdom oriented toward the achievement of desired ends. This type of interaction was emphasized by Faraj, Jarvenpass, and Majchrzak (2011), who suggested that the defining feature of the OC is the dynamic nature of *knowledge collaboration*, the "sharing, transfer, accumulation, transformation, and co-creation of knowledge" (p. 1224). In knowledge collaboration, individuals engage in multiple acts of "adding to, recombining, modifying, and integrating knowledge that others have contributed," often and especially "when standard answers are insufficient to help participants with their problems" (p. 1224). The dynamism of knowledge collaboration is closely tied to the sustainability of the community, which evolves and adapts in response to the ongoing integration of ideas. In "fluid" OCs, "boundaries, norms, participants, artifacts, interactions, and foci continually change over time—in the sense of Heraclitus' pronouncement of not being able to step twice in the same river" (p. 1226). This kind of dynamism was especially salient in the OCs that, responding to the dearth of help and guid-ance from banks, invited victims of the unfolding mortgage crisis to share difficul-ties and collaboratively generate solutions.

In what follows, we apply and extend the concept of knowledge collabora-tion by examining interactions in a specific mortgage help forum, LoanSafe. Faraj et al. (2011) suggested that five consequential tensions illustrate a commu-nity's generative potential, including its framing of problems and possibilities for action: (1) the strength of commitment to the community's shared goals; (2) the time that users are able to devote; (3) the social ambiguity of user identities; (4) the disembodiment or decontextualization of content as it becomes indepen-dent of its creator; and (5) the temporary convergences of users around a central goal or direction. Yet while they acknowledged expertise and participation only as potential additional tensions, LoanSafe models a form of knowledge collabo-ration intensely dependent upon both. Nearly wholly defined by the deficiency of "standard answers," LoanSafe users attempted to make an intensely indeter-minate situation knowable by placing extended participation and experiential authority at the center of their social writing endeavors. In particular, seasoned users were needed to help new users craft effective negotiatory discourse through the collaborative rhetorical practice we call *social composing*.

It bears noting that LoanSafe is a site of some motivational conflict. Unlike social movements related to the housing crisis, its intentions were neither to sway public sentiment nor mobilize protest action, but to facilitate dialogue between homeowners and lenders. Though it forwards primarily legal and administrative means of fighting foreclosure, many are not precisely institutionally sanctioned: Like Bailey's email blast, LoanSafe has tended to endorse strategies that, in seeking to outwit financial institutions or exploit loopholes in their processes, are also designed to cause them annoyance. Moreover, founder Moe Bedard has something of a mixed reputation on the Internet. In addition to potential conflict between the site's negotiatory stance and Bedard's own public rhetorical actions—including activist endeavors like organizing "Save the Dream" protests at financial institutions during the heart of the crisis—some Internet commentary (Dibert, 2010) raised questions about the sincerity of his dedication to homeowners. Without discounting these tensions, we maintain our focus on participant usage of the site within its defined parameters.

SOCIAL WRITING & COMPOSING IN THE LOANSAFE FORUM

A rich space in which to examine the networked discourses of financial hardship, LoanSafe.org, according to its mission statement, "protects, strengthens and promotes homeownership" by means of the Internet, providing individuals "tools and help to stop foreclosure" without cost or obligation (Bedard, 2007b). Claiming more than 13 million users in its short history, the site grew from an initially small community in 2007 to an extensively utilized resource boasting over 140,000 members and nearly half a million posts as of September 2014. In broadening from its initial focus on loan modification to its current focus on general mortgage help, it has simultaneously become more commercialized: The home page today displays advertisements, mortgage calculators, and other sales tools, and most employee profiles mention a secondary availability as mortgage brokers, realtors, or other industry professionals. Nevertheless, it remains not-for-profit, and the foundational commitment to fighting foreclosure is sustained especially in the discussion forums, where users and moderators discuss and troubleshoot individuals' financial situations with an eye to new and expiring laws and programs as well as potentially suspicious or predatory practices.

LoanSafe's discussion forums announce key elements of its organizational culture: the entwined, fundamental commitments to collegiality and paying it forward. As Bedard (2007a) articulated:

> The reason I created this website was to create a safe place
> where homeowners can visit and get legitimate free help and
> also to learn from others who are going through similar situa-

tions. It's a simple concept of bringing everyone together and uniting them to produce solutions to our mortgage problems.

The emphasis on safety prescribes an internal dynamic for the community, appealing to user behavior in a way common to OCs. At the same time, it underscores a contrast between LoanSafe and the uncertain terrain of the post-bubble financial services industry, particularly the predatory acts of those who sought to profit in it. Threatening that those who troll, scam, or advertise for-profit services will be "banned forever," Bedard (2007a) sought to inculcate a staunch distrust of corporate influence. At the same time, he constructed an understanding of legitimate help as experience-based, altruistic, and built foremost on the continual participation of users, who must not only draw from communal wisdom but, by reporting back on the outcome of its application, continue to grow and refine it.

With extended engagement intrinsic to its mission, the site uses several mechanisms to recognize and reward participation. Registered members (there are no participatory benefits for unregistered lurkers) may "like" posts much as Facebook users "like" status updates or comments—though here, "likes" are not used cursorily but as a meaningful indicator that a response was useable or appreciated. The concurrent "Trophy Points" system celebrates quantitative milestones, with both "likes" and posts advancing users through levels with corresponding accolades. One earns the "First Message" status and one point, for instance, by posting an inaugural message, while "Somebody Likes You" commemorates a first like and conveys two points. As participation ramps up, so do points: At the 20-point level, "Addicted" commemorates 1,000 messages and "Can't Get Enough of Your Stuff" celebrates 250 likes. A track record in any of these tripartite measures of participation—messages posted, likes received, and points earned—can earn a user "Notable Member" status.

These interlocking mechanisms replicate the status-conveying and community-building features of SNSs: Much like Reddit's karma system, they reward participation and visibly mark expertise for the benefit of others. As Figure 5.1 illustrates, all earned accolades are displayed with each post, as are taglines denoting affiliation and expertise level: LoanSafe Member and LoanSafe Guide are default designators, but many individuals choose to self-identify according to their place in the negotiation process—e.g., as a "Successful Homeowner." While it is difficult to say how earning accolades might motivate users, such mechanisms provide a framework for displaying and celebrating key stages and achievements in the process of becoming a knowledgeable user.

As with many networked spaces, LoanSafe is a rich site of social writing. Participants engage in a range of discursive practices by sharing background information, posing queries and requesting assistance, offering feedback and encouragement, and narrating lender interactions. Yet discourse is not just the means of community exchange; it is an end in and of itself. Specifically, as members strategize to obtain lender attention and cooperation, they rehearse communication and work in highly conscious ways to craft the discourse they anticipate negotiatory interactions will entail. Thus, the practices of social writing are enmeshed and interwoven with what we, to call attention to the intentionality at play, call social composing. This term is not new to scholarship on web-based pedagogies: It recurs, for instance, as Jason Ranker (2008, 2014) explored the classroom processes by which young students engage multiple media and modalities. However, recalling Mathieu's (2005) insistence on attending to composing beyond the academy, LoanSafe expands our understanding of the non-academic urgencies that can be ameliorated by online interactive networking. Common practices in its forums bring explicit attention to inventive and generative processes, including informal acts of peer review: Participants plan appeals, post drafts, exchange feedback, and revise documents to reflect input from other knowledgeable contributors. In accordance, we define social composing as networked rhetorical action that layers attention to the writing process along with the goal of producing persuasive communication.

Figure 5.1. Freedomwon's profile snapshot.

Social composing in LoanSafe serves a number of ends, but most conspicuous is a highly personal example of what Sheridan, Ridolfo, and Michel (2012), drawing on Bruce McComiskey (2000), called a "written rhetorical intervention" (p. 825): the hardship letter, which details the borrower's difficulties so as to persuade the lender to modify the loan, accede to a short sale, or make another desired accommodation. To date, there is little research linking a well-written hardship narrative to the outcome of an appeal, and lenders rarely dictate what the document should do or be. Absent definitive understandings, a wealth of anecdotal and sometimes contradictory lore is found on the Internet—some specialists doubt the document's relevance, while others emphasize its vital importance in stopping foreclosure. LoanSafe tends to take the latter position, and its participants devote considerable energy to shaping *phronetic* understandings of the genre. Indeed, the hardship letter is seen as a complex rhetorical challenge: From the raw material of personal, often painful experience, the supplicant must construct her narrative with circumspection, striking a balance between accepting responsibility and depicting circumstances beyond control, between giving detail and making a quick case to the "over worked, $12 an hour loss mitigation employee" that is her likely reader (Bedard, 2007c). Little is known about how precisely hardship letters compel, and thus the work of crafting them always coincides with the work of attempting to discern what constitutes persuasion in a given circumstance.

In this milieu, success stories are more than inspiration—they provide glimpses into the veiled decision-making of lenders, producing rhetorical knowledge that others can use to act. To support these claims, we turn to the cases of two influential LoanSafe users: Andrew, the forum's first successful loan modification, and freedomwon. While the methodological complexities of analyzing OC interactions (Grabill & Pigg, 2012) mean we can offer only a limited snapshot, these users begin to illustrate how the social composition of negotiatory discourse is inseparable from the processes of enculturation enacted by social writing. Through arcs of extended participation, users constructed mutable identities, moving back and forth between more and less knowledgeable subject positions even as their interactions shaped and were shaped by community norms and expectations.

It is worth noting that in LoanSafe, success meant different things to different users. Most participants sought help from their lenders, but some pursued loan modification or short sale agreements while others (in a trend increasingly common over the site's life) wished merely to delay foreclosure as long as possible. While it may be tempting to impose a moral distinction on these goals, we avoid doing so ourselves: We are highly wary of the neoliberal tendency to erase contextual rhetorical influences, cast systemic problems as failures of individual risk management, and reduce complex decisions to a simple matter of rational choice. Our intent, therefore, is not to comment on the motivations for or acceptability of default. We would, however, agree that the connectivity afforded by LoanSafe allowed individuals to apprehend, experience, and address mortgage financial hardships collectively, illustrating the multivalent capacity of social web technologies to socialize hardship by making it more habitable, knowable, even survivable.

BECOMING KNOWLEDGEABLE PEERS: ANDREW AND FREEDOMWON

Andrew joined in August 2007, early in LoanSafe's life, under the original user name "sswiz." His inaugural post (Andrew, 2008) follows typical introductory patterns: In keeping with the promise of a judgment-free community and the need to provide specific details to facilitate problem-solving, he was forthcoming with loan information—though when asked by Bedard, he opted to provide expense and income information privately. Along with details of his wife's difficult pregnancy and other financial constraints, he described his failure to obtain a loan modification from Countrywide before an impending monthly payment increase. Posing no specific queries, Andrew seemed initially uncertain of what to expect from LoanSafe, and after his first welcome and reassurance from Bedard, he was at first an infrequent poster.

Over the next several months, Andrew intermittently updated, expressing frustration with a drawn-out process where his file was bounced among bank negotiators, his calls went unanswered, and his important documents were misplaced. In January, after being urged by user Evelyn to send a letter to the bank, Andrew replied that he has already taken that step. Illustrating social composing at play, he described writing his hardship letter by adapting from other users' examples, accepting guidance from user Brian K., and finally distributing his missive widely by email, mail, and fax to bank personnel, public figures, and organizations including "Angelo Mozilo, all the board members, most execs within countrywide, ca attorney general, pa attorney general, bbb, 995hope, naca, acorn, vice president of the us, my senator and congressman, ny attorney general" (Andrew, 2008).

Early evidence of how the community's emergent knowledge could be effectively directed at strategic action, Andrew's letter proved a turning point both in his bank negotiations and for his role in the LoanSafe forum. The very next day, he posted multiple times (one example is displayed in Figure 5.2) to describe receiving a series of phone calls from Countrywide, more attention than he had "ever received throughout this dilemma," and ultimately an acceptable modification offer (Andrew, 2008).

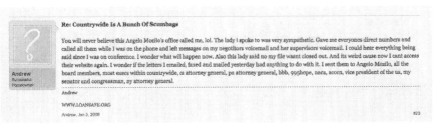

Figure 5.2. "Countrywide Success!"

Andrew's success—billed as LoanSafe's first—has a transformative effect on his interactivity. His sudden status as a successful negotiator cues others to the value of his input: He is promptly asked to share his letter by users hoping to incorporate his strategies into their own negotiatory discourse. Though he initially has more questions than answers, he becomes an increasingly valued and active contributor over the next several years, identifying himself as a "Successful Homeowner" and discarding "sswiz" in favor of the more formal Andrew. Something of a hometown hero—one user tells him, "you are a legend for me now" (elusha, 2008)—Andrew assumed a progressively more authoritative presence, and his "success story" thread was often co-opted by information-seekers to whom he assumed the role of the more knowledgeable peer, asking questions, giving advice, and helping users shape appeals and strategies.

Member "freedomwon" was similarly influential. After joining in October of 2010, his first posts appeared nearly a month later, a common trend among new users who observe and browse before speaking up. His first thread reflected the convention of providing key information and narrating his personal struggle to attain a "quiet title action" (2010). From the start, freedomwon appeared to have self-educated extensively on the foreclosure process, but nevertheless evidenced his desire to acquire and build new knowledge. Over time, he became more vocal about the goal of locating and exploiting loopholes in the foreclosure process and more strategic in the written communication that helped him exhaust all courses of action to avoid foreclosure without making payments. In June 2011, he shared the appeal letter that helped him successfully postpone the foreclosure on his property (freedomwon, 2011). As with Andrew, freedomwon's success quickly led to requests for participation in acts of social composition, with other users complimenting his letter and seeking his input on their own processes.

Over the course of his interactions, freedomwon alternated between coaching and being coached, asking and answering questions about laws, processes, and strategies. Increasingly, he took up moderator-like tasks that served to not only maintain the culture and safety of the site but ensure the currency and availability of its knowledge—actions like marking threads for violating forum rules and "bumping," the standard practice of bringing a thread up to date by posting in it. Into the often-technical advice he gave others, freedomwon continued to draw on the successes and failures of his own long process, enjoining others to "study" (freedomwon, #386, 2012) his work and avoid strategies that failed him (Figure 5.3). Yet even "tried and true" knowledge remains contingent; recognizing that many contextual factors determine how strategic actions will be received, freedomwon and other users often engaged in extended interchange, interpreting the success or failure of different appeals at length. Threaded through with an emphasis on "learning . . . from those that have gone before" (freedomwon, #386, 2012), freedomwon's exchanges, much like Andrew's, show how LoanSafe's "pay it forward" principle can work to its desired effect. More importantly, they illustrate how knowledge collaboration occurs not only through social writing but social composing, where extended participation and reciprocal expertise lie at the heart of communal efforts to curate phronesis, craft persuasive discourse, and achieve desired outcomes.

6/9/11 - Another update. Received a v.m. msg from a negotiator at BofA yesterday. Simply wanted to introduce herself & give me her contact info. She said she just received my file & would be back in touch in a couple of days.

Oh, and my loan was transferred from BAC to BofA. This was revealed in an (undated) letter I received by regular snail mail on 6/6/11.

Also got a case file # opened by Ca AG's office (they made reference to it in their acknowledgement correspondence to me). Also received letter from the OCC office with a Case file # as well. So we shall see what develops. ReconTrust was the last to sign for my CMRRR letter.

freedomwon
LoanSafe Member

Figure 5.3. "My Recent letter to BofA (Part 2)."

FINAL THOUGHTS: RISKS & REWARDS OF SOCIAL COMPOSING IN THE ONLINE COMMUNITY

LoanSafe's distinctive approach to knowledge collaboration, built on the recurrent participation and expertise of individual users, resulted in a considerable body of practical wisdom. Spanning an impressive array of legal, political, and organizational topics, it was most often espoused by founder Moe Bedard, his family member and co-moderator Evan Bedard, and other employees of the site, who drew on and re-circulated the results of countless reported experiences when responding to new situations. Frequently, Bedard couched his advice as a product of time-tested, communally vetted knowledge: For instance, in answer to a query about one user's underwater second mortgage with GreenTree (smpjaf, 2014), Bedard replied, "The strategy for settling 2nd mortgages here on LoanSafe has always been to just sit and wait for them to come to you with an offer or talks of a settlement" (Bedard, 2014). Access to *phronetic* knowledge also enabled respondents to speak honestly about the potential for successful negotiations—in this instance, not high: "We have had very few successes here with GreenTree" (Bedard, 2014). It was also frequently synthesized and disbursed by long-term, active members like Andrew and freedomwon, whose "success story" status marked them as especially valuable collaborators in social composing endeavors. Both profiled users illustrate how LoanSafe participants navigated lender negotiation via collaborative acts of social writing and composing, even as their own knowledge-gaining processes constituted and were constituted by the site's "pay it forward" culture.

While LoanSafe's many participants attest to the value of its *phronesis*, our analysis suggests that the convergence of social writing, social composing, and knowledge collaboration is not without potential risks; we close this chapter by briefly discussing them and highlighting potentials for future research. Perhaps most obviously, the Mozillo incident raises questions about the public rhetorical implications of communally cultivated discourses. While Daniel Bailey appeared to have triumphed—one news story (Reckard, 2013) claimed that he was able to stay in his home for five years without making a mortgage payment after Countrywide's damage-control team induced him to stop speaking to the media—Mozilo's response nevertheless appeared to devalue LoanSafe's processes of social composing, invalidating its collaboratively produced understanding of rhetorical effectiveness within the hardship letter genre by marking it as formulaic. Indeed, the common injunction that hardship letters must "grab the reader's attention," engaging and persuading recalcitrant bank employees with compelling narratives would seem somewhat at odds with the emphasis on templates and recycled appeals that arose from the "success story" approach. Such tensions invite further consideration of social writing and composing in OCs and other online networks. While we should continue to explore the role of individual participation and expertise in knowledge collaboration, we may also ask how over-reliance on experiential evidence may discount the needs of external audiences.

Finally, we hope that this chapter will invite a broadened conception of networked discourse and public rhetoric, one combining inquiry into the highly visible public rhetorics surrounding social and political problems with attention to the rhetorical ways in which individuals achieve change in their daily lives. While Bailey benefited from LoanSafe's willingness and ability to exert public pressure on financial institutions via the media, users like Andrew and freedomwon benefited more directly by translating the community's collective wisdom into strategically composed written rhetorical interventions. We see room for more research not only on rhetoric and hardship generally, but on the ways that social interaction online can inform the rhetorical resolution of individual problems—which are often, as we see in this case, collective as well. Given that the volatile economic situation of contemporary capitalism is not likely to become more stable, it is critically important for rhetorical studies to account for related discourses and seek to better understand the ways that networked rhetorical activity can socialize and ameliorate hardship within communities, even as it mobilizes individuals to act beyond them.

REFERENCES

Alexander, B. (2006). Web 2.0: A new wave of teaching and learning? *EDUCAUSE Review, 41*(2), 32–44.

American Dialect Society. (2007). "Subprime" voted 2007 word of the year. Retrieved from http://www.americandialect.org/subprime_voted_2007_word_of_the_year.

Andrew. (2008). Countrywide Success! [Msg 23] [Forum post]. Retrieved from http://www.loansafe.org/forum/threads/countrywide-success.452/.

Bedard, M. (2007a). Forum Rules and Regulations [Forum post]. Retrieved from http://www.loansafe.org/forum/threads/loansafe-org-forum-rules-and-regulations.1/.

Bedard, M. (2007b). About LoanSafe.org and My Mission [Forum post]. Retrieved from http://www.loansafe.org/forum/threads/about-loansafe-org-and-my-mission.50/.

Bedard, M. (2007c). Example of a Hardship Letter [Forum post]. Retrieved from http://www.loansafe.org/forum/threads/examples-of-a-hardship-letter.135/

Bedard, M. (2008). A real Countrywide email from the office of Angelo Mozilo—email below calls homeowner disgusting [Forum post]. Retrieved from http://www.loansafe.org/forum/threads/a-real-countrywide-email-from-the-office-of-angelo-mozilo-email-below-calls-homeowner-disgusting.2785/.

Bedard, M. (2014). Greentree Services Underwater 2nd Mortgage. [Msg 2] [Forum post]. Retrieved from http://www.loansafe.org/forum/threads/greentree-services-underwater-2nd-mortgage.89010/.

Bailey, D. (2008). This is what mozillo thinks [Forum post]. Retrieved from http://www.loansafe.org/forum/threads/this-is-what-mozillo-thinks.2759/.

boyd, d. m. (2007). Social network sites: Definition, history, and scholarship. *Journal of Computer-Mediated Communication, 13*(1), 210–230.

Buckels, E. E., Trapnell, P. D. & Palhaus, D. L. (2014). Trolls just want to have fun. *Personality and Individual Differences, 67*, 97–102.

DeLuca, K. M., Lawson, S. & Sun, Y. (2012). Occupy Wall Street on the public screens of social media: The many framings of the birth of a protest movement. *Communication, Culture & Critique, 5*(4), 483–509.

Dibert, S. (2010, November). Just because a website claims to be a foreclosure advocacy site, it does not mean it is. Retrieved from http://mfi-miami.com/2010/11/just-because-a-website-claims-to-be-a-foreclosure-advocacy-site-it-does-not-mean-it-is/.

elusha. (2008). New WAR with Countrywide. [Msg 1] [Forum post]. Retrieved from http://www.loansafe.org/forum/threads/new-war-with-countrywide.731/.

Faraj, S., Jarvenpaa, S. L. & Majchrzak, A. (2011). Knowledge collaboration in online communities. *Organizational Science, 22*(5), 1224–1239.

Fay, S., Hurst, E. & White, M. (2002). The household bankruptcy decision. *The American Economic Review, 92*(3), 706–718.

Freedomwon. (2010). Best strategy on when to file a quiet title action during the foreclosure process [Forum post]. Retrieved from http://www.loansafe.org/forum/threads/best-strategy-on-when-to-file-a-quiet-title-action-durring-the-foreclosure-process.35511/.

Freedomwon. (2011). My recent letter to BofA (Part 2) [Forum post]. Retrieved from http://www.loansafe.org/forum/threads/my-recent-letter-to-bofa-part-2.41283/.

Grabill, J. T. & Pigg, S. (2012). Messy rhetoric: Identity performance as rhetorical agency in online public forums. *Rhetoric Society Quarterly, 42*(2), 99–119.

Gross, D. B. & Souleles, N. S. (2002). An empirical analysis of personal bankruptcy and delinquency. *The Review of Financial Studies, 15*(1), 319–347.

Guiso, L., Sapienza, P. & Zingales, L. (2013). The determinants of attitudes toward strategic default on mortgages. *The Journal of Finance, 68*(4), 1473–1515.

Hawisher, G. E. & Selfe, C. L. (1998). Reflections on computers and composition studies at the century's end. In I. Snyder (Ed.), *Page to screen: Taking literacy into the electronic era* (pp. 3–19). New York, NY: Routledge.

Jackson, B. & Wallin, J. (2009). Rediscovering the "back-and-forthness" of rhetoric in the age of YouTube. *College Composition and Communication, 61*(2), W374-W396.

Mathieu, P. (2005). *Tactics of hope: The public turn in English composition*. Portsmouth, NH: Boynton/Cook.

McComiskey, B. (2000). *Teaching composition as a social process*. Logan, UT: Utah State University Press.

Morgenson, G. (2008). Silence of the lenders: Is anyone listening? *The New York Times.* Retrieved from http://www.nytimes.com/2008/07/13/business/13mail.html?_r=0.

Penney, J. & Dadas, C. (2014). (Re)Tweeting in the service of protest: Digital composition and circulation in the Occupy Wall Street movement. *New Media & Society, 16*(1), 74–90.

Potts, L. (2014). *Social media in disaster response: How experience architects can build for participation.* New York, NY: ATTW.

Rainie, L. & Wellman, B. (2012). *The new social operating system.* Cambridge, MA: MIT Press.

Ranker, J. (2008). Composing across multiple media: A case study of digital video production in a fifth grade classroom. *Written Communication, 25*(2), 196–234.

Ranker, J. (2014). The emergence of semiotic resource complexes in the composing processes of young students in a literacy classroom context. *Linguistics and Education, 25*, 129–144.

Reckard, E. S. (2013). Lender forgave payments to avert Mozilo PR crisis, borrower insists. *Los Angeles Times.* Retrieved from http://articles.latimes.com/2013/dec/14/business/la-fi-live-for-free-20131214.

Sheridan, D., Ridolfo, J. & Michel, A. (2012). The available means of persuasion: Mapping a theory and pedagogy of multimodal public rhetoric. *JAC, 25*(4), 803–844.

smpjaf. (2014). Greentree services underwater second mortgage [Forum post]. Retrieved from http://www.loansafe.org/forum/threads/greentree-services-underwater-2nd-mortgage.89010/.

Spinuzzi, C. (2007). Guest editor's introduction: Technical communication in the age of distributed work. *Technical Communication Quarterly, 16*(3), 265–277.

Warnick, B. (2007). *Rhetoric online: Persuasion and politics on the World Wide Web.* New York, NY: Peter Lang.

Warnick, B. & Heineman, D. S. (Eds.). (2012). *Rhetoric online: The politics of new media* (2nd ed). New York, NY: Peter Lang.

White, M. & Dorman, S. M. (2001). Receiving social support online: Implications for education. *Health Education Research, 16*(6), 693–707.

CHAPTER 6

STILL FLYING: WRITING AS PARTICIPATORY ACTIVISM CIRCULATING ACROSS THE FIREFLY 'VERSE

Liza Potts
Michigan State University

INTRODUCTION

The production and circulation of fan culture is entering a moment when fans, entertainers, and copyright holders are renegotiating the terms of participation. No longer bound by traditional means of making and delivering content, content producers and content consumers are blurring the lines between their roles by co-producing material to share, spread, and celebrate the object of their enjoyment. Much of this activity takes places across digital spaces such as Tumblr, Twitter, Facebook, Etsy, meet-ups, and conventions (or cons). Sometimes, such blurring has resulted in the production of music videos (amandapalmer, 2009) and funding movies (Thomas, 2013). At other times, the results have met with resistance in the form of cease-and-desist letters and the threats of lawsuits (Gibson, 2007). In many of these cases, it is the self-organizing activity of the fans—sometimes in cooperation with artists and producers—that create networks for knowledge sharing and collaboration.

Negotiating participation, fans work within and across various digital spaces to contribute to their fandoms. Many scholars have examined this kind of labor, including Henry Jenkins' (1992) groundbreaking work on fan fiction, Matt Hills' (2002) examination of fandom's anti-commercial ideology, Jonathan Gray's (2010) work on paratexts, and Abigail De Kosnik's (2013) work on the free labor of fandom. The activities fans partake in and the objects they invoke across physical and digital spaces alter the context in which they can participate. And while these activities are in abundance online and many are protected by Fair Use, the copyright holders do not always appreciate such participation from fans. As Tabetha Adkins mentioned in this collection, it is through social media that these participants are able to communicate and change social activism dramatically.

For fans of the short-lived science-fiction television show *Firefly* and the movie *Serenity*, this fandom has far outlived the show and produced more original content than the show ever will. From podcasts (*The Signal*) to edited collections whose authors include a mix of fans and academics who are fans (Espenson, 2004, 2007; Wilcox & Cochran, 2010), these participants are as prolific as they are passionate about the source material.

A hat worn by a main character in *Firefly* has become a symbol of their fandom. The "Jayne hat" is worn by fans to identify each other, celebrate the show, and demonstrate their allegiance to *Firefly*. In 2013, that hat was claimed by the copyright holders, licensed to a third party to produce "official" hats, and sold by a "nerd company" (Chaney, 2013) that may have regretted it. Before the official version was produced, the crafters of these hats were primarily fans selling their knitted caps to and sharing patterns online with other fans. The making of the official hat led *Firefly*'s copyright holder, 21st Century Fox, to send cease-and-desist letters to crafters selling their homemade hats on Etsy (Hall, 2013). It also inspired fans and allies to take to social media to vent their frustrations and come up with solutions together.

In analyzing these activities, I explain how individual members of this event participated, illustrating how groups mobilized by shifting their movements across and between strategies and tactics. To discuss these issues, I predominately apply the concept of enunciation from Michel de Certeau's *The Practice of Everyday Life* (1984) as well as my own work studying fandom, social media (Potts, 2012, 2015), and disaster (Potts, 2014). Through their *social* writings across *social* media, their acts are exhibited through their enunciation of the conflict and the translation of activity across the network of the fan community.

As Ann M. Blakeslee and Rachel Spilka (2010) have noted, "digital audiences are complex, requiring processes of analysis and accommodation that embrace and take full account of this complexity" (p. 223). By making these moves more visible through this type of analysis, I explain why this kind of social web participation is a significant site of study for digital rhetoric, one that can help expand how we teach social media writing practices to our students. Examining how social media can be a space for activism and shared experience can provide examples of how writing works in these digital spaces. Understanding how writing works in social media can bring practical examples to our classes, whether we are teaching courses on content strategy, digital writing, experience architecture, new media, or technical communication.

PARTICIPATORY CULTURE'S STRATEGIES AND TACTICS

Concepts from Michel de Certeau's (1984) *The Practice of Everyday Life* have received much attention from scholars studying participatory culture. In particular, Henry Jenkins (1992, 2010a) and others (Jenkins et al., 2009) have used it to discuss expectations for engagement for students, fans, and everyday people. Participatory culture examines how communication is networked, how everyday people can connect and engage with others, and how collaborative activities work across these networks. In the case of this research, I am examining the collaborative, participatory writing space of social media and social networks. This section will look specifically at de Certeau's concept of enunciation as it relates to writing and communicating in digital spaces. Here I suggest that we consider a hybridized model that would help us negotiate the space between a strategy and a tactic. That is, I question whether the emergence of social media, participatory culture, and activism gave rise to other models of activity outside of the binary presented by many scholars when they think of de Certeau's work. The writers in this case study see themselves as participating in a fandom where their key text focuses on rebellion, survival, and chosen family. Through their participation, they rebel with the help of actors, magazine writers, and other fans against a corporate giant that had betrayed them.

DEFINING STRATEGIES AND TACTICS

In *The Practice of Everyday Life*, de Certeau (1984) created a framework by which he could discuss power relations and communication. His work on the concepts of strategies and tactics is often seen as a binary. He defined a strategy as "the calculation or manipulation of power relationships that becomes possible as soon as a subject with will and power (a business, an army, a city, a scientific institution) can be isolated" (pp. 35–36). In defining a strategy, de Certeau linked these acts to a space, an environment, the "place of its own power and will" (p. 36). The place of major organizations and corporations is the space of power in which strategies can be executed. In contrast, de Certeau defined a tactic as "a calculated action determined by the absence of a power locus" (pp. 36–37). The tactic is an "art of the weak" in this power relationship (p. 37), the "space of the other" in which everyday people reside (p. 36). This binary establishes corporations as producers of power and knowledge, and everyday people as operating under these conditions and constraints.

It is useful that de Certeau situated his analysis as a way of examining "contexts of use" (p. 33), something familiar to scholars of Internet studies, where the interfaces, platforms, and devices are often studied as part of an ecosystem of activity. De Certeau pointed to context as a way of describing traits, and he framed a model of *enunciation* as a way of understanding these traits. In that model, he discussed issues of language and linguistics, and we would say, as scholars of participatory action, rhetoric. He lays out four elements (Table 6.1) that collectively comprise enunciation and thus use and context: realizing, appropriating, inscribing relations, and situating in time (p. 33). The concept of realizing refers to how a speech act can actualize its potential. A speaker's appropriate language and an interlocutor create a contract between speakers. Finally, establishing a moment in time, a *kairos*, roots the enunciation in a fixed present—a "now" in which the speakers can contextualize activity.

Table 6.1. Four Elements of Enunciation

Element	Definition
Realizing	How a speech act can actualize its potential
Appropriating	How speakers take and fit language
Inscribing	Creating a relationship between speakers
Situating	Contextualizing speech within an activity

Each presupposition to enunciation—which all four of these elements describe—works to create meaning through language and context through use. We can see this kind of activity in online communities, as inside jokes, shared values, and memes are used repeatedly to layer community knowledge and create context for conversations. Other studies of Internet communication have discussed such communication issues across spaces such as YouTube (Gal, Shifman & Kampf, 2015), Reddit (Potts & Harrison, 2013), and other social networking spaces (De Ridder, 2013), as well as fandoms and digital spaces, such as the work of Richard McCulloch, Virginia Crisp, Jon Hickman, and Stephanie Janes (2013).

PARTICIPATION AS A HYBRID MODEL OF STRATEGIES AND TACTICS

In considering participatory cultures, Jenkins (2013) described how "the 'digital revolution' has resulted in real, demonstrable, shifts in media power, expanding the capacity of various subcultures and communities to access the means of media production and circulation" (p. xxiii). It is through this revolution that we see a collapse in de Certeau's model of strategy and tactics. Participation and activism can be resituated as neither a strategy nor a tactic, but an ability to flex and adapt to conditions. Jenkins et al. (2009) defined participatory culture as having

1. relatively low barriers to artistic expression and civic engagement
2. strong support for creating and sharing creations with others

3. some type of informal mentorship whereby what is known by the most experienced is passed on to the novices
4. members who believe that their contributions matter, and
5. members who feel some degree of social connection with one another (at the least, they care what other people think about what they have created). (p. 50)

Axel Bruns (2008) referred to participatory culture activities as "produsage"—combining the terms "production" and "use" (p. 2), which is relevant when considering the crafting community and participation across social media in this case study. (See Estee Beck's chapter in this volume for a discussion of produsage vis-à-vis labor issues in social media spaces.) Here, we have participants who are both producing material objects as well as using objects created earlier by content producers. In some instances, fans take these objects and work them into remixes; in other examples, the materials created by fan crafters are based on props from the object of their adoration—television shows, movies, books, etc. In his recent work, Jenkins looked at participatory culture and how spreadable media can empower consumers (Jenkins et al., 2013). Spreadable media refers to the circulation of content within commercial and participatory culture, examining issues of economics and meaning making (p. 1). Such issues are key to communicating across digital spaces as a form of social activism.

Combining these key definitions of participatory culture, a framework can begin to emerge when discussing activities that take place across social media. For example, we can examine using Twitter to chat directly with content producers or creating websites to share fan community knowledge, such as design patterns for creating costumes. This activity is not bound to specific strategies or tactics by participants so much as it is a shifting of power relationships across spaces where traditional claims are not so easily enforced. So by their production, use, and ability to spread information, the fans in these communities can participate in ways that can often circumvent these traditional power relationships.

IMPLICATIONS FOR STUDYING DIGITAL RHETORIC

For fans to build their identities and align themselves with their communities, there are specific practices that they take up in various digital spaces. In particular, different social media tools can support this kind of work. For example, fan scholars and scholar fans have traced the use of technologies and sites such as LiveJournal (Busker, 2008), blogs (Chin & Hills, 2008), and, more recently, Twitter (Deller, 2011). Throughout the history of social web technologies and fandoms, conflicts have arisen between fans and copyright holders—from the early example of Fox's takedown of the *X-Files* fan-produced multimedia archive the Treehouse to the lawsuit brought against the fan-organized Harry Potter Lexicon (a website that the fans wanted to turn into a physical encyclopedia). And while these conflicts are certainly troublesome, the ways in which fans are able to circumvent these issues and continue to keep their communities active is noteworthy, both as spaces where digital rhetoric can be studied and where pedagogy can be developed. There are also many instances where the collective actions of fans and content producers have led to the creation of new content, as in the case of Whedon's *Serenity* and more recent examples on Kickstarter such as the fan-supported movie for *Veronica Mars*.

Given the case study in this chapter, it becomes clear that the strategies and tactics of crafters and their supporters are deploying a mixed model, a hybrid of sorts of the two terms. They are writing their participation in social media as a form of activism, where both strategies and tactics are required to circumvent traditional channels of content distribution, sales, and support. This form of activism is made more visible by their use of social media and through these writings. This is participatory action.

PARTICIPATORY ACTION: THE CASE OF *FIREFLY*

Fans of *Firefly* have created their own community around the television show and movie. *Firefly* is a show focused on a group of heroes who are often fearless in the face of opposition, although all of them have faced some major loss in their lives. In describing *Firefly* creator Joss Whedon's take on heroes, actor and star of *Firefly* Nathan Fillion stated, "Joss Whedon's version of a hero doesn't always win. He loses more than he wins, and when he wins, the victories are tiny, but he takes 'em" (as cited in Pascale, 2014, location 78). This understanding is useful in examining strategies, tactics, and participation—the activities undertaken by the fandom to support, protect, and defend members of the community in this case study. These fans adopt personas similar to the characters in *Firefly*, and thus share an ethos regarding heroics, family, and independence. The object that is central to this particular case study is a symbol of both fandom and family for *Firefly* fans: a hat worn by one of the main characters, Jayne Cobb, a gift given to him by his mother. It is a key example of how posthuman objects can impact communities and writing and how they can become the interlocutor necessary to enunciate meaning in a community. As *Firefly* scholar Elizabeth L. Rambo (2014) noted, the "*Firefly* fandom has come to associate Jayne's hat with devoted family ties and with fearlessness in the face of opposition, such as the corporate interest that doomed *Firefly*" (p. 191). The care for and wearing of this hat is one way in which these fans enact and embody their fandom.

In April 2013, the fan community of *Firefly* faced off against Fox through various spaces across the social web. Wanting to sell an authorized, official version of Jayne's hat, online retailer ThinkGeek contacted the copyright holder, Fox. Fox worked with third-party supplier Ripple Junction to create the hat, which ThinkGeek could then sell in their online store. The need for the official hat triggered Fox to then go after the "unofficial" versions sold by fan crafters on Etsy, sending cease-and-desist letters in an effort to stop the sale of the unofficial hats. By tweeting on Twitter, renaming items in Etsy, writing articles in geek news sources such as *Buzzfeed* (Hall, 2013) and the *Mary Sue* (Pantozzi, 2013; Polo, 2013), and responding on websites, fans and their allies deployed various strategies and tactics in response to Fox's moves. By participating, they were at once enunciating their fandoms, finding a route around a corporation, and deploying long-term strategies for the crafters' sustainability.

Looking specifically at the incident discussed in this case study, we can see how fans, fandoms, and copyright holders collide. Such understandings can help us be better researchers of these kinds of social media writing genres as well as explore issues of intellectual property and the crafting community. Analyzing the activity that occurred during the summer of 2013, we can better understand how fans construct their social networks, share crafter knowledge, and distribute information across these networks to support one another using a hybrid model of strategy and tactic: participation.

BACKGROUND ON *FIREFLY*

Firefly was a television show created by Joss Whedon that was aired for three months by Fox, premiering in the fall of 2002. The show did not receive much support from the network; episodes were broadcast out of order, confusing viewers and failing to gain an audience large enough to satisfy Fox. Even so, *Firefly* garnered fan support. These fans persuaded the rights holders to produce and release the film *Serenity* and a reunion special in 2012 on the Science Channel. In between those years and since, the *Firefly* universe has produced various merchandise and media. These objects include official and unofficial objects such as compendia, comic books, and various fan-made products such as fan fiction, fan videos, books, and merchandise.

These details about *Firefly* are important, as the values and mores of the characters in the show help construct the ways in which the fans have constructed their fan community. Set in the year 2516, *Firefly* presents a futuristic world where Earth was destroyed and people spread out across the universe (referred to as the 'Verse in the show). Fighting in the Unification War, the Browncoats lost to the Alliance at the Battle of Serenity. The Alliance continued to assert their control to varying degrees across the 'Verse, while the losers of this civil war were pushed to the boundaries, taking up a pioneer lifestyle reminiscent of the American Western society. The time and space in which this show took place, a reconstructed Old West, and the inscription of rebellion against a monolithic superpower are key elements in understanding the ethos of the fans and allies in this case study.

The main characters of the story are self-proclaimed "Big Damn Heroes" who survived the war in their own ways: soldiers, a mercenary, a mechanic, a religious leader, and fugitives. They are "by and large irrelevant in the grander scheme of the universe" (Rowley, 2007, p. 319), while being representative of survivors strewn across the 'Verse. Whedon's characters are purposefully ambiguous about good and evil; they defy the Alliance, steal when necessary, and come to the aid of the weak when needed. In a similar way, the fans of the series share these values themselves, especially in the case study. By referring to themselves as Browncoats, the fans are appropriating the language of the show and using this term to realize their community. They are pointing to the image of central character Captain Malcolm "Mal" Reynolds, still wearing his brown coat long past his group's loss at the Battle of Serenity, as a way to show unity with the greater cause of freedom and independence in opposition to the overwhelming control and loss of agency that the Alliance represents. A similar tactic is taken by the crafters and their allies in opposition to Fox in this case study.

These actions leading to enunciation are critical moments for the fandom to shape itself and become coherent. In describing their community, one of the fans states, "When you meet a Browncoat for the first time they don't shake hands, they hug you right away. It's like a family, and you feel that from the actors, too" (Hadlock et al., 2006). These fans gather at conventions, chat in various digital spaces such as FireflyFans.net, and talk to the stars, producers, writers, and costume makers over Twitter. The fandom's culture often replicates the *Firefly* 'Verse, with many noting that "the fans of *Firefly* are in fact sort of these characters on the show" (Hadlock et al., 2006). This further enunciates the sense of family and belonging within this fandom and *Firefly*.

As characters, they are also constructing a different kind of fan community. This concept of "family" and community is one that is central for the fans, fan scholars, scholar fans, and the cast and crew of *Firefly*. Other scholars in Whedon Studies have explored these ideas (Koontz, 2008; Rambo, 2014; Wilcox & Cochran, 2008), and the idea of strong community ties is central to the fan-produced video celebrating the *Firefly* fandom (Hadlock, Heppler, Neish & Wiser, 2006). The phrase "Done the Impossible" is a line of dialogue spoken by Mal in reference to a temporary victory during the Battle of Serenity during the *Firefly* pilot episode. In that way, it is also the shared ethos of the fandom that they had done the impossible by uniting themselves as Browncoats and produced the video to showcase their community. This concept of family is pervasive throughout many of Whedon's works, and it has an effect on the fans and scholars who study his work. A central leader of the Whedon Studies Association, scholar Rhonda V. Cochran (2014) noted that she was "especially drawn in by the abiding theme of chosen family" (p. 392). This theme is central to the ways in which these fans enunciate their community's ethos through communication moves they make across social media and the symbols they choose to rally behind.

FANDOMS AND SYMBOLS

The main characters use the ship to smuggle goods and protect their stowaways. In the words of the ship's captain, Mal: "You got a job, we can do it, don't much care what it is" (Minear, 2002). This continued ambiguity about right and wrong permeates the show. It also shows up in Nathan Fillion's response to a fan crafter regarding the Jayne hat issue (Fillion, 2013b). As the actor who played Mal, he is a central figure for the fandom, and his involvement in this case lent weight to the fan crafters' cause. As for the owner of the hat itself, Jayne Cobb is a character described as a "doltish mercenary" and a "lovable sonuvabitch," (Chant, 2012, p. 224). In the twelfth episode of the series, he receives a gift from his mother: A winter hat she has knitted for him in various shades of orange. As a material symbol, this hat became the focus of the event in this case study. In an authorized book about *Firefly*, costume designer Shawna Trpcic described the hat as a "labor of love," noting that "you can tell that he loves it because it's from his mom, and he doesn't even think about the fact that here he is, this hired killer, wearing a pom-pom on his head" (Twentieth Century Fox, 2007, p. 140). When Jayne puts it on, his crewmates are amused, while Jayne is proud to wear something handmade by his mom, softening his tough-guy persona. Here is the rugged mercenary with a family and backstory.

The hat is an important object to the Browncoat fandom, one which they have poached, as a form of fan crafting, from the show while also crafting their own versions of the hat. This kind of poaching was first discussed by de Certeau (1984) and later elaborated on by Jenkins in discussing fan fiction (1992, 2012). The fans inscribe their fandom through the hat across various kinds of media, both physical and digital. People can download patterns to make the hat (Fung, 2012), listen to a podcast dedicated to the hat ('dillo, 2013), cosplay about the hat (blaster, 2013), and listen to fan-produced music (known as filk) dedicated to the hat (Peal, 2008). In these ways they have reached enunciation—realizing the need for an object to unite the fandom, appropriating from Jayne as a central object within the fandom, inscribing the hat as a relationship-making object among fans, and situating the hat as a way of cementing their connections to each other.

The hat was taken up by the fandom, with one fan crafter noting that "every fan who sees them knows I'm a fellow traveller in the 'Verse" ('dillo, 2013), signaling to the term used to describe the *Firefly* Universe. Describing the hat and how to craft one in a podcast, one fan states: "Is there anything more symbolic of firefly than a cunning yellow-orange hat with red earflaps? When a browncoat walks down the street wearing a Jayne's hat, you can tell they're proud of their fandom" ('dillo, 2013). These statements by fans both align them with their fellow fans and point to the symbol as central to the fandom, thus walking through the four elements of de Certeau's enunciation. During the episode where Jayne's character received the hat, he asked, "How does it sit? Pretty cunning, don't you think?"

Fans have poached the artifact from *Firefly* and made it part of their "lexicon of use" (de Certeau, 1984, p. 31)—a way to ascribe meaning to their fandom while prescribing the ways in which they can participate and show their loyalty to their fan community. Responding to the actions of Fox, fans appropriate the language of *Firefly* by using the phrases used in the show, situating and inscribing meaning between the show and the events happening in real life as a way of the larger fan community and their allies. On Twitter, the #jaynehat hashtag was used as an interlocutor during the time and space of the case study, and it is still in use today for fans to talk about the hat, the controversy, and the fandom. Someone is even running a Twitter account under the name of the hat, spelled backwards (EnyajTah), in reference to Nathan Fillion's suggestion that crafters rename their hats EnyajTah to avoid Fox's interference (Fillion, 2013a). But it is the physical manifestations of the hat—the official one sold on ThinkGeek (2013a) and the crafter fan-made versions on Etsy—that cause the controversy in this case study.

Eynaj Stahs for Sale

This kind of "entrepreneurial feminism" (Jenkins, 2013, p. xxx) is supported by *Firefly*'s creator, Joss Whedon. This term refers to "feminists' conflicted ability and desire to engage with and intervene in capitalism" (Sheridan-Rabideau, 2009, p. 128). As the creator of *Firefly* and several other cult television shows, including *Buffy the Vampire Slayer*, Joss Whedon has notably generated strong female characters and shown support for the DIY community. On a crafter blog called Crochet Me, he stated that seeing the hats "fills me with tiny knitted joy" (Werker, 2008). In that same article, Whedon (2008) acknowledged the crafter culture within *Firefly*, noting the "pioneer spirit" of the show and explaining that "we were really trying to evoke the idea of things you make for yourself, of a life that you create with your own two hands" (as cited in Werker, 2008). It is unsurprising that the fandom would also show signs of this kind of participation, making their own hats, selling hats to fellow Browncoats, and sharing information with each other about how to make these hats. In that way, the hat itself becomes both a symbol and a genre form for the fans to show their allegiance to the show and each other.

Etsy is a space for crafters to sell handmade objects and connect with fans. Through this case study, we can see how the *Firefly* fandom is similar to a folk culture, which, "as they historically operated . . . [was] highly participatory, with skills and norms passed down informally across generations and with no sharp division between expert and novice" (Jenkins, 2013, p. xxvii). It is through this kind of activity that we can also see how sellers might alter the genre of Etsy by posting new listings that take up the language of their fandom—appropriating this language to fit the situation—rather than using the specific name of the copyrighted material. So here we see listings for "cunning hats" rather than "Jayne hats," pointing to the catch phrases of their fandoms—the interlocutors of their fandom—rather than pointing to Fox's "official name" for the hats. In this way, they are inscribing the relationship between object and fandom, situating it within this context to enunciate the connection. Whether or not this can continue will be up to Fox's lawyers and Etsy's policies, but many of the fan crafters, the fans, and the Big Damn Heroes all seem willing to support these exchanges.

CRAFTERS AND ETSY

Crafters are artists who create handmade objects, as opposed to mass-produced creations made in factories. Similar to the do-it-yourself (DIY) maker community, the crafter community is an online and offline phenomenon attracting the attention of researchers across Internet studies, participatory culture, and digital rhetoric. These communities are useful locations for examining how crafters use technology to share, remix, and mentor other participants. Within the crafter community is a sense of openness and sharing, a similar attitude found in fan fiction communities (Busse & Hellekson, 2006, p. 6). Scholars such as Jenkins (2010a) have considered DIY culture as part of a longer historical movement that he referred to as DIO (Do it Ourselves), a component of participatory culture and community-based action. Colin Lankshear and Michele Knobel referred to how "new technologies make it possible in principle for everyday people to produce artifacts that have the kind of sophistication that could previously only be obtained via very high cost infrastructure" (as cited in Jenkins, 2010b). It is that kind of activity that led to the activism in this case study, crafting and writing to align themselves with a particular fan community. While the Jayne hats are derivatives of *Firefly* and not fan fiction, the similarities between these two types of production are clear in terms of ideology, values, and orientation. Like the "female fanzine editors" that Jenkins (2013) talked about in his work, these crafters are mostly women who are "asserting their rights to create and manage their own small-scale business within the support structure fandom provided" (p. xxx).

While crafter fans create hat patterns (Fung, 2012) and share advice through websites and podcasts ('dillo, 2013), it was the crafters on Etsy who garnered the ire of Fox. A space for crafters, Etsy encourages shoppers to "buy from creative people who care about quality and craftsmanship" (2014a). Etsy is a supporter of the DIY/DIO movement, creating a space for crafters to sell their products and asking its shoppers to participate in a "marketplace where people around the world connect to buy and sell unique goods" (2014b).

It is within this space that we can often witness "fan culture as folk culture" (Jenkins & Scott, 2013, p. xxvii) as crafters create objects for different kinds of fans. It was in a space where such folk culture flourishes—Etsy—that crafters selling their Jayne hats received notification of cease-and-desist orders sent by Fox (Pantozi, 2013). Although many of these takedown notices were not documented, most of them have one element in common: They all referred to the hats using the name Jayne and hat or noted the *Firefly* connection. Here, Fox is exercising their power as a major corporation and media company as a strategy to stop the sale of the hats by the fan crafters. But they are taking action by invading a space known for building communities and relationships through selling handmade products. The crafters who set up shop on Etsy do so through a number of rhetorical moves. First, they must create their shop, using images and text to create an ethos as a crafter and seller of products that are distinctive and compelling to other community members. Then they must do the same for each object they list, describing the item and encouraging others to see it as a unique product that will convey a sense of homemade crafting legacy that normally would only be found at art fairs or one-of-a-kind style art shops. In fact, many of the Etsy crafters offer customization of their products, both in made-to-order and personalization options. This all occurs within this community that encourages crafting.

Undeterred, many of these crafters wanted to continue selling their hats. In discussing how to circumvent the issue, *Firefly* actor Nathan Fillion suggested in a tweet that crafters "Maybe just call them Enyaj hats from Erifylf" (Fillion, 2013a). Here, the star who plays the central leader on the show appropriates the language of the fandom in ways that would signal an attempt to deploy a tactic to circumvent the strategy of Fox. Is Fillion a strategist or a tactician? As the star of the show, he could be considered part of Fox's strategic machine, but as an independent actor on Twitter, he is aligning himself with the tactics of the fandom and the Etsy crafters.

The most vocal of these Etsy crafters referred to herself as Ma Cobb, the mother of *Firefly* character Jayne Cobb who crafted his hat. This act of enunciation aligns her with the fandom and the show through her appropriation of the character. In order to protect themselves, the crafters asked *The Mary Sue* to remove their names from their geek news articles. Some of these crafters were more reluctant to oppose Fox publicly, possibly due to the risk of litigation given the wording of the cease-and-desist orders. However, many of them continue to sell hats similar to the one worn by Jayne in *Firefly*, just under different names, as mentioned earlier in this case study. Again, these names would be easily recognized by other fans of *Firefly*, an act of poaching and appropriation that becomes both a strategy (as a business on Etsy) and a tactic (as a fan of the television show).

"OFFICIAL" AS A STRATEGY

Fox is the copyright holder for *Firefly* material and merchandise, and legally speaking, they are the entity who can issue an "official" Jayne hat. Working with third-party manufacturer Ripple Junction, an official hat was made for ThinkGeek. Ripple Junction has stayed largely silent about the incident, and Fox has spoken to fans—whether they realize it or not—through their cease-and-desist orders sent to Etsy to shut down the fan crafters. Fans were upset at Fox for sending these letters; the letters effectively shut down the Jayne hat listings on Etsy. Some crafters, taking lead *Firefly* actor Nathan Fillion's advice (2013a), sought to route around this issue by reworking the genre on Etsy to serve the *Firefly* fans and become an activist that supported them. It is unclear how long this resistance can last, as Jenkins (2013) noted that a "utopian imagination often fuels fandom's resistances to corporate efforts to commodify its cultural productions and exchanges" (p. xxix).

While it is not disputed that Fox holds the copyright to the show, fans and some of the writers, producers, and actors in the show—known to fans as the Big Damn Heroes—disagree over whether the hat is a an item that Fox can copyright. Fox believes they can copyright the hat, and they have the weight of their production company and the lawyers to enforce it. In this situation, "the company still seeks to set the terms of our participation and fans are by and large still refusing to play by those rules" (Jenkins, 2013, p. xxvi). Their strategy was to deploy letters through lawyers, attempting to silence their fandom and crafters alike. Siding with the fans, actor Nathan Fillion tweeted, "How do you license hats? I don't think FOX invented hats" (2013a). His tweet contained a link to the article about the incident, attaching an image from an article of a baby wearing a tiny Jayne hat. His move here is clear, following de Certeau's framework for enunciation. Fillion realized the efforts of the fans through this speech act and went on to appropriate the language of the fandom in further tweets mentioned in this article. He worked to act as an interlocutor connecting fans with geek news websites, the ThinkGeek operation, and the fandom itself.

Sussing Out the Reactions across Digital Spaces

The *Firefly* fandom is known for being activists for women's rights. In describing these moves, one scholar notes that many "Whedon fan activists have cultivated a distinctive character: specifically, a feminist one" (Cochran, 2012). These fans are active and activist across a number of causes, most notably Can't Stop the Serenity, a fan-based charity that supports Equality Now and other organizations promoting "human rights of women around the world." The ways in which they use digital spaces as a community promotes these kinds of values. It is notable that the crafters in this case study are mostly women, and several of the digital spaces where this story was told and participation the most visible were woman-centered in both demographics and design: Etsy and geek news sites such as *The Mary Sue*, *io9*, and *Buzzfeed*, and to a lesser extent, Twitter.

Some fans reached out to the Big Damn Heroes of the show, contacting Nathan Fillion, Adam Baldwin, and others asking for their support. In one example, a crafter asked Fillion to help "unload illegal hats" in Twitter. This tweet also included an image of knitted Jayne hats. Fillion retweeted this tweet, adding "You got a job? We'll do it. Don't much care what it is" (Fillion, 2013b). That phrase is one uttered by the character he played in *Firefly* to indicate his crew's feelings towards smuggling, a necessary ambiguity towards right and wrong. In making this move, Fillion and the fan acknowledged each other's roles within the fandom with Fillion as the smuggler captain and the crafter in need of moving her merchandise: appropriating the language of the show and fandom, inscribing it to create a relationship, and situating it within the context of this case study. And it did not go unnoticed; his tweet, an act of participation and activism, was favorited 2,324 times and retweeted 2,145 times. Both numbers are significant in showing how fans were acknowledging this use of Twitter and sharing them with others. Here they used this social media genre in useful ways by not-so-subtly stating which side they are on: The crafter calling him- or herself by the handle PirateKnits, and Fillion reposting the material in his *Firefly* captain persona. It was through this kind of work on Twitter and their rework-ing of hat names on Etsy that the crafters and allies showed their ability to use these genres to rally fan community members.

During the events of April 2013, these Big Damn Heroes (BDH) expressed their concern for the situation by either tweeting or retweeting content on Twitter. Fillion was outspoken about the treatment of the show's fans, post-ing numerous times about the hats and fan crafters (Fillion, 2013a, 2013b). Like Nathan Fillion, the actor who played Jayne, Adam Baldwin, also tempo-rarily aligned himself with the crafters, retweeting a post by a fan that states, "I don't have a 'Jayne' hat. I have an Adam Baldwin Hat" (Baldwin, 2013). This retweet has since been removed from Baldwin's Twitter feed, while Fillion's tweets remain. The tweet and the retweet are interesting conventions on Twitter, with the former being a statement made directly from the participant and the latter being the resending of a tweet made by a different participant. The tweet is authorship, while the retweet can be considered endorsement or at least inter-est by the retweeter. These tweets are interlocutors that enunciate the fandom's activism. Various geek news outlets speculated about the various stands taken by the BDH, with one stating, "it seems clear that they're all a little nervous about biting the hand that feeds, but it's also clear that they're not happy, either" (Roth, 2013). This insight may point to why Baldwin initially retweeted and then deleted the tweet.

FUTURES FOR DIGITAL RHETORIC, WRITING, AND PARTICIPATION

Spaces where fans congregate, pushing and pulling against the fandoms that they collectively enjoy, are a compelling site of study for researchers wanting to under-stand digital rhetoric, power relationships, genre conventions, and new models for participation. Understanding how fans draw on rhetoric, realizing a system of communication, connecting to one another through interlocutors, appropriating language, contextualizing speech, and establishing a sense of time and space for their fellow fans can help us piece together activity, use, and genre. Through this understanding, we can become better researchers and teachers of and in digital spaces. These kinds of explorations can tell us how our students might be pro-ducing content, remixing, and participating across digital spaces. We can learn about best (and worst) practices to teach and inform. Bringing in these kinds of case studies to the classroom helps students see the connections between how they might play in these spaces and the work they might produce in practice. Questions about ownership, intellectual property, and participation are all up for discussion both in thinking about social media use and crafter culture.

In this case study, Fox is aligning itself with *Firefly*'s Alliance by deploying strategies where they are trying to control the power in their relationship with fans—fans that they see as consumers, and not crafters or makers. *Firefly* fans—makers, actors, writers, costumers—align themselves with their fandom while deploying a combination of strategies and tactics and enunciating their fandoms through their activities in various digital spaces. Short of a limited understanding of fans, the Internet, and rhetoric, it is unclear why *Firefly*'s rights holders would want to do further injury to their relationship with *Firefly*'s fans. As Jenkins (2013) noted, "we are seeing far fewer cease-and-desist letters as media companies have come to value networked audiences" (p. xxv). Why go after these fan crafters? As one geek news reporter noted, "Fox has actually decided to license merchandise based on the ten-year-old television series" (Polo, 2013). Why now, when these hats have been available online for years? Are they really a threat to Fox's ability to sell licensed hats on ThinkGeek? While not embracing their short-lived show's fandom, Fox continues to look like an adversary to the Browncoats. Through the use of the genre of a cease-and-desist letter, Fox missed an opportunity to network across these crafters, creating the possibility of licensing their work or at least allowing them to continue their comparatively low output without conflict or interruption. How do these issues of intellectual property, the rights of a community, and the ability to spread this kind of content alter the relationships between content owners, content producers, and fan crafters?

As with these kinds of case studies for research purposes, the implications for teachers of social media is clear: Understanding how students participate in these spaces, providing them the tools to understand how to use various digital genres, and guiding them through the elements of enunciation in professional spaces is a critical part of the writing and rhetoric classroom. By paying attention to these practices, we can create pedagogies for social media (Daer & Potts, 2014) and continue to research these spaces with an understanding of the participants who inhabit them and often route around established practices for social activism, feminist entrepreneurship, and community.

REFERENCES

amandapalmer. (2009). if you want to sing out, log in (Amanda & co. in L.A.) [YouTube video]. Retrieved from http://youtu.be/0W25uK-TETU.

Baldwin, A. (2013). RT @monsterhunter45 I don't have a "Jayne" hat. I have an Adam Baldwin hat. [Tweet]. Retrieved from http://www.blastr.com/sites/blastr/files/styles/blog_post_in_content_image/public/adambaldwintweet.png?itok=oGh8eZap.

Blakeslee, A. M. (2010). Addressing audiences in a digital age. In R. Spilka (Ed.), *Digital literacy for technical communication: 21st century theory and practice* (pp. 199–229). New York, NY: Routledge.

blaster. (2013, March 22). Cosplay we love: Most insanely awesome Firefly recreation we've ever seen. *Syfywire*. Retrieved from http://www.blastr.com/2013-3-22/cosplay -we-love-most-insanely-awesome-firefly-recreation-weve-ever-seen.

Bruns, A. (2008). *Blogs, Wikipedia, Second Life, and beyond: From production to produsage*. New York, NY: Peter Lang.

Busker, R. L. (2008). On symposia: LiveJournal and the shape of fannish discourse. *Transformative Works and Cultures, 1*(1). Retrieved from http://journal.transforma tiveworks.org/index.php/twc/article/view/49.

Busse, K. & Hellekson, K. (2006). Introduction: Work in progress. In K. Hellekson & K. Busse (Eds.), *Fan fiction and fan communities in the age of the Internet* (pp. 5–32). Jefferson, NC: McFarland & Company.

Chaney, J. (2013). ThinkGeek: The nerd company at a crossroads. *The Washington Post*. Retrieved from http://www.washingtonpost.com/lifestyle/magazine/thinkgeek-the -nerd-company-at-a-crossroads/2013/12/11/c7d579ba-4b12-11e3-9890-a1e0997 fb0c0_story.html.

Chant, I. (2011, March 16). Joss Whedon 101: Firefly. Retrieved from http://www .popmatters.com/feature/137607-joss-whedon-101-firefly/.

Chin, B. & Hills, M. (2008). Restricted confessions? Blogging, subcultural celebrity and the management of producer-fan proximity. *Social Semiotics, 18*(2), 253–272.

Cochran, T. R. (2012). "Past the brink of tacit support": Fan activism and the Whe- donverses. *Transformative Works and Cultures, 10*. Retrieved from http://journal .transformativeworks.org/index.php/twc/article/view/331/295.

Cochran, T. R. (2014). Whedon studies: A living history, 1999–2013. In R. V. Wilcox, T. R. Cochran, C. Masson & D. Lavery (Eds.), *Reading Joss Whedon* (pp. 371–392). Syracuse, NY: Syracuse University Press.

Daer, A. & Potts, L. (2014). Teaching and learning with social media: Tools, cultures, and best practices. *Programmatic Perspectives, 6*(2), 21–40.

de Certeau, M. (1984). *The practice of everyday life*. Berkeley, CA: University of Califor- nia Press.

De Kosnik, A. (2013). Fandom as free labor. In T. Scholz (Ed.), *Digital labor: The Internet as playground and factory* (pp. 98–111). New York, NY: Routledge.

De Ridder, S. (2013). Are digital media institutions shaping youth's intimate stories? Strategies and tactics in the social networking site Netlog. *New Media and Society, 17*(3), 356–374.

Deller, R. (2011). Twittering on: Audience research and participation using Twitter. *Participants: Journal of Audience & Reception Studies, 8*(1). Retrieved from http:// www.participations.org/Volume%208/Issue%201/deller.htm.

'dillo. (2013, March 26). 101 uses for a Jayne's hat [Audio podcast]. *The Signal, 9*(2). Retrieved from http://signal.serenityfirefly.com/mmx/show/view.php/244.

Fillion, N. (2013a, April 10). How do you license hats? I don't think FOX invented hats. Maybe just call them Enyaj hats from Erifylf. http://io9.com/fox-bans-the

-sale-of-unlicensed-jayne-hats-from-firefly-471820413 . . . [Tweet]. Retrieved from https://twitter.com/NathanFillion/status/322106561382191104.

Fillion, N. (2013b, April 11). "@PirateKnits: Captain, looking to unload illegal hats. pic.twitter.com/fR1V0wJA9b" You got a job? We'll do it. Don't much care what it is. [Tweet]. Retrieved from https://twitter.com/NathanFillion/status/32220118840 3671040.

Fung, V. (2012). Make your own Jayne hat. Retrieved from http://qmxonline.com /blogs/news/13844233-make-your-own-jayne-hat.

Gal, N., Shifman, L. & Zohar, K. (2015). "It gets better": Internet memes and the construction of collective identity. *New Media and Society, 18*(8), 1698–1714. doi: 10.1177/1461444814568784

Gibson, O. (2007). Prince threatens to sue his fans over online images. Retrieved from http://www.theguardian.com/uk/2007/nov/07/musicnews.topstorics3.

Gray, J. (2010). *Show sold separately: Promos, spoilers, and other media paratexts.* New York, NY: NY University Press.

Hadlock, T., Heppler, J., Neish, J., Nelson, J. & Wiser, B. (Directors). (2006). *Done the impossible: The fans' tale of* Firefly *&* Serenity [Documentary]. US: Done the Impossible Studios.

Hall, E. (2013). "Firefly" hat triggers corporate crackdown. Retrieved from http:// www.buzzfeed.com/ellievhall/firefly-hat-triggers-corporate-crackdown.

Hills, M. (2002). *Fan cultures.* New York, NY: Routledge.

Jenkins, H. (2013). *Textual poachers: Television fans and participatory culture* (2nd ed.). New York, NY: Routledge.

Jenkins, H. (2010a, May 24). Why participatory culture is not Web 2.0: Some basic distinctions [Blog]. Retrieved from http://henryjenkins.org/2010/05/why_partici patory_culture_is_n.html.

Jenkins, H. (1992). *Textual poachers: Television fans and participatory culture.* New York, NY: Routledge.

Jenkins, H. (2010b, May 26). What can teachers learn from DIY cultures: An interview with Colin Lankshear & Michele Knobel (part one) [Blog]. Retrieved from http://henryjenkins.org/2010/05/diy_learning.html.

Jenkins, H., Clinton, K., Purushotma, R., Robison, A. J. & Weigel, M. (2009). *Confronting the challenges of participatory culture: Media education for the 21st century.* Chicago, IL: MacArthur Foundation.

Jenkins, H., Ford, S. & Green, J. (2013). *Spreadable media: Creating value and meaning in a networked culture.* New York, NY: New York University Press.

Jenkins, H. & Scott, S. (2013). Textual poachers, 20 years later: A conversation between Henry Jenkins and Suzanne Scott. In H. Jenkins (Ed.), *Textual poachers: Television fans and participatory culture* (20th anniversary ed.) (pp. vii–xlii). New York, NY: Routledge.

Koontz, K. D. (2008). *Faith and choice in the works of Joss Whedon.* Jefferson, NC: McFarland.

McCulloch, R., Crisp, V., Hickman, J. & Janes, S. (2013). Of proprietors and poachers: Fandom as negotiated brand ownership. *Participation: Journal of Audience and Reception Studies, 10*(1), 319–328.

Whedon, J. & Minear, T. (Writers) & Minear, T. (Director). (2002). The message [Television series episode]. In J. Whedon & T. Minear (Executive producers), *Firefly*. Los Angeles, CA: Fox Broadcasting Company.

Pantozzi, J. (2013). Updated: Are you a *Firefly* fan who makes Jayne hats? Watch out, Fox is coming for you. Retrieved from http://www.themarysue.com/jayne-hats-fox/.

Pascale, A. (2014). *Joss Whedon: The biography*. Chicago, IL: Chicago Review Press [Kindle Edition].

Peal, S. (n.d.). Jayne's hat [Video file]. Retrieved from http://signal.serenityfirefly.com /mmx/segment/view.php/2032.

Polo, S. (2013). ThinkGeek will donate all Jayne hat proceeds to Firefly charity. Retrieved from http://www.themarysue.com/thinkgeek-jayne-hats-charity.

Potts, L. (2012). Amanda Palmer and the #LOFNOTC: How online fan participation is rewriting music labels. *Participants: Journal of Audience & Reception Studies, 9*(2). Retrieved from http://www.participations.org/Volume%209/Issue%202/20%20 Potts.pdf.

Potts, L. (2014). *Social media in disaster response: How experience architects can build for participation*. New York, NY: Routledge.

Potts, L. (2015). Can't stop the fandom: Writing participation in the *Firefly* 'verse. *Kairos: A Journal of Rhetoric, Technology, and Pedagogy, 19*(2). Retrieved from http:// technorhetoric.net/19.3/topoi/potts/.

Potts, L. & Harrison, A. (2013). Interfaces as rhetorical constructions: Reddit and 4chan during the Boston bombings. *Proceedings of the 31st ACM international conference on the Design of Communication* (pp. 143–150). New York, NY: ACM.

Rambo, E. L. (2014). Sending and receiving *Firefly*'s last "message." In R. V. Wilcox, T. R. Cochran, C. Masson & D. Lavery (Eds.), *Reading Joss Whedon* (pp. 185–197). Syracuse, NY: Syracuse University Press.

Roth, D. (2013). *Firefly* cast and crew weigh in on DIY Jayne hat ban (and they're not happy). Retrieved from http://www.blastr.com/2013-4-10/firefly-cast-and-crew -weigh-diy-jayne-hat-ban-and-theyre-not-happy.

Rowley, C. (2007). *Firefly/Serenity*: Gendered space and gendered bodies. *The British Journal of Politics & International Relations, 9*(2), 318–325.

Sheridan-Rabideau, M. P. (2009). *Girls, feminism, and grassroots literacies: Activism in the GirlZone*. Albany, NY: State University of New York Press.

ThinkGeek. (2013, April 10). Jayne hat proceeds to Can't Stop the Serenity. Retrieved from http://www.thinkgeek.com/blog/2013/04/jayne-hat-proceeds-to-cant-sto.html.

Thomas, R. (2013). The *Veronica Mars* movie project. Retrieved from http://www .kickstarter.com/projects/559914737/the-veronica-mars-movie-project.

Twentieth Century Fox. (2007). Firefly: *The official companion, volume two*. London, England: Titan Books.

Werker, K. (2008). Joss Whedon on crafts and craftiness: Interview transcript [Blog entry]. Retrieved from http://www.crochetme.com/blogs/kim_werker/archive/2008/12/6/joss-whedon-on-crafts-and-craftiness-interview-transcript.aspx.

Wilcox, R. V. & Cochran, T. R. (2010). *Investigating* Firefly *and* Serenity*: Science fiction on the frontier*. New York, NY: I.B. Tauris & Co. Ltd.

PART 2: PRESENTATION OF SELF, GROUPS, AND DATA

CHAPTER 7

HAVING A FEEL FOR WHAT WORKS: POLYMEDIA, EMOTION, AND LITERACY PRACTICES WITH MOBILE TECHNOLOGIES

Bronwyn T. Williams

University of Louisville

Sarah is using her phone to have a conversation.[1] To read this sentence will, for many people, conjure an image of a person holding a device to her head where she can speak and listen with another person holding a similar device. Yet, like so many secondary and university students (not to mention many of the rest of us), the concept of both "phone" and "conversation" are more flexible and capacious than we might initially imagine. During the course of the two hours in which I am observing and interviewing her, Sarah uses no fewer than five modes of communication (phone call, Twitter, Snapchat, Instagram, text message) to converse with friends and family. She trades text messages with three different people, receives and looks at photos on both Snapchat and Instagram (and writes comments on two of the Instagram photos), responds to a comment on her Twitter feed that is part of an ongoing conversation thread with two friends (one of whom she is also texting), and even takes a traditional phone call ("From my mother," she explains. "She still likes to call me"). In addition to her interactive uses of communication technology, Sarah also uses apps on her phone to look up information for school and check the traffic situation before she has to leave for her restaurant job.

Sarah's use of her phone, which is not unusual among her peers, makes clear that when we say "phone" and "conversation" now we are describing a set of practices very different from those we would have been describing even a decade ago. A "phone" today is a hand-held computer on which one can also make the occasional voice call, and a "conversation," in which one has interactive communication with others using such a device, may involve spoken words, images, audio, and video, or some combination of all of these.

---

1   The names used are pseudonyms chosen by the individuals.

Watching Sarah navigate the variety of modes and media through which she communicates raises the question of how and why she makes the choices she does. When does she decide to post to social media rather than text? What rhetorical factors does she weigh when she decides to use one social media platform, such as Twitter, over another, such as Instagram? How does she interpret and respond to the communicative choices made by others, from a friend's Snapchat post to her mother's phone call?

In recent years, scholars in rhetoric and composition and literacy studies have often turned to the concept of affordances as a framework through which to interpret and analyze the practices and pedagogy of composing with multiple media and modes (Cooper, 2005; Keller, 2007; Pahl & Rowsell, 2010; Wilson, 2011). Affordances, with their focus on rhetorical concepts such as purpose, genre, and audience, have offered a way to connect the concerns that shaped the teaching of traditional print-on-paper literacy with the burgeoning range of digital media available for creating texts. In this way, affordances have provided—and will continue to provide—productive frameworks for the theorizing, research, and teaching of multimodal composing.

Yet, as useful as the concept of affordances has been, the scholarship and pedagogy developing from the idea has often approached such composing choices as if they were limited and made one at a time. Do I use video or print? Sound or blog? Employing this concept of affordances, however, misses the ways that many people today approach the use of digital media in their daily lives. Rather than making singular choices, they move back and forth among social media and modes quickly, changing from one to another as the content and emotional register of their communication shifts. Their actions are fast, mobile, and grounded in social and emotional needs and relationships. Like Sarah, they may move, in one conversation with a friend or relative, from texting to photo sharing to phone call and back again, depending on the emotional register, power relations, and cultural genres of the situation.

In this chapter, I draw on Mirca Madianou's and Daniel Miller's (2012) concept of polymedia to explore how students negotiate these fluid movements among media in their literacy practices with social media. Polymedia assumes that people with multiple media, when communicating, make choices that, though including considerations of functional communication, are also shaped by material conditions, social contexts, relationships, and emotional responses (Madianou & Miller, 2012). In my chapter, drawn from interviews and observations with university students in the United States and United Kingdom using digital media such as mobile devices, I focus on how the rhetorical and compositional moves people make in communicating with others are shaped by concerns and responses of emotion and their relationships with audience members.

For example, a person choosing to tweet rather than text is not only deciding how best to convey information, but may also weigh the emotional dispositions toward the medium, such as the desire to establish or obscure intimacy. Such dispositions are constructed over time through experiences in specific cultural contexts as well as individual relationships. At the same time, emotion as a rhetorical performance (Micciche, 2007) also influences student choices, as the choice of media may be intended or interpreted as having a particular emotional impact. A person circulating news to friends may employ multiple media to friends and acquaintances (Twitter, Instagram, Facebook, text, phone call) with the intent that different media will not only convey different information, but that the choice of media will also be read as rhetorical and with emotional impact. Focusing on the role emotion plays in individuals' polymedia literacy practices helps illuminate the embodied and affective impact of such practices and deepens our understanding of the role of social media in shaping and sustaining relationships and identities.

RETHINKING AFFORDANCES WITH DIGITAL MEDIA

There is no doubt that the concept of affordances has provided us with a productive way of studying and teaching how to compose with multiple media and modes (Cooper, 2005; Keller, 2007; Werner, 2013; Wilson, 2011). As Kate Pahl and Jennifer Rowsell (2010) defined the term, "An affordance describes the specific possibilities resident within a mode, whether these are determined by the material or cultural possibilities of the mode" (pp. 4–5). In theory and pedagogy, the work on affordances has often focused on the rhetorical possibilities a mode offers, particularly in terms of concepts of audience and genre. The framework of affordances has been useful in reminding us that composing with digital media, as well as with print on paper, is not just about having choices, but about making thoughtful choices with regard to how a text can best convey particular ideas to a particular audience. The popularity of affordances in our field, with its frequent focus on pedagogy, also comes in part from its utility in talking about how digital media can and should be used in academic settings. Talking about affordances provides traction in such discussions by focusing on easily comprehensible rhetorical goals and principles, such as purpose, genre, audience, and impact. Such arguments have been useful to the field, useful to me, and I am in no way arguing that we stop using the idea and language of affordances when it is useful to our scholarship and teaching.

Yet affordances as a concept emerged in the 1990s, along with desktop computers and particular ways of engaging with software; as such, it has led to certain kinds of discussions and pedagogical practices that it may be time to complicate. First, the focus on affordances in terms of pedagogy has often meant missing or discounting literacy practices that take place outside the classroom. What's more, many discussions of affordances approach composing with digital media as an activity that involves engaging one technology at a time in a series of choices that take place sitting at a computer, composed for a classroom. Each delivery system, such as a podcast, or genre, such as remixed video, is offered as a single choice. Yet new technologies, such as smartphones and tablets, have created more fluid and mobile practices that are not reflected in this more traditional approach to affordances and do not address or consider the role of emotion—both as individual responses and as social and rhetorical practices—in how and why a particular medium or genre might be chosen.

During the past two years, I have been involved in a research project exploring issues of literacy, identity, and perceptions of agency. The research, conducted both in the United States and the United Kingdom, has involved interviews and observations with a wide range of individuals, more than 100, from secondary school students, to community college and university undergraduates, to graduate students. The people I am quoting in this chapter were all participants in these interviews and observations and covered a broad range of backgrounds and social settings. I am drawing from a wide range of responses, rather than just focusing on one or two people, to underscore the range of participants and contexts. I did not set out in this research specifically to study the use of mobile technologies, but their ubiquitous presence and use made them an integral part of most of the conversations and practices I encountered.

I quickly realized that the widespread and mainstream concept of affordances can only partially help us understand or respond to a moment such as this:

> Aaron sits in the cafeteria area of his community college in a mid-sized city in the United Kingdom while he waits for his next class. Like many others in the large room, he has earbuds in his ears and is using his mobile phone. He is scrolling through his Facebook feed when a text comes in from his girlfriend, which he reads and answers. For the next few minutes, he moves back and forth between the text conversation with his girlfriend and his Facebook feed, smiling to himself at several moments. At one point, in response to one of his texts, she posts a link to his Facebook page and he comments on the link and then texts a private comment about his social media comment. During this exchange he also notices that another friend has posted a link to a song on Facebook and he likes the link and listens to the song.

As this moment indicates, the choices of people—in particular, many young people—are fluid and shifting. Rather than address one affordance at a time, mobility and software allow individuals such as Aaron to move back and forth among media and genres quickly within a day, or even a conversation. What's more, while the rhetorical choices people make certainly involve considerations of audience, genre, purpose, and what a particular technology allows them to do, such considerations are not limited to detached, logic-driven concerns. Emotions and relationships are also integral to the choices individuals make, from embodied responses to emotion as a rhetorical and social factor involving networked, mobile communities. When Aaron described what he had been doing, he said that because he was in school and his girlfriend was at work, they did not get to spend as much time together as they would like:

> So any time we can, we get in touch. Mostly texting, but when
> she posts things on my (Facebook) page I like it because it's
> usually some joke or movie we like and so it takes more think-
> ing to do it than just text. I know she's thinking about me.

It's clear that Aaron's considerations of how and why he makes particular choices in communicating and responding with his girlfriend require an approach, in addition to rhetorical affordances, for understanding how emotions and relationships mediate his literacy practices.

In their concept of polymedia, Madianou and Miller (2012) offered a useful approach for considering the role of emotion and relationships in the choices people make while composing with digital media. For Madianou and Miller, polymedia focuses "less on the affordances of each particular medium and more on how users exploit the contrasts between media as an integrated environment in order to meet their relationship and emotional needs" (p. 128). To put it another way, deciding on whether to text or tweet or post a photo online to communicate with friends is not only a matter of considering the technological affordances of each medium and mode and making a single choice about how best to communicate a message. Smartphones, tablets, and laptops all now routinely offer the capacity to switch quickly among different media and modes, making the material constraints and considerations less important in shaping such choices. In the pre-digital era, deciding between mailing a letter and making a long-distance phone call was often determined by cost as much as it was by rhetorical impact. Even ten years ago, creating a video or posting a photo often took special software and skills and high-end technology that would influence decisions about composing messages. Once a person had made a choice about medium and mode, it took time and a deliberate change in work and often location to move to another way of communicating.

Material costs obviously are not absent with smartphones—first you have to own one and then the cost of data plans can vary widely. A smartphone without a generous data plan is much more limited in how it can be used. As with other technologies, recent research reinforces the fact that one's level of affluence and location as well as identity factors such as race and gender influence the kind of technology to which a person has access (Dugan, 2014; Smith, 2012, 2013; Williams, 2018). In other words, you're most likely to have a powerful smartphone if you're a white, urban, male professional. While mobile devices themselves have become a pervasive part of the culture in the United States and Europe, levels of affluence now determine who can afford a device and plan that allow for more varied multimodal applications and practices. Almost all the university students I spoke with and observed in the United States and the United Kingdom owned smartphones. The universities in question are urban institutions that include many first-generation university students or students working one or two jobs in addition to going to school. Even those who, in other contexts, told me about their struggles making financial ends meet while at university were not deciding to economize by doing without a smartphone. Indeed, several students said it was easier to get by without a laptop or home computer—and use computers on campus—precisely because they could get so much done with their smartphones. While it is important not to overlook issues of access, it is also clear that recent trends indicate that smartphone ownership and use is going to continue to increase and that we must pay attention to how people are communicating on these devices and over these networks (Dugan, 2014; Smith, 2012, 2013). Smartphone ownership in the United States is increasing rapidly, from 35 percent of the population in 2011 to 56 percent just two years later (Smith, 2013). Among young people the trend is even more telling, with 84 percent of adults between the ages of 18–29 reporting owning smartphones (Smith, 2013). In the United Kingdom, smartphone use in 2014 was reported at 62 percent of the population (Ofcom, 2014). Of course, not all smartphone use involves social media sites. However, polymedia practices illustrate that people often move quickly from social media use to individual communication such as texting and back again. At some moments, the networks of social media sites become important factors in these decisions, as I will discuss below, but not always. Yet given how much social media participation comes from people using smartphones, it is important to explore these practices even if at some moments they are communicating by individual text or phone call.

In addition to more widespread adaptation of smartphones, a number of the students I interviewed, like Eric, said that they used their smartphones for most of their digital work, using a more traditional laptop or desktop computer only for writing papers and other school work. Young people with smartphones say they often do not need to consider cost and time to the same degree when deciding whether to post a video or photo. Applications that allow for posting messages from different modes and through different media are often free and many of the people I talked to did not regard data speeds and costs as prohibitive. Smartphones and tablets are also set up to allow users to open, close, and move among applications quickly. For many young people, including most of the people I reference in this chapter, most of their activity with their smartphones is done through apps rather than by using more traditional Internet browsers such as Google or Safari. "My apps give me what I have to have (to communicate and find information). I pretty much never use Google," Leslie said. The processing power of new phones, and the convenience of apps that open with a single tap, mean that more applications can be kept open at any one time. As Daniel Keller (2013) pointed out, we live in a "culture of acceleration" in which speed is privileged and celebrated in most aspects of life, including literacy practices and rhetorical choices. Speed in using digital media is a consistent theme in scholars studying students' online literacy practices (Carrington, 2012; Davies, 2014; Keller, 2013; Rowsell, 2013; Williams, 2009). The value placed on speed has only increased as mobile devices provide individuals with the ability to have a device immediately accessible that allows them to move rapidly among apps, and know that all of them can be used in fast, interactive communication with friends.

SOCIALITY AND EMOTION

If the material and technological conditions are not as central to the choices people make in communicating through digital devices, then, as Madianou and Miller (2012) argued, other considerations become more important, such as sociality, emotion, and power. As they pointed out, "Polymedia is not a range of technical potentials, it is a series of cultural genres or emotional registers that make these contrasts into significant differences in communication by exploiting them for various tasks within relationships" (p. 148). To think about sociality is to consider how relationships are coordinated and sustained. Such relationships are formed within what the conventions of what Madianou and Miller called the cultural genres of sociality, which include the roles and expectations within relationships that are shaped by culture. For example, a mother is both someone in a personal relationship with an individual child as well as someone acting within and shaped by the cultural genres of the role of motherhood. To think about polymedia literacy practices within the context of sociality is to consider how the medium and mode, as well as the message, will be read within the context of the particular relationship.

For example, when Sarah's mother calls Sarah on her smartphone, the mother's choice—and the daughter's reaction—reflects not only their individual relationship but their roles in culture. When the call is over Sarah rolls her eyes slightly and says:

> Mom always calls because people her age do that and I know that, pretty much, if I get a phone call it's her or my grandma. And I have to always try to answer it or she'll get worried about what's happened to me.

Sarah's response places the actions of her mother in the context of cultural generalizations about the practices of people of different generations with digital media. Sarah does the same thing when talking about email when she says that the only emails she gets are from her boss or official university information, including from professors. Email, in her eyes, is an older person's technology she only checks for work or school purposes. Sarah's reaction to her mother's phone call also illustrates the roles mothers are supposed to play with their daughters—the latter worry about the former, who in turn try to be reassuring. Cultural genres also privilege certain forms of technology, or adapt them for uses in ways that conform to social expectations. In Jamaica, the popularity of mobile phones reinforced cultural values of individuality and privacy that are less possible when using a landline phone in a shared household space such as a kitchen (Madianou & Miller, 2012). And in Qatar, young women adapt Facebook pages to conform to local cultural genres. Instead of posting photos of themselves in the space for the profile photo, which would be considered immodest and inappropriate for a young woman, they instead post photos of younger siblings, celebrities, or designer fashion items (Rajakumar, 2012).

While the social relationships that are sustained by digital media use are shaped by larger cultural conventions—such as the role expected of mothers—they are also shaped by the often-varied cultural genres of local groups of friends and acquaintances. Within a particular group of friends, there often emerge specific expectations of what kind of information gets posted on a particular social media site. While some of these social conventions reflect broader cultural practices, sometimes they can end up developing practices that are quite specific to one local community or group. For example, Alia, a U.S. student at a public urban university in the Midwest, had a specific set of criteria for what media she used for what kinds of communications:

> Texting is for daily life, so I use it when I'm just trying to communicate news to people—"I'm just leaving" or "Where should I meet you." And jokes. Lots of jokes and being stupid

with friends. A phone call is usually just for a crisis. And
when I post pictures on Instagram that's for friends to enjoy,
sappy pictures, selfies, you know.

Robert, a student at the same university in the United States, had a slightly
different set of categories and preferences. He also said he used texting for informal conversation and communication with friends. "I like Twitter for getting
news and ideas about the world. I find out most of my news from there," he said.
"I use Facebook for sharing photos and for posting new music I hear or what I'm
listening to at the moment."

Both Alia and Robert said that they would not post information on any site
that would be at odds with what people there expected. Alia said, for example,
that her friends would be surprised if she posted anything on her Instagram
account aside from social photos of friends. "It would be weird if I posted something serious on there, like from the news, or even about me," she said. This
sentiment was shared by many of the students with whom I spoke and echoes
the work of Ilana Gershon (2010) on how, for many young people, the management of a breakup of a relationship through texting and social media—or how
they broke the news and let their friends know about the breakup—is judged
by their peers in terms of what the local community perceives as the appropriate
use of medium and platform. As another student told me, it would be wrong to
post a photo online of herself with a new boyfriend until everyone knew about
the previous breakup. The considerations of timing, social response, and rhetorical effect that students demonstrate in these kinds of actions and comments
supports Keller's (2013) observation that students exhibit "awareness of *kairos*,
which involves choosing the best discourse for the situation, taking into consideration, timing, audience, and context" (p. 93). As Kristin L. Arola's chapter on
indigenous interfaces in this volume also points out, students, like the rest of us,
develop a keen sense of the kinds of rhetorical moves they need to make in their
social groups to not only communicate information but to sustain community
relationships.

Yet the sustaining and coordinating of relationships through polymedia practices involves considerations of emotion and the rhetorics of emotion as much
as a rational weighing of affordances and kairotic opportunities. As Madianou
and Miller (2012) pointed out, "Being in an environment of polymedia matters
because polymedia allow the choice of medium or combination of media that
best conveys one's feeling and intentions" (p. 147). Individuals often discuss
their choices of social media and digital communication in terms of emotions.
In my interviews and observations, I came across quote after quote in which
people used phrases such as "it made my day," "I love to laugh at that," "that

made me depressed," "it would be embarrassing," "I wanted to show I cared," and so on. Megan's quote is typical of the kinds of things students talk about:

> I worry sometimes about how people are going to react if I tweet about having a bad day, or feeling bad about myself, that they'll think it's self-centered or annoying. But most of the time when I do, I get favorited, or my friends reply with something nice and, I know it sounds lame, but that makes me feel better.

Megan's comment reveals the complex interaction of the personal and the social in how people experience and conceive of emotion. Although there is a tendency in the culture at large to regard emotion as an individual, embodied experience, in fact the experience and communication of emotion are inextricable from social practices and conventions. As Margaret Wetherell (2012) argued, while we may feel emotions as embodied responses, they are reinforced and gain meaning in relationships with others and agreed upon social contexts: "The affective pattern is in fact *distributed* across the relational field and each partner's part becomes meaningful only in relation to the whole affective dance" (p. 87, emphasis in original). The posts students make on social media, from photos to written sentiments to popular culture links, reflect a shared conception of emotion. Their communicative acts not only reflect a sense of how the content will transmit emotion, but also how the act itself will be read emotionally. So, for example, when Aaron sees a post on his Facebook page from his girlfriend of a funny article from *The Onion*, it amuses him, but it also makes him feel cared for that she took time to post it, and that she posted it where it can be seen by their friends as a public display of affection. Emotion, then, is relational and dynamic, and rarely far from the minds of students when they are communicating with their mobile devices.

Any moment or phenomenon that is social is very often rhetorical, and emotion is no exception. We communicate our emotions to others for rhetorical ends, but we also learn and shape our emotions in the context of the rhetorical conventions of the culture in which we live. To feel and communicate outrage, for example, is shaped by cultural and rhetorical expectations as much as by the embodied feelings that follow a particular event. The feelings are real, but to process them as outrage, rather than shame or even indifference, is learned and then performed for, and interpreted by, others. As Laura Micciche (2007) pointed out:

> Performing emotions suggests that emotions are not already *in* us or others, waiting to be externalized. It means that

they take form, become recognizable, and enter the realm of rhetoric when they are bodily enacted and lived, which always entails some degree of performance. (p. 62, italics in original)

Emotions have their social component, but explicitly enter the realm of rhetoric when they are performed and enacted. Enacting emotions does not mean they are not genuinely felt, but that they become knowable to others, and gain rhetorical power, through how we perform them to others. I may feel impatient if I am waiting in a long line, but the way I fold my arms, plant my feet, and roll my eyes is a performance of that emotion meant to communicate my thoughts and feelings to others in the line—or to the person at the airline ticket counter refusing to help any of us.

It's easy to think about embodied performances of emotion as the kind I described above, but for young people, the rhetorical performance of emotion also takes place online in both the choice of social media and what is posted there. Young people in particular are mindful that making the wrong rhetorical choices online, in terms of media or tone, can have social and emotional consequences (Davies, 2014; Keller, 2013; Williams, 2009). Robert said that he had made posts on both Facebook and Twitter that were meant to be read ironically. When some people misread his posts as sincere, he found he had to explain his meaning—and apologize: "I have to be a lot more careful now if I'm going to make a joke. It's not worth the trouble for people to misunderstand it and get all in your face over it." Anxiety over being misread, or over having posted material interpreted in ways they had not intended, came up a number of times in interviews, as it has in other research (Buck, this volume; Williams, 2009).

Conversely, people talk about how making the right rhetorical choices can be emotionally fulfilling and sustain relationships. Leanna, a university student in the United Kingdom, said that getting texts from her boyfriend "never gets old. It doesn't always matter what he says, but I like hearing from him. When I walk out of class and look at my phone, I'm hoping I hear from him. That's what I want to see." Leanna's comment reflects not only the way the texts and posts from her boyfriend make her feel when she reads them, but also how the use of social media builds a sense of anticipation that individuals feel about what might be waiting for them when they go online. Just as people used to wait for the mail to arrive by post for word from loved ones, Leanna's sense of opening her text and social media accounts on her phone once she leaves the classroom indicates the same kind of anticipation and even excitement. Such an understanding of how social media facilitate daily relationships provides a substantially different perspective than the critiques of social media that have received so much attention in popular media (Carr, 2011; Turkle, 2011). In addition to the rhetorical considerations that shape the composition and reception of individual posts and messages, the students' comments also indicate that they began to see different social media sites as more appropriate for performing particular emotions. For example, a number of the people I interviewed talked about Instagram as a place where more sentimental and traditionally emotional material was posted, such as photos of friends and family or notable events. Twitter, on the other hand, was described more in terms of humor or politics and Facebook as a place to share popular culture as well as the kind of photos that go on Instagram. For these students, posting sentimental testimonies to friendship on Twitter would "hit the wrong note," Robert said, "You'd be embarrassed and look stupid." Different sites had definable emotional registers and were part of students' calculations about the rhetorical moves they made online. Although emotion in discussions of rhetoric often is addressed in terms of how it helps people communicate ideas—and that is certainly happening when students are deciding what to post to friends—it is the case that emotion in polymedia practices also functions as a rhetorical matrix that shapes the messages that sustain relationships. For these young people, emotion as performance, as context, as interpretive framework, is always present in their online conversations.

POWER, EMBODIMENT, AND MOBILITY

Of course, in any relationship and in any cultural context, power is always present. In terms of polymedia, power is evident from a number of perspectives. Certainly the most obvious position of power is that of the corporations who own, shape, and set the terms of use of social media sites. However, it is also the case that the practices through which users choose and engage in sites and the relationships they foster and develop there can, in turn, result in changes from the owners of the sites (Madianou & Miller, 2012). Rather than focus on this perspective in this chapter, which has been addressed at length elsewhere, I find it also useful to consider power in terms of the relationships of the users. For example, the person who buys and pays for the technology and the data plan, which for some university students is still their parents, controls what kinds of choices are available. Peter did not have a smartphone, and so was excluded from Instagram and did more of his social media communicating on Facebook. Power can also be seen in how the media choices influence a sense of the context of a site. As more parents and grandparents have established Facebook accounts, some young people used Facebook less frequently (boyd, 2014). On the other hand, the inability of Google+ to gain enough users as a social media site meant it never once came up in interviews or observations.

In addition, the power in relationships in terms of polymedia can be seen when one person insists on a particular medium and the other person feels obliged to acquiesce to that choice. Students often note that their professors are among the few people they know who use email. Amber Buck's discussion in this collection of graduate students' considerations of how and when to use social media also reflects the impact of power relations between student and instructor. Or, as in the scene that opened this chapter, when Sarah's mother makes a phone call, Sarah always answers. When I ask if she ever ignores her mother's calls, she says:

> I'd like to sometimes when I don't want to have to deal with
> her. But I know if I do then there would be problems that I'd
> have to deal with a lot. So it's better I do what she wants.

Sarah's response highlights both the power dynamics involved in the relationship as well as the social factors involved in the emotions. She feels an obligation to answer the call from her mother, and in doing so both mother and daughter are acting out the social roles they understand in their relationship. Later in the conversation Sarah mentions that many of her friends get phone calls rather than texts from their parents. At the moment of getting the call, though, the tone of Sarah's voice and the rolling of her eyes indicate a measure of embarrassment and slight exasperation that is the cultural and relational marker many contemporary students and parents would recognize in such an exchange. Power, or resistance, can be enacted in many different ways, however, and are reflected in the choice and control of the media through which one chooses to communicate. Sarah also said that she often chooses to text her mother rather than call, particularly "if I don't want to talk and talk and have to answer all kinds of questions when I don't have time." In many relationships, the text rather than the phone call, the phone call rather than the email, are understood by both sides of the relationship to have implications about both message and relationship. Sarah used texts to her mother to establish distance and indicate her independence (and while we don't know her mother's response, I am sure she interpreted the texts through a particular set of emotions). And several students said that, if they received a phone call from a friend it indicated a level of seriousness to the message or situation that required immediate response. By contrast, an email might be used to defer emotion or distance.

Sarah's response to her mother's call, while illustrating the social and relational aspects of emotion, also reminds us that emotion is very much an embodied experience—as I could see as she rolled her eyes and hear in the mild tone of exasperation in her voice. Having an embodied, emotional response to composing or reading a text is certainly nothing new. Yet the mobility provided by digital technologies such as smartphones means that we now encounter and engage in digital literacy practices through a broad range of our daily experiences—and, by extension, a broad range of our daily emotions. Mobile technologies, and the variety of media they allow individuals to use in rapid succession or even simultaneously (sound, text, image, video), illuminate how online literacy practices are deeply entwined with the embodied lives of the person holding the mobile device. Immediate experiences, language histories, or geographical locations shape online practices, which in turn affect embodied, physical responses and interpretations of the surrounding world. Eric, for example, said that what he looked at outside the window of the bus as he rode home could affect how he responded to people, both in terms of the content of his messages and how much he could focus on what he was reading and writing. And, while a number of the students talked about how messages from friends and family could make them feel happy or cared for, several also said that getting a message at the wrong time and place could lead to problems. Alia said that, more than once, she had posted comments to people on both Instagram and Twitter that were critical in tone because of the stress she was feeling in her embodied life at the moment:

> Like, I'm in a traffic jam, late, late, late, and I'm looking at
> stuff that hits me wrong and I say something sort of bitchy.
> And it's all because of where I'm at at that moment. It's not
> them. I've got to stop doing that because I always regret it.

The dual mobilities (Nordquist, 2014) of simultaneous physical movement along with the virtual movement of digital texts mean that the emotional and relational impact of communication feels immediate and sometimes unpredictable. In addition, the cultural emphasis on acceleration and speed means that people often feel the pressure to respond right away to texts and posts. To not respond quickly to a message can be regarded as its own emotional message of neglect or indifference.

CONCLUSION

To bring the perspective of polymedia to our discussions of people's daily digital media practices helps foreground the role emotion plays in the rhetorical choices individuals make with speed and facility. Whether it is with friends or authority figures, the decisions made by people using mobile devices and social media are made with an ongoing evaluation of how they will affect social relationships. Understanding sociality means thinking about the "social" as more than just the implications of culture, institutions, and power that have dominated much of our conversations in rhetoric and composition over the past two decades.

Instead, sociality, while not ignoring power, also asks us to think about how people create and maintain meaningful relationships with others in their lives, online and off. Certainly the social media networks people establish and nurture through polymedia literacy practices are quite often about sustaining relationships. When I talk to people about why they decide to sign on, or not sign on, to a particular social media site, the answer is more often than not a variation of "because that's where my friends are." What's more, once on a site, people are willing to invest time to learn how to use the site and to understand the cultural genres that shape the rhetorical conventions people employ there. The importance of relationships for motivating learning and perceptions of agency offer us an important perspective for exploring how and why people use social media in their lives. At the same time, the understanding of those social relationships mediates how people decide to shift from one app to the next, from one social media network to another.

Emotion is always a presence in the cultural genres people learn and negotiate to maintain these social relationships. To think about emotion in this way—as not a matter of a single person's feelings, but as an ongoing system of embodiment and social response—also helps us understand how integral it is to our rhetorical choices. Our understanding, interpretation, and performance of emotion happen through a continuing pattern of feelings, actions, and responses from others. We learn what an emotion is not just from how it feels to us, but also from how others respond to our performance of that emotion. It is, as Wetherell (2012) maintained, a "joint, coordinated, relational, activity" (p. 83). What we can see in the polymedia practices of young people with their mobile phones is that these patterns of performance and response now take place regularly through digital media and social media networks, and that digital media has become an essential part of those patterns. Emotion is not optional in these choices and communications, nor is it a less important or less intellectual rhetorical consideration. Emotion is both the motivator and the framework through which the communication and rhetorical choices are made that build and sustain relationships. In addition, these recurring emotional patterns create dispositions that are an essential part of what we think of as identity and, as such, are also bound up in individual perceptions of agency.

Finally, in understanding the role of mobile digital technologies in creating and nurturing relationships, we should see it not as a replacement, nor an add-on, but as an integral part of daily life. The social networks and embodied feelings people have are not divided into online and offline experiences, but are part of the ongoing flow of experience. The development and popularity of mobile devices allows online experiences to be accessed and engaged with almost as consistently and continually as face-to-face encounters. Mobile technologies are embedded in the lives of many of the people I observed and interviewed, and have entwined themselves in their relationships and supporting social structures.

People choose to communicate through particular media or modes not solely—or perhaps even primarily—in terms of the traditional rhetorical affordances. Instead their choices "come much more from the wider social context of their communication rather than the narrower issues of technology and function" (Madianou & Miller, 2012, p. 137). In our conceptions of the motivations that drive particular rhetorical choices, and the affordances that people perceive in a given medium or mode, we have to include considerations of emotion and sociality.[2]

REFERENCES

boyd, d. (2014). *It's complicated: The social lives of networked teens.* New Haven, CT: Yale University Press.

Carr, N. (2011). *The shallows: What the Internet is doing to our brains.* New York, NY: W. W. Norton.

Carrington, V. (2012). "There's no going back." Roxie's iPhone: An object ethnography. *Language and Literacy, 14*(2), 27–40.

Cooper, M. M. (2005). Bringing forth worlds. *Computers and Composition, 22*(1), 31–38.

Davies, J. (2014). (Im)material girls living in (im)material worlds: Identity curation through time and space. In C. Burnett, J. Davies, G. Merchant & J. Rowsell (Eds.), *New literacies around the globe: Policy and pedagogy* (pp. 72–87). London, England: Routledge.

Dugan, A. (2014). American's tech tastes changing with times. Retrieved from http://www.gallup.com/poll/166745/americans-tech-tastes-change-times.aspx.

Gershon, I. (2012). *Breakup 2.0: Disconnecting over new media.* Ithaca, NY: Cornell University Press.

Keller, D. (2007). Thinking rhetorically. In C. Selfe (Ed.), *Multimodal composition: Resources for teachers* (pp. 49–63). Cresskill, NJ: Hampton Press.

Keller, D. (2013). *Chasing literacy: Reading and writing in the age of acceleration.* Logan, UT: Utah State University Press.

Madianou, M. & Miller, D. (2012). *Migration and new media: Transnational families and polymedia.* London, England: Routledge.

Micciche, L. R. (2007). *Doing emotion: Rhetoric, writing, teaching.* Portsmouth, NH: Boynton/Cook.

Nordquist, B. (2014). *Composing college and career: Mobility, complexity, and agency at the nexus of high school, college and work* (Unpublished doctoral dissertation). University of Louisville, Louisville, KY.

---

2   The research reported in this chapter was supported in part by a 2013 Fulbright Research Fellowship at the University of Sheffield's Centre for the Study of Literacies in the United Kingdom.

Ofcom. (2014). *Adults' media use and attitudes report.* Office of Communication. London, England: United Kingdom.

Pahl, K. & Rowsell, J. (2010). *Artifactual literacies: Every object tells a story.* New York, NY: Teachers College Press.

Rajakumar, M. (2012). Faceless Facebook: Female Qatari users choosing wisely. In B. T. Williams & A. A. Zenger (Eds.), *New media literacies and participatory popular culture across borders* (pp. 125–134). London, England: Routledge.

Rowsell, J. (2013). *Working with multimodality: Rethinking literacy in a digital age.* London, England: Routledge.

Smith, A. (2012). The best (and worst) of mobile connectivity. *Pew Internet Research Project.* Retrieved from http://www.pewinternet.org/2012/11/30/the-best-and-worst-of-mobile-connectivity/.

Smith, A. (2013). Smartphone ownership 2013. *Pew Internet Research Project.* Retrieved from http://www.pewinternet.org/2013/06/05/smartphone-ownership-2013/.

Turkle, S. (2011). *Alone together: Why we expect more from technology and less from each other.* New York, NY: Basic Books.

Werner, C. L. (2013). *Dear Professor X, This is not my best work: Multimodal composition meets (e)portfolio.* Computers and Composition Online. http://www2.bgsu.edu/departments/english/cconline/WernerPortfolios/HomePort.html.

Wetherell, M. (2012). *Affect and emotion: A new social science understanding.* London, England: SAGE.

Williams, B. T. (2009). *Shimmering literacies: Popular culture and reading and writing online.* London, England: Peter Lang.

Williams, B. T. (In 2018). *Literacy practices and perceptions of agency: Composing identities.* London, England: Routledge.

Wilson, A. A. (2011). A social semiotics framework for conceptualizing content area literacies. *Journal of Adolescent & Adult Literacy, 54*(6), 435–444.

CHAPTER 8

VISUALIZING BOUTIQUE DATA IN EGOCENTRIC NETWORKS

Douglas M. Walls

North Carolina State University

INTRODUCTION

We do more than write in social media platforms. We "Like" posts and pictures.[1]
We share and move information along by tapping "Share" or "Retweet." Each of
these actions has meaning, so sometimes we hedge in our profiles, writing things
like, "Retweets are not endorsements," or making sure our networks are not
too close, saying things like, "Views represented here are only my own," in an
effort to avoid confusion over responsibility. Our bodies move across interfaces,
frequently through tapping/clicking; this movement shows, if not our approval,
certainly our attention as we push content along or announce to others and
ourselves that what we are liking or reposting is important and worth paying
attention to. The scale of such activity can be daunting. We care about our own
networks and the activity in those networks more than larger trends.[2] As Mark
Zuckerberg once famously said, "A squirrel dying in front of your house may be
more relevant to your interests right now than people dying in Africa" (as cited
in Pariser, 2011). And we care about our networks because of relevance. Our
networks are the way we stay in touch with friends and, increasingly, they are
the way we get our jobs done.

This chapter focuses on visualizing the social networks around individuals,
or "egocentric" networks, as well as producing a way to measure and visualize
the embodied rhetorical production of egocentric network behavior. I began
this project as a way for people to understand and visualize rhetorical activity
in their own networks. This chapter takes as a starting point that social media
networks and platforms record rhetorical behavior beyond linguistic production. Emerging from a larger project about culture and professionalism, my goal

---

1   I use capitalization here and through this chapter for actions that are available in Facebook
and Twitter such as "Like" or "Retweet."

2   Unless, of course, it is one's job to pay attention to social media trends.

was the development of a research model that attempts to measure embodied rhetorical performances on social media platforms. Such measures are needed to capture both sharing or liking as well as more traditional semiotic rhetorical production. Trying to develop a way to capture and measure all forms of rhetorical interactions within a network became one of the deliverables of the project. In other words, I am attempting to answer the following question: How does one recognize, capture, and measure both linguistic and nonlinguistic rhetorical performances in a social network? And so, my goal in this chapter is to provide a visual method of displaying embodied and semiotic rhetorical activity in egocentric networks.

EGOCENTRIC NETWORKS AND EMBODIED RHETORICAL ACTIVITY

Bonnie A. Nardi, Steve Whittaker & Heinrich Schwarz (2000) claimed that networks that are egocentric are "mapped around an individual rather than a full network scope" (p. 437). That is to say, they are network activities traced around single individuals. Nardi, Whittaker & Schwarz are particularly interested in how workers rely on and maintain effective professional networks outside of their employers and within cross-organizational contexts. They found that the maintenance of such key cross-organizational networks is important to the fundamental way that business is done. Recently, Toni Ferro, Doug Divine, and Mark Zachry (2012) found that knowledge workers frequently use publicly available online services (Facebook, Twitter, etc.) even in situations where their employer has given those workers access to similar enterprise-level, proprietary systems. In their survey, Ferro, Divine, and Zachry also discovered that the knowledge workers used publicly available online services "to develop associations with others and to learn new information" in professional contexts, allowing "workers to develop and maintain associations with experts and peers they would not have been able to meet without" (p. 18) these networked tools. In other words, platforms like Facebook and Twitter allowed knowledge workers to maintain important professional- and task-centered networks beyond their organizations.

In a more fine-grained mode of data collection, Stacey Pigg (2014) found in her case study of "Daniel" that, as a freelance writer, significant amounts of Daniel's time were dedicated to using socially networked writing platforms both to access communities of practice but also to coordinate people and technologies to circulate texts. Away from technical and professional contexts, Amber Buck (2012) found in her case study of an undergraduate that "Ronnie" described himself "as a 'publisher,' someone who creates content online for others" (p. 14);

he mentioned his multiple online identities and his work as a producer of content rather than a consumer matching each platform's specific audience with specific content. Buck went on to note that "Ronnie envisioned different audiences with different concerns and interests on both Facebook and Twitter and constructed his identity on both sites with these audiences in mind" (p. 18). This shows Ronnie's rhetorical savviness in maintaining a specific egocentric network of consumers of his content. What is clear is that socially-network writing is more than just large patterns of networks; it is also about how individuals build and maintain networks around themselves for specific purposes regardless of the type or nature of the content circulated. Socially-network writing and its attendant technologies assist not only with the circulation of content but also with the maintenance of relationships. Looking at the nature of networked activity around individuals can help us see how each egocentric network depends on different kinds of rhetorical activities. These rhetorical activities are not just that of the individual but of the network around multiple individuals and can be captured and displayed in total. Successful egocentric networks do not flow one way. People share as much as they get in a healthy network as rhetorical performance flows multiple ways. It is perhaps worth noting that egocentric networks are not about individuals but are instead about the work of networks around them.

These egocentric networks depend on nonlinguistic responses often left out of work in rhetoric and composition. Rhetoric has a long and deep tradition of nonlinguistic activity, often forgotten by modern writing studies. Projects like Cheryl Glenn's (2004) pointed to the importance of nonlinguistic-based rhetorical activity, like silence (Monberg, 2008; Ratcliffe, 2006), as essential and meaningful. Debra Hawhee (2004, 2009) has examined the place of the body not only in ancient Western rhetorics but also how the body as a site of communicative meaning-making has gone unnoticed in the work of Kenneth Burke. Cultural rhetorical scholars like Malea Powell et al. (2014) drew on bodies and their connections and relationships from Native scholarship to engage in the importance of rhetorical production and meaning. Particularly important to Powell et al. is Michel de Certeau's *The Practice of Everyday Life*. De Certeau (1984) declared the importance of movement in something as mundane as walking when he wrote, "There is a rhetoric of walking. The art of 'turning' phrases finds an *equivalent* in the art of composing a path . . . like ordinary language, this art implies and combines styles and uses" (p. 100, emphasis mine). Like walking a city, deciding what to "Like" and what to comment on has meaning. We see the breadcrumbs of rhetorical activity in our feeds constantly. It means more to us when a friend or a senior colleague likes a photo on Instagram than it does when a stranger or a robot account does.

VISUALIZING NETWORKS AND DATA

The majority of scholars interested in the visualization of data dwell in big data, large data sets that are relatively recent developments. As Cheryl E. Ball (2013) noted, these large data sets are indeed what drive much of the funding in digital humanities research itself. Efforts like that of Karissa McKelvey, Alex Rudnick, Michael D. Conover, and Filippo Menczer (2012) aimed to visualize caches of data. Networked relationships may be visualized based on content or associations. Such visualizations show large trends and strengths of association. Ben Schneiderman noted that that data tools should be able to provide an overview of the data, allowing for zooming and filtering as well as details-on-demand, should be able to show relationships between objects, and should be able to extract data about subsets (as cited in McKelvey et al., 2012). This complexity of data and tool display, however, makes meaningful visualizations difficult. Gema Bello-Orgaz, Jason J. Jung, and David Camacho (2016), for example, have pointed out that data captured in social contexts presents new problems of "data processing, data storage, data representation" (p. 45). Like most computer scientists, their goal is to reduce that information to make it knowable. One can hear their disciplinary values when they discuss the data visualization tool MapReduce: "MapReduce [a data cutting tool] is presented as one of the most efficient big data solutions" (Bello-Orgaz, Jung & Camacho, 2016, p. 3). In other words, because data sets are large, the reduction of the data to efficient transactions and visualizations is most important. MapReduce functions by examining content analysis but fails to recognize relationships between other values like tools or accounts in social media spaces.

Many scholars have struggled with representing the complicated media ecology of social media networks at large scales. That is not to say that there is no space for smaller data sets and their visualization in work. For example, researchers like Heli Aramo-Immonen, Jari Jussila, and Jukka Huhtamäki (2015) have used metadata and tools like Gephi to analyze both topic sharing as well as the activity streams of conference learning with relatively small data sets. However, these data sets represent struggles with meaningful information. Such visualizations often look like a jumble of lines and intersecting accounts. In other words, they look interesting but we remain unsure of what they say. Large-scale projects, such as following eleven million people and looking at how eleven million users enact social networking sites (Mislove, Marcon, Gummadi, Druschel & Bhattacharjee, 2007) are not useful methodologies for understanding how egocentric networks happen or what is going on in them. Such work may demonstrate trends within large groups, rather than trends among individuals, in relation to technologies or culture.

A NOTE ABOUT ORIENTATION

Much of what happens in Facebook is not, in fact, writing in the strictest sense as much as it is some other form of embodied rhetorical performance. An advantage of Facebook is that the activities cohere nicely across physical places as rhetorical technologies. What we mean by "Facebook" is not tied to a single platform or type of technology but exists in multiple places with similar types of rhetorical performances. Clicking "Like" on a laptop is similar to pressing "Like" on a mobile device. Designers perform a great deal of work to make an application experience coherent, mobile, and always available in a variety of spaces with web-based technologies and the rise of smartphones. Mastery on one piece of hardware leads to understanding one another in terms of user experience. So coherent is the experience of Facebook that a user doesn't even need to own his or her own computer to log in! If I am in a library or a coffee shop and I have not taken my computer with me, I can use someone else's computer to log in and I see nothing different in the window from my own arrangements. My network will be there. My profile picture of myself and all the other decisions I have negotiated with Facebook will greet me when I log in. The goal with visualizing boutique data is to understand, locate, and visualize a network's rhetorical activity, both embodied and linguistic, around individual accounts. These visualizations are complex measures of types of embodied rhetorical behavior.

With a focus on the egocentric network and the task of visualizing boutique data in mind, I want to take a moment to carefully articulate assumptions. Networking is hard to see and is distributed across ideological, material, embodied, and linguistic relationships. These facts make tracing networks difficult. Networks are enacted between people, things, and places in a non-metaphorical ecology. No one actor can enact a network by him- or herself; instead, the totality creates an object, an object we have learned to call a network. We can learn how networks are enacted at specific kairotic moments. Therefore, we can attempt to see how an enacted network is distributed between work and home, between social and cultural subjectivities like social networking sites because they enact the "invisible work" (Harquail, 2011) of networks. So, then, we can "see" moments in networks through embodied rhetorical activity as indexed by the social media platform.

In other words, Facebook records when people press buttons to make associations within a network. We can see what counts as effort by identifying how a network reacts to information, new content, and new users' embodied actions, be they linguistic or embodied in nature. My focus on boutique data attempts to account for content that a user generates both as a presence (that is, how others respond to their content), as well as content they generate themselves such as status updates or responding to others' posts. I developed an analytic to be able to visualize moments in networks by tracing the frequency of interactions, the activity around individuals' content, and individuals' activities around the content of others.

VISUALIZING BOUTIQUE DATA IN EGOCENTRIC NETWORKS: METHOD

What follows are small-scale visualizations (what may also be called boutique data) of egocentric networks. While my participants engage actively or passively in these networks, the views I present here are not of individuals. These visualizations are of networked rhetorical activity around individuals. Data collected were part of a larger set of case studies on social/professional boundary activity in social media. In the data I represent here, I followed one online social writing network from two professional and professionalizing women of color for a one-week period. Due to the nature of social media writing, these networks involve the accounts of other people. I then followed up this data collection with semi-structured interviews about data views and asked participants to categorize people involved in their social media feed as professional acquaintances, personal friends, or somewhere in between.

What advantages can be gained through boutique views? Examining smaller-scale interactions allows for a fine-grained view of traceable rhetorical behavior. The visualization I employ here enables comparisons of moments across accounts as well as moments within individual networks. The polargram visualizations (see Figure 8.1) enable two important moves in that regard.

First, by using a simple five-point sliding ordinal scale, numbers can shift across users' networks as a group (e.g., this network had more "Likes" than that network). Additionally, different time increments can provide different views of network behavior (e.g., Sunday may have more networked activity than Tuesday in someone's network). The polargrams are sorted into three large categories: accounts involved, tools used, and activity in total. "Accounts involved" are the amount of people/accounts contributing, commenting, or posting during a visualized moment around that user's account.[3] For example, if one post elicited the responses of three people/accounts, the total number of accounts involved for that particular time would be four. "Tools used" lists the material components mentioned as forms of rhetorical delivery in those moments (e.g., "sent from

---

3   I use people/accounts to be accurate in terms of activity measures. Online 'bots can, and do, emulate rhetorical behavior online in social media sites. While these behaviors can assume to be behaviors of people, I still think it a necessary caution to avoid collapsing people and their social media accounts.

iPhone" or "via Web"). I counted applications separately, so if a person/account used Tweetdeck for iPhone as well as Twitter for iPhone such activity would be counted as two tools. "Activity," specifically rhetorical activity, constituted the production of or reaction to content. Activities such as liking or sharing, status updates, or posting and commenting were counted here.

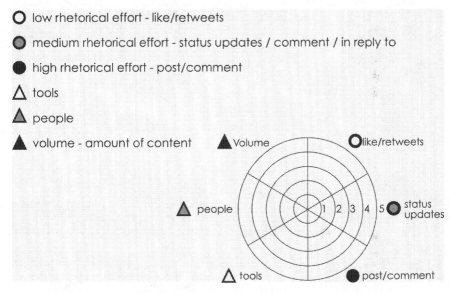

Figure 8.1. Egocentric network view.

The right side of the polargram indicates an even more fine-grained account of activity based on the amount of embodied rhetorical effort involved on the part of network participants. By embodied rhetorical effort I mean how much of the body had to move to engage in the activity as well as how much time the body took to engage in said activity. For example, to "Like" something in Facebook merely requires a single click of an onscreen button. Status updates require more complicated embodied actions like the movement of fingers to type out messages. For example, the embodied and cognitive complexity of posting a status update requires people to move their fingers and bodies. To take pictures, then upload them, then frame those pictures rhetorically by placing captions under them or using filters involves more embodied movement than tapping "Like."

These polargrams show patterns of rhetorical behavior in a variety of situated and enacted types of networks based on what networks value. Figure 8.2 shows fictional representations of how egocentric networks form and are enacted in certain online spaces.

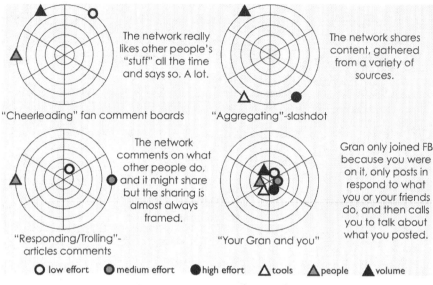

Figure 8.2. Fictional examples.

Various forms of networks enact change in different rhetorical situations. Visualizations such as this one compare different microtransactions of networks measuring different forms of rhetorical activity. Figure 8.3 shows what these different types of networked views look like for two of my participants, Lana and Barbara.[4]

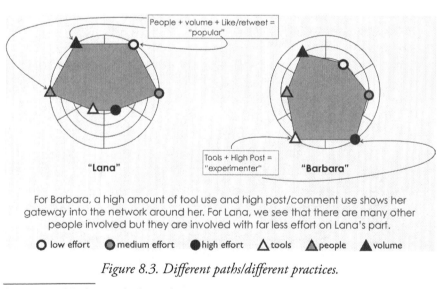

Figure 8.3. Different paths/different practices.

The visualization in Figure 8.3 allows us to see the area of network activity as it occurs in different users' egocentric networks. We can use the grey area between data points to think about how and what kind of rhetorical activity is taking place as well as the strength and nature of ties in the egocentric network. In Figure 8.3, similar amounts of space are covered but the networks are shaped by different kinds of rhetorical activity.

Figure 8.4 also shows us the different nature of those egocentric networks in terms of types of rhetorical activity.

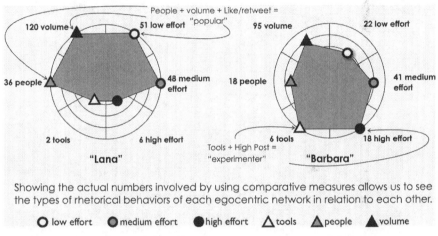

Showing the actual numbers involved by using comparative measures allows us to see the types of rhetorical behaviors of each egocentric network in relation to each other.

○ low effort　◐ medium effort　● high effort　△ tools　△ people　▲ volume

Figure 8.4. Numbers in networks.

For example, we can see that Lana's network is engaged in a high volume of activity with a small amount of rhetorical effort. Barbara's network contains a high number of different technological tools as well as high rhetorical effort. Most of this effort comes from Barbara herself as she provides content and comments on and "likes" other people's posts. Showing the actual numbers involved by using comparative measures allows us to see how each set of networks is distributed in relation to other sets. Such a view also helps us understand how different forms of networked rhetorical activity look in relationship to each other. The sliding numeric scale shows which moments are comparable to other moments located in time or by level of scope. As a method of data visualization, this display allows scale to shift easily between data sets and still remain meaningful. Different numbers tell different stories of network activity that do not isolate or exclude relevant information from comparative cases. For example, while Lana's network coordinates differently from Barbara's, we can still see that Barbara's network engages in a lot of activity.

FINE-GRAINED VIEWS OF INDIVIDUAL USER NETWORKS: BARBARA'S NETWORK

While comparisons between networks are useful, comparisons of moments within networks can also tell us a great deal. Visualizing boutique data allows for different scales to become meaningful. For example, Barbara's network is mostly a result of her own activity. Most of the content created in her network came from her, with most comments coming from people in her old graduate program. Barbara's network maintains itself by her own practices that people/accounts respond to. Almost all of the "high effort" content (16/18) came from Barbara. By following the associations made by groups in Facebook, we can learn a great deal about how networks are enacted through rhetorical activity. In my follow-up interview with her, I discovered that the most prominent accounts in her network belonged not to her current employer but instead to colleagues from her graduate program. Barbara is not tailoring her posts toward that audience, however. More than likely Facebook is maintaining a connection by feeding her content into her old colleagues' streams.

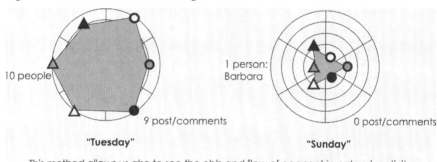

This method allows us also to see the ebb and flow of egocentric network activity within a single user's account because of its relative scale. Here we can see that Barbara's network is not active on Sunday. This allows us to ask questions about why, where, and when egocentric networks maintain their associations.

Figure 8.5. Everybody's working for the weekend.

Boutique data views allow the researcher to understand the nature of each network being created by understanding the relationship between effort and types of people. In this case, Barbara, along with Facebook, is creating the space of her peers and their graduate program online, even though the network is dislocated from a geographic reality. As a new Ph.D., she teaches, literally, a continent away from her old graduate program's physical location, and even its members are distributed across the country. Posts and friendships are maintained in Facebook but little is being done to make connections in her current geographical work place. A boutique view of the data suggests that Barbara, with Facebook's help, is doing a lot of work to maintain those career friendships by producing content to which her former colleagues respond.

Figure 8.5 shows us just how much "Facebooking" ends up happening at work for her. Again, this method of viewing enacted access helps us to see the recursive nature of enacted access within a single user's account because of its relative scale. Here we can see that Barbara's network is not active on Sunday. This allows us to ask questions about why, where, and when egocentric networks maintain contact with users. In our follow-up interview, Barbara related to me that she spent Sundays watching football and calling family. When Barbara shuts down, her network shuts down. As we will see with Lana's network, that is not always the case.

FINE-GRAINED VIEWS OF INDIVIDUAL USER NETWORKS: LANA'S NETWORK

As we can see, Lana's network generates a great deal of activity and involves many people. Out of all of the Facebook users I studied, her network had the most activity (represented here by volume) as well as the most comments and the most people involved. While her personal number of posts was average and her content mundane, her network responded to those posts a great deal. With just a little more information, we can learn much about how this network functions both professionally and privately.

I followed Lana's Facebook feed during the end of the semester. Lana's activity remained constant during this period. She had a series of posts, all of them made from her Blackberry phone, where she described a trip about two hours away from her university and then to her home state. Some of these were textual in nature, while some of them were photo posts. Unlike Barbara, Lana doesn't post links, nor do the people in her network. All high rhetorical effort came from Lana in the nature of a photo post with comments. When I asked Lana to categorize the people/accounts involved in her network, an interesting pattern developed (see Figure 8.6).

In this view, we see the people/accounts that Lana categorizes as professional-only contacts that indicate a great deal of activity. In fact, Lana's "professional" network, in just three days, produced more activity than most of the other participants' networks in my study. Here we see how the effect of embodied presence manifests itself in the activity of the "primarily professional" network. As Lana leaves the embodied space of the network, the "primarily professional" network's online activity becomes non-existent. The "primarily professional" network no longer "wants" to be part of Lana's social writing. Figure 8.7 displays the activity of peers (both friends and professional relationships).

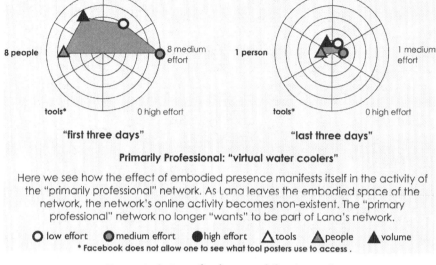

Figure 8.6. Out of sight, out of (hive) mind.

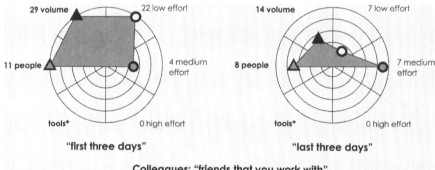

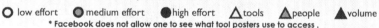

Figure 8.7. Peer pressure.

We can see that, again, embodied presence affects how the network reacts to Lana. Here though, we see that the network continues to maintain itself through activity, although nowhere near as heavily as when Lana is physically present, and the change is not as dramatic. The network is altered, but is not lost. In fact, there is a higher level of rhetorical effort used in terms of comments. Interestingly, what we don't see here is that only three current colleagues engaged in any sort of activity in the last three days, replicating the pattern we see in her "professional-exclusive" network but not to such a frequency.

Interestingly enough, Figure 8.8, which shows the friendship exclusive network view, shows almost no difference between the first part of the week and the second part of the week.

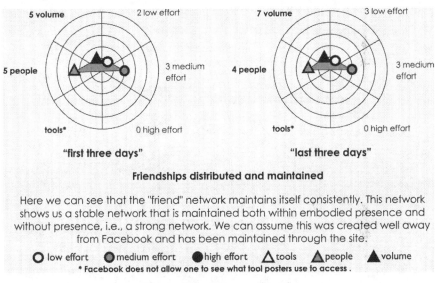

Figure 8.8. Constant friends.

Likes, comments, and posts remain almost constant. Lana's friendship network remains constant whether members are physically present or not. Here we can see that the friend network maintains itself consistently. This network shows us a stable network that is maintained both within embodied presence and without embodied presence (i.e., a strong network). We can assume this network's relationships were created well away from Facebook and have been maintained through social media use. We can also see here that pure friendship-related activity is a small percentage of Lana's writing network's volume. Lana's network is mostly a professional one with little to no professional content.

IMPLICATIONS & CONCLUSIONS

My hope is that this visualization method supports a trajectory that incorporates embodied rhetorical performance as the field moves beyond the fact that socially-network writing platforms are worthy of disciplinary interest. Attempts to visualize egocentric network activity show that there is no one type of egocentric network, technological or ideological. There is no one space that is "professional" or "personal" but many that are negotiated, collapsed, and expanded based on networked behaviors and the collective rhetorical production of multiple human and nonhuman rhetors. By visualizing Barbara and Lana's egocentric network data, we see possibilities in the types of networks that people are a part of. Lana's network, with little effort on her own part, generates large amounts of rhetorical activity while Barbara's network is carefully curated. Visualizing comparative boutique egocentric network data allows us to measure and visualize the embodied rhetorical production of networks. Such visualizations also allow participants and researchers to understand networked rhetorical activity at a personal scale beyond the felt sense of how one's network functions.

Visualizing boutique data of successful professionals has the potential to make certain kinds of discursive rhetorical behaviors and identity performances knowable. Such information is especially valuable for those attempting to enter into professions. For such people, large but personalized patterns in socially networked rhetorical action index the communicative patterns of professionals not just in task-centered activities but also around those activities. Visualizing these behaviors can help unpack "water cooler" discourses, discourses around professional and task-based work. Visualizing and making the back and forth of such discourses knowable could, potentially, help groups who have traditionally been marginalized by such discourses.

Two important factors are essential for the field of rhetoric and composition going forward as we study socially networked rhetorical choices. First, we begin to account for networks and, by extension, ecologies as useful metaphorical abstractions, as well as traceable collections of influences. Social media and social network platforms rely on embodied rhetorical performances to make meaning as surely as they rely on information architecture back ends and the TCP/IP protocols of the Internet. Rhetorical theory is especially well suited to study and understand how and when bodies and technologies interact and respond to each other as points of theorization. In other words, rhetorical theory can help us move beyond metaphors of ecologies and into the tracing of nonmetaphorical material rhetorical ecologies.

Second, as a field we have, to some degree, moved between the small and the large with our preferred levels of scope with our objects of inquiry. We have moved between the close reading of rhetorical texts and large cultural patterns to understand and theorize rhetoric as semiotic acts and cultural warrants. While many fields are focused on big data, including scholars of digital humanities and rhetoric, the discipline of rhetorical studies has the potential to provide important lessons learned from medium-scale projects. Such a robust middle ground of inquiry could provide rhetorical studies research that moves between online and offline rhetorical activity through measuring embodied and material forms of rhetorical activity. In larger conversations about how social networks function and circulate content, rhetoric and composition has a great deal of theory to share about embodied rhetorical performance. More work should be done in the field to understand the connection between language, bodies, and meaning making that takes place in social networks at the medium/boutique level of scale.

REFERENCES

Aramo-Immonen, H., Jussila, J. & Huhtamäki, J. (2015). Exploring co-learning behavior of conference participants with visual network analysis of Twitter data. *Computers in Human Behavior, 51*, 1154–1162. http://dx.doi.org/10.1016/j.chb.2015.02.033.

Ball, C. E. (2013). From big data to boutique data. *Gayle Morris Sweetland Digital Rhetoric Collaborative*. Retrieved from http://www.digitalrhetoriccollaborative.org/2013/11/12/from-big-data-to-boutique-data/.

Bello-Orgaz, G., Jung, J. J. & Camacho, D. (2016). Social big data: Recent achievements and new challenges. *Information Fusion, 28*, 45–59. http://dx.doi.org/10.1016/j.inffus.2015.08.005.

Buck, A. (2012). Examining digital literacy practices on social network sites. *Research in the Teaching of English, 47*(1), 9–38.

de Certeau, M. (1984). *The practice of everyday life* (S. F. Rendall, Trans.) (2nd ed.). Berkeley, CA: University of California Press.

Ferro, T., Divine, D. & Zachry, M. (2012). Knowledge workers and their use of publicly available online services for day-to-day work. *Proceedings from SIGDOC '12: The 30th ACM International Conference on Design of Communication* (pp. 47–54). http://dx.doi.org/10.1145/2379057.2379068.

Glenn, C. (2004). *Unspoken: A rhetoric of silence*. Carbondale, IL: Southern Illinois University Press.

Harquail, C. (2011, January 27). How social media reveals invisible work. Retrieved from http://www.socialmediatoday.com/content/how-social-media-reveals-invisible-work.

Hawhee, D. (2004). *Bodily arts: Rhetoric and athletics in ancient Greece*. Austin, TX: University of Texas Press.

Hawhee, D. (2009). *Moving bodies: Kenneth Burke at the edges of language*. Columbia, SC: University of South Carolina Press.

McKelvey, K., Rudnick, A., Conover, M. D. & Menczer, F. (2012). Visualizing communication on social media: Making big data accessible. Retrieved from http://arxiv.org/abs/1202.1367.

Mislove, A., Marcon, M., Gummadi, K. P., Druschel, P. & Bhattacharjee, B. (2007). Measurement and analysis of online social networks. *IMC '07: Proceedings of the 5th ACM/USENIX Internet measurement conference*. Retrieved from http://citeseerx.ist.psu.edu/viewdoc/summary?doi=10.1.1.109.4432.

Monberg, T. G. (2008). Listening for legacies; or, how I began to hear Dorothy Laigo Cordova, the Pinay behind the podium known as FANHS. In L. Mao & M. Young (Eds.), *Representations: Doing Asian American Rhetoric* (pp. 83–105). Logan, UT: Utah State University Press.

Nardi, B. A., Whittaker, S. & Schwarz, H. (2000, May 1). It's not what you know, it's who you know: Work in the information age. *First Monday, 5*(5). Retrieved from http://pear.accc.uic.edu/ojs/index.php/fm/article/view/741/650.

Pariser, E. (2011, May 22). When the Internet thinks it knows you. *The New York Times*. Retrieved from http://www.nytimes.com/2011/05/23/opinion/23pariser .html.

Pigg, S. (2014). Coordinating constant invention: Social media's role in distributed work. *Technical Communication Quarterly, 23*(2), 69–87. http://dx.doi.org/10.1080 /10572252.2013.796545.

Powell, M., Levy, D., Riley-Mukavetz, A., Brooks-Gillies, M., Novotny, M. & Fisch-Ferguson, J. (2014, October 25). Our story begins here: Constellating cultural rhetorics. *Enculturation: A Journal for Rhetoric, Writing, and Culture*. Retrieved from http://www.enculturation.net/our-story-begins-here.

Ratcliffe, A. P. K. (2006). *Rhetorical listening: Identification, gender, whiteness*. Carbondale, IL: Southern Illinois University Press.

CHAPTER 9

GRAD SCHOOL 2.0: PERFORMING PROFESSIONALISM ON SOCIAL MEDIA

Amber Buck

University of Alabama

Graduate students often perform dual roles within universities while earning their degrees. While they remain students, they occupy professional positions at the university through research or teaching positions as they develop as scholars contributing research to their fields. Allison D. Carr, Hannah J. Rule, and Kathryn Trauth Taylor (2013) emphasized the informal mentoring networks through which graduate students develop identities as teachers and scholars, describing these professionalization processes as often "patchworked" and ad-hoc. Graduate students develop professional identities not only through formal instruction, but also through informal networks of collaboration and mentoring. These informal professionalization practices become more complicated as students enter digital spaces with fewer established rules for interaction (Carr et al., 2013).

This chapter explores the implications for extending this professionalization process into online spaces through social media. The role of online digital media in graduate students' ongoing development as scholars is an open and continually evolving question. Communication within academic fields has expanded beyond professional listservs to conversations on social media. Twitter has become an important platform not only to connect with scholars who share research interests, but also to interact at conferences. An archive of tweets using the hashtag for the 2016 Conference on College Composition and Communication, for example, contained over 12,000 tweets over the course of the conference (Chen, 2016). While the field of writing studies has frequently examined graduate student literacy practices, using social media in a professional context is far from a settled question within the field and in the profession as a whole.[5] The process of professionalization remains ad hoc for established

---

5   Indeed, the situation of Professor Steven Salaita at the University of Illinois, Urbana-Champaign provides a worst-case scenario for even established scholars using social media, and this example may have a chilling effect for graduate students and younger scholars who choose to use social media in some professional capacity.

scholars as well as graduate students, with little to no formal mentoring provided from graduate programs on using social media (Carr, Rule & Taylor, 2013).

Closely examining graduate students' social media use can provide insight into the informal processes through which graduate students develop professional academic identities. In this chapter, I focus specifically on the professional identities of three graduate students in writing studies to explore how these graduate students developed distinct methods of joining professional communities and developing identities as teachers and scholars. Much scholarship in the field emphasizes the ways that graduate students develop professional identities through a formal process of enculturation. Social media revises traditional processes and allows us to see these identities as more dynamic. They are constantly revised and created in dialogue with other communities of which they are a part. Representing a scholarly and professional identity in online spaces, I contend, requires a delicate balance between the personal and professional. The findings from these case studies suggest that a successful professional persona on social media must cultivate an identity I call "personally professional."

PRACTICE THEORY OF IDENTITY: JOINING FIGURED WORLDS

Much scholarship within writing studies, beginning with Carol Berkenkotter, Thomas N. Huckin, and John Ackerman (1988), has explored the processes through which graduate students learn to write academic genres common at the postgraduate level, but the focus of this work is primarily focused on writing instruction rather than identity construction. Contributing to a professional community, however, requires more than just a familiarity with the genres of academic writing. As Paul Prior (1998) described, graduate students develop professional identities through participation in disciplinary communities of practice (p. 139). This process is not monolithic but instead is situated within particular programs and disciplines. As Christine Pearson Casanave (2002) explored, this process of enculturation requires a negotiation of identity as these students develop as professionals and enter academic communities of practice. Within the literature, this development is usually presented as a progress narrative; students learn the discourse of the profession to become part of a scholarly community.

Mentoring practices within writing studies often follow graduate students beyond the discourse and genres of the profession into less formal digital spaces. Kendall Leon and Stacey Pigg (2011) and Patrick W. Berry, Gail E. Hawisher, and Cynthia L. Selfe (2012) described how graduate students attempt to manage personal connections and maintain identities as students within a peer group through social media at the same time that they network with scholars in their fields through those same platforms. Leon and Pigg (2011) used the concept of digital time/space to emphasize the central role of digital media in assisting graduate students in navigating a multiplicity of tasks within the academy. Digital writing, they contended, serves as the "connective thread" through which graduate students do both personal and professional work (p. 4). For the graduate students they studied, digital technology provided a place not only to participate in the more informal aspects of graduate student enculturation discussed by Carr et al. (2013), but also a location for the more formal aspects of professionalization and networking.

Much work has been done within the field on cultural identity and its connection to literacy (Cushman, 2008; Richardson, 2003; Smitherman, 2000; Villanueva, 1993). Jay Lemke (2008) called attention to the increased references to identity in scholarship, noting the "theoretical burden" that the term identity has to carry when used as the primary term to describe notions of selfhood. He demonstrated a need to understand identity in how it functions as a mediating term between social-structural phenomena and lived, interactional experiences (p. 17). Indeed, there is a tension between scholarship that discusses identity that is tied to gender, racial, and class categories and a professional identity that is situated within a specific workplace or professional community of practice. Lemke highlighted this distinction between "identity-in-practice on the short timescales of situated small-group activity" (p. 18) and concepts of identity that exist over a lifetime and are framed according to "larger institutional scales" (p. 18). Patricia Boyd (2013) discussed professional identities by drawing on Herminia Ibarra and Jennifer L. Petriglieri's (2010) definition as centered in "the various meanings attached to oneself by self and others" in professional spaces, combining a social identity, centered in social roles and groups, with a personal one.

Casanave (2002) and Prior (1998) both described identity creation within academic disciplines as created through practice, as Lemke suggested. Casanave (2002) saw identity as created through the socially situated practice of writing within a particular discipline. Both Casanave (2002) and Prior (1998) described scholarly identity as created in interaction with Lave and Wenger's concept of scholarly communities of practice. Identities are multiple and negotiated through practices and "modes of belonging" (Casanave, 2002, p. 22), through which graduate students become part of these disciplinary communities.

Dorothy Holland, William Lachicotte, Debra Skinner, and Carole Cain (1998) posited a practice theory of identity that is particularly productive for considering the ways that individuals represent themselves in social media for different audiences. Holland et al.'s (1998) framework sees identity as "lived through activity and developed in social practice" (p. 5), constantly negotiated through social activity and individual agency. These scholars posit an internal, intrinsic identity that interacts with a cultural one. This socially constructed self is based in one's subject position, the influences of the culture in which one lives, and the powerful discourses an individual encounters (pp. 26–27). These individual elements do not in and of themselves make an individual, but they are "living tools of the self" (p. 28). Interactions between an individual and a group of people create what Holland and her colleagues called "figured worlds" (p. 41), through which individuals create identities that fit within a particular group but are still based in that individual's embodied experience.

In my analysis below, I use the term figured worlds to describe the different communities that each research participant connected to through their social media activity. These communities are created through this dialogic interaction Holland et al. described. Considering how graduate students within writing studies conceive of and enter figured worlds in their professional development and identity representation allows us to examine more closely how they navigate multiple audiences and consider their own identities within these different disciplinary communities. This practice-based, dialogic identity revises a process narrative of enculturation within professional communities and instead considers how individuals navigate a representation of self that is in constant negotiation with these different figured worlds. After a discussion of the research methodology for this study, I examine each of the case studies individually, describing the ways each graduate student negotiated personal and professional boundaries in representing their identities as graduate students.

METHODOLOGY

This research is part of a larger longitudinal study of undergraduate and graduate students' digital literacy practices on social network sites. The graduate student participants were recruited from among teachers of writing courses at a large Midwestern university. One of the primary research questions of this study concerned identity representation across different social network sites, and one criterion for inclusion in this study was an active presence on more than one social network site. Through this study, I followed three graduate students on social media for a total of ten months and collected data from the following four sources:

Digital texts: I followed research participants on social network sites and collected the digital writing they posted on these sites. I collected frequent still image screen shots of participants' profile pages and updates and also collected all tweets sent over the ten months of the study.

Detailed interviews: I conducted periodic, face-to-face interviews with each research participant, which provided deeper context and reflection on the material these participants shared through social media.

Time use diaries: Following Bill Hart-Davidson's (2007) example of time-use diaries to trace distributed writing tasks, I asked participants to complete a log of all uses of social networking sites over a typical three-day period in order to get a better sense of how they integrated their writing practices on social network sites within their daily activities.

Profile tours: Using a video screen capture program, I asked each research participant to show and describe each profile on every social network site they used. This tour was a means through which to discuss identity representation and allowed participants to speak from specific elements of their identity representation—for example, profile pictures or specific written descriptions—but also to gain insights into participants' attitudes towards privacy settings, friend lists, and other elements of social network sites.

These multiple sources of data were analyzed first through open coding and "clustering," described by Casanave (2002) as a process through which common trends and threads from each research participant's experience came together in similar ways to suggest common conclusions (p. 33). I used this open coding and clustering method to then create specific coding categories that were used in a second pass through the data. Utilizing these multiple sources of data, I was able to explore participants' identity representations on different social media sites, to explore how they integrated their social network site use into their daily lives, and to consider how these identities changed over time.

In the rest of this chapter, I will focus on specific aspects of three different graduate students' social media use. While these three case studies are not representative of all graduate students in writing studies, they remain what Dorothy Sheridan, Brian Street, and David Bloome (2000) called "telling cases" that work "not through empirical generalization, but by revealing the principles that underlie relationships between specific writing practices, the local events of which they are a part, and the institutional contexts in which they take place" (p. 14). Each of these individual case studies provides important situated, descriptive information through which we can learn more about the ways that some graduate students in the field use social media. While each student worked to present a digital professional identity within the figured world of the academic field of writing studies, they each had different approaches for managing more personal and more professional audiences.

THE ROLE OF SOCIAL MEDIA IN PROFESSIONAL IDENTITY REPRESENTATION

JACK: DIVIDING AUDIENCE ON TWITTER

Jack, a 33-year-old graduate student in writing studies at the time of the study, was a musician, blogger, and also a father of three. Jack had profiles on the following social media sites: Facebook, Twitter, MySpace, Google, Tumblr, Flickr, Picasa, Vimeo, YouTube, and lala—a music sharing social network site. He also contributed to another music-themed blog that provides music reviews for regional concerts, but Twitter represented the social media platform he used most frequently.

While Jack used Facebook primarily for personal use, Twitter provided him with an opportunity to connect with those he did not know in real life, and he sought opportunities to build new connections with scholars in his area. Jack had three different Twitter accounts over the course of this study, which was a result of his concerns about negotiating his different professional and personal figured worlds: a long-standing personal Twitter account, a more professionally focused Twitter account about academic research interests, and one account for teaching. Jack identified specific figured worlds and their corresponding audience groups, and he represented his identity in relation to them: as a teacher on one account, an academic on another, and a musician and music critic on what he labeled his primary account.

Jack's primary Twitter account blended personal and professional figured worlds: musicians, music bloggers, friends, academics and students. Jack explained his About Me blurb on Twitter as being an important part of his identity representation, where he mentioned his position as a graduate student, a teacher, a researcher, and a music writer. Some sample tweets from Jack's main account reflect these mixed interests. The following tweets share more of his personal reflection on his life as a student:

> Still have 8 students' double-papers to grade—Got Willie
> Nelson promoting his new b'grass album in concert on the
> dvr. Let's do this. 8:31 PM Feb 27th via TweetDeck
>
> ahhh.. just registered for 8 hours of "thesis research" for next
> semester. Feels good. (as I'm sure it will until I begin said
> research) 2:24 PM Nov 18th via TweetDeck

These updates represent Jack's Twitter practice of combining his activities as a graduate student with comments on his daily, lived experience, such as watching the Willie Nelson concert, presenting a casual perspective on his activities as a graduate student.

As Jack began to write more music reviews, connecting to the music community on Twitter became more important, which also gave him new writing opportunities. With his music connections, Jack was able to attend almost fifty concerts for free, which he saw as a testament to the networking power of Twitter:

> This whole network of maybe these music writers that I've
> become associated with because of Twitter, like I got this

job writing for this blog through Twitter, and I've kind of, I
don't necessarily have any kind of notoriety and clout, but
every once in a while there's a little bit of like, oh, I wrote
this piece for this blog and it gets picked up, you know, and
retweeted, and that's the first time I'm ever had any of that,
right? Like most of us . . . don't get our stuff published kind
of across the web.

As Jack progressed through his academic program and worked on scholarly publications, Twitter and the access it provided to a different figured world
allowed him to reach a different public audience and to publish in spaces beyond
academic journals.

In order to manage the different figured worlds to which he belonged, Jack
frequently experimented with the ways he reached audiences on Twitter, and
he created and abandoned separate teaching and academic Twitter accounts.
Jack developed the teaching account to communicate with his advanced composition class without "subjecting students to personal tweets." He required his
students to check the class Twitter account frequently, but only about four or
five students tweeted actively. Despite low participation, Jack found tweeting a
valuable activity to engage in with his class, which was an advanced composition
class focused on multimodal composition. Keeping the class Twitter posts on a
separate account was a way for Jack to manage his different audiences on Twitter.
Jack stated that he didn't want class announcements going out to all of his other
Twitter followers:

> So I mean, I could have created like a hashtag or something
> like that that would have made that specific tweet go to my
> students, but still if I sent that through my regular account,
> everybody that follows me would see it, and like what, what
> would the point of that be? I don't really know. It's weird, and
> so I don't know that I would be comfortable sending out that
> kind of tweet that obviously has an audience that can respond
> to it and the information there is important, um, but I always
> feel less comfortable just sending it out to the world.

Jack noted that he often saw other academics tweeting with their students
on a regular Twitter account but didn't feel comfortable doing the same, even
as he worried he wasn't giving students a good example of how most people use
Twitter. After about a month, however, Jack noted that he kept missing his students' messages because he did not log into his class account regularly enough,
and he stopped using the account specifically for his students. The following are

tweets he sent from primary account after he moved class information back to his primary account:

> #classhashtag students: All but done w grading your projects. Look for them back tomorrow sometime. Great work overall, guys. I'm super impressed. 12:09am March 1 via TweetDeck
>
> #classhashtag folks: Love this video a girl made stranded in the Pittsburgh airport. Check out her editing/music choices. 8:35 AM Feb 23rd via TweetDeck
>
> #classhashtag students: don't forget I need ur (double)write-ups tonight by midnight (& hey, rest of the world: I teach. I tweet. why not both?) 8:59 PM Feb 19th via TweetDeck

The final tweet here shows Jack acknowledging "context collapse," which Alice Marwick and danah boyd (2011) described as the practice of social media sites unifying different communities and audiences under one "friends" or "followers" list. While this merging of figured worlds made Jack a bit self-conscious, he relied on the activity of other Twitter users, his followers, and other academics to justify that what he was doing was a common practice, something he refers to in this final tweet directly.

At the beginning of this study, Jack had recently retired his academic Twitter account. He noted that he had already made connections with academics through his personal account before starting the second one, so he had few follows through the academic account that became primarily a "container for links." When Jack was required to tweet for a graduate course, however, he revived the account. At times, he tweeted material from both academic and personal Twitter accounts simultaneously, but at other times, these two accounts had distinct topics and audiences. Jack described this decision as one he made as his research interests developed: Both the academic tweets and the music tweets were becoming more specialized. Given the success he had in networking with musicians and writers through his primary Twitter account, he saw the potential for a Twitter account focused specifically on academic issues to work the same way. He commented on this audience distinction in an interview:

> I guess I sense the power of Twitter in that way, and so I want to represent myself to this other group of people when I'm becoming more comfortable talking about academic things there, and I suppose as I get more and more comfortable in that community, that I'll want to interact with those people more often as I get to know them, and meet them maybe at conferences, or read their work or whatever. I see the Twitter

network as a way of staying connected and interested and having people know who I am and that kind of thing. All this stuff is kind of important when I get a job.

As these interests developed, he saw the increased tweets about music and musicians as separate from and distracting to a more academic tweeting audience. Jack considered the change as successful, as several scholars he had connected with on his primary Twitter account had already switched to sending links and communicating with him primarily through his academic account. The tweets he sent from this academic account ranged from reflections on academia and academic culture:

> being a successful academic is about learning to celebrate (not envy) your colleagues' brilliance & w/out spite or fear daring to add to it 5:45 PM Dec 8th via TweetDeck

> That may be the secret of life, actually. 5:45 PM Dec 8th via TweetDeck

> Been thinking about the observation of new grad student that everybody talks about how busy they are. Academics have a culture of busyness. 9:07 PM Oct 6th via TweetDeck

> It's true, but why? Is our projected busyness evidence of our "seriousness" or devotion to our work? Or a trick to guard against more work? 9:18 PM Oct 6th via TweetDeck

> If you have an answer, I'll have to read it tomorrow. I'm busy grading right now. 9:19 PM Oct 6th via TweetDeck

Along with the tweets presented here, Jack also often discussed scholarship through his academic Twitter account, sometimes tweeting questions for his own research or quotations from his reading. Jack saw this account as a way to discuss his developing research interests, connecting them to material he found online, and most importantly, connecting with like-minded scholars. Distinguishing boundaries between "colleagues" and "friends" remained one of the challenges of Jack's split Twitter accounts. Parsing out this inevitable overlap was something that Jack constantly struggled with in representing his identity with a number of different figured worlds on Twitter.

He anticipated using this academic account more actively as he became more established as a scholar himself. After he published something, he said, he would feel "more justified in interacting with people. I just kind of feel like the new kid, you know, that's not a very good metaphor. I don't know all the dance moves yet." As Jack developed his scholarly interests and planned to contribute to the field in more traditional ways through academic publishing, he anticipated that his scholarly Twitter identity would also contribute more to the scholarly conversations he saw happening on this social network site as well. Here Jack describes developing an identity for the figured world of an academic field as happening gradually on Twitter. While he began to participate in conversations, he was not yet a central figure.

Jack was excited, though, to receive some attention from someone he referred to as a star academic and a frequent tweeter:

> He replied to me once. And I was kind of like, this guy isn't responding to me, this is crazy. And it was also something really stupid too, like I was joking that my hair was getting long enough that I could comb it and look like Justin Bieber, and he said something, congratulations, or something like that.
> But it felt cool to be noticed, you know, by this person.

Even though the conversation was about something completely innocuous, Jack was excited that this academic noticed him and commented, as he felt it gave him some sort of notoriety. It is also notable that the tweet that drew the attention of this scholar was not a professional tweet or one connected to Jack's research or teaching, but a more casual tweet about a celebrity. This example demonstrates that using Twitter successfully sometimes means blending personal and professional content. In his Twitter use, Jack saw himself connecting to and shaping his online identity in connection to multiple figured worlds, a practice that developed continually through each update he sent. Jack saw these different figured worlds as flexible in sometimes blending personal and professional content, and this approach seems to have been his most successful one.

ESTHER: ACADEMIC ENTRY INTO PERSONAL SPACES

Esther, a graduate student in writing studies and a teaching assistant, was also a blogger and a knitter, sharing projects and participating in events with her fellow knitting friends online. Esther had mostly lapsed profiles on MySpace and Orkut, and she used Facebook, Twitter, and blogged through LiveJournal and WordPress. The social network site she used most frequently, however, was Ravelry, a site specifically for knitters. Esther joined all of these sites in graduate school, prompted by friends (Orkut, Twitter), musicians she enjoyed (MySpace), and even students (Facebook). Esther considered herself an occasional user of Facebook, with Ravelry consuming the majority of her online time and attention.

Esther first presented more of a teacher persona on Facebook when she joined the site in 2005. She described her initial interest in Facebook as based on her students' activities on the social network site:

> They were kind of influencing me to do it. I didn't really have any curiosity about it per se; I think I was more interested in this thing my students were using to do certain kinds of writing. I mean I had already been kind of attuned at that point to talking about students' writing in lots of different settings, so I was just kind of interested in seeing this format that they were writing in and what it was like. So my interest in it was more about them than something I thought I would use for myself.

At the time, Facebook membership was restricted to those with an .edu email address, and many of Esther's friends were no longer in college. She noted that there was resistance among her graduate student friends for other reasons as well:

> I even knew there was lots of resistance to it at that point, and this idea of having your personal life in any way displayed in a public forum was really, by some people I think, frowned upon and supposedly affects your ability to get a job, or you know, you have to represent yourself in certain ways.

Esther first joined Facebook as a teacher, interested in her students' literate activity on the site and interacting with them about writing in this location. Esther first approached this site, then, through the figured world of writing instruction. She used Facebook to keep in touch with former students and also to consider the type of writing they engaged in on the site. Esther, therefore, had a number of former students who were still friends with her on Facebook, and she was connected with other writing classes through the site, joining a Facebook group formed by her business and technical writing students one semester, for example.

As a graduate student, Esther had concerns about her representation as a scholar. While Jack worked to develop a professional identity in interaction with a specific community of scholars on Twitter, Esther did not cultivate an academic scholarly identity connected to an academic field and professional figured world in the same way. Although Esther cited knitting as her primary influence in joining Twitter, she also observed her colleagues tweeting professionally from conferences. She tweeted from her phone at one primary conference in her field and preferred tweeting live events:

> I tweeted a lot during 4Cs, and then I haven't since then. So I would say I'm kind of interested in using it for academic

purposes, but I kind of like it for more of the live stuff, like it was really fun at 4Cs. I liked when people were tweeting from presentations I couldn't go to. I liked tweeting from presentations myself. Um, and it was fun, there was like different other kinds of exchanges that happened. Like I tweeted that we were going to have Ethiopian food, and somebody—so somebody did the mention for me, asking what restaurant it was, and then I did that for her telling her where to go. So just like stuff like that. It's kind of cool, it feels very live.

Esther only connected to a few academics on Twitter and saw it primarily as a tool to enhance her conference experience, rather than a place where she could join academic conversations on a regular basis. She expected other academics to see her tweets not because they were her followers on Twitter, but because they were using the common conference hashtag. She occasionally tweeted when she was frustrated about academic topics, however, particularly dissertation writing:

today's agenda: coffee, writing, breakfast, writing, lunch, writing, knitting break, writing, potluck, Mexican food, board game, writing. 1:37pm, Sep 18 via Tweetdeck

How am I supposed to be brilliant if Microsoft word won't save? What do mean insufficient memory? Trust me, the diss is not that long yet. 3:19pm, Sep 24 via Tweetdeck

That came out terribly wrong. Should read: what do you mean there's insufficient memory. In my defense, I only slept 4 hours last nite. 3:20pm, Sep 24 via Tweetdeck

Like Jack, Esther also sent updates from her daily lived experience as a graduate student. She noted that for these tweets, for example, the figured world she reached was a closer community of friends and fellow graduate students. While Jack described entering conversations on Twitter as a way to enter a scholarly community, Esther saw her own connections in this area to be entered around a particular event and bounded by that event rather than developed over time.

Esther also experimented with integrating Twitter into her teaching practices. A few of the other instructors of this course were using Twitter to communicate with students, and Esther started using it in the classroom to explore its possibilities. These tweets were minimal, however, and she only used the class hashtag eight times herself. As an optional part of the class, her students' use of Twitter was minimal, primarily to tweet about links and connections to the class, and Esther stopped using it several weeks into the course. While Esther joined Facebook as a writing teacher, she used Twitter for live events and less formal uses.

Esther was finishing her dissertation at the time of the study and was actively applying for academic positions. Esther did not have a professional digital presence beyond her graduate student profile page on her university's website, which she found sufficient for her purposes. Our conversations about the job market and her social media usage, though, primarily occurred within the context of censoring information about the interview process and her campus visits. She noted on several occasions that she had to remove or censor family members' posts on her Facebook wall regarding her travel. She was concerned about privacy regarding her status as a job candidate, and she worked to ensure none of that information was available to her Facebook friends. Rather than promoting a professional academic identity in order to connect to other scholars, she instead managed her online identities by removing information. While Jack was hypersensitive to audience and considered a number of different figured worlds with which he was communicating on Twitter, Esther primarily conceived of her updates as reaching primarily friends, and she represented her academic life through a personal lens.

BECCA: NEGOTIATING PERSONAL AND PROFESSIONAL

Becca was a graduate student in writing studies and a teaching assistant in the undergraduate rhetoric program, and she participated in a university belly-dancing troupe and uploaded some of their performances online. She also maintained a store on Etsy where she sold jewelry. During this study, Becca was active on Facebook, Etsy, and Academia.edu.

Of Becca's roughly 300 Facebook friends, she connected with a few family members and friends from high school and college, as well as with groups of friends at her university: graduate student friends, former students, professors, and members of her belly-dance troupe. While Becca thought frequently about her identity representation on Facebook, she valued the connections she made with each of these different figured worlds and sought to represent herself in ways that would work with these different audience groups.

Becca's use of Facebook required her to negotiate a number of different audience groups that straddled her personal and professional life. She connected with former students on Facebook, some of them her own dissertation research participants. She had strict policies for friending current students; she would accept friend requests from current students but not initiate them. She placed these current students in a special group on Facebook by using the Facebook

Groups feature available at the time that restricted content to this group.[1] Becca noted that she used to do the same with her professional contacts, and she connected to both her own professors and other scholars in her field of study. She gave up using a specific Facebook group with this figured world and allowed her information to be shared more widely with her professional connections. Part of Becca's approach to social media use where she blended her personal and professional figured worlds was a result of a larger argument she had about academic culture:

> I don't know, this is generally something that bothers me
> about academia that we're not supposed to be entire people.
> We're just supposed to be academics and we can't have person-
> al lives, and families, and hobbies, and emotions and all that
> kind of good stuff like real people might have. I think that's
> crap, and if anyone were to find me on Facebook who was
> a potential employer and have some problem with anything
> I was doing, I get the feeling I wouldn't want to work with
> them anyway, so it's like, I'm not going to make two separate
> profiles.

Rather than reaching segmented audiences on different social media profiles, Becca saw blending these identities and figured worlds not only as a personal preference, but also as a statement about blending personal and professional concerns within the academy. While she came to this conclusion for different reasons than Jack, Becca also cultivated a kind of personally professional identity on social media.

During the second half of my study, Becca was preparing for the academic job market and was actively searching for and applying for jobs. As she began to envision a professional identity for herself as a faculty member rather than a graduate student, these identity concerns led her to make revisions to her identity representation online. She joined Academia.edu, a social network site for academics, primarily to enhance her professional online presence and to connect with other scholars with similar research interests. While Becca found little interaction happening on that social network site, she found the site to be an important way for her to direct information about herself online to this location.

Becca also restricted access to her Facebook profile during her job search process, noting that she tried to influence and direct the first impression search

---

1   In 2010, Facebook allowed users to separate their own friend list into separate groups; users were not notified about being placed in a group. When sharing content on the site, users had the opportunity to either restrict a particular group from seeing certain content or could share updates with just that group.

committees might have of her when looking for her online, and she changed her privacy settings to make her Facebook profile hidden to those who were not her friends on the site. While Becca attempted to maintain her philosophy of representing her whole person rather than separating her personal and professional identities, she acknowledged that controlling this first impression was an important part of her online representation and crucial for representing herself as a professional, a teacher, scholar, and writing researcher:

> I didn't want someone searching the web for me and being
> their first, their first introduction to me to be a picture of me
> belly dancing when they're looking for a writing teacher. You
> know, it just seems incongruous in ways that are not incon-
> gruous to me but may be to other people.

Here Becca noted that blending figured worlds in online environments can be confusing and disruptive. While Becca has a number of different personal and professional interests, she attempted to separate them in online spaces while she was on the job market. As she began to represent herself beyond her local and personal networks to others in her professional community, Becca found it necessary to construct an identity more specifically for a professional, academic figured world and to promote this identity in online spaces. While she blended personal and professional in most of her social media use, managing her persona for the job market meant directing specific parts of her identity for specific professional figured worlds.

REPRESENTING AND REVISING
PROFESSIONAL IDENTITIES

In Alice Marwick's (2013) ethnography of the tech industry in Silicon Valley, she argued that social media self-branding strategies result in online identities that become safe for work, removed of any personal or potentially embarrassing information to become bland, corporate versions of individuals in online spaces. While her argument remains specific to the tech industry, concerns about professional identity and audience have the possibility of creating a similar situation for graduate students.

Rather than considering a digital professional identity to be a monolithic concept, the experiences of these graduate students instead suggest a multiplicity of different ideas of what it means to be a writing researcher and academic. Esther's introduction to Facebook was through her identity as a writing teacher, and she took the most conservative approach in connecting with scholars in her field on social media. Becca ultimately changed her privacy settings and her profile picture as she prepared for the academic job market, but she also expressed a conscious effort not to censor other aspects of her identity in academic circles. Jack continually revised how he represented his identity for the different audiences he connected with on Twitter. The experiences described here suggest viewing the ways that graduate students develop professional identities not as a process narrative of enculturation, but instead through dialogic interactions with the different figured worlds graduate students are a part of in digital spaces. The approach that seemed most successful for Jack, and to a lesser extent for Becca, was a "personally professional" identity that combined more professionally oriented content with everyday minutiae.

Developing a professional identity through social media does not happen just through building a profile, but in the accumulation of specific moments of interaction with different communities. Esther and Becca chose to manage their professional identities as they approached the academic job market by revising privacy settings and removing information. While these activities may change one's initial identity presentation at the surface level of the profile, the approach does not consider the ways that this data can persist online, through tagged photos, information shared by other social media users, and archives or databases. This digital record, so to speak, becomes even more important for younger students. The graduate students featured here all joined these social media platforms during graduate school. As students develop a longer history of online activity, stretching to high school and even before, the persistence of personal information affects one's ability to manage or alter it, thus becoming an even more important consideration in developing professional digital identities.

While this study has taken a practice approach to identity, this identity construction also interacts with individuals' other identity categories, including race, class, gender, ethnicity, and sexual identity as well. While Jack's more personal updates were well received, and Jack more actively sought out professional communities on social media, both Esther and Becca were ultimately concerned about presenting some aspects of their personal identities to professional audiences. While the three case studies presented here cannot offer conclusions about the role of gender in professional identity representations, the data presented here cannot be separated from these identity categories either.

This balance between the personal and professional has important implications for graduate student mentoring as they begin to network with other scholars through social media. Developing a professional identity in coordination with social media requires graduate students to navigate multiple audiences and figured worlds as they work to develop their own sense of identity as teachers and scholars. Yet digital spaces are always in flux, and the rules for acting within them are contested and constantly changing. Studying digital professional identities requires similarly flexible frameworks. Viewing digital professional identity as multiple and enacted through interactions that strike a balance between more professional and more casual content can help writing researchers better understand the role of social media as part of students' professional identity representation. This research suggests a personally professional identity as an effective one for graduate students developing professional digital identities through social media. More research is needed to better understand the social media use of scholars at all levels and the perceptions of that use among graduate faculty and hiring committees. More research on the use of social media in professional contexts can help us better understand its influence on graduate student identity and professional development.

REFERENCES

Berkenkotter, C., Huckin, T. & Ackerman, J. (1988). Conventions, conversations, and the writer: Case study of a student in a rhetoric Ph.D. program. *Research in the Teaching of English, 22*(1), 9–41.

Berry, P. W., Hawisher, G. E. & Selfe, C. L. (2012). *Transnational literate lives in digital times*. Logan, UT: Computers and Composition Digital Press/Utah State University Press. Retrieved from http://ccdigitalpress.org/transnational.

Boyd, P. (2013). Online discussion boards as identity workspaces: Building professional identities in online writing classes. *JiTP: The Journal of Interactive Technology and Pedagogy, 4*. Retrieved from http://jitp.commons.gc.cuny.edu.proxy.library.csi .cuny.edu/online-discussion-boards-as-identity-workspaces-building-professional -identities-in-online-writing-classes/.

Carr, A. D., Rule, H. J. & Taylor, K. T. (2013). Collecting, sharing, and circulating graduate literacy narratives. *Computers and Composition Online*. Retrieved from http:// www2.bgsu.edu/departments/english/cconline/winter2013/literacy_raw/index.html.

Casanave, C. P. (2002). *Writing games: Multicultural case studies of academic literacy practices in higher education*. London, England: Erlbaum.

Chen, C. (2016). *#4C16*. Tweet archivist. Retrieved from https://www.tweetarchivist .com/chenchen328/6.

Cushman, E. (2008). Toward a rhetoric of self-representation: Identity politics in Indian country and rhetoric and composition. *College Composition and Communication, 60*(2), 321–365.

Hart-Davidson, B. (2007). Studying the mediated action of composing with time-use diaries. In H. McKee & D. N. DeVoss (Eds.), *Digital writing research: Technologies, methodologies, and ethical issues* (pp. 153–170). New York, NY: Hampton.

Holland, D., Lachicotte, W., Jr., Skinner, D. & Holland, C. C. (1998). Identity and agency in cultural worlds. Cambridge, MA: Harvard University Press.

Lemke, J. (2008). Identity, development, and desire: Critical questions. In C. R. Caldas-Coulthard & R. Iedema (Eds.), *Identity trouble: Critical discourse and contestations of identification* (pp. 17–42). London, England: Macmillan/Palgrave.

Leon, K. & Pigg, S. (2011). Graduate students professionalizing in digital time/space: A view from "down below." *Computers and Composition, 28*(1), 3–13.

Marwick, A. (2013). *Status update: Celebrity, publicity & branding in the social media age.* New Haven, CT: Yale University Press.

Marwick, A. & boyd, d. (2011). I tweet honestly, I tweet passionately: Twitter users, context collapse, and the imagined audience. *New Media and Society, 13,* 96–113.

Prior, P. (1998). *Writing/disciplinarity: A sociohistoric account of literate activity in the academy.* Mahwah, NJ: Erlbaum.

Richardson, E. (2003). *African American literacies.* New York, NY: Routledge.

Sheridan, D., Street, B. & Bloome, D. (2000). *Writing ourselves: Mass-observation and literacy practices.* Cresskill, NJ: Hampton Press.

Smitherman, G. (2000). *Black talk: Words and phrases from the hood to the amen corner.* Boston, MA: Houghton Mifflin.

Villanueva, V. (1993). *Bootstraps: From an American academic of color.* Urbana, IL: National Council of Teachers of English.

CHAPTER 10

WRITING TO HAVE NO FACE: THE ORIENTATION OF ANONYMITY IN TWITTER

Les Hutchinson

Michigan State University

> I am no doubt not the only one who writes in order to have no face. Do not ask who I am and do not ask me to remain the same: leave it to our bureaucrats and our police to see that our papers are in order. At least spare us their morality when we write.
>
> —Foucault

Foucault isn't the only one. This chapter is a story about how I wrote to have no face; it is my anonymity story. Late in 2011, I became fascinated by the Guy Fawkes/pirate flag avatars that I saw all over social media. Who were these people behind the mask? Why did they choose to show themselves online as this figure? And, what motivated them to protest online? The answers to these questions inspired me to study the online protest rhetoric of Anonymous through a developing research methodology I detail in this chapter.

The methodology has shaped my research practices as a rhetoric and writing scholar. In order to study anonymity, I had to study Anonymous. One cannot be separated from the other, not on the Internet. However, with studying Anonymous came great risk.

It meant the recurrence of an unmarked van parked down my street. It meant hearing strange clicks through my phone receiver every time I made or accepted a call. It meant my Internet going down, usually mid-conversation in a chat with my research participants. It meant [still] being intrusively checked by TSA every time I flew anywhere for work. It meant worrying that I could be doxxed by someone on social media and have my private personal information exploited—an incident that happened in the summer of 2012 when a particularly talented hacker from within the Anonymous community found out the name and location of my son's school, which he used as information collateral to threaten another person in the community. I was terrified, angry, and confused. At the time, I had no idea why studying Anonymous meant a continual lesson of how to keep my information private and why anonymity is so important, especially for researchers who work in online communities.

Despite these lived risks, this experience also taught me why some choose anonymity online and what anonymous identities afford users in social media spaces. I have made many life-long connections by joining the larger Anonymous community and those acquainted with others around it. I learned what it means to do research with vulnerable participants who are very much also at risk— some of whom are serving sentences, or worse, today.

And, most of all, I learned the importance of telling my story about anonymity.

A METHODOLOGY FOR EMBODYING ANONYMITY

I open this chapter with an explanation of the repercussions I experienced as a way of guiding you into how my scholarship on anonymity has unfolded. My purpose is to show that at no point in my research was my body separated from my work. Who I am online as an academic has inseparably connected my body with other bodies. Additionally, the dichotomy between online and offline bears no relation to my lived reality as a scholar or as a person. The bodies I inhabited in Twitter to study anonymity cannot be quantified within a unified, single theory of identity or selfhood.

A methodology capable of addressing anonymous embodiment starts from Sara Ahmed's (2006) discussion of orientations in *Queer Phenomenology*. Ahmed explained that "bodies as well as objects take shape through being oriented toward each other, as an orientation that may be experienced as the co-habitation of sharing space" (p. 54). My methodology begins with Ahmed's focus on orientation. By theorizing orientation as a spatial relationship between bodies, the selves around one's body (in all their identifiable forms) provide context for us to theorize how our own body takes shape. Cohabitation, then, centers theorizing of the relationships between bodies as collaborative. The orientations of anonymous bodies with other bodies shape one another, but also shape their communal social landscape together.

Within this methodology of anonymous embodiment, I rely on the combination of feminist and queer rhetorical practices as tactics. Because I am specifically working with autoethnographic data from my own rhetorical performances of identity in Twitter, I primarily theorize the way I came to embody anonymity through the deployment of tactical strategies for activism acquired from my disciplinary knowledge as a rhetorician. In this chapter, I employed two specific tactics as methods for doing my work: *strategic contemplation* and *chusmeria*.

Jacqueline Jones Royster and Gesa E. Kirsch (2012) defined the term *strategic contemplation* in order to reclaim a genre of scholarly practice that emphasizes meditation and reflection as a heuristic (p. 84). Strategic contemplation reorients us as academics to cultural practices that exist within our space of research. As I reflect on the various re-compositions of myself in Twitter, I participate in the reclaiming of this genre of scholarly practice. Royster and Kirsch asserted that we need to reflect on the experiences and sensations of our bodies that are relevant to the research we are doing and contemplate them at every step of our project (p. 95). They provided me a new way—an embodied feminist way—of approaching the work I do as an academic. As I began applying this approach to my own study of anonymity, I better understood the experience of becoming anonymous by contemplating it as a scholarly body I needed to inhabit. I was able to use strategic contemplation in this chapter to reflect on anonymous embodiment as a tactic that infuses my work with practical meaning. Such practical meaning takes shape as I reflected on the relationship my body had *in* Twitter.

Through strategic contemplation, I am able to reflect on how what my body had undergone in Twitter—as revolutions of various Twitter selves—resembled a model of identity theorized by José Esteban Muñoz (1999). Muñoz explained that *chusmeria* is a practice of embodiment that blends exaggerated antinormative and inappropriate behaviors with professional, normative ones to "spoil" an identity construction (pp. 184–185). He defined *chusmeria* as "a tactical refusal to keep things 'pristine' and binarized, a willful mismatching of striped and floral print genres, and a loud defiance of a rather fixed order" (p. 191). *Chusmeria*, as a rhetorical tactic with Latina/o Caribbean roots, allows a Spanish-speaking Caribbean identity to resist being defined (and even defiled) by hegemonic power; it is the embodiment of a Latina/o queer performativity that provokes confusion and even discomfort from its audience. The tactic of *chusmeria* explains how I navigated the blending of my own clashing identities in Twitter. As a queer, light-skinned (Mexican) Latinx, I live by mitigating such navigation anyway. I am fascinated by how this navigation shifted into embodied performances of my selves in Twitter while I was doing academic research.

TWITTER AS A PLACE FOR EMBODIMENT

I chose Twitter as my location of study because I was socially located there when I began doing my research. Everyday interactions within that space permitted me to notice my experiences with identity boundaries blurring—unfolding constantly anew—in real, living time. When I joined Twitter in 2009, I immediately felt the possibility for interaction with anyone. Upon logging in, I was opted into following news organizations and celebrities. I unfollowed most of them once I realized that I could find and follow people who discussed topics more in line with my interests. At the time, I was an English literature senior studying literary theory, struggling with theorists such as Derrida and Foucault. A simple search for people discussing these Western thinkers brought me to three men discussing them in detail. I followed them, then started "listening" to their conversation. After some time, I joined them as a fellow educated conversant.

The friendship with these men and many others taught me that Twitter operates differently than other social networks I inhabit. I recall Michael Warner's (2005) statement that "a public is a relation among strangers" (p. 75). The public space of Twitter has a distinct emphasis on connecting strangers with one another. Twitter does not differ much from online social spaces like Instagram or Tumblr in its abilities to provide opportunities to meet strangers. However, Twitter has distinct differences that make it representative of a public where identities converge to converse. The main difference between Twitter and other online spaces is Twitter's timeline. Though many social media technologies have timelines where users scroll through posts written by people they follow in real time, Twitter's timeline surpasses others in sheer pace. The Twitter timeline runs fast, relying on the speech of news and events for acceleration. The temporal materiality in its timeline conforms conversation to the fixed structure of seconds, minutes, hours, and days. Twitter makes news go viral like no social space we have today. Most of the speech of virality depends upon the number of people Twitter users follow.

For instance, my main Twitter account currently follows upward of over 800 Twitter users. I cannot keep up with every post in my timeline, so I have adjusted my experience with Twitter by using lists where I sort this account's friends from news and research. Lists allow me to connect with the people I follow in uniquely specific ways based upon my relationships with them. To return to Ahmed, I have adjusted my orientations in Twitter to the people in my community and these orientations shape my interactions with them. I will explain this further in the sections that follow.

Comparing the algorithmic allowances for identity in Twitter to those in Facebook illuminates the technical function of anonymity in Twitter. Facebook has a history of not accepting—even downright opposing—people who present nontraditional identities to use its service. In the fall of 2014, Facebook received mainstream criticism for deleting accounts belonging to drag queens who did not present as their given names. It even requires users to submit state-issued identification as proof their names are *their* names. Such blatant opposition to giving users the right to select the names they present in their own accounts makes Facebook an unsafe, inhospitable place for people who live on the margins of traditional heteronormativity. And it also grants its users little control over their own information, which is devastating for people with personal reasons that require they retain a sense of privacy. In contrast, Twitter does not require ID to use its service. Twitter prioritizes connection not as a relationship with people users already know, but as a relationship with people and organizations who say something users want to hear. Twitter's digital architecture revolves around a communal desire for shared, global conversation with strangers and friends alike. And it remains special for being one of the few places on the Internet where identity play is not only possible, but accepted.

Like other online social spaces such as Tumblr and Instagram, Twitter users can choose their name to be [nearly] whatever they want. These names follow the @ symbol and can be anything from their given names, aliases, or even names made of combined letters and numbers that are otherwise unpronounceable. People can choose to present themselves as a character, a parody account, an inanimate object, anonymous, or even pseudonymous. The nominal choices are nearly infinite in Twitter, making for a unique temporal user experience with anonymity in ways that even spaces like Tumblr and Instagram do not quite match, which is what I use this chapter to explain.

WHAT'S THE IDENTITY IN A NAME?

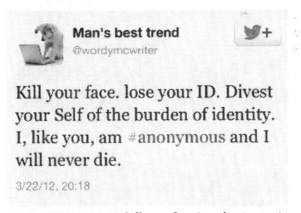

Man's best trend
@wordymcwriter

Kill your face. lose your ID. Divest your Self of the burden of identity. I, like you, am #anonymous and I will never die.

3/22/12, 20:18

Figure 10.1. How to kill your face (wordymcwriter).

I first began studying Twitter having no idea what I was beginning would turn into a serious scholarly practice. During the fall of 2011, I was there studying how the Occupy Wall Street movement used this space to perform social activist rhetoric (for more conversation on Occupy, Caroline Dadas has an excellent chapter about the movement's hashtag activism in this collection). I kept coming across Twitter accounts using pseudonyms, alternate identities, and avatars with Guy Fawkes masks. I wondered why people were electing to *not be* themselves in this space and what these alternative representations meant within and outside of Twitter.

That was when I came across Bertolt Brecht's (1996) use of dialectical materialism for his Marxist analysis of theatre. My wondering helped me form theory-based questions about how the construction of our selves online visually reflects our social relationships. Brecht employed dialectical materialism as a performance method to help his characters project their social situations as processes. He felt that

> [dialectical materialism] regards nothing as existing except
> in so far as it changes, in other words is in disharmony with
> itself. This also goes for those human feelings, opinions, and
> attitudes through which at any time the form of men's life
> together finds its expression. (p. 122)

By emphasizing change as a natural orientation among social relationships, Brecht explained how the desires and drives collectively constitute our material bodies. Pathos is not merely a second-rate subjectivity to Brecht, but a valid orientation that connects us with one another through sharing our histories.

Brecht's theoretical approach taught me what dialectical materialism means in regard to Twitter avatars. I turned critically to my own Twitter account to question how I was employing pathos in my visual representation of self. Some time has passed since this self-critique began. I have further evaluative distance to strategically rhetoricize the transitions my Twitter account underwent.

Figure 10.2. Avatar transitions of the original @LesHutch Twitter account (#1).

Figure 10.3. Avatar transitions of the original @LesHutch Twitter account (#2).

Each picture in Figures 10.2, 10.3, and 10.4 served as an avatar for different iterations of my original Twitter account. The first photograph represented @LesHutch's Twitter identity in 2009—an image composition of me going to work at the emergency room (my career prior to academia), wearing scrubs, and with stylized artifice drawn over the image thanks to a nifty photo app. @LesHutch's avatar shows me playing with my identity even then, though I still held a name closely resembling my given name. Through strategic contemplation now, I see that I clearly held an understanding that identity play through self-presentation was possible in Twitter. The way I played with my identity then signals Twitter as a place where I felt comfortable not taking myself too seriously.

The next photograph marks a transition I made after three years on Twitter. This was one of the avatars I had once I started studying Occupy Wall Street and had connected more with activists and anonymous individuals. I had changed my name to @LesHeme, a writing alias I have used in the past. I adopted this name to distance my account from my "real" identity in an effort to protect my son's. Ironically, @LesHeme's avatar, arguably, more closely resembles my face than the one preceding it. It appears to be nearly all me. But it isn't. @LesHeme's avatar was photo manipulated from an original. One of my Twitter friends offered to put her in sepia with a light rose blush imposed upon it. This friend altered this image to celebrate one of my tweets making over fifty retweets. I wore this avatar to project some semblance of "classic beauty," while maintaining a sense of sass; at the time, this was true to the me I chose to present.

Figure 10.4. Avatar transitions of the original @LesHutch Twitter account (#3).

To symbolize my first full detachment from myself, the last photograph of this incarnation stands in for the final name change this account had: @tumblesweed. Capturing me sitting on the sand at Dog Beach, California, wearing sunglasses on a day off from school and work, this avatar again represented a true representation of a form of myself. @tumblesweed's avatar is simultaneously Leslie Hutchinson and a person I cannot be anywhere else. In a way, she represents me in an idealized form.

Yet @tumblesweed contradicts a normative visual narrative of "realness." She rejected any affiliation with my nominal self; she was the end-stop of @LesHutch's identity. @tumblesweed was someone I was not fully able to be in my "real life." Rather, I became her in order to embody anonymity for my research. @tumblesweed *blended* my personal identity with a scholarly one I did not quite know yet: a researcher without a face.

In June of 2012, I deleted my @tumblesweed Twitter account and started two new ones. I created a private account for @leslieheme, so I could keep in touch with some of the people who knew me. Then I made a public anonymous account: @s0undbomb3r.

Figure 10.5. Who is @tumblesweed (the exphilosopher).

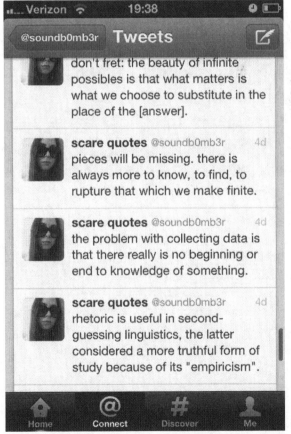

Figure 10.6. The rhetoric of @soundb0mb3r (scare quotes).

Figure 10.7. The rhetoric of @soundb0mb3r (not Victor's girl).

@soundb0mb3r's Twitter body, shown here in Figures 10.6 and 10.7, allowed me to present a mixed, *chusmeria* representation of my anonymous and academic selves. I look at these tweets through strategic contemplation and see how I blended an anonymous identity with my academic one. These timeline screencaptures show @soundb0mb3r speaking in Twitter to project a mismatched, clashing (loudly, defiant even) self. While it feels a bit odd to reflect on an identity of mine in the third person, Muñoz (1999) proposed what a practice of *chusmeria* could mean:

> Disidentificatory performances opt to do more than simply tear down the majoritarian public sphere. They disassemble that sphere of publicity and use its parts to build an alternative reality. Disidentification uses the majoritarian culture as raw material to make a new world. (p. 196)

I won't go as far as saying that my little Twitter account made a new reality on its own. However, I will contextualize the academic practice I engaged in *with* the culture I participated *within*: Anonymous. Having used the @soundb0mb3r identity to study anonymity, I adopted the same rhetorical practices of its culture, and I find this practice akin to a method of disidentificatory, *chusmeria* performance.

ORIENTATIONS OF ANONYMITY

This is the moment when I remind readers of my earlier discussion that identities orient to their communities and cultures of anonymity that go beyond individuality. As I discussed, no Twitter account exists there without connections to other accounts. Therefore, I have an imperative to orient @soundb0mb3r with a community of anonymity by discussing Anonymous.

Witchy
@nagoul1

Why is it #AnonCulture? Because we already have our own language, art, music, videos, news and many other forms of expressions.
#anonymous
4/28/13, 11:45

Figure 10.8. @nagoul1 refers to Anonymous as a culture and a family (Witchy).

In this stream of tweets in succession (see Figure 10.8), @nagoul1 takes the mainstream definition of Anonymous as a group of hackers and resituates it as a form of expression by their use of the hashtag #AnonCulture. The use of a hashtag, in this instance, creates a conversation where before there was none. Hashtags establish a place—a location—where people who share similar ideas can collect around to speak together. Like FoolishReporter expresses in Figure 10.10, hashtags operate similar to an empty vessel. And, to be *in* Twitter is equally about being a Twitter @ as it is about speaking as an @. When hashtags emerge in Twitter in real time, they provide a chance for people to participate in speech acts together. @nagoul1's speech acts, therefore, execute what Muñoz (1999) called *reterritorializing*: when a subject takes injurious speech such as a name or label used pejoratively, and embraces it as a sense of self (p. 185). @nagoul1 reterritorializes the anonymous label by pointing out that not every anon is a hacker, despite popular opinion. According to @nagoul1, a well-respected anon within the community, a majority of anons have careers producing texts and art. I see what @nagoul1 says as an enactment of Brecht's dialectical materialism. These tweets change the relationships anyone reading them may have with this account by changing the definition of Anonymous—a definition that has led to many an arrest.

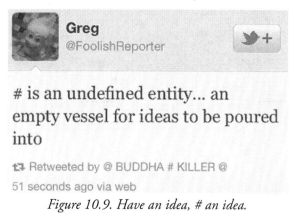

Greg
@FoolishReporter

is an undefined entity... an empty vessel for ideas to be poured into

⟳ Retweeted by @ BUDDHA # KILLER @
51 seconds ago via web

Figure 10.9. Have an idea, # an idea.

Anonymous
@AnonyOps

What? You want to join Anonymous? Do something. Don't tell anyone.
#YoureNowAnonymous
WELCOME ABOARD.

5/14/13, 11:07

125 RETWEETS **65** FAVORITES

Brian Henley @houstonbch 🗩 4d
@AnonyOps it's possible to do something and not talk about it on Twitter? #MindBlown

Figure 10.10. Do something and that's you. (@houstonbch 14 May 2013 11:12 am).

@nagoul1 used the hashtag as a forum to reorient anonymity in this space, and even arguably outside it. Their tweets allow for a reconsideration of anonymous Twitter accounts as identities with more to them than just being identified as hackers or trolls. Rather, they can be seen as people with rich cultural lives outside of their Twitter selves. By using the #AnonCulture hashtag, @nagoul makes room for our social relationship with anonymity to change. Now, move with me as I bring in @AnonyOps to further change the identification with this label.

In Figure 10.10, @AnonyOps uses the hashtag #YoureNowAnonymous as a syntactical construction that reorients the possibility for anyone to wear the Anonymous identity. *Doing* something without talking about it, without defining the action by one's name and thus one's ego, characterizes the Anonymous ethos. The Anonymous form of anonymity symbolizes identification with a performed political ethos—an activism resisting fame or publicity.

Anonymous
@YourAnonNews

We are mothers & daughters. We are you. You are us. We are Legion. @SaraMandil: Do you have female members too in your organization? #AskYAN

1/4/13, 20:28

Figure 10.11. Three tweets about the Anonymous Identity (YourAnonNews).

BrazilAnon
@BrazilAnon

We are Fathers. We are Mothers. We are Sisters. We are Brothers. We are Aunts. We are Uncles. It's time to fight back #Anonymous.

9/3/11, 23:10

Figure 10.12. Three tweets about the Anonymous Identity (BrazilAnon).

Joshua Corman
@joshcorman

Resolved: If you've not seen "Fight Club" you're missing a huge piece of why #Anonymous is a bigger deal than you suspect

5/4/13, 19:46

Figure 10.13. Three tweets about the Anonymous Identity (Corman).

The tweets in Figures 10.11, 10.12, and 10.13 further highlight Anonymous' ideological ethos. By opening discussion through the #AskYAN hashtag, @YourAnonNews' engages with @SaraMandrill to project a feminist rhetoric of inclusion into the Anonymous identity. Listing "mothers & daughters" alongside the plural pronouns of "you," "us," and "we" includes @SaraMandrill in not just a conversation, but with constructing Anonymous as part of her own identity. Meanwhile, @BrazilAnon articulates their tweet in a patriarchically centered discourse by listing "Fathers" before "Mothers," but then complicates that dominant discourse by choosing to list "Sisters" before "Brothers" and "Aunts" before "Uncles." Both tweets imply that the reader or viewer as identifying with Anonymous through the use of the collective personal pronoun "we," which is part and parcel of the "We Are All Anonymous" ethos.

To explicate this ethos further, we can look at @joshcorman's tweet. Anonymous has appropriated the film *Fight Club* as a cultural artifact because of the film's representation of an underground society initiating chaos and revolution. *Fight Club* purposely disrupts the audience's conception of the performer's identities because it portrays the protagonist and the antagonist as separate people. Surprise and/or shock ensues once the audience learns that they are one and the same person. Yet, The Narrator and Tyler Durden are as separate as they are one; each man acts on his own for personal motive. @joshcorman implied this in his tweet. And it is this paradox of blending individuality with a collective identity that composes the Anonymous ideology. Muñoz (1999) explained how such a paradox can be an identity: "Performance is capable of providing a ground-level assault on a hegemonic world vision that substantiates the dominant public sphere. Disidentificatory performance willfully disavows that which majoritarian culture has decreed as the 'real'" (p. 196). So long as majoritarian culture (exemplified in instances such as how Facebook handles identity presentation in its platform) asserts that a person can only be one self, anonymous performativity can resist hegemony via a collective identity. Anonymity says that identity need not be singular in order to appease majoritarian culture. To embody anonymity performs resistance against the reading of identity as limited.

EMBODYING ANONYMITY FOR POLITICAL AGENCY

I arrive at this place in my scholarship, and I have to ask: What about our society makes us need anonymity as an identity in the first place? What affordances does anonymity provide us? Why would some of us need to hide who we are? In Figure 10.14, @AnonyNewsNet reasons why some people need anonymity.

Inkosi Inkosikazi
@AnonyNewsNet

"A desire for privacy does not imply shameful secrets ... without anonymity in discourse, free speech is impossible, & hence also democracy"

4/30/13, 6:10

Figure 10.14. Inkosi on our social necessity for anonymity (Inkosikazi).

By placing these two statements in quotes with no nominal acknowledgment, they read like a character's lines in a play: open for embodiment. I pay critical attention to what the performance of these lines say. For one, they say what they literally say—that anonymity is democratic and necessary to keeping free speech safe. Incidentally, they also say that one can only be safe to say such a thing if one is anonymous. Because @AnonyNewsNet wears anonymity, they perform the very anonymity to which one needs to speak. The performativity of anonymity here is ideologically meta-representative.

Anonymity provides a person with a possibility to speak against the majoritarian expectations of the self. Wanting this for oneself is not rare. In fact, Michel Foucault (2010) wrote with a longing for anonymity:

> At the moment of speaking, I would like to have perceived a
> nameless voice, long preceding me, leaving me merely to en-

mesh myself in it, taking up its cadence, and to lodge myself, when no one was looking, in its interstices as if it had paused an instant, in suspense, to beckon to me. (p. 215)

Foucault essentially asked for anonymity to absorb him and define his identity. I want to argue that his desire to have this anonymity *long preceding him* imprints a history onto anonymous desires. Perhaps this was Foucault's response to Western culture's overwhelming idolatry of him as a celebrity, or maybe it was a deeper desire to resist the reification of a singular identity in general. Perhaps it was both, meshed irrevocably together.

Being in a place of confusion about Foucault's desire for anonymity recalls me back to the body—my body. I consider why I gave up my @soundb0mb3r identity in early 2013, and made a new, queered and feminist version of myself: @codemesh.

Figure 10.15. The chusmeria of @codemesh circa Spring 2013 (chusma).

This screenshot from 2013 of my current Twitter account shows the visual collection of all my Twitter identities in one; @codemesh best embodies the continuous revolutions of my selves. She represents a simultaneous disassociation from my legal name by hiding all identity markers, but also hints toward a blending of my professional and anonymous identities. I change my avatar, secondary name (pictured here as *chusma*) and profile descriptions often. I do this because I am, indeed, "in a self i don't know yet." Constant visual changes emphasize that my Twitter identity is always in a process of developing based on continual reorientations. I practice an identity ethic that Steve Urbanski (2011) used Foucault to define:

> Foucault sees ethics as an entity that is pushed and pulled by the binary oppositions of constraint and freedom: Too much of oneself constrains ethics and the freedom of a multitude of voices propels an ethic of action. On the other hand, an unbridled collection of voices can be just as restrictive. The answer resides in a balance between the two undergirded by critical thinking. To achieve this ethical salvation, one must first know

oneself well enough to break free of the bonds of self and discover an agency that can bring about change. (p. 8)

The queer feminist in me believes in the ethics of rejecting a reification of a single
identity while maintaining a distance, at times, from being consumed by the multi-
tude. It is a tricky dance of personal politics, but it is a dance that never limits what
I can do, who I can study, or what I can say. The trick, as Urbanski (2011) argued,
requires knowing oneself well—a method strategic contemplation encourages.

During this time in 2013, I found myself confronted with a moment of reori-
entation that required new contemplation. On a whim, I had made @codemesh's
avatar a picture of my face—the first time I had done so since I was @LesHeme.
I unmasked myself to see what would happen. Quickly after switching avatars,
a Twitter friend told me in a private message of their surprise to learn that I was
"female" (see Figures 10.16 and 10.17). I responded by being curious about
what part of my Twitter identity previously performed masculinity.

Figure 10.16. The @codemesh gender identity problem (@codemesh).

Figure 10.17. The @codemesh gender identity problem (@codemesh).

This conversation taught me that instances where my gender, sexual, or nominal identities become apparent forces an awareness of the instability of anonymity. At that very moment, I knew that further analysis required a refocus on feminist rhetorics of identity.

Feminist scholars have emphasized publishing subjectivity-based narratives as a discursive form of activism against patriarchy. A mentor of mine, Jacqueline Rhodes, profoundly influenced the subjectivity I chose to inhabit in this paper. Rhodes (2002) analyzed the embodiment of the feminist subjectivity within Internet history. She held that being a feminist body online allows for certain politics:

> This emphasis on the situatedness of text, technology, and subjectivity, as well as the rejection of a hierarchical infor-

mation structure, can make the World Wide Web a particularly rich site for feminist action, particularly the ambiguous yet purposeful collaboration—a type of "collaborative
interruption," that is—that was the hallmark of radical
feminism. (p. 20)

Rhodes connected an embodied feminist subjectivity to the process of hypertextual production of texts. Rhodes taught me that to embody a digital, feminist identity makes feminist action online possible. Therefore, having a feminist
Twitter identity brings me into a history of feminist subjectivity.

With Rhodes' work, I am inclined to ask: What kinds of orientations does
an anonymous feminist Twitter body create? As anyone who has been subject
to harmful discourse, online trolling, or harassment knows, having "no face"
allows people to say terrible things online. However, I want to challenge us
to pause and reflect before we simply write off the wielding of anonymity as
solely indicative of harmful behavior. Before I answer that question, I want us
to consider how anonymity occurs as a natural attribute of our everyday lives.
We must read anonymity rhetorically because the anonymous body is a body
that can be read.

Studying anonymity in Twitter focuses my attention to tweets about anonymity. Even people who project seemingly "literal" versions of themselves fail
to recognize *why* someone would want to be anonymous in the first place, which
is ironic because they are not literally *themselves* in Twitter either (note Figure
10.12). Misnomers about anonymity surface in my timeline every day, which is
why I began this work in the first place. I return to Rhodes (2002), who pointed
out that "the online interplay of fixity, fluidity, text, and identity has much to
do with the particular textual ambiguities of online discourse, particularly as
evidenced in the preferred medium of hypertext" (p. 118). Twitter's nature of
bringing people together by making account names and hashtags hypertextual
reinforces this fluidity between identities that Rhodes described.

I offer that we can embody a feminist form of anonymity since anonymity
keeps the foundational structures of radical feminist practices intact. Combatting
misogynistic and patriarchal discourse online through anonymity as an online
practice empowers women with a sense of communal agency. I attempted my
own study of this practice myself by joining feminist activists in the hashtag
conversation #KillAllMen in 2014. The harassment from misogynist trolls in
my mentions because of tweeting with this hashtag grew to such high numbers
that I had to temporarily change my @codemesh name and make my account
private. I also deleted the one tweet that received a bulk of the attention, and
then posted this one in response (see Figure 10.18).

Figure 10.18. Mistakes were made. (codemesh)

My use of the #killallmen hashtag contributed to a pre-existing conversation started by feminist activists in Twitter. They purposefully employed hyperbole in this hashtag to emphasize the lived reality of violence that women experience every day. By speaking in this hashtag, feminists are able to express their anger and fears about misogyny and patriarchy. I contributed to this conversation as a feminist, a woman who has experienced violence by men, and as an academic who questioned why my first tweet with this hashtag led to nearly debilitating harassment.

I learned about the fragility of feminist embodiment from the trolling and harassment that followed. I had my face as my avatar, which *told* the world that I was a woman using this hashtag. Had I been fully anonymous, I do not know what the responses would have been. However, I have a suspecting belief that had I presented as male, I would not have had to change my @ name and hide. Combatting misogyny online is scary. Being anonymous online can also have its terrifying moments. The fragility in both identity presentations has its share of consequences. Neither provides full safety or security for saying something that might upset someone else. The difference is that when I use an anonymous body to speak, no one in Twitter can tell if I am a boy or a girl (a play on the 30th rule of the Internet, "There are no girls on the Internet").

WHEN WORDS ARE OUR IDENTITY

Because of this experience, I discovered that none of us are exempt from others questioning *who* we are or *what* we say. If anything, a conversation with a stranger has made me all the more aware of the instability of identity. Therefore, it is vitally important to the health of our shared public spaces that we remember that the harmful discourses of dominant, majoritarian culture follow us by our ways with language.

I emphasize that the Anonymous community is as guilty of using harmful discourses as anyone else. Let me discuss the content in Figure 10.19 as an example. (Trigger warning: homophobic slurs and discussion of sexual violence follow.)

Fag is one of the most, but certainly not the only, well-known slurs within many Anonymous communities. In Figure 10.19, @TheLulzDeptxx connects it to the act of unmasking (a person coming out as their legal identity; such an act can happen when a person is doxxed or arrested) and wanting fame. Within the Anonymous ethos, the desire for fame is an antithetical sin. We can see an example of this when Deric Lostutter acquired fame and recognition for his part in doxxing a group of high school football players who gang-raped a sixteen-year-old girl in Steubenville, Ohio. Lostutter's embodiment of the Anonymous ethos suffered a loss of credibility when he used his name to garner public attention.

Figure 10.19. The nearly synonymous use of "fag" with Anons.

Figure 10.20. Who wrote on my Tumblr as anon?

In addition to fag being used as a pejorative for people who "unmask," the use of it as unnecessary commentary often surfaces throughout the Internet, as I have tried to capture in @HeavenMacArthur's tweet (see Figure 10.20). I find @HeavenMacArthur's point that she "know[s] like 4 people" who call her fag very interesting. What *know* means here is ambiguous. The people posting such comments in her Tumblr have obvious knowledge of the rhetorical affordances of anonymity when speaking.

Because anonymity masks names, it focuses attention on the speech as the primary means of identification. Both tweets in Figures 10.19 and 10.20 demonstrate the investments of these anonymous speakers. @TheLulzDeptxx displays the amount of anger they reserve for people who use Anonymous as an instigator for fame. The screen capture of her Tumblr comment in @HeavenMacArthur's tweet expresses the person's desire for affect, not conversation. That comment serves no purpose other than to incite @HeavenMacArthur's emotion—a ploy of pathos through a slur, pure and simple.

In this instance, we grasp the negative aspects of these affordances. Like Bill Reader (2012) noted, many people often equate anonymity with incivility. Nevertheless, Reader also acknowledged that anonymity allows people to speak truth to powerful institutions (p. 503). I take this conflicting data to mean that anonymity reflects the myriad of ways people use discourse whether they present as anonymous or not. After all, people say horrible things both online and offline every day under their own names. People also attempt to speak truth to power and powerful institutions when they feel oppressed. Therefore, anonymity doesn't mask speech; it masks names.

The masking of names permits people to say many things they would normally not be able to articulate. Anonymity provides a realm of safety from consequences. It also provides people with the ability to comment on the way anonymity allows for people to say horrible things. @Kilgoar's tweet, as seen in Figure 10.21, is one instance of this.

K̂ILGOAR
@Kilgoar

You Anons might think it's really cute to "fag" this and "faggotry" that but to everyone else you just look like a homophobic bigot.

5/28/13, 16:17

Figure 10.21. @Kilgoar's reminder goes +9000 (@Kilgoar).

@Kilgoar argued against the way people identifying as Anonymous use fag as part of their discourse. @Kilgoar used anonymity to make these statements, yet again reiterating the meta-representative function of anonymity as an ethos. @Kilgoar's anonymous identity permitted them to speak as part of the anonymous community in Twitter. Such a speech act encourages the discourse about anonymity to change by creating new articulations. @Kilgoar intimates that the use of fag does not necessarily operate as a slur in this community. Rather, it is a use of the term that "everyone else" misunderstands.

Without putting unwanted attention on individuals I have conversed with about this topic, I cannot show tweets that further represent the use of fag as a term of endearment. I can, however, talk about it abstractly. @Kilgoar's intimation of fag having a specific meaning within Anonymous culture is sound. Many anonymous Twitter accounts specifically reserve words like fag and cunt for their comrades and friends. From the outside, though, this use is easily misunderstood. Even I find it off-putting and unnerving at times. Those are the moments when I come to terms with the conflicting identities I embody in this space. Sometimes they just don't mesh. This is when I embrace the ways my discomfort teaches me something new.

WHEN IDENTITY GETS REAL

Not every Twitter user has the same privilege to participate in online conversations freely without consequences. Most of us have to account for our social positions, genders, politics, even our sexualities when we speak online. Therefore, anonymity is one way to protect oneself from the restrictions of speaking publicly as a regular, everyday person. I call anonymity a form of identity encryption because it allows anyone who wears it to keep parts of themselves safely hidden while still enabling them to speak online.

Figure 10.22. Hamster is always in swallow mode.

I showcase @SwallowRedux's tweet (in Figure 10.22) about their accidental embodiment of a hamster in Twitter to point to Twitter's capacity to let users play with the personal connections they have to its platform. @SwallowRedux takes on a hamster as an identification. Twitter's ability for play and identification gives users who identify as "real" versions of themselves different options.

This policeman in Granada (see Figure 10.23) has the opportunity to wear a patch of his Twitter @ name on his arm, an opportunity not many people can adopt in their everyday lives. @Umair_Aziz refers to the image of @PoliciaJun as a "pretty amazing approach to Twitter," to which I heartily agree. There's a blurring of online and offline boundaries here that I especially appreciate, but I additionally note something more. @PoliciaJun is not this policeman's sole identity. Surely, he has more to his life than his career. I have a small inclination to ask: Is he, by chance, anyone else online? A problem might arise if I were to use Twitter to ask him, for admitting a personal online identity through his professional one would conflate the two. And, it could also bring harassment and trolling his way. Through embodying his professional *policia* identity, @PoliciaJun adopts an air of law enforcement and legal protection—something very few of us can adopt ourselves.

Figure 10.23. @PoliciaJun plays himself IRL (@Umair_Aziz).

Twitter affords comedians, celebrities, and politicians another kind of difference for speaking there. In Figure 10.24, we see a conversation scaffold among all three kinds of identities I listed above. Writer @MacMoreno participates in a conversation that Patrick Stewart, Rob Delaney, and David Cameron have adapted in sequential order. Both Delaney and Stewart play with the seriousness of Cameron's original tweet showing him talking to @BarackObama about the situation in Ukraine. Stewart's tweet usurps Delaney's in hilarity by his use of a Wet Ones container as a phone. @MacMoreno further adds to this comedic conversation by using his dog. The tweet scaffold stops at Moreno because he is not a celebrity, but simply a writer. His name does not precede his identity. In this way, the scaffolding works backwards. Cameron can tag the United States President in earnest, even expecting a response. Delaney, however, cannot expect the same from either Obama or Cameron. Sir Patrick Stewart could, theoretically expect a response from any of these men, and knows it. Instead, he uses his name for play with the picture he has added. Moreno's tweet marks the end of the conversation because the men preceding him may not even know who he is and did not acknowledge his addition to their tweets. This tweet proves that in Twitter, even if others are available to us, identities are not equal.

Figure 10.24. Calling in to a conference call.

WHERE CAN IDENTITY IN TWITTER GO?

My embodied research on anonymity in Twitter taught me that new identities have the potential for embodiment in a moment of random happenstance. The space of Twitter enables our @ identities to become bodies they could not be otherwise and speak as voices we have yet to hear. Our timelines bring strangers to us just as hashtags open spaces for shared values that do not yet exist. Every day in Twitter is a new day for expressing collective pain, anger, happiness, resistance, and even humor.

Anonymity gives us the opportunity to participate in Twitter without worry that what we say might affect who we are. I affirm this by admitting that this chapter wouldn't exist if I was still employed at a university in Kansas. Late in 2013, the Kansas Board of Regents adopted a social media policy severely limiting the freedom of its tenured and non-tenured employees to speak online. I was temporary faculty then, which made my scholarship on anonymity a legitimate cause for concern. I felt fear, repression, and hesitation when this policy came into effect, knowing I needed to leave after my contract was over if I was to continue developing my methodology for anonymous embodiment.

The social media policy exists because the Kansas Board of Regents did not appreciate professor David Guth tweeting with anger and emotion in response to a violent shooting incident. Like him, Steven Salaita suffered a termination of his tenure-line contract with the University of Illinois for tweeting with anger and emotion about violence in Palestine. Both Salaita and Guth used Twitter as a space to discuss their feelings about tragedies that held personal significance to their lives. They were punished professionally for their speech.

Such instances tell me that academics need anonymity more than ever.

Considering these accounts of silencing and repression that have happened, anonymity may be one of the only forms of resistance many of us have for speaking online. My life has been shaped and continues to be shaped by these risks. Risk orients my body.

And I recognize that I am not alone in experiencing this risk. The solidarity I feel with my fellow academics, journalists, Internet researchers, and anyone who experiences the consequences of speaking online matters. Solidarity keeps us going. We submit ourselves to these risks because we believe in the potential of our work to create change. I believe we have a right to it. To return to the Foucault (2010) quote at the beginning of this chapter, "leave it to our bureaucrats and our police to see that our papers are in order. At least spare us *their* morality when we write" (p. 17, emphasis mine).

I conclude this chapter with an urging that we, as academics, continue to theorize the relationship between our bodies and our digital, social platforms. How we speak affects who we are, and vice versa. To enact agency online lies in the ability to define our own identity and choose our orientations to one another. For us to have power to be heard, we have to value our various embodiments of this agency. I can only hope that the work I have started here with my own experience of embodying anonymity is a beginning—that scholars continue to make space for questioning who we are online. I also have hope that the risks we incur for speaking decrease. These tumultuous times beg for our active participation. This chapter is just one perspective in the conversation.

ACKNOWLEDGMENTS

As this is my first academic publication, I wanted to extend my gratitude to a few people for helping me create this work. I would first like to thank my children, Ben and Zia, for living through the moments I will have put you at risk and for all of the joy you bring me; you are my very life. To Josh, for his friendship and insight in the technical and emotional moments of this work. To Rhodes, who gave me the room to think through the beginning of these ideas in her Gender, Sexuality, and Rhetoric course at Cal State San Bernardino in 2013. To Malea Powell, for providing eternally beneficial advice and inspiration on the development of my writing. To Doug and Stephanie, for taking a chance on me right at the beginning and for seeing me through to the end. To the kindness of the reviewers of this chapter for their guidance and patience with my introduction. Lastly, to all my research participants from the Anonymous community and beyond for all of their work, dedication, and humor. This chapter was made possible because of all of you.

REFERENCES

Ahmed, S. (2006). *Queer phenomenology*. Durham, NC: Duke University Press.

Anon Receptionist. [@TheLulzDeptxx]. (2013, November 1). Every "unmasked" anon is just another fame fag that failed to understand what Anonymous is. Fuck you [Tweet]. Retrieved from https://twitter.com/thelulzdeptxx/status/396464581217775616.

Anonymous [YourAnonNews]. (2013, January 4). We are mothers & daughters. We are you. You are us. We are Legion. @SaraMandil: Do you have female members too in your organization? #AskYAN [Tweet]. Retrieved from https://twitter.com/YourAnonNews/status/287415280190242817

Anonymous. [@AnonyOps]. (2013, May 14). What? You want to join Anonymous? Do something. Don't tell anyone. #YoureNowAnonymous WELCOME ABOARD [Tweet]. Retrieved from https://twitter.com/anonyops/status/334339264852664320.

Aziz, U. [@Umair_Aziz]. (2014, March 3). Pretty amazing approach to Twitter in Granada. All police officers have their Twitter handle on their uniform [Tweet]. Retrieved from https://twitter.com/umair_aziz/status/440704498752028672.

BrazilAnon. [@BrazilAnon]. (2011, September 3). We are Fathers. We are Mothers. We are Sisters. We are Brothers. We are Aunts. We are Uncles. It's time to fight back #Anonymous [Tweet]. Retrieved from https://twitter.com/brazilanon/status/110233126801915904.

Brecht, B. (1996). A short organum for the theatre (J. Willett, Trans.). In D. Milne & T. Eagleton (Eds.), *Marxist Literary Theory* (pp. 107–135.) Malton, MA: Blackwell Publishing. (Original work published 1949)

@codemesh. (2013, June 11). [Tweet]. Retrieved from https://twitter.com/codemesh.

Codemesh. [@codemesh]. (2014, March 9). if the phrase #killallmen and/or the term "mansplainer" upsets you, you're actually upset at feeling othered. welcome to THIS world [Tweet]. Retrieved from https://twitter.com/codemesh/status /44275616943036416O.

Corman, J. [@joshcorman]. (2013, May 4). Resolved: If you've not seen "Fight Club" you're missing a huge piece of why #Anonymous is a bigger deal than you suspect [Tweet]. Retrieved from https://twitter.com/joshcorman/status/33087614325741 5681.

the exphilosopher. [@tumblesweed]. (2012, June). [Tweet]. Retrieved from https:// twitter.com/tumblesweed.

Foucault, M. (2010). *The archeology of knowledge and the discourse on language.* New York, NY: Vintage Books. (Original work published 1972)

Heaven. [@HeavenMacArthur]. (2013, December 16). But really who wrote me on my tumblr as anon? I know like 4 people who call me fag just about everytime we talk. Lol [Tweet]. Retrieved from https://twitter.com/heavenmacarthur/status /412636229180481536.

Hutchinson, L. (2013). *The Internet, anonymous, and our public identities: Recreating democracy* (Unpublished master's thesis). California State University San Bernardino, San Bernardino.

Inkosikazi, I. [@AnonyNewsNet]. (2013, April 30). A desire for privacy does not imply shameful secrets . . . without anonymity in discourse, free speech is impossible & hence also democracy [Tweet]. Retrieved from https://twitter.com /anonynewsnet/status/329221311320707073.

Inkosikazi, I. [@AnonyNewsNet]. (2013, April 30). The right to speak truth to power does not shield one from the consequences of doing so; only comparable power or anonymity can do that [Tweet]. Retrieved from https://twitter.com/anonynewsnet /status/329221293859827715.

Kilgoar. [@kilgoar]. (2013, May 28). You Anons might think it's really cute to "fag" this and "faggotry" that but to everyone else you just look like a homophobic bigot. [Tweet]. Retrieved from https://twitter.com/Kilgoar/status/339520843543617536

Moreno, M. [@MacMoreno]. (2014, March 5). Sorry, guys, had to take a call. https:// twitter.com/macmoreno/status/441354571701448704 [Tweet]. Retrieved from https://twitter.com/macmoreno/status/441359292638056448.

Muñoz, J. E. (1999). *Disidentifications: Queers of color and the performance of politics.* Minneapolis, MN: University of Minnesota Press.

Reader, B. (2012). Free press vs. free speech? The rhetoric of "civility" in regard to anonymous online comments. *Journalism & Mass Communication Quarterly, 89*(3), 495–513.

Rhodes, J. (2002). "Substantive and feminist girlie action": Women online. *College Composition and Communication, 54*(1), 116–142.

Royster, J. J. & Kirsch, G. E. (2012). *Feminist rhetorical practices: New horizons for rhetoric, composition, and literacy studies.* Carbondale, IL: Southern Illinois University Press.

SwallowMode. [@SwallowRedux]. (2014, June 5). Twitter: my life as an accidental hamster [Tweet].

Urbanski, S. (2011). The identity game: Michel Foucault's discourse-mediated identity as an effective tool for achieving a narrative-based ethic. *The Open Ethics Journal, 5.* Retrieved from https://benthamopen.com/contents/pdf/TOJ/TOJ-5-3.pdf.

Warner, M. (2005). *Publics and counterpublics.* New York, NY: Zone Books.

Witchy [@nagoul1]. (2013, April 28). A lot of #AnonCulture was created right here on #twitter by you. #Anonymous [Tweet]. Retrieved from https://twitter.com/nagoul1/status/328587358511452160.

Witchy [@nagoul1]. (2013, April 28). #Anonymous evolved from an idea into a movement and then into a form of cultural expression in 2011. #AnonCulture [Tweet]. Retrieved from https://twitter.com/nagoul1/status/328584575846580225.

Witchy [@nagoul1]. (2013, April 28). In just a few years the #anon mask become recognized worldwide, even in places that don't have internet access #AnonCulture #Anonymous [Tweet]. Retrieved from https://twitter.com/nagoul1/status/328581606019325952.

Witchy [@nagoul1]. (2013, April 28). Many #anons are writers, musicians, designers, visual artists, DJs, movie directors, street artists and pop culture-makers. #AnonCulture [Tweet]. Retrieved from https://twitter.com/nagoul1/status/328585527672578049.

Witchy [@nagoul1]. (2013, April 28). We became the new culture of resistance spreading worldwide in 2011 when #anon became an integral part of mainstream culture. #Anonoculture [Tweet]. Retrieved from https://twitter.com/nagoul1/status/328593864711614465.

Witchy [@nagoul1]. (2013, April 28). We occasionally do have some domestic disputes *giggles*, but we are—first and foremost—a worldwide family. #Anonculture #AnonFam [Tweet]. Retrieved from https://twitter.com/nagoul1/status/328588087477276674.

Witchy [@nagoul1]. (2013, April 28). We're often labeled as a "hacker group." About 10–15% of us are hackers, and as far as I know there are about 120–150 "groups." #Anonymous [Tweet]. Retrieved from https://twitter.com/nagoul1/status/328583932515860480.

Witchy [@nagoul1]. (2013, April 28). Why is it #AnonCulture? Because we already have our own language, art, music, videos, news and many other forms of expressions. #anonymous [Tweet]. Retrieved from https://twitter.com/nagoul1/status/328582034748489728.

CHAPTER 11
INDIGENOUS INTERFACES

Kristin L. Arola
Washington State University

This is a story about what happens when college-aged American Indians are asked the question, "What would Facebook look like if it were designed by and for American Indians?"[2] This story emerges from my embodied experiences as a Finnish and Ojibwa woman, and my desire for digital spaces where I can compose myself and my relations with rhetorical sovereignty (Lyons, 2000). This story also emerges from my own explorations of how the design of online spaces invites certain ways of being and understanding (K. L. Arola, 2010, 2011, 2012). While I continue to believe the design of online spaces is rhetorical and does encourage certain compositional affordances and relations between and amongst users, I'm less inclined than I once was to believe in the rhetorical sway of interface design itself. That is, while an interface can encourage certain uses, this small study illustrates how the visual design of an interface, in this case the social media interface, does not necessarily imply one set of compositional affordances. Instead, visual design is only one element within the web of relations within which communication and representation occur.

Not so long ago, I returned to my hometown in order to attend the Spirit of the Harvest Powwow—a powwow sponsored by my alma mater, Michigan Technological University, and largely attended by members of the Keweenaw Bay Indian Community Lake Superior Band of Chippewa Indians, one of whom includes my mother, a powwow jingle dancer (among other things). I spent a week with Michigan Tech's American Indian student group attending regalia-making workshops, helping make frybread for the powwow, and interviewing powwow participants (both dancers and those organizing the event) about their cultural crafting practices. While my work was most focused on material crafting practices, I concluded most interviews with the question, "What would Facebook look like if it were designed by and for American Indians?" Overall, I interviewed twelve people, and while these results are of course by no means representative of one fixed American Indian worldview, I share here the answers in order to problematize a conception of race and representation based solely on

---

2   Within my own tribe, "theory" as we know it within academe is generally told through stories. This is common within indigenous cultures. See M. Powell et al. (2014).

the visual; as well, I interrogate the compositional affordances encouraged by the visual design of a social media interface.

RACE AND THE INTERFACE

The idea of an ideological rhetorical interface—that is, that the design of a digital space persuades users to engage in particular actions, representations, and relations, and that it is always already embedded in existing belief systems—is not new. Consider Cynthia L. Selfe and Richard J. Selfe's (1994) exploration of the ways in which graphical user interfaces are always political and ideological, or Anne F. Wysocki and Julia I. Jasken's (2004) look at the rhetorical work of the interface, or Teena A. M. Carnegie's (2009) understanding of the interface as exordium. Those of us who work with digital rhetorics understand that interfaces are value-laden and work to position us and relate us to information, ideas, and each other in particular ways.

I've argued before that "the act of composing a [social media] profile is an act of composing the self" (K. L. Arola, 2010, p. 8). I would add that the act of composing *within* a social media space—be it to post a picture, respond to a posted link, post a status update, etc.—is also an act of composing the self in relation to, and with, other people and ideas. However, the fixed template-driven design of most social media platforms appears to limit the ways in which one is able to compose oneself and one's relations online. Lisa Nakamura (2002, 2007) has done a good deal of work exploring the ways in which race and representation are figured and refigured through the use of digital media. Nakamura and Peter Chow-White (2011) have argued that "the digital is altering our understandings of what race is as well as nurturing new types of inequality along racial lines" (p. 2). Nakamura (2002) has suggested that this inequality comes, in part, through cybertyping, or a menu-driven identity whereby certain prefixed racial categories are available for one to choose from when composing the online self. Her claims about race online—that it doesn't simply go away but is reinscribed with similar baggage from offline spaces—hold true today. However, her work on menu-driven identities is now a bit dated. While it was true in early versions of MySpace and Friendster that one was encouraged to define oneself from a limited set of racial categories, Facebook doesn't even have a category for race or ethnicity. The categories Facebook does have for self-identification, such as language, religious views, and political views, include both drop-down options and the ability to both fill in the blank and add a description. Additionally, there is no requirement that one fill out these categories to have a profile. You can simply ignore them. The menu-driven identity of Nakamura's early 2000s Internet is no longer as visibly fixed as it was once, but the choices a social media site offers afford particular types of representations and relations.

Rhetoric and composition's exploration of the ideological interface, along with Nakamura's exploration of race online, both suggest that the design of online spaces function from a "white as default" premise, as well as an arguably straight and male premise (Alexander, 2002, 2005; Alexander & Banks, 2004; Barrios, 2004; Blair & Takayoshi, 1999; McKee, 2004; Rhodes, 2002, 2004). This interface presumes a monolithic user. I asked the question, "what would Facebook look like if it were designed by and for American Indians?" as I was curious how this supposed default white position presumed by many digital cultural scholars was understood by American Indians themselves. Would they imagine a space differently? And if so, how?

BEING/SEEING INDIAN

In asking what Facebook would look like if it were designed by and for American Indians, I was largely relying on the assumption that visual design guides a user's composing practices in a space. That is, I was thinking that were a social media interface to "look" a certain way, it would attract a specific set of users and would enable a specific set of uses. I presumed that an interface could, in some ways, *be* Indian. Within American Indian Studies as it is found in the halls of academe, as well as American Indian thought generally, there is an ongoing tension between this sense of *being* Indian and *doing* Indian. Ellen Cushman (2008) suggested this shift from *being* Indian to *doing* Indian so as to move the focus of "Indianness" away from preoccupations with blood quantum and phenotype, and toward issues of what's at stake and for whom when Indianness is categorized in particular ways.[1] Similarly, in interrogating the notion that there is something identifiable and representable to *being* Indian, Scott Richard Lyons (2010) reframed the question, "what is an Indian?" to "what should an Indian do?" This shift from *being* to *doing* "would mean a move away from conceptions of Indians as 'things' and toward a deeper analysis of Indians as human beings who *do* things" (p. 59). In short, the presumption that one can *be* Indian tends to fall prey to notions of the visible as a burden of proof. For example, one must

---

1   Blood quantum, a colonized conception of race, remains a frequent battleground for Indianness. The question "so how Indian are you?"—as though a certain percentage will satisfy someone's desire for one to be a "real" Indian—exemplifies this problem. Meanwhile, tribes have varying requirements for quantum, some requiring ¼ or ½ to enroll as a tribal member, whereas other tribes focus on lineage (if a direct descendent is on the Dawes Roll, you can enroll). This "proving" of race, be it through percent blood or a family name on a document, has been interrogated and challenged by many native scholars (Bizzaro, 2004; Garroutte, 2003).

have a certain skin tone, a certain color and length of hair, and be adorned in the proper jewelry to be *seen as* Indian.

Given the visible burden of proof that many Natives live with on a daily basis, it's perhaps not surprising that the most common answer I heard to my Facebook question referred to the four colors important to most tribes.[2] [3] Five respondents simply answered, "Red, black, white, and yellow." Another suggested it would "definitely [be] colorful, I know that one. . . . It would definitely have deeper meaning." And yet another respondent described that "I think you'd definitely have the four colors somewhere associated with it, probably eagle feathers, and, um, just overall . . . more colorful instead of the typical blue and white." These answers provide a seemingly straightforward visible way to envision how Indianness might be represented through an interface. That is, the use of a specific design element recognizable as Native—be it the four colors or an iconic image like a feather or medicine wheel—suddenly makes the site visibly Indian. Rather than the colorful feathered design suggested by these respondents (a design that to them would make Facebook feel more Indian), the design elements of many social media sites—from LinkedIn to Facebook to Instagram to Twitter—use "the typical blue and white." While the template can be changed in some sites, the default design is blue and white. In fact, these colors are so common that in some ways they become nearly invisible. While perhaps a bit audacious of a claim, in some ways blue-and-white interfaces function as the white privilege of online design. For those who enjoy its benefits, it remains invisible, a means to an end, a way of doing and being that is normalized and routinized into everyday digital practice. Similar to Dennis Baron's (2009) idea that writing technologies become invisible as we acclimate to them, or Michel Foucault's (1991) broader claims that power becomes invisible as it is diffused and embodied through discourse, the design of interfaces becomes an invisible background upon which we compose ourselves—invisible, at least, to those for whom it feels a natural space within which to interact. As Paula S. Rothenberg (2008) described of white privilege, "Many [whites] cannot remember a time when they first 'noticed' that they were white because whiteness was, for them, unremarkable. It was everywhere" (p. 2). Yet for those who desire another type of space, another way of being, this blue-and-white interface can in fact be very visible.

---

2   If you claim to be Native but don't phenotypically present as dark-haired, dark-skinned, and appropriately adorned, be prepared to be told by white folks, "but you don't look Indian."

3   Most North American tribes hold culturally important the four directions and ascribe four colors to those directions. Each direction and color comes with its own teachings and stories. My own tribe uses yellow (east), red (south), black (west), and white (north); however, other tribes (including the Navajo) use blue, white, yellow, and black.

When faced with the question of how an interface might visibly welcome a defined population of users such as American Indians, the normalized blue-and-white interface becomes visible. On the one hand, this visibility is important in that it helps us see and interrogate the design of our interfaces. Blue and white is a genre convention for social media design, and it's worth considering whom this genre convention supports. On the other hand, when the normalized interface is called into question and placed against the notion that it is somehow *not* American Indian, it is not particularly surprising that the answer to my question "what would an American Indian interface look like" became "white, yellow, red, and black." For if my question assumes that the current Facebook interface is somehow *not* Indian (and I think it does), then it asks the participant to describe what Indian looks like as represented through a visual design. The four colors and an eagle feather serve as a visible promise of Indianness.

Using particular images as a representation of American Indians speaks to Gerald Vizenor's (1999) understanding of the category "Indian" as an absence. For as he described, "Indians are simulations of the discoverable other . . . the simulations of the other have no real origin, no original reference, and there is no real place on this continent that bears the meaning of that name" (as cited in Vizenor & Lee, 1999, p. 85). The Indian as a category that bears quantifiable meaning, meaning imbued from the outside (though sometime also the inside), is a product of colonization. The absence of "Indian" as One Real Thing is often filled with stereotypical images such as the warrior or the Indian princess, or sometimes with a visual metonymy such as the teepee or the peace pipe.[4] Granted, these symbols do often carry significant meaning within particular tribes. Yet, assuming one symbol, such as the teepee, or one set of colors can stand in for "Indian" and thus represent all native peoples is a rhetorical act of colonization.

The visible is not necessarily a promise of any one identity. In discussing issues of racial passing in the African American community, Amy Robinson (1994) described that "in hegemonic contexts, recognition typically serves as an accomplice to ontological truth claims of identity in which claiming to tell who is or is not passing is inextricable from knowing the fixed contours of a passing identity" (p. 722). For, as she argued, "the 'problem' of identity, a problem to which passing owes the very possibility of its practice, is predicated on the false promise of the visible as an epistemological guarantee" (p. 716). The promise of the visible in an interface, while not exactly the same thing as a physical passing (though in many ways still embodied) becomes a question of how and if design carries with it an implied race and ethnicity. And, more specifically, it assumes

---

4   That is, there is not one type of person who can stand in for what American Indian looks like, is, and does. We can't necessarily point to one image and declare, "THAT is an Indian."

there are clear visible choices that guarantee Indianness. I believe we should interrogate our interfaces and question any system that becomes so normalized so as to be invisible, yet I am hesitant to say that American Indians cannot and do not make a white-and-blue interface their own. In fact, there is a long history of post-colonized American Indians taking agency over new technologies. As Kade Twist (2000) described, "Indian people have always made new technologies reflect their own respective world views." That being said, as Angela M. Haas (2005) asserted, there is a great "rhetorical and cultural value of online digital rhetorical sovereignty" for American Indians. That is, there is power in composing the self within a design of one's own making.

To be fair, it is entirely possible that the participants who suggested that a Facebook designed by and for American Indians would include images of eagle feathers or the four colors were speaking from a tribal sensibility whereby these images are incredibly significant for many of their own spiritual practices. And, in this way, these visual cues in an interface may signify a space that is native-friendly. Yet, such answers indicate a somewhat serious problem—not so much with the answers themselves, but instead with my question. My question, "what would Facebook look like if it were designed by and for American Indians?" presumes that, first, it is not; second, it led participants down a path whereby I requested a visible promise of Indianness. I suggested that there was a way that one can *be* Indian and thus be visibly recognized through an interface.

While in some ways different than a body physically appearing "Indian"—be it through phenotype or wearing the right clothes or jewelry—the idea that a design can be Indian is intimately connected to issues of embodiment and race. Many native scholars have discussed in great detail the issues surrounding American Indian identity and representation (Clifton, 1990; P. Deloria, 1998; V. Deloria, 1990, 1998; Garroutte, 2003; Mihesuah, 1996). While not always in full agreement, these scholars do agree that stereotypical visual representations—the noble savage, the wise medicine man, the Indian maiden—serve to distance, or in Malea Powell's (2002) words, "unsee" the contemporary Indian. As native artist and scholar Erica Lord (2009) described, these images function as "an attempt (even if unconscious) to keep the Native in the past, easily recognizable, simple, and, essentially, separate and different from 'us'" (p. 315). An interface tailored to visually appeal to one set of users falls prey to similar issues, as it suggests an interface can embody a recognizable and uncomplicated visual racial identity.

Returning to Lyons' (2000, 2010) and Cushman's (2008) suggestions that we understand Indianness as something one *does* (that is, through a certain set of actions or relations) as opposed to something one *is* (through being a certain skin tone or blood quantum) shifts how we understand race as embodied, and also shifts how we might understand the interface as visually composed for one set of users. Acknowledging how one might go about *doing* Indian instead of *being* recognizable as Indian via the interface suggests a rephrasing of my question from "what would Facebook *look* like?" to "what would Facebook allow you to *do?*" In spite of not asking this question, this is precisely how some respondents answered.

DOING/ACTING INDIAN

Carnegie (2009) asked us to think of the interface as an exordium in the ways that Cicero envisioned the exordium; that is, an interface can exist to make the audience/user "well-disposed, attentive, and receptive" and "open to persuasion" (p. 171). Thinking about the Facebook interface as exordium, as something that might persuade us to represent ourselves in a self-determined way, or relate to one another in particular ways, then my question about an American Indian interface should focus less on *being* Indian and more on how the interface positions American Indians and what it allows them to do.

The concept of *doing* Indian still contains the possibility of essentializing what counts as Indian insofar as certain actions (powwow dancing, basket weaving, wild ricing, etc.) might be seen as something a Real Indian does. As one respondent described, laughing, "it would look ghetto, and what I mean by ghetto [laughs] is that it wouldn't look like a white person designed it! It would have 'teepee creepin' as an option for your away message, 'snaggin' would also be an option, all the status updates would be about frybread, going outside, eating frybread, making frybread, chillin' at someone's house." While partially a tongue-in-cheek answer given how often the respondent laughed during this answer, there is a sense here that certain actions equate with Indianness. What I find interesting about this answer is that she considers both the interface design—options related to her sense of what American Indians do—as well as the content that people post within the interface. Similarly, another respondent suggested how the interface might allow users to compose themselves and their relations in ways important to American Indians (specifically Ojibwe): "Creating ways that it could allow for Ojibwemowin or different cultural stuff, like the sharing groups . . . that'd be nice." In both cases, the respondents imagine an interface that doesn't necessarily look a certain way but that allows and encourages certain actions important to a group of people. Another respondent appeared excited by the idea that a social media site might be designed by and for someone like him, and after spending a few seconds smiling and pondering, he said, "I think it'd be neat, it definitely wouldn't be, um, so formal." I wasn't clear at first if he meant the design or the content, but in a follow-up question it became clear he wished for a social media space where users would be more playful and informal, not trying so hard to compose a perfect and uncomplicated sense of self.

The idea that a social media site wouldn't be so formal, would allow for various cultural connections between people, would have built-in away messages that use the vernacular of many American Indians, and would allow for the use of native languages indicates that some respondents understood the idea of a space designed *for* a certain group to mean much less about *looking* American Indian and more about *doing* (even if in a bit of a tongue-in-cheek way, as the "ghetto" response implied). Lyons' (1996) work on rhetorical sovereignty seems particularly apt in considering what American Indians might want from composing within social media. Lyons asked a broader question of composing: What do American Indians want from writing? His answer is "rhetorical sovereignty," which he defines as "the inherent right and ability of *peoples* to determine their own communicative needs and desires in this pursuit, to decide for themselves the goals, modes, styles, and languages of public discourse" (pp. 449–450, emphasis in original). In describing sovereignty as it relates to Indian nations, Lyons suggested that "the sovereignty of individuals and the privileging of procedure are less important in the logic of a nation-people, which takes as its supreme charge the sovereignty of the group through a privileging of its traditions and culture and continuity" (p. 455). That is, the individual's communicative acts gain importance as they are understood as furthering, and positively transforming and sustaining, the group's culture. A space that affords and encourages American Indians to compose and relate in a self-determined way, one that supports and sustains one's culture, seems an important way of *doing* Indianness within a social media space.

In addition to affording rhetorical sovereignty, a social media interface that is welcoming to American Indians would also allow for a sense of relationality. As perhaps a side note, but worth mentioning as I am somewhat flattening indigenous epistemology to be one thing (tribal customs and belief systems do vary), consider American Indian philosopher Viola F. Cordova's (2007) suggestion that while tribes do certainly vary, this doesn't mean the category of American Indian is an empty one. She suggested that while at the beginning of the colonization of the Americas, "there was no such thing as the singular notion of all indigenous peoples being 'Indians,' there is now such a thing" (p. 102). She went on to state that

> this has come about through the fact that Native Americans find that, despite forced attempts to assimilate them conceptually as well as physically, they have more in common with other indigenous groups, regardless of their obvious differences,

than they do with the conceptual framework of the European colonizer. So it is possible to identify some of the conceptual commonalities shared by Native Americans. (p. 102)

Cordova suggested that one of these conceptual commonalities is the idea of relatedness: "A statement that 'all things are related' reminds us that we are not separate from all other things and that our actions have far-reaching consequences" (p. 30). Phillip J. Deloria (1999) echoed this notion, saying that "everything in the natural world has relationships with every other thing and the total set of relationships that make up the world as we experience it" (p. 34). These relations and the "we" within these relations are not static, nor are they relegated to just humans. Everything is related, and our place within these relations is constantly shifting. Issues of identity and truth are terms best understood through how we conceive of our relations. In most native thought, "the identity of any particular entity in the world can never be discovered by distilling the essence out of a particular object such that one could arrive at an eternal *eidos* that shines out of this particular encapsulation; rather, identity emerges through the constant act of relating" (A. Arola, 2011, p. 567, emphasis in original). While we can't know what an American Indian is insofar as we might want to perceive him/her as an autonomous entity in the world, we can know ways of being and doing that tend to be more enacted within Native cultures. One of these fundamental ways of being and doing is acknowledging the web of relations that make us who we are.

If enacting Indianness involves understanding oneself within a web of relations, then an American Indian interface would acknowledge these relations, and acknowledge that our selves, our families, our cultures, our homelands are only knowable insofar as we have an understanding of the whole in which the thing participates. That is, "the universal is (rejected) in lieu of knowledge of the network that [the thing] sustains, and that in turn sustains [the thing itself]" (A. Arola, 2011, p. 567). An American Indian interface, then, isn't so much about visually presenting as Indian as it is about doing Indian, about encouraging composing practices within a preexisting and shifting web of relations. This type of interface would afford opportunities for rhetorical sovereignty, for one to compose and understand oneself within a web of relations where things only have meaning insofar as they are connected to other things.

THE INDIGENOUS NETWORK: BEING AND DOING

Shortly after my interviews with powwow participants about what an American Indian Facebook would look like, I received a request from a native friend to join the Indigenous Network. The Indigenous Network was a social networking site "powered by the indigenous to share their culture and promote solidarity" (Indigenous Network, n.d.). Essentially, it was a social networking site designed by and for American Indians and other indigenous peoples. Angelica Chrysler, from the Delaware Nation in Ontario, Canada, created the site as a way for native communities to reach out to each other "inspiring action for common goals" (Indigenous Network, n.d.).

In many ways the site looked and acted like a more flexible version of Facebook (see Figures 11.1 and 11.2).

Figure 11.1: Main Page of Indigenous Network.

Similar to Facebook, users had a home screen that displayed other user activities (Figure 11.1). The design used blue and white but also included a banner photo of an eagle wing, providing both the genre expectation for color on a social media site as well as a visible promise of Indianness. Users also had a profile page that displayed activity directly posted by and to the user herself (Figure 11.2). Unlike Facebook, however, a user could choose her profile template (notice mine used a concentric leaf pattern) and, similar to the MySpace options of the early 2000s, it was also incredibly easy to post and share music. The media (such as music, art, or videos) that a user posted were automatically accessible to all users for viewing and listening. Additionally, the activities— including the media posted by users—displayed on the home screen were from all users of the network, not just those designated as one's friends in the network. This sharing from one-to-many both on the home screen itself (what the design affords) and the links themselves (what the functionality affords) embodied a very indigenous sensibility. It automatically put one in relation to others in the space, even if you hadn't actively made someone a friend. You were, by nature of being there, visibly part of something bigger than yourself.

Figure 11.2: My Indigenous Network profile page.

This interface not only put one in a visible relationality with others, it relied on a built-in spirit of sharing and reciprocity. As Cordova (2007) explained, one aspect of a Native American worldview is questioning "what is the good of having anything if you can't share it?" (p. 65). Sharing is necessarily related to the notion of being-in-relation insofar as, as Cordova explained, "If humans were solitary individuals, then there would be no need for cooperative behavior and there would be no social groups. . . . it is 'natural' for humans to be cooperative"

(p. 184). And while she used the term "humans" here, she defined this characteristic as an ethical rule of Native American society, which she set against a Western/Christian perspective. Not that those raised in the latter can't, and don't, learn to be otherwise. Yet, the idea of a sharing society is in many ways an indigenous way of being, and was a way of being embraced by the Indigenous Network. One's postings were constantly in-relation-to everyone else's. I find this aspect of the design and functionality to be inspiring and exciting, yet much of it was possible because of the small numbers of Indigenous Network participants. (Imagine seeing every link *every* single Facebook user posted!)

In May 2012 there were 257 Indigenous Network users. While there was nothing preventing non-indigenous users from using the space, all participants had, up until this point, filled in the question, "What Nation/Tribe are you from?", leading me to believe that all users were indigenous. There is power in affinity groups and cultural empowerment, and a space designed by and for indigenous users definitely has its place. Yet, unfortunately, this limited audience for the site is where the Indigenous Network broke down for me. It took me a while to notice, but after eagerly signing up, I realized I would go weeks at a time without checking the Indigenous Network; those weeks became months, and truthfully until I started writing this chapter in spring 2013 it had been six months since I last logged in. I noticed that my friend who invited me to join has not logged on in over 11 months. And today, as I continue working on this chapter in 2015, I came to discover the Indigenous Network is no more. It folded in April 2013, lasting only two years. The space, while intriguing at the onset, did not keep our attention. In spite of appearing to be and do Indian, it was not an online place to call home.

FACEBOOK AS ALWAYS ALREADY INDIGENOUS?

So if stand-alone social networking sites like the Indigenous Network aren't sustainable, can preexisting social media sites provide a space for rhetorical sovereignty? While seven of my interview participants provided answers that suggested a design could somehow be Indian, and three suggested a site could somehow enact Indianness, two participants challenged the notion that a site designed by and for American Indians would look any different. One looked a bit perplexed at my question, answering, "Honestly, I think it would look exactly the same as it looks now." Another elaborated on this point by saying that "Natives are pretty good at taking existing technologies and using them to their advantage, so I guess I don't really know if it would be different." At the time I found these answers curious, but the more I've worked with and reflected on this material, the more these answers make perfect sense.

Being raised by an indigenous mother and a father of European descent in a Western culture means I tend to have a mixed way of being. Yet, my mother's influence was quite strong and I do often find myself, for better or for worse, understanding myself as I exist in relation to and with the world around me. I often find it difficult to disentangle myself from the larger community of which I'm a part. For example, I recently met with my chair to discuss taking on a larger administrative function in the department. He asked if I really wanted the job, and I described in detail how I only wanted it if it what was best for the department and for our students. He kept returning to the question, "but do *you* want it?" I honestly found it impossible to answer this question without returning to understanding myself as but a piece in the larger whole. I found myself exclaiming to my chair, "but I don't exist apart from this!" Returning to Adam Arola's (2011) description of indigenous thought: "The universal . . . is [rejected] in lieu of knowledge of the network that [the thing] sustains, and that, in turn, sustains [the thing itself]" (p. 567). The network that sustains me, that I cannot understand myself without, changes based on my particular context, but it often includes my colleagues, the 26 people I went to school with from K-12 in a small rural town in Upper Michigan, my immediate and extended family, my college roommates, my first boyfriend, my graduate school buddies, my coauthors, my students, my friends both old and new. This network also includes my hometown, Lake Superior, the Palouse hills, the chickadees, the magpies, the black bear, my dog, the pool I swim laps in, my car, my laptop, and all the others. This network is large and shifting, and at different times in different places it functions in different ways. Yet this is my network, and nearly all of the humans from this network exist on Facebook. When I compose on Facebook, the interface positions me in relation with my relations, thus making Facebook for me an arguably indigenous space, one that provides a sense of being-in-relation to one another and sharing amongst these relations.

If we think about Indianness as something that one does instead of something that one is, and if we think about those characteristics that distinguish indigenous cultures and epistemologies, we must also think of the interface not as something that can necessarily visually promise a sense of Indianness, but as something that allows for indigenous ways of being and doing. While the Indigenous Network's sharing functionality encouraged indigenous ways of being, separating oneself out from all of my relations—be they indigenous or otherwise—brackets my relations to one slice of who I am. The fact that the Indigenous Network is no more indicates I was not alone. And even though Facebook is a corporate entity designed within a Western culture, as the Seminole-Creek art historian Mary Jo Watson put it, "what makes Indian people so unique and so persistent is their ability to take foreign material, or a foreign technology, and make it Indian" (as quoted in Haas, 2005, n.p.). Similarly, Lyons (2010) described his conception of the x-mark (that is, the signature made by many American Indians on treaties) as "more than just embracing new or foreign ideas as your own; it means consciously connecting those ideas to certain values, interests, and political objectives, and making the best call you can under conditions not of your making" (p. 70). The interface is but one player in a web of relations, one that may not be of one's own making but can be put into relation with ideas, people, and the world in a very indigenous way. The act of posting a social networking profile allows, in danah boyd's (2007) words, users to "write themselves and their community into being" (p. 2). However, composing the self is never an act free of context. In the case of social networking, the interface provides a visual context wherein the self is composed. And while the interface affords certain opportunities and understandings—consider the Indigenous Network's entry page which visually represented all user's posts (a one-to-all relationship) versus a news feed in Facebook which visually represents a predefined subset of posts (a one-to-some relationship)—indigenous users will always already place themselves in-relation-to so long as a space allows for it.

What would Facebook look like if designed by and for American Indians? An American Indian interface doesn't necessarily have to be red, white, black and yellow, nor does it have to include eagle feathers, nor does it necessarily mean that one will talk about frybread (but it might) or that it will "have a point" (but it might) or that one will talk about teepee creepin' (but it might), but instead it means an acknowledgement of the network that I sustain, and that sustains me back. And, you know what my network looks like? It looks a lot like Facebook. Miigwetch.[5]

REFERENCES

Alexander, J. (2005). *Digital youth: Emerging literacies on the World Wide Web.* New York, NY: Hampton Press.

Alexander, J. (2002). Homo-pages and queer sites: Studying the construction and representation of queer identities on the World Wide Web. *International Journal of Sexuality and Gender Studies, 7*(2–3), 85–106.

Alexander, J. & Banks, W. P. (2004). Sexualities, technologies, and the teaching of writing: A critical overview. *Computers & Composition, 21*(1), 273–293.

Arola, A. (2011). Native American philosophy. In J. L. Garfield & W. Edelglass (Eds.), *The Oxford handbook of world philosophy* (pp. 562–573). New York, NY: Oxford University Press.

Arola, K. L. (2010). The design of web 2.0: The rise of the template, the fall of design. *Computers & Composition, 27*(1), 4–14.

5   Miigwech means "thank you" in Ojibwemowin.

Arola, K. L. (2011). Listening to see: A feminist approach to design literacy. *The Journal of Literacy and Technology, 12*(1), 65–105.

Arola, K. L. (2012). It's my revolution: Learning to see the mixedblood. In K. L. Arola & A. F. Wysocki (Eds.), *Composing(Media) = Composing(Embodiment)* (pp. 115–142). Logan, UT: Utah State University Press.

Baron, D. (2009). *A better pencil: Readers, writers, and the digital revolution.* New York, NY: Oxford University Press.

Barrios, B. (2004). Of flags: Online queer identities, writing classrooms, and actions horizons. *Computers and Composition, 21*(3), 341–361.

Bizzaro, R. C. (2004). Shooting our last arrow: Developing a rhetoric of identity for unenrolled American Indians. *College English, 67*(1), 61–74.

Blair, K. & Takayoshi, P. (1999). *Feminist cyberscapes: Mapping gendered academic spaces.* Stamford, CT: Ablex.

boyd, d. (2007). Why youth (heart) social network sites: The role of networked publics in teenage social life. In D. Buckingham (Ed.), *MacArthur foundation series on digital learning—Youth, identity, and digital media volume* (pp. 1–26). Cambridge, MA: MIT Press.

Carnegie, T. A. M. (2009). Interface as exordium: The rhetoric of interactivity. *Computers & Composition, 26*(2), 164–173.

Clifton, J. A. (1990). *The invented Indian: Cultural fictions and government policies.* New Brunswick, NJ: Transaction.

Cordova, V. F. (2007). What is the world? In V. F. Cordova, K. D. Moore, K. Peters, T. Jojola & A. Lacy (Eds.), *How it is: The Native American philosophy of V. F. Cordova* (pp. 100–106). Tucson, AZ: University of Arizona Press.

Cushman, E. (2008). Toward a rhetoric of self representation: Identity politics in Indian country and rhetoric and composition. *College Composition and Communication, 60*(2), 321–365.

Deloria, P. J. (1998). *Playing Indian.* New Haven, CT: Yale University Press.

Deloria, V. (1990). Comfortable fictions and the struggle for turf: An essay review of the invented Indian: Cultural fictions and government policies. *American Indian Quarterly, 16*(3), 397–410.

Deloria, V. (1998). *Custer died for our sins: An Indian manifesto.* Norman, OK: University of Oklahoma Press.

Foucault, M. (1991). *Discipline and punish: The birth of a prison.* London, England: Penguin.

Garroutte, E. M. (2003). *Real Indians: Identity and the survival of Native America.* Berkeley, CA: California University Press.

Haas, A. M. (2005). Making online spaces more native to American Indians: A digital diversity recommendation. *Computers and Composition Online.* Retrieved from http://www.cconlinejournal.org/Haas/sovereignty.htm.

Indigenous Network. (n.d.). Retrieved from http://indigenousnetwork.net/.

Lord, E. (2009). America's wretched. In M. S. T. Williams (Ed.), *The Alaska native reader: History, culture, politics* (pp. 309–317). Durham, NC: Duke University Press.

Lyons, S. R. (2000). Rhetorical sovereignty: What do American Indians want from writing? *College Composition and Communication, 51*(3), 447–468.

Lyons, S. R. (2010). *X-Marks: Native signatures of assent.* Minneapolis, MN: University of Minnesota Press.

Mihesuah, D. A. (1996). *American Indians: Stereotypes and realities.* Atlanta, GA: Clarity International Press.

McKee, H. A. (2004). "Always a shadow of hope": Heteronormative binaries in an online discussion of sexuality and sexual orientation. *Computers and Composition, 21*(1), 315–340.

Nakamura, L. (2002). *Cybertypes: Race, ethnicity, and identity on the Internet.* New York, NY: Routledge.

Nakamura, L. (2007). *Digitizing race: Visual cultures of the Internet.* Minneapolis, MN: University of Minnesota Press.

Nakamura, L. & Chow-White, P. L. (Eds.). (2011). *Race after the Internet.* New York, NY: Routledge.

Powell, M. (2002). Rhetorics of survivance: How American Indians use writing. *College Composition and Communication, 53*(3), 396–434.

Powell, M., Levy, D., Riley-Mukavetz, A., Brooks-Gillies, M., Novotny, M. & Fisch-Ferguson, J. (2014). Our story begins here: Constellating cultural rhetorics. *Enculturation: A Journal of Rhetoric, Writing, and Culture, 17*(1). Retrieved from http://www.enculturation.net/our-story-begins-here.

Rhodes, J. (2002). "Substantive and feminist girlie action": Women online. *College Composition and Communication, 54*(3), 116–142.

Rhodes, J. (2004). Homo origo: The queer manifesto. *Computers and Composition, 21*(2), 387–390.

Robinson, A. (1994). It takes one to know one: Passing and communities of common interest. *Critical Inquiry, 20*(4), 715–736.

Rothenberg, P. (2008). *White privilege: Essential readings on the other side of racism.* New York, NY: Worth.

Selfe, C. L. & Selfe, R. J. (1994). The politics of the interface: Power and its exercise in electronic contact zones. *College Composition and Communication, 45*(4), 480–504.

Twist, K. (2000, December 4). Four directions to making the Internet Indian. Retrieved from http://www.digitaldivide.net/articles/view.php?ArticleID=241.

Vizenor, G. & Lee, A. R. (1999). *Postindian conversations.* Lincoln, NE: University of Nebraska Press.

Wysocki, A. F. & Jasken, J. I. (2004). What should be an unforgettable face. *Computers & Composition, 21*(1), 29–48.

CHAPTER 12

THE INTIMATE SCREEN: REVISUALIZING UNDERSTANDINGS OF DOWN SYNDROME THROUGH DIGITAL ACTIVISM ON INSTAGRAM

Kara Poe Alexander and Leslie A. Hahner

Baylor University

When Christy and her husband Danny found out that their unborn child had Down syndrome (Ds), they were devastated. Their only knowledge about Ds at the time had come from the media's mostly negative portrayal. As a result, all their initial thoughts were negative and they feared the worst. These feelings transformed, however, when their daughter Bailey was born. After getting to know her, they realized how false their perceptions had been. Danny and Christy enjoyed life with Bailey so much that two years later they were on a plane to Lithuania to adopt another child with Ds—an almost-three-year-old girl named Abby who had lived all of her life in an orphanage. Largely because of her personal experiences, Christy has become an advocate for children with Ds and for the adoption of children with special needs. Her activist work is most visible on the social media platform Instagram (www.instagram.com/cjpics), a primarily visual site that allows users to post pictures and videos, compose captions, and create hashtags that link individuals and communities together. Christy's rhetorical purpose on Instagram is to overcome dominant, mostly negative perceptions of Ds perpetuated through the media and popular culture and to raise awareness.

In our rhetorical analysis of her CJPICS Instagram page, we find that Christy seeks to overcome these stereotypes by including images, captions, and hashtags that challenge viewers' understandings of Ds and that instill a sense of intimacy with her audience. In contrast to more direct forms of advocacy, Christy's activism is more understated and organic, encouraging viewers to change their misperceptions by recoding the unfamiliar into that which is known and celebrated. We suggest that such digital activism employs what we call the "intimate screen"—an extension of Kevin Michael DeLuca's and Jennifer Peeples' (2002) concept of the public screen—that cultivates a supportive, empathetic public through familiarity. Christy's purposeful engagement with social media encourages audiences to adopt new ways of understanding not only Ds but also the people defined by this label. We argue that Christy's intimate screen is a form of digital activism that invites the public into her life through personal imagery, thus undermining dominant perceptions of Ds and promoting special-needs adoption. Christy creates a community of like-minded individuals by visually and narratively transforming the foreignness of Ds into a life that is celebrated and familiar, reframing what it means to live with a disability. Extensive work has been conducted about the intersections of writing with disability studies (Brueggemann, 2001; Fox, 2013; Lewiecki-Wilson, 2003; Lewiecki-Wilson & Brueggemann, 2008; Price, 2011). This essay suggests one way that social media advocacy for children with disabilities can proceed, especially when the goal emphasizes awareness. We propose that digital activism with the goal of awareness can employ different rhetorical structures than direct political protest. We conclude by making applications from this study to digital activism through Instagram and other social media.

TOWARDS A THEORY OF THE INTIMATE SCREEN

Scholars have begun to interrogate how digital activism works and the ways it commonly mirrors grassroots protest. Inquiries into social media events such as the Arab Spring and Occupy Wall Street suggest that such activism is often explicitly political and effective through the quick circulation of information (Dadurka & Pigg, 2011; Eltantawy & Wiest, 2011; Howard & Parks, 2012; Khondker, 2011; Lotan, Graeff, Ananny, Gaffney & Pearce, 2011; McKee, 2011; Obar, Zube & Lampe, 2012; Tufekci & Wilson, 2012). More recent studies have begun to illuminate the unique features of social media activism, maintaining that such advocacy often operates via online networks that democratize media communication and thereby enable effective dissent (Buck, 2012; Carroll & Hackett, 2006; Forbes, 2014; Gerbaudo, 2012; Harb, 2011; Peary, 2014; Scott & Welch, 2014). In order to understand how media is imbricated in activism, DeLuca and Peeples (2002) introduced a productive supplement to the well-known concept of the public sphere, which describes the social formation of favored policies and mores. While the public sphere emphasizes the ways public talk shapes culture, the "public screen" accentuates the importance of media and dissemination. As they wrote, "Such a concept takes technology seriously. It recognizes that most important, public discussions take place via 'screens'—television, computer, and the front page of newspapers" (DeLuca & Peeples, 2002, p. 131). DeLuca and Peeples underscored that instead of talk, audiences come to understand major public issues largely through the circulation of images and videos. The imagistic aspect of the public must be accounted for in discussions about the social formation of culture. In particular, DeLuca and Peeples insisted that the public screen is an important component of effective twenty-first-century activism. Through the public screen, protestors can organize "image events," or staged acts of protest designed for mass media dissemination that dramatically expose injustice by garnering media attention to shock the audience (DeLuca, 1999). DeLuca and Peeples (2002) attended to the 1999 World Trade Organization protestors in Seattle who used violence to attract television news agencies to cover their cause. For these authors, this strategy anticipated the national media attention necessary to galvanize further activism. The lesson afforded by thinking about the public screen is that successful activism must contend with the constraints and opportunities of the mediums through which audiences come to understand their cause. In this regard, effective digital activism must grapple with the affordances of social media and the various screens users engage.

As such, we would reconfigure DeLuca and Peeples' concept by suggesting that Christy deploys an "intimate screen" as a form of digital activism. DeLuca and Peeples were writing in a time shortly before the explosion of social media and much of their discussion was focused on how the public screen aggregates mass attention. In the contemporary moment, however, screens are not solely directed at mass audiences. Indeed, most social network users—particularly for Facebook, Twitter, and Instagram—are engaging with these media on smaller, individualized screens such as smartphones and tablets. A number of studies and scholars have contended that smartphone users interact with these devices on a deeply personal level (Acheson, Barratt & Balthazar, 2013; Lambert, 2013; Perlow, 2013). To peruse social media or play games on these devices cultivates a particularly intimate relationship with the device and a mediated or mobile intimacy with friends and others (Hjorth & Richardson, 2014; Ito & Daisuke, 2005; Siebert, 2013). Given how users interact with social media, it behooves scholars to consider how digital activism engages with the privacy of the individualized screen. On our read, Christy deploys the personalization of digital devices in her rhetorical imaging strategies to cultivate an intimate public. These activist images and captions are not shocking image events that garner mass media attention like traditional forms of public screen activism. Rather, Christy's rhetorical imaging strategies assume an individual viewer interacting with her Instagram page in a particularly personal manner. Her visuals are serene, even quotidian, revealing the joy and contentment in raising children with Ds. As we will show, such tactics operate as a clandestine invitation that encourages the audience to feel at home, even comforted, by her depictions. Here, digital activism is not the mass spectacle of the public screen but rather an approach that impacts the viewer through familiarity and intimacy with her life.

In this chapter, we take seriously the way the audience accesses and experiences images. Because Instagram is designed for the smartphone, successful activist strategies must impact the viewer as she scrolls through a barrage of photographs. We argue that Christy's activism highlights several characteristics of intimate screen activism: the use of images that engender familiarity with Ds; images that counter misperceptions of Ds through their subject and depiction; the use of visually stunning or shocking images to aesthetically impact the viewer; and images that allow the viewer to peek in on the banal, creating a sense of identification with the cause. These strategies are devised to capture the personal attention of the smartphone viewer. In this way Christy's awareness campaign encourages viewers to see Ds differently and to become intimately invested in her family and their cause.

To better understand how Christy deploys the intimate screen, we collected data from Christy's Instagram page, including the images, captions, and hashtags she uses. We also conducted two interviews with Christy.[1] We coded the images and the interviews using a grounded theory approach (Glaser & Strauss, 1967; Strauss & Corbin, 1998) where we examined the data, identified common themes, and made generalizations about the rhetorical tactics Christy used. To analyze these data, we employed the tools of visual rhetorical analysis and grounded theory to demonstrate what activism that uses an intimate screen looks like. Cara A. Finnegan (2004) described visual rhetoric as a "project of inquiry that considers the implications for rhetorical theory of sustained attention to visuality" (p. 235). We use visual rhetorical analysis to consider how the images on Christy's page cultivate an intimacy with her audience while simultaneously encouraging that audience to see Ds differently. We attend to Christy's imaging tactics, which include the visual style and composition of the images on CJPICS, the specific appeals Christy uses, the relationship between the image and the accompanying text, and the themes that emerge in the photographs and videos.[2]

DEPLOYING THE INTIMATE SCREEN

Christy began using Instagram when it first appeared in 2010, mostly to document her son's and daughter's lives. However, when she and her husband

---

1   We first learned about Christy's Instagram page through Kara's sister. Kara started following Christy's page three years ago as Christy's family was adopting Abby.

2   We have secured appropriate IRB approval and Christy has given us permission to use her words and images. We use "CJPICS" to refer to the Instagram page; we use "Christy" to refer to the person who shapes the Instagram page.

adopted Abby from Lithuania in 2013, her page became much more focused on Ds and special needs adoption. Her current Instagram description reads, "Finding humor and experiencing joy every day as the mama to three extraordinary kids. Adoption and Ds have blessed our lives!" Through her posts and hashtags, Christy has gained a following. As of May 15, 2016, Christy has more than 21,000 followers on Instagram.

In much the same way as Christy and her husband discovered the truth of their new life with a Ds child, Christy invites her followers to rethink prevailing assumptions. Priya Lalvani (2008) argued that mothers of children with Ds commonly resignify the meaning of Ds in order to counter negative stereotypes. Likewise, Christy primarily uses Instagram to overcome the dominant perceptions and unnecessary anxieties about Ds that she readily admits she and her husband felt when they were told their unborn daughter had Ds. In this section, we illustrate how Christy counters these assumptions through her digital activism.

Our analysis highlights the characteristics of the intimate screen and the hashtags Christy employs by using these as section headings. On Instagram, hashtags classify content, enable users to search for particular sets of images, and as with CJPICS, create a sense of community when users adopt, search for, or click the hashtag link. Thus, we organize our analysis by highlighting the different modes of rhetorical activism at stake on CJPICS.

ENGENDERING FAMILIARITY: #DOWNSYNDROMEROCKS AND #DOWNSYNDROMELOVE

One of the main purposes of Christy's Instagram feed is to counter the notion that children with Ds are all that dissimilar from other children. An important aspect of her visual strategies is to illustrate the intelligence of her two daughters. The images posted on CJPICS do not simply announce the acumen of Christy's children but rather present everyday images that highlight how Abby and Bailey master early education tasks. In effect, her rhetorical tactics do not assert arguments or directly address misperceptions. Instead, her advocacy operates by inviting the viewer to engage with scenes that familiarize the audience with what it means to live with Ds and to recognize that her children's lives are filled with many of the same struggles and joys as other children.

In one short video from March 2014, Christy's three-year-old daughter, Abby, counts to ten. The scene is rather ordinary: the child faces a set of foam numbers and repeats the numbers as her mother prompts her. The shot is cropped to create a cozy vignette. The child's face remains out of the frame, with the camera pointed at the lower portion of her body. The framing of the image conveys the intimacy we argue is essential to Christy's advocacy. The tight cropping encourages the viewer to engage with the sheltered scene as though she were in that same moment. The realism of the video highlights the quotidian nature of the interaction. Similarly, the caption announces, "Abby counts!" with the hashtag #downsyndromelove. As emphasized by this hashtag, the scene is sweet, even charming—its warmth attracts viewers and asks them to see the child's accomplishments as typical. The intimacy of the scene enables the viewer to share that same triumph while the content of the video situates the child as a learning, intelligent pupil.

CJPICS also creates familiarity with her audience by showing the normalcy of her kids' lives. In most of the images presented on CJPICS, the girls are shown in common childhood activities. In one image from February 2014, Abby, Bailey, and two friends play with an interactive light wall while visiting a children's museum. Four girls with mesmerized faces are lined up at the exhibit. The image is grainy, shot by a smartphone camera while the photographer was moving. The quality of the image adds to the realism of the moment, positioning the viewer as peeking in on a typical day in the life of these children. The viewer finds herself not just an impartial observer but lucky enough to feel connected to these children and their private moments. Similarly, a video from January 2014 shows the girls sitting together in a plastic tub, giggling and being silly. The short film centers on the two girls and, much like the previous photograph, situates the viewer as secretly watching the world constructed between two imaginative children. These rhetorical imaging strategies counter the notion that children with Ds are different from other kids in negative ways. Instead, the viewer is encouraged to view these children with a sense of wonder—as original, clever, and curious children. Here, CJPICS emphasizes the precocity of her daughters through these intimate, connective moments.

COUNTERING MISPERCEPTIONS: #BRINGINGTHESUNSHINE AND #SOSTINKINGCUTE

In addition to challenging the perception that Ds is a burden by showing how her children are similar to other kids, Christy also uses Instagram to show how her daughters are unique. Linda Gilmore, Jennifer Campbell, and Monica Cuskelly (2003) argued that public perceptions of Ds indicate that many believe children with Ds have relatively similar personalities and are always happy and affectionate. Likewise, Christy's use of the intimate screen works by deploying images that counter the notion that children with Ds are all similar by showing the distinct personalities of her daughters and applauding their differences from other children. Christy regularly includes images and captions that show and describe their personalities and challenging moments categorized by #bringingthesunshine.

In one video, for instance, Christy shows the mischievous side of her daughter. She asks Bailey, "What do you want to eat?" Bailey replies, "Fries." Christy laughs and says, "What about something else that is more healthy?" Bailey says, "Cay-cay [candy]." Christy giggles again and says, "No, what else can we eat?" And Bailey repeats "cay-cay" over and over again with a big smile on her face while her mother laughs. The caption reads, "Her suggestions for an after-nap snack include fries and candy. What happened to the little girl that refused to eat sugar?!? #dailybailey #bringingthesunshine." Such posts underscore the idea that Bailey's sassy personality brings sunshine to her family and, by extension, to us. By focusing on her children's individual attributes, Christy redirects and challenges the viewer's understanding of Ds and of children with Ds.

When Christy uses the hashtag #bringingthesunshine, she often includes another hashtag with it: #sostinkingcute. In these posts, Christy highlights how the girls' appearance is actually a positive attribute, not something to be viewed as negative. Images with this hashtag demonstrate how cute she views her children to be—how her kids' eyes smile when they laugh; how their laughs are infectious; how the faces they make can brighten up a room; how flexible they are because of their syndrome; how even when they're in trouble, they're still grinning. Christy's emphasis on joy aims to challenge the notion that families with special needs children are miserable. Once again, Christy repeats one of the main misperceptions of Ds: that those living with Ds are always happy. Indeed, the vast majority of images on CJPICS show the girls smiling and laughing. Yet, her general tactics also emphasize the complexity of her children's emotions, the combination of happiness and deviousness, the difficult days spent in the hospital after surgeries, the cute arguments that emerge between her children, and the fits that can be thrown. Although her kids are young and have challenges still to come, Christy emphasizes how their physical appearance and sweet spirits bring joy and sunshine to those around them. Christy defies the perception that children with Ds are a burden. Not only are the lives of family members impacted by Ds not miserable or dismal, but they are actually happy, blessed, and lucky. This point is also indicated by her use of the hashtags #blessingnotburden and #theluckyfew. Throughout these imaging strategies, Christy uses the intimacy of the personal screen to connect to audiences and challenge their inaccurate assumptions. However, instead of explicitly condemning her viewers' assumptions, she uses intimacy to emphasize how fortunate she is to be raising these children, a strategy that invites her viewers to be less defensive or suspicious about Christy's motives.

USING STUNNING IMAGES: #ADOPTIONLOVE AND #SPECIALNEEDSADOPTION

Yet another goal for Christy includes the promotion of special needs adoption. While Christy is more explicit with her advocacy in this area, most of her rhetorical tactics are less assertive and often rely on the aesthetic appeal of the image or an appeal to her audience's emotions to make her case. For instance, in a post from June 2014, CJPICS presented an image of her daughter Abby from her Lithuanian identification card. Christy acknowledges, "This is only one of three pictures we have of her from before we started the adoption process." Yet instead of focusing on the child's living conditions or even her adoption process, Christy writes, "Oh my word! Those cheeks! That hair!! #adoptionlove #specialneedsadoption." Through the use of a still image, Christy can displace the anxieties surrounding international or special needs adoption by focusing on the cute infant. Thus, while the viewer may certainly know the obstacles involved in adoption and in the transition process, she can delight in the precious imagery presented. With this image, the intimacy of the personal device comes to the fore. Social media is well known for how users oversupply cute images of children. Christy certainly uses this strategy, but here the cute image emphasizes the happiness of adoption, not the larger system and difficulties at play, and appeals to the viewer's emotional capacities for sympathy. Thus, the intimate screen works as a form of advocacy by trafficking in charming photographs but shifting the focus to the positive aspects of international special needs adoption.

One of the strategies CJPICS uses to visually show how special needs adoption can change a life is to show side-by-side images of Abby before she was adopted and afterwards. Though they only have three images of Abby before they met her at the orphanage, the images are striking when compared to Abby after she was brought home. In the orphanage images, three-year-old Abby is rarely smiling, and her mouth turns downward. Her brown eyes seem empty, almost lifeless. She is well fed, well clothed, and cared for as well as the orphanage workers could, but she is often serious, cold, and withdrawn. Contrast this child with images even five months later where Abby is beaming, laughing, happy, and full of life. Her entire demeanor seems to have changed. Christy attributes this transition to being loved and wanted and, through stunning images, often pleads with her followers to consider adopting extraordinary children like Abby. Christy uses these stunning images to cause strong feelings of affection and sympathy in her viewers and hopefully move at least one person to act. In one particular side-by-side image comparison (see Figure 12.1), Christy writes,

> Honestly, until we were blessed with Bailey . . ., we were
> never interested in adopting. That was for families with more

money, more free time, [etc.]. But when we realized parenting a child with special needs was a blessing, not a burden, and then found out about all the children with Ds wasting away in orphanages across the world, how could we not say yes?

Figure 12.1. Abby in the orphanage and Abby with her new family. Reprinted with permission.

Christy's comparison photographs visually arrest the viewer, demonstrating that this child's life was dramatically changed through adoption. The point is to impact the viewer emotionally through glimpsing the visual change that occurred. Her appeal to pathos confirms the argument made by Bronwyn T. Williams in this collection that social media writers are concerned with emotional responses from their audience. As CJPICS has gained more followers, Christy's Instagram page now features other children with Ds who are available for adoption. Often, the images Christy selects are close-ups of children who could be adopted. The images center on the cute infant or are visually arresting images of children in need of help. One post from July 2014 shows two infants cuddled together in a Ukrainian orphanage. The close shots are similar to newborn photography, and the glow lens Christy uses gives the photographs a romantic air, a style that deploys intimacy to evoke viewers' affections. Christy likewise appeals to her followers when they have an opportunity to give financially. In one post, she features a three-month-old child with Ds named Finnley, showing an image of the baby in a hospital bed with tubes in his little body. After briefly telling his story, she writes: "One thing I love about this little IG community is how supportive everyone is, and this is a member of our community that could really use some support and encouragement. Will you please help me by reaching out to them?" Christy appeals to her followers on behalf of another "Ds mama" who reached out to Christy about her sick child. By highlighting the need for community support, she creates group identification for the cause.

In sum, much of Christy's activism and imaging strategies for special needs adoption focus on the joy of adoption. Children with Ds are not portrayed as helpless or difficult; instead, they are presented in visually stunning modes that encourage viewers to recognize the happiness entailed in growing alongside these children. Such images on the smaller, hand-held screen are intimate in that they connect the audience to Christy's family and her advocacy in a personal way. Much like a wallet photograph, the viewer can pull out her personal device and visually relate to this mother, her family, and her causes.

ENCOURAGING IDENTIFICATION THROUGH THE BANAL: #THELUCKYFEW AND #BLESSINGNOTBURDEN

Yet another aspect of the intimate screen is that the imagery is not shocking, but rather banal, quotidian. The point of such a tactic is to create identification between the viewer, the subject, and the larger cause. Such identification is important on social media platforms like Instagram because, except in cases where the page is set to private, anyone can follow a page, whether you know the person or not. As a result, strangers can find and follow pages (see Les Hutchinson in this collection for more on the stranger and anonymity online), and it is up to the social media user to keep them from unfollowing. For Christy, she keeps her followers by encouraging them to identify with her images. Much like other social media users, Christy rarely photographs the less appealing aspects of child rearing and family life, or if she does, it's to note the humor in the situation. Instead, her purpose is to familiarize the viewer with raising children with special needs. Bernie Hogan (2010) wrote that social media often enables users to curate their lives in ways that only exhibit positive qualities. With CJPICS, such an imaging strategy is not simply to aggrandize her own life but rather to present visual evidence that minimizes the negative perceptions of Ds. Christy uses photo-editing techniques that make her images charming and warm. She also uses glow filters, black-and-white photographs, cropping, and other tactics that highlight the happiness of her life, not the struggles. She occasionally overlays text or hashtags on photos to emphasize a particular point or to promote a hashtag she wants her viewers to see.

Throughout these imaging strategies, Christy rhetorically frames her life as an intimate scene that invites her viewers to rejoice with her rather than to pity her or her children. For instance, in May 2013, Christy posted an image of her daughter Bailey minutes after leaving the hospital. Bailey had been hospitalized for ten days with a respiratory illness. The shot is a close-up of Bailey's smiling face outside beside grass. The image is cropped with rounded edges, a technique that mimics photographs from the mid-twentieth century. On top of the photograph, Christy has included the word "freedom!" and a heart that looks as though it has been hand-drawn. While the viewer might be obliquely aware that children with Ds often experience respiratory conditions and are prone to infection, this image highlights the joyful aftermath of hospitalization. The child is grinning from ear to ear, and the viewer understands her life as difficult but joyful.

Another way Christy utilizes the intimate screen is by posting pictures of Abby and Bailey to encourage viewers to connect to her girls as individuals—to see them beyond their diagnosis—and also to nuance her audience's view of children with Ds. When the children achieve a new goal, Christy posts about it, praising them for their progress. Her praise then shows readers that these girls are working hard to grow and change: When they do reach a goal or overcome some difficulty, it is to be celebrated. Viewers are cheering for these girls to make progress rather than focusing on their differences from other children. Not only is this tactic persuasive rhetorically, but it also offers viewers a way to feel that they, too, are advocating for these issues. In one post from June 2014, Abby and Bailey are sitting in chairs in a waiting room eating popcorn and sitting in the same contorted position. Christy's caption reads: "Two little pretzels eating popcorn. #abbyandbailey #downsyndromelove." In this image, Christy tries to highlight the humorous aspect of one feature of Ds—flexibility. The viewer comes to see flexibility as a positive, and to see these children as more than their condition. Once again, the point is to foster identification between the audience and children.

Once she has helped to cultivate identification, Christy encourages the viewer to see Ds differently. In one image posted in February 2014, the girls are on a playground that has a divided slide (see Figure 12.2). Bailey is lying on her tummy on one side of the slide, poised to slide down headfirst. Abby is standing on the slide next to Abby, holding onto the rails and looking timidly down it.

Figure 12.2. Abby and Bailey going down the slide. Reprinted with permission.

Christy's caption reads, "One has an over abundance [sic] of caution and one has not a cautious bone in her body. But I'll never tell who is who. #abbyandbailey #downsyndromerocks." By describing each girl's approach to the slide, Christy shows how the girls are dissimilar. Readers are able to see Bailey as someone without fear and Abby as a girl who takes things a little more carefully, thus seeing them as individuals with distinct interests, personalities, and behaviors. Christy subtly shows how the girls are different, once again focusing on the "girls as people" rather than the "girls as their condition." In short, although Christy often uses the hashtag #morealikethandifferent to show how people with Ds are more similar to those without than we might think, she uses #abbyandbailey to point out how people with Ds are not all the same.

In these images, the strategy of identification through the banal is part of the overall activism of the intimate screen. The girls are shown doing everyday activities and while their Ds is noted as part of their unique personalities, the fact that they have Ds is not the main focus. Instead, the noticeable, distinct personalities of each girl come to the fore and allow readers to glimpse their individual charms, an important distinction to make for viewers unknowledgeable about people with Ds. Christy thus uses one rhetorical affordance of social media—the ability to make both visual and verbal comparisons—to make viewers not only empathetic with the girls about their condition but also to make us smile about their distinctive characteristics. Because viewers are engaging with these girls on a personal screen, they become further connected to them. In all, the intimate screen offers Christy a way to engage in digital activism in subtle, nuanced, and personal ways. By embracing familiarity, countering misperceptions, using stunning images, and celebrating banal scenes, Christy not only invites her audience into her life but she also seeks to develop awareness and connection. As such, her Instagram page is rhetorically persuasive.

DISCUSSION: ADVOCACY AND INSTAGRAM

As our analysis indicates, Christy uses an intimate screen to advocate for Ds and special needs adoption. By showing everyday pictures of her family's life and by including captions and hashtags that further elaborate on the image, she cultivates an intimate public that invites this audience to journey with her as she navigates what she calls "blessings" of both. All the while, these visual tactics aim to encourage her audience to revisualize people with Ds as individuals who can live vibrant lives and to be more knowledgeable about Ds. Furthermore, the understated way in which she encourages social change by sharing the private details of her life leaves space for viewers to change their perceptions without direct confrontation. Instead, the change comes by inviting the viewer to peek in on her life and feel connected to the happy, domestic scenes she includes.

In addition, Christy's Instagram account indicates her understanding of how this medium creates opportunities and constraints for advocacy. She has thousands of followers; each image she posts is liked by hundreds, and dozens offer written responses. More generally, we know that the more followers someone has, the more influential they can be (Bakshy, Mason, Hofman & Watts, 2011). Thus, activists who take technology seriously must consider how their audiences interact with them and how mediation changes their cause. Instagram is a unique site. Its market valuation at 35 million eclipses Facebook and Twitter with users that surpass 300 million (Alba, 2014). A December 2014 *Wired* article proclaimed Instagram's popularity as attributable to its reliance on photographs. Up against the recognition of the impersonal aspects of social networks—the bots that comprise millions of Twitter users, that Facebook is largely a conduit for data mining and advertising—the photographic aspects of Instagram seem more personal, more human (Woollaston, 2014). Christy understands all too well the power of the photograph and short video. The image allows the viewer to connect to her cause and her children on a personal, intimate level. Thus, in some sense Christy relies on the aesthetic appeal of the visual in order to cultivate a sympathetic public. Awareness changes via the intimate screen must invite the public to identify with the people in the images. In a broader sense, then, activists who wish to enact similar awareness campaigns must stylize photographs and videos with a similar appeal.

While Christy's rhetorical acumen is very different to that of traditional activism that requires mass attention and overt action, our analysis counters a number of authors who insist that social media networks merely birth clicktivism. Slacktivism and clicktivism are terms often applied to social media networks such as Facebook, Twitter, and even Instagram (Jeong & Lee, 2013; Portman-Daley, 2010, 2011; Scott & Welch, 2014). It is a term that suggests users of these sites are only invested in self-presentation, not participating in true activism. Christy's deployment of images on Instagram, by contrast, helps to change misperceptions of Ds. Indeed, the fact that Christy is working to change awareness of Ds might indicate one reason why her strategies are important. Given that Christy seeks to change perceptions that she once held, she understands all too well that what is needed is a more intimate understanding of Ds, which she is glad to provide. Recent research indicates that one of the most effective, inexpensive, and dramatic ways to change public perception is to foster a personal relationship between opposing viewpoints (Hocks, 1999; Issenberg, 2014). Such scholarship has argued that people change their opinions on same-sex marriage, abortion, and a whole host of hot-button issues if they know someone who can identify with the cause and tell their story (Issenberg, 2014). In this way, intimacy is a particularly important activist strategy particularly for awareness campaigns that are conducted via screens.

Significantly, Christy's deployment of the intimate screen does not often focus on direct change. Instead, her subtle techniques revisualize Ds. On her Instagram feed, Christy's children are not depicted as a burden; they are intelligent, creative, joyful, adorable individuals who complete their family. The viewer comes to see Christy's family as a happy one in which both children and adults thrive. With her hashtag #morealikethandifferent, Christy uses implicit comparison to rewrite the narrative that people with Ds have unique capabilities, interests, and personalities that make them distinct and that complicate the presumed sameness of all people with Ds. This approach and the visual imaging strategies Christy uses inspires viewers to see her children as human beings rather than as a genetic condition. As one of Christy's posts makes clear, she would like all people to see her kids as "just Bailey" or "just Abby." Indeed, Christy encourages the audience to see her children as individuals through how she visually creates a personal relationship with the viewer. Asimina Vasalou, Adam Joinson, and Delphine Courvoisier (2010) noted that photographs on Facebook prompted users to visit the site more often and to invest in it. They claim that more experienced users see photographs as dramatically important to their social network experience. Such an argument helps explain the exponential rise in the use of Instagram, whose daily smartphone users surpass Twitter (Russell, 2014). With CJPICS, the use of intimate imaging strategies doesn't simply increase use but rather works to congeal a community and build an advocacy network. By allowing viewers to glimpse daily life, CJPICS creates a new world where people can become more educated and reconsider their assumptions about the people impacted by Ds and special needs adoption.

The intimate screen, then, is a form of activism that works by inviting the audience to reconsider how they see particular peoples, issues, and causes. With Christy, that invitation is presented through photographs and videos that familiarize the viewer with Ds while countering misperceptions. In this sense, the intimate screen works by first acknowledging how users glimpse the images of Instagram and then recognizing that to affect viewers the image must prompt them to pause and engage with what is shown. Christy's Instagram feed is a significant rhetorical artifact because it highlights the visual architecture of such intimacy. Intimacy via screens can be fashioned by understanding the way viewers interact with their smartphones, by creating visually stunning images that engender familiarity and counter misperceptions, and by allowing viewers to identify with a story.

CONCLUSION

This brief analysis has only begun to illuminate the ways social media digital activism can cultivate intimate networked publics. Christy uses a less overt activist approach that redirects biases against Ds and encourages viewers to celebrate the unique personalities of her children—and, by extension, others with Ds. Importantly, Ds is a remarkably misunderstood condition that can constrain the opportunities for those living with Ds. The advocacy on CJPICS, then, is not simply an imaging strategy that shows how children with Ds live. Instead, these imaging strategies rejoice in the small miracles of everyday life, the optimism of childhood, and the fact that assumptions can be false. Christy's rhetorical tactics are significant here in that she does not fall prey to universalizing children with Ds or simply relaying her own assumptions. While there are moments that might rehearse exclusionary narratives, her overarching rhetorical tactics account for the uniqueness of those amazing children in her care.

The value of our analysis highlights the importance of intimacy as a mode of digital activism. Certainly, there is a vast amount of scholarly investment in traditional forms of direct civic action and even digital forms of explicit protest. Yet, this chapter illuminates the ways rhetorical tactics that create an affectionate bond between viewer, scene, and subject preclude those othering strategies entailed in assumptions about Ds. In other words, once the viewer comes to see Abby and Bailey as singular children, it becomes more difficult to label them with the stigmas associated with Ds. This is not to suggest that the viewer necessarily transforms their entire vision of children with disabilities. Indeed, more research is needed to determine the broader effects of these imaging strategies. But what this short analysis does emphasize is that even the most quotidian of rhetorical imaging strategies can impact the lives of viewers. As with CJPICS, followers invest in these children and their promise—a hopeful vision of the future that can open even more possibilities. We hope that writing and rhetoric scholars and students can apply this notion of the intimate screen to both interrogate and construct forms of digital activism on social media.

ACKNOWLEDGEMENTS

We are extremely grateful to Christy McDonald for her openness with us and her permission to use her words and images. We also thank Douglas M. Walls, Stephanie Vie, Beth Allison Barr, and Theresa Kennedy for their insightful feedback. Finally, we express appreciation to Shane Alexander and Scott Varda for their steadfast love and support.

REFERENCES

Acheson, P., Barratt, C. C. & Balthazar, R. (2013). Kindle research in the writing classroom. *Computers and Composition, 30*, 283–296.

Alba, D. (2014, December 22). Instagram's £22 billion valuation eclipses Twitter. *Wired*. Retrieved from http://www.wired.co.uk/news/archive/2014–12/22/instagram-eclipsing-twitter.

Bakshy, E., Mason, W. A., Hofman, J. M. & Watts, D. J. (2011). Everyone's an influencer: Quantifying influence on Twitter. *Proceedings of the Fourth ACM International Conference on Web Search and Data Mining*. New York, NY: ACM.

Brueggemann, B. J. (2001). An enabling pedagogy: Meditations on writing and disability. *JAC, 21*(4), 790–820.

Buck, A. (2012). Examining digital literacy practices on social network sites. *Computers and Composition, 47*(1), 9–38.

Carroll, W. K. & Hackett, R. (2006). Democratic media activism through the lens of social movement theory. *Media, Culture, and Society, 28*(1), 83–104.

Dadurka, D. & Pigg, S. (2011). Mapping complex terrains: Bridging social media and community literacies. *Community Literacy Journal, 6*(1): 7–22.

DeLuca, K. M. (1999). *Image politics: The new rhetoric of environmental activism.* New York, NY: The Guilford Press.

DeLuca, K. M. & Peeples, J. (2002). From public sphere to public screen: Democracy, activism, and the "violence" of Seattle. *Critical Studies in Media Communication, 19*(2), 125–151.

Eltantawy, N. & Wiest, J. B. (2011). Social media in the Egyptian revolution: Reconsidering resource mobilization theory. *International Journal of Communication, 5*, 1207–1224.

Finnegan, C. (2004). Review essay: Visual studies and visual rhetoric. *Quarterly Journal of Speech, 90*(2), 234–256.

Forbes, C. (2014). Caribbean women writing: Social media, spirituality and the arts of solitude in Edwidge Danticat's Haiti. *Caribbean Quarterly, 60*(1), 1–22.

Fox, B. (2013). Embodying the writer in the multimodal classroom through disability studies. *Computers and Composition, 30*(4), 266–282.

Gerbaudo, P. (2012). *Tweets and the streets: Social media and contemporary activism.* London, England: Pluto Press.

Gilmore, L., Campbell, J. & Cuskelly, M. (2003). Developmental expectations, personality stereotypes, and attitudes towards inclusive education: Community and teacher views of Down syndrome. *International Journal of Disability, Development and Education, 50*(1), 65–76.

Glaser, B. G. & Strauss, A. L. (1967). *The discovery of grounded theory: Strategies for qualitative research.* Chicago, IL: Aldine.

Harb, Z. (2011). Arab revolutions and the social media effect. *M/C Journal, 14*(2). Retrieved from http://journal.media-culture.org.au/index.php/mcjournal/article/view/364.

Hjorth, L. & Richardson, I. (2014). *Gaming in social, locative and mobile media.* New York, NY: Palgrave Macmillan.

Hocks, M. E. (1999). Feminist interventions in electronic environments. *Computers and Composition, 16*(1), 107–119.

Hogan, B. (2010). The presentation of self in the age of social media: Distinguishing performances and exhibitions online. *Bulletin of Science, Technology, and Society, 30*(6), 377–386.

Howard, P. N. & Parks, M. R. (2012). Social media and political change: Capacity, constraint, and consequence. *Journal of Communication, 62*(2), 359–362.

Issenberg, S. (2014, October 6). How do you change someone's mind about abortion? Tell them you had one. Retrieved from http://www.bloomberg.com/politics/fea

tures/2014-10-06/how-do-you-change-someones-mind-about-abortion-tell-them
-you-had-one.

Ito, M. & Daisuke, O. (2005). Intimate connections. Contextualizing Japanese youth and mobile messaging. In R. Harper, L. Palen & A. Taylor (Eds.), *The inside text: Social, cultural and design perspectives on SMS* (pp. 127–145). New York, NY: Springer.

Jeong, H. J. & Lee, M. (2013). The effect of online media platforms on joining causes: The impression management perspective. *Journal of Broadcasting & Electronic Media, 57*(4), 439–455.

Khondker, H. H. (2011). Role of the new media in the Arab Spring. *Globalizations, 8*(5), 675–679.

Lalvani, P. (2008). Mothers of children with Down syndrome: Constructing the socio-cultural meaning of disability. *Intellectual and Developmental Disabilities, 46*(6), 436–445.

Lambert, A. (2013). *Intimacy and friendship on Facebook.* New York, NY: Palgrave Macmillan.

Lewiecki-Wilson, C. (2003). Rethinking rhetoric through mental disabilities. *Rhetoric Review, 22*(2), 156–167.

Lewiecki-Wilson, C. & Brueggemann, B. J. (Eds.). (2008). *Disability and the teaching of writing: A critical sourcebook.* Boston, MA: Bedford.

Lotan, G., Graeff, E., Ananny, M., Gaffney, D. & Pearce, I. (2011). The revolutions were tweeted: Information flows during the 2011 Tunisian and Egyptian revolutions. *International Journal of Communication, 5*, 1375–1405.

McDonald, C. (n.d.). CJPICS. Retrieved from http://instagram.com/cjpics.

McKee, H. A. (2011). Policy matters now and in the future: Net neutrality, corporate data mining, and government surveillance. *Computers and Composition, 28*, 276–291.

Obar, J. A., Zube, P. & Lampe, C. (2012). Advocacy 2.0: An analysis of how advocacy groups in the United States perceive and use social media as tools for facilitating civic engagement and collective action. *Journal of Information Policy, 2*, 1–25.

Peary, A. (2014). Walls with a word count: The textrooms of the extracurriculum. *College Composition and Communication, 66*(1), 43–66.

Perlow, L. (2013). *Sleeping with your smartphone: How to break the 24/7 habit and change the way you work.* Boston, MA: Harvard Business Press.

Portman-Daley, J. (2010/11). Reshaping slacktivist rhetoric: Social networking for social change. *Reflections, 10*(1), 104–133.

Price, M. (2011). *Mad at school: Rhetorics of mental disability and academic life.* Ann Arbor, MI: University of Michigan Press.

Russell, J. (2014, March 27). Instagram now has more mobile users in the US than Twitter, according to new report. Retrieved from http://thenextweb.com/twitter/2014/03/27/instagram-now-mobile-users-us-twitter-according-new-report/.

Scott, T. & Welch, N. (2014). One train can hide another: Critical materialism for public consumption. *College English, 76*(6), 562–579.

Siebert, A. (2013). How non-Western consumers negotiate competing ideologies of sharing through the consumption of digital technology. In R.W. Belk & R. Llamas

(Eds.), *The Routledge companion to digital consumption* (pp. 137–148). New York, NY: Routledge.

Strauss, A. & Corbin, J. (1998). *Basics of qualitative research: Techniques and procedures for developing grounded theory* (2nd ed). Thousand Oaks, CA: SAGE.

Tufekci, Z. & Wilson, C. (2012). Social media and the decision to participate in political protest: Observations from Tahrir Square. *Journal of Communication, 62*(2), 363–379.

Vasalou, A., Joinson, A. & Courvoisier, D. (2010). Cultural differences, experience with social networks and the nature of "true commitment" in Facebook. *International Journal of Human-Computer Studies, 68*, 719–728.

Woollaston, V. (2014, August 12). Rise of the Twitter bots: Social network admits 23 million of its users tweet automatically without human input. *The Daily Mail*. Retrieved from http://www.dailymail.co.uk/sciencetech/article-2722677/Rise -Twitter-bots-Social-network-admits-23-MILLION-users-tweet-automatically -without-human-input.html.

PART 3: PEDAGOGY

CHAPTER 13

THE RHETORIC OF DISTRACTION: MEDIA USE AND THE STUDENT WRITING PROCESS

Patricia Portanova

Northern Essex Community College

One often-heard concern that has gained a great deal of traction over the past decade by journalists and teachers alike is that our 21st century students, so-called "digital natives," are increasingly distracted by portable media technologies. It seems as though popular media reports almost daily about the implication of our distracted lives, from a lack of social connections to decreased productivity. This rhetoric of distraction frequently posits tech-savvy millennials as mindless media-consumers—unable to unplug or power down.[1,2] Books like Mark Bauerlein's *The Dumbest Generation* (2009), Nicholas Carr's *The Shallows* (2011), and Sherry Turkle's *Alone Together* (2012) warn of the negative effects of a digital world on our students' social lives as well as on their ability to read comprehensively and think critically—two skills necessary to the composing process of any strong writer. Despite the popularity of these claims, there have been no empirical studies that show a negative correlation between both social and general media use and students' writing performance.

Why is it important to complicate the rhetoric of distraction? For one, educators across the country are paying attention to these reports. Many, as both Michael J. Faris and Lilian W. Mina show in subsequent chapters, take advantage of social media as a pedagogical tool critical to the development of student writers in a digital world. Others, influenced by what Chris M. Anson referred to as "concerns about the fragmentation of attention," may banish the use of social media and portable technologies in the classroom altogether. Yet there has been little research on how the writing process has been altered or adapted

---

1   The rhetoric of distraction is a term I devised to describe public discourse via mass media regarding the current generation's inability to pay attention as a result of advancements in portable technology.

2   The generation dubbed millennials refers to today's "teens and twenty-somethings," according to the Pew Research Foundation's extensive research, which may be found here: http://www.pewresearch.org/millennials/.

as a result of negotiating such accessible and portable media technology. In this chapter, I share the results of a survey and quasi-experiment that explored the impact of media use on student writing. Student participants in the study did not consistently perform worse on writing tasks when distracted by portable media technology. The variability in performance and complexities in media use suggest that twenty-first-century students may have a much more complicated relationship with media multitasking than the narrative of distraction suggests. The design and subsequent findings of this study will, I hope, encourage several future empirical studies examining media use and student writing.

RELEVANT RESEARCH

We know from a long history of research on cognition and writing that writing is a complex cognitive act of problem-solving involving several mental processes and sub-processes within working memory (Alamargot & Fayol, 2006; Bereiter & Scardamalia, 1987; Berninger & Swanson, 1994; Britton, 1978; Flower & Hayes, 1981; Hayes, 1996, 2006, 2012). Writing is particularly challenging because research on information processing (Rohrer & Pashlar, 2003; Ruthruff & Klaassen, 2001; Ruthruff & Pashlar, 2010) shows that individuals can only hold a certain amount of information within working memory before experiencing cognitive overload. Therefore, it is not surprising that recent studies on media multitasking (Bowman, Levine, Waite & Gendron, 2010; Jeong & Fishbein, 2007; Levine, Waite & Bowman, 2007; Lin & Lee, 2009; Ophir, Nass & Wagner, 2010) indicate that we do not have the cognitive ability to multitask more than one medium at a time, which writing with media distractions requires.

It is understandable, then, why writing instructors would be concerned about students multitasking with social media while writing based on the current research on multitasking during academic tasks. Helene Hembrooke and Geri Gay (2003) and Yvonne Ellis, Bobbie Daniels, and Andres Jauregi (2010) found that students who multitasked during lectures suffered on traditional memory tests and performed significantly lower on exam scores than non-multitasking students. Ulla G. Foehr (2006) suggested multitasking might have an impact on one's ability to comprehend content (p. 2). Laura E. Levine, Bradley M. Waite, and Laura L. Bowman (2007) also found that chronic IMing (instant messaging) was positively related to higher ratings of distractibility for academic tasks. Another study comparing reading comprehension while multitasking among expert and novice readers found that both expert and novice student performance decreased while reading with a video game playing in the background (Lin, Robertson & Lee, 2009). In a follow-up study, Bowman, Levine, Waite, and Michael Gendron (2010) also found that although test performance did not suffer, students who IMed while reading took significantly longer to read passages. These studies indicate that media multitasking increases student distractibility and time on task, and inhibits a student's ability to comprehend content. These studies look at reading performance and overall academic performance; however, there have been no studies that look specifically at the impact of media distractions on the quality of student writing produced while distracted by social media or technology in general.

RESEARCH DESIGN

To investigate the relationship between media use and writing specifically, I designed a two-part study that included a Media Multitasking Survey (MMS) and a quasi-experimental study of ten traditional college-level student participants. The MMS was adapted from a Stanford University study to include domain-specific questions that measure day-to-day media multitasking and media multitasking while writing academic texts.[1] The survey provided a general picture of the media multitasking habits of college-level students while writing academic texts, but did not provide a holistic picture of student writing behavior. To augment the survey, I collected qualitative data in the form of ten participant case studies that included interviews, writing samples, and observations to illustrate how media distractions impact the writing process and product.

First, I conducted a pre-experiment interview with each participant, ranging from approximately 20 to 40 minutes in length. The pre-experiment interview asked participants to reflect on their writing literacy (how they learned to write), their technology history (access to technology in school and home), and current relationship with media technologies (e.g., television, music, phone, and social media). Each participant also completed a form indicating the kinds of music they typically listen to while writing academic texts. From this information, I created a custom playlist for each individual participant on iTunes. Music genres ranged from country to hip-hop to modern folk music. To ensure music would provide a distraction, I also included one unfamiliar song with lyrics on each participant playlist; these songs were purposely selected from a genre vastly different than the participant's typical music.

After completing the initial interview, each participant was asked to compose an essay in response to a written prompt on a MacBook Pro laptop in an observation room on four separate occasions (what I refer to as writing modules). Each writing module was restricted to 45 minutes in length and asked participants to

---

1   The Media Multitasking Survey was adapted from Ophir et al.'s (2010) study, "Cognitive Control in Media Multitaskers."

respond to one of four different prompts in writing while negotiating various media multitasking conditions. For example, during one module, participants responded to a written prompt while listening to familiar music with lyrics from their customized playlist (Conditions B). During a different module, participants responded to a new written prompt on my laptop while listening to familiar music with lyrics and responding to text messages that I sent every ten minutes (Conditions C). In the most extreme module, participants responded to a written prompt on my laptop while listening to familiar music with lyrics, responding to texts every ten minutes, and checking Facebook every fifteen minutes (Conditions D). I chose these three media variables for two reasons: 1) based on interviews, these are the kinds of media distractions participants typically engage with while writing and 2) each kind of media (audible music, texting, and Facebook) require a different form of engagement (e.g., responding to a question through text versus scrolling through a Facebook newsfeed). In addition to the three modules that included some form of media distraction, one module asked participants to write under no conditions, or in silence (Conditions A). This module served as a baseline for each participant; the writing produced under various media conditions could be compared to the writing produced under no conditions.

Each participant had an individualized combination of conditions and writing prompts. No two participants responded to the same prompts in the same order, nor did they write under the same conditions in the same order. Additionally, four different writing prompts were used to avoid practice effects, or the ability to perform a task more proficiently simply by repeating the same task. If participants responded to the same prompt in all four events, the participant would naturally produce stronger writing and/or erase any discernable impact of media use. For the same reason, the conditions were randomized. Simply adding one more stimulus during each event, in chronological order, may minimize impact.

The writing prompts were designed to emulate first-year writing placement exam prompts.[2] I chose placement exam prompts because they ask students to perform the same kind of thinking across each module (e.g., choose a side in a debate and write a letter to a specific audience). This allowed me to compare the scores of written products from each module to the baseline (writing with no media stimuli) of each participant. It is important to note that participants were not compared to each other in terms of performance (i.e., this participant is a stronger

---

2   Three of the writing prompts were taken in full from Bridgewater State University's writing placement exam, 2008–2010. BSU's Writing Program Administrator, Anne Doyle, granted permission to use the writing prompts in this study. The fourth writing prompt was designed to elicit the same kind of response as the three BSU prompts.

writer than another participant). Rather, the writing of each individual participant was compared to his/her own writing in other conditions within the modules.

The additional variable of a timed writing event was purposeful. As the literature indicates, media multitasking may impact performance in two ways: increased time to carry out each individual task and decreased proficiency on each task. Therefore, the timed event limited participants' ability to mitigate the impact of distractions in terms of time away from task. If participants had the freedom to revise at their own pace, the effects of media distractions may have become difficult to discern. Ultimately, most writing is completed under some form of time restraint; the restraint of 45 minutes allowed for uniformity in writing opportunity across participants and modules.

During each module that required text messaging, participants were instructed to leave their cell phones on the table near the laptop on which they composed. I told participants that they were free to respond to any texts or alerts that appeared on their phone, but were not required to do so. They were, however, required to respond to any text message that I sent. In an effort to create a sense of real-life text conversation, I asked questions through text messages that required some level of processing to form a response. In modules that required Facebook checks, I sent a text to remind the participant to check Facebook. As was the case with the cell phone, I told participants that while Facebook was available, they were free to check alerts at will in addition to my reminders. Ultimately, my reminders were meant to ensure participants were engaged with media while writing, but several participants were engaged regardless of my reminders. During these modules, participants were instructed to scroll through their Facebook newsfeed and interact with Facebook as they would typically.

All modules were screen-recorded on my laptop using QuickTime software as well as video-recorded using a digital video camera. QuickTime is a pre-installed software program on Apple's MacBook Pro. When the software is running, the program will record everything that occurs on the computer screen in real time as well as capture (through microphone) all audible noises in the nearby vicinity. Using this program, I could watch student participants compose their essays—including pauses, deletions, revisions, spellchecks, and Facebook activity. Additionally, I could hear the sounds of the keyboard while they typed, the sound of music playing in the background, any verbal noises made by the participants (sighs, groans, singing, reading aloud, etc.), and the sound of every cell phone alert, including vibration. The software allowed me to review composing in process and pinpoint the exact moment a participant stopped composing to engage with media.

The screen video was cross-referenced with digital video footage also collected during each module. After each module, participants were invited to join me in reviewing portions of the video and to report on their writing process as well as the perceived impact of media distractions on their writing. During the review, I asked students to self-report on moments in their writing process where they appeared to make decisions (including the decision to stop writing) as well as on their general impressions of writing under various conditions. I also asked participants to comment on the writing prompt, how they approached the writing task, and whether or not they were satisfied with the final product, given time limitations.

The participant pool for the writing modules included six females and four males. Of the ten participants, four were freshmen, two were sophomores, two were juniors, and two were seniors. Participants represented a range of academic majors. All participants were of traditional college age for their year with 90 percent of the participant pool identifying as Caucasian (White) and 10 percent reporting as Caucasian (White) and African American. The average GPA was 3.52 with a low GPA of 2.9 and a high GPA of 3.83. The participants represent a range of college students, but it should be noted that this is representative of a certain kind of institution—a northeastern, research-focused state university. A lack of racial, cultural, and linguistic diversity is indicative of this particular university, but would not be representative of universities in other regions or other types of institutions in the same region.

All writing produced during the writing modules was stripped of identification, coded, and reviewed by three normed first-year writing instructors using the same six-point-scale holistic rubric. The holistic scoring rubric was created by the College Board and outlines criteria of successful academic writing often valued by writing instructors. For example, a five-point essay showing a "high degree of competence" demonstrates the following:

- Essay addresses the writing task effectively
- Essay is well developed, using appropriate reasons, examples, or details to support ideas
- Essay is generally well focused and well organized
- Essay demonstrates facility with language, using appropriate vocabulary and some sentence variety
- Essay demonstrates strong control of the standard conventions of grammar, usage, and mechanics but may have minor errors

Although the rubric is not perfect (no holistic rubric is, in my estimate), it has been tested nationally and proven valid. Again, the purpose of this study is not to evaluate writing performance in terms of grading or ranking. Rather, scores were used to indicate trends in writing under different conditions (e.g., students scored lower under several conditions than no conditions).

The act of composing a text involves several variables and not all of these variables could be accounted for in the design of this study. The two main areas of limitations include the size and scope of the participant pool and features of the multimodal study. First, the size of the participant pool is low with only ten quasi-experimental student participants with a high GPA average. Results of the study may also be impacted by the genre and topic of the writing prompts, time constraints imposed on the writer, the kinds of media distractions chosen for the study, as well as the controlled and unfamiliar setting participants composed in. Writing is produced under a complex set of cultural, social, and historical variables. All of these variables could not be controlled for. As a result of these limitations, I have avoided making broad conclusive statements when reporting findings. The data collected using these methods has raised several questions requiring further study by writing researchers.

FINDINGS

The Media Multitasking Survey (MMS) completed by participants prior to completing the writing modules showed that participants engage with media less while writing than in general, hinting at metacognitive awareness of the cognitive burden associated with writing.[3] In other words, students have some sense that media multitasking while writing poses cognitive challenges if they make the decision to decrease this behavior while writing. And it is this awareness that plays a role in whether or not students are successful in their academic writing. In fact, the participants in this study who showed metacognitive awareness of their writing process and ability, or inability, to engage with media while writing during interviews appeared to be able to mitigate the impact of such behavior on their written product. This is substantiated through the holistic scores of the writing produced by participants, which did not show a systematic negative correlation between writing and increased media distractions. The holistic scores of writing produced by participants *did not* decrease as the media variables the participant negotiated increased, giving the impression that writing with media distractions has little impact on a student's written product. That is not to say, however, that media distractions had *no* impact on the composing *process* of participants.

---

3   I used Ophir et al.'s (2010) equation to calculate a media multitasking index score for each participant. The mean of all participant index scores was 3.11. Individual participants with an index score higher than 3.11 are described as heavy media multitaskers, participants with scores around 3.11 are moderate media multitaskers, and participants below 3.11 are light media multitaskers. I also calculated a media multitasking index score for domain-specific questions that measured media multitasking while writing. The media multitasking while writing mean index score was 2.44.

In fact, participants were impacted in several significant ways: They showed difficulty transforming information (invention) and lost ideas through task switching.[4] These detriments may be related to difficulty drawing from long-term memory and other resources as well as limited capacity working memory.[5] In short, when students write with distractions, their ability to manage the cognitive processes involved in writing appears to be significantly impacted. The impact of distractions is apparent in student behavior exhibited during the writing modules. Although most students believe they are able to manage media use while writing, observations suggest their writing process is actually impaired.

One participant, Brian, is an excellent example of the deleterious effects of media distractions on the participants' writing process. By his own account, Brian's relationship to social media and text messaging is limited to organization. In other words, Brian uses texting and Facebook messaging to schedule meet-ups with friends, but does not engage in idle conversation or "creeping" through media. Brian's self-description of his engagement with media illustrates the differences he sees in their function:

> I personally don't like texting just to text and Facebook; it is
> just doing that just to do it. There is no point; you are not
> trying to accomplish anything. If you go on, like I've gone on
> before cus [sic] someone is sending me a message relating to
> classwork or . . . I want to see if someone is on there because
> I don't have their number and I need to get something from
> them, but I could see how that would be more efficient
> because you can type everything out in a quick chat, but . . .
> all those five text messages can be done in, I'll say, ten min-
> utes. And then beyond that the rest of the time is yours. The
> Facebook is just; it is like a black hole.

Brian does not self-initiate engagement with media; he responds to notifications of activity such as updates on his Facebook page, text message alerts, and cell phone game notifications—all of which send an audible alert to Brian's smartphone.

---

4   Observations of participant behavior also suggest that they struggled to comprehend new information through reading. However, the impact of media distractions on reading comprehension is outside the scope of this project. Please see Lin et al.'s (2009) study on reading performance between novices and experts in different media multitasking environments for empirical scholarship in this area.

5   John Hayes' (2012) most recent model of the cognitive processes involved in composing provides a nuanced illustration of the processes involved in writing discussed here.

It is equally important to note that Brian's typical writing process does not include media use beyond listening to familiar music. He writes academic essays in the library while wearing headphones as a deterrent for distraction. As is the case with many writers, Brian uses consistent and familiar noise to mask sudden or inconsistent sounds that may distract him. Brian is relying on selective attention, the cognitive ability to reject familiar stimuli unrelated to a task. He either listens to hip-hop or instrumentals because he feels as though he can "zone out" the music. While writing, Brian keeps his cell phone silenced and tucked away in his backpack. He does not visit websites such as Facebook while producing an essay.

Because Brian rarely multitasks while writing, distractions imposed on his writing process during the study had a significantly negative impact on his process. As Brian was faced with media conditions not typically present in his writing process, his writing process began to break down. With increased distraction Brian showed physical signs of agitation (e.g., sighing, stretching, rubbing his face with hands) while writing. By Brian's own account, stopping to check media disrupted his thought process, frequently caused him to lose track of his next sentence, and created difficulty when task switching to resume writing. Even unfamiliar music (a Johnny Cash song purposefully included on his music list) caused Brian to stop writing completely. Screen video shows that as the unfamiliar song becomes audible, Brian finishes a sentence and then spends time clicking aimlessly on a misspelled word and scrolls up and down the page a few times before stopping the task altogether; he did not resume writing for approximately five minutes.

When receiving text alerts under Conditions C (writing while listening to music and texting) and D (writing while listening to music, texting, and checking Facebook), Brian physically stopped writing, leaned back in his chair, and slowly typed his responses on his cell phone. As an infrequent text message user, Brian took longer to compose his text message responses (presumably due to graphomotor skills) and had to reread his entire essay draft after each text message to reconstruct his thought process. Although Brian attempted to rely on the organizational pattern used in his baseline condition and Condition B (listening to music), the overall text produced was shorter and his paragraphs became increasingly underdeveloped. By Condition D, Brian's final paragraphs made little sense and were incomplete.

In Brian's estimate, media distractions that caused him to "think about something else" undermined his writing process. When he heard a song that reminded him of an ex-girlfriend or the Johnny Cash song that reminded him of his brother, he found that his mind focused on those memories, disrupting the development of his ideas. When a distraction required retrieving information from long-term memory (e.g., the Johnny Cash song or a text message asking,

"Did you get anything good for Christmas?"), Brian had difficulty returning to the written text without spending some time deciphering what he was trying to say or erasing text to start over. Rather than compensating for distraction (e.g., waiting to finish/start a new idea before responding to a text), Brian was easily thrown off task by incoming alerts or unfamiliar music. In his own words: "I just remember like everything, like all the songs I knew were up-tempo, like, and just mainstream kind of pop, hip-hop, and then all the sudden it was just like: 'What the hell is this?' (Laughs)." It appears that the impact of media multitasking may be linked to the writing process already developed by the writer. In other words, the ability to manage media distractions is dependent on an established writing routine.

A similar scenario occurred with Sam, a participant who typically composes in complete silence; he was adamant about writing without media distractions when carrying out writing tasks outside of this study. This suggested that media distractions would have a significant impact on Sam's process. In his first module, Sam developed a pre-writing strategy to mitigate the impact of media distractions on his performance. While reading the prompt, Sam composed a detailed outline for his composition to provide direction while carrying out the writing task. However, this strategy did not mitigate the impact of media on his reading comprehension. In his post-interview, Sam stated:

> I thought [the experience] was pretty interesting. I sort of had trouble reading [the prompt] while listening to the music. Like I found myself like listening to music while I was mid-sentence and then I had to read it over again and like go back over the sentence.

This struggle is particularly evident when one prompt asked Sam to compose a letter to Google CEO Larry Page about his new privacy policies. After Sam read the prompt and composed a full paragraph, he re-read the prompt and realized that he had failed to recognize Larry Page as his intended audience. At this moment in the screen-capture footage, Sam stopped composing; there is a brief pause before Sam was heard audibly swearing ("oh, fuck"), and he was heard slamming his pen onto the table. In the follow-up interview Sam said:

> And like right here it says "in a well-organized essay addressed to Larry Page . . ." I completely skipped over that and I just started writing . . . and then I read that after I wrote a paragraph and I was like oh this is going to be a letter so now I need to address it to him and put it in first person and everything so, yeah. I completely botched that.

Because Sam was distracted while reading and inventing his text, he missed a central component of the rhetorical situation: the audience. When reviewing the writing prompt to find direct evidence to support his claims, Sam realized his mistake and had to delete his initial paragraph. This realization derailed Sam's process momentarily before he started to scramble to adjust the direction of his essay. Ultimately, Sam's attempt to mitigate the impact of media distractions by creating an outline prior to writing was undermined when he was essentially forced to revisit a stage of invention.

For Brian and Sam, media distractions were an imposition—taking cognitive resources away from the writing task. Brian struggled to return to task when distracted by a media variable that spurred a memory, an act that drew information from his long-term memory. Meanwhile, Sam struggled to integrate new information with information in his long-term memory to formulate a text aligned with the rhetorical situation while faced with media distractions. Both had their thinking processes derailed by media distractions, a trend found among several participants in this study.

The response of Brian and Sam to media distractions, among other similar responses by participants in this study, aligns with studies on divided attention, which show that when we attempt to attend to two complex cognitive tasks or two unrelated stimuli simultaneously, performance on both tasks and processing both stimuli suffers. Even participants that performed the same or better with the addition of multiple media distractions noted in post-interviews that they frequently lost their train of thought or were forced to delete sentences as a result of media multitasking. For example, Kristen, a heavy media multitasker, said in response to receiving a text message:

> Um, it didn't bother me much, but I did notice having to
> reread the previous couple of sentences that I had written each
> time I answered a text just to get back on track of where I was
> going with my writing.

When I asked Mark, who typically composes essays for school while listening to music and checking Facebook, if he had any trouble returning to his writing after a Facebook check he argued:

> It would kind of depend because I definitely start going back
> and looking over the prompt again. It was more so deciding
> when, how much I wanted, how long I wanted it to be, and
> what exactly I wanted to use in there. What I wanted the let-
> ter to exactly say, because it was kind of tough to decide that
> with everything going on.

For several participants media stimuli distracted enough to disrupt the writing process.

Despite the detrimental impact of media on the writing process, media distractions imposed on participants in this study created no discernable systematic impact on the written product. In other words, if we look at the pattern produced by the holistic scores, it appears that the normed readers could not distinguish between texts written under no conditions and texts produced under several conditions. As Table 13.1 indicates, some participants scored lower under increased media conditions while others flat-lined or even improved their scores.

Table 13.1: Participant Holistic Scores

	Silence	With Music	With Music and Texts	With Music, Texts, and Facebook
Brian	3	4	2	2
Evelyn	4	3	3	2
Theresa	4	5	4	5
Sam	4	2	2	2
Kristen	4	3	3	4
Erica	3	4	2	2
Nina	4	3	4	4
Derek	3	3	3	2
Mark	2	2	3	4
Haley	3	4	3	4

The strongest potential explanation for the phenomenon of students scoring highest under various conditions comes from student participant self-reporting during the pre-experiment interview. In pre-interviews, I asked students to describe their media use during their composing process for academic writing assignments. Their accounts were then paired with holistic scores. A striking trend emerges from this correlation: Students appear to have performed well under the conditions that most closely match their typical writing environment. As noted previously, Brian's self-description of his writing environment and his holistic scores illustrate this relationship. In Brian's estimate, he performs best with music playing in the background. Indeed, his holistic scores support this preference.

The relationship between typical, self-reported writing environments and holistic scores holds true for Sam, who must write in complete silence as he explained in our initial interview:

> In high school I liked to have music playing while I was writing, but I found that very distracting. I like to . . . find one of those desks that have the blinders on it and then I'm focused and it's my place where I go. I don't go on Facebook when I'm there. If go on Facebook then I get seriously distracted creeping on people.

Sam quite eloquently articulates his reasons for creating his typical writing space. He has tried alternative methods and, based on self-reflection, they proved too distracting. Consequently, Sam creates a space devoid of distraction and his holistic scores reflect this need; Sam performed significantly better when writing in silence. His performance markedly decreased as media variables were introduced into his environment. For Sam to be successful, he is aware that he must write academic essays in both silence and solitude.

Finally, we look at Mark who is an anomaly in terms of trends in holistic scores. Mark's scores actually increased as more variables are introduced. This seems perplexing until hearing Mark's self-assessment of his writing process:

> Usually . . . I'll check all my social media and stuff before I start writing. I'll put on my music and I'll find the song I really want to listen to . . . When I get texts or something, unless it's something important I'll usually look at it and see if it's important. Then I'll respond if it is, or if not. Sometimes when I'm sitting there and I can't think of what I want to put down next, instead of just getting up and coming back a few hours later I'll kind of take my mind off it and scroll through Twitter . . . then just get back into it. That way I'm not completely taking myself away from it but I can just calm down a little bit and get back to work and actually think about what I want to write.

Mark's media use is such an integral part of his writing process that he has difficulty concentrating in silence. Mark uses media distractions to take mental breaks. While he is carrying out a task that requires little awareness ("scroll through Twitter"), he is presumably processing his ideas so that he may return to the written text at hand. Again, this student performed best under his typical writing conditions—in this case, a media-rich environment.

It is important to note that participants who showed a strong correlation between normal writing conditions and high holistic scores in that condition provided responses that clearly describe stages of the writing process and different genres of writing. They made clear links between media use and reading, brainstorming, and drafting as well as made distinctions between kinds of writing—informal and formal. It is equally important to note that although the participant pool represented a range of majors, years in school, and an equal mix of gender, all ten participants in this study were high-performing students based on GPA; the average GPA of the participant pool was 3.52. Lower-achieving students may need more guidance to build the awareness exhibited by these participants.

CONCLUSIONS

As mentioned before, the lack of consistent negative impact on the scores of writing produced in this study suggests that twenty-first-century students have a much more complicated relationship with media multitasking than the narrative of distraction suggests. Not only is there high variability among student participants in terms of their relationship with media technologies, access to such technologies and writing process, but students may also have a much stronger awareness of the impact of media distractions on their lives than we often give them credit for. Although I cannot draw broad generalizations from such a small sample of student participants, the data suggests that like all of us who are negotiating twenty-first-century technologies, our so-called "digital native" college students make frequent decisions to attend to some stimuli while ignoring others. Few student writers seem to frequently multitask in its truest sense: carrying out two tasks simultaneously. Rather, student writers in this study appeared to rapidly switch between tasks—finishing a text before talking to a friend, checking Facebook before resuming academic work, stopping to compose an email on a cell phone before walking, etc. These decisions were made purposefully and reflect the individual's self-efficacy when writing with potential distractions. In short, the student writers who participated in this study appear to be aware of the cognitive challenges posed by writing with media stimuli dividing their attention and have strategies for adapting or mitigating the impact of those distractions.

This study is just the first of many, I hope, that explores how the writing process has been altered or adapted as a result of portable media technology. Future writing research on composing processes must consider the physical conditions texts are developed under. Even John Hayes' (2012) recent iteration of his model of cognitive processes involved in composing written texts did not account for the physical environment—distractions and all—the text is composed in. Although this study provides some initial insight into the twenty-first-century media-rich student writing process, the intersection of media use and writing process research is a rich and compelling area for continued investigation.

REFERENCES

Alamargot, D. & Fayol, M. (2006). Modeling the development of written transcription. In R. Beard, D. Myhill, M. Nystrand & J. Riley (Eds.), *Handbook of writing development* (pp. 23–47). London, England: SAGE.

Bauerlein, M. (2008). *The dumbest generation: How the digital age stupefies young Americans and jeopardizes our future (or, don't trust anyone under 30).* New York, NY: Penguin.

Bereiter, C. & Scardamalia, M. (1987). *The psychology of written composition.* Hillsdale, NJ: Lawrence Erlbaum.

Berninger, V. & Swanson, H. L. (1994). Modifying Hayes and Flowers' model of skilled writing to explain beginning and developing writing. In E. Butterfield (Ed.), *Children's writing: Toward a process theory of development of skilled writing* (pp. 57–81). Greenwich, CT: JAI Press.

Bowman, L., Levine, L., Waite, B. & Gendron, M. (2010). Can students really multitask?: An experimental study of instant messaging while reading. *Computers & Education, 54*, 927–931.

Britton, J. (1978). The composing processes and the functions of writing. In C. Cooper & L. Odell (Eds.), *Research on composing: Points of departure* (pp. 13–28). Urbana, IL: National Council of Teachers of English.

Carr, N. G. (2010). *The shallows: What the Internet is doing to our brains.* New York, NY: W. W. Norton.

Ellis, Y., B. Daniels & A. Jauregui. (2010). The effect of multitasking on the grade performance of business students. *Research in Higher Education Journal, 8.* Retrieved from http://www.aabri.com/manuscripts/10498.pdf.

Flower, L. & Hayes, J. (1981). A cognitive process theory of writing. *College Composition and Communication, 32*(4), 365–387.

Foehr, U. G. (2006). Media multitasking among American youth: Prevalence, predictors and pairings. *Henry J. Kaiser Family Foundation.* Retrieved from www.kff.org/entmedia/upload/7592.pdf.

Gay, G. & Hembrooke, H. (2003). The laptop and the lecture: The effects of multitasking in learning environments. *Journal of Computing in Higher Education, 15*(1), 46–64.

Hayes, J. (1996). A new framework for understanding cognition and affect in writing. In E. Cushman, E. R. Kintgen, B. M. Kroll & M. Rose (Eds.), *Literacy: A critical sourcebook* (pp. 172–198). Boston, MA: Bedford.

Hayes, J. (2006). New directions in writing theory. In C. A. MacArthur, S. Graham & J. Fitzgerald (Eds.), *Handbook of writing research* (pp. 28–40). New York, NY: The Guilford Press.

Hayes, J. (2012). Modeling and remodeling writing. *Written Communication, 29*, 369–388.

Jeong, S. & Fishbein, M. (2007). Predictors of multitasking with media: Media factors and audience factors. *Media Psychology, 10*, 364–387.

Levine, L. E., Waite, B. M. & Bowman, L. B. (2007). Electronic media use, reading, and academic distractibility in college youth. *CyberPsychology & Behavior, 10*(4), 560–566.

Lin, L., Robertson, T. & Lee, J. (2009). Reading performances between novices and experts in different media multitasking environments. *Computers in the Schools, 26*(3), 169–186.

Ophir, E., Nass, C. & Wagner, A. (2010). Cognitive control in media multitaskers. *Proceedings of the National Academy of Sciences, 106*(37), 15583–15587.

Rohrer, D. & Pashler, H. (2003). Concurrent task effects on memory retrieval: A cumulative latency analysis. *Psychonomic Bulletin & Review, 10*, 96–103.

Ruthruff, E. & Pashler, H. (2010). Mental timing and the central attentional bottleneck. In A. C. Nobre & J. T. Coull (Eds.), *Attention and time* (pp. 123–135). Oxford, England: Oxford University Press.

Ruthruff, E., Pashler, H. E. & Klaassen, A. (2001). Processing bottlenecks in dual-task performance: Structural limitation or voluntary postponement? *Psychonomic Bulletin and Review, 8*, 73–80.

Turkle, S. (2011). *Alone together: Why we expect more from technology and less from each other.* New York, NY: Basic Books.

CHAPTER 14

SOCIAL MEDIA IN THE FYC CLASS: THE NEW DIGITAL DIVIDE

Lilian W. Mina

Auburn University at Montgomery

In the spring 2015 semester, I was teaching a second-semester writing course focused on the rhetoric and culture of social media. In one class, students were asked to tweet their initial analysis of a chapter by danah boyd (2014). In order to protect both my and students' privacy while using Twitter, I created the hashtag #eng112GB (the course code, number, and section). By creating this hashtag, neither students nor I had to follow each other. Students got in groups, discussed the assigned chapter, and tweeted to the designated hashtag as seen in Figure 14.1. After they finished tweeting, I pulled up the Twitter feed on the screen as a springboard for a whole-class discussion of the chapter.

Figure 14.1: Students' Tweets to a Designated Hashtag.

Meanwhile, at the University of Colorado Colorado Springs, another English professor, Ann N. Amicucci, created a Facebook page for her 400-level course on social media. As demonstrated in Figure 14.2, the description of the page states that Facebook is serving "as a public forum for communication" (Social Media 4880, 2015). Both the professor and students post photos, concepts, and ideas for class discussion.

Figure 14.2: The Description of a Facebook Page Used in a Writing Class.

These two activities are examples of writing teachers' genuine interest in using various social media sites in their classes. One characteristic of social media is the possibility of producing content easily. That being the case, using social media in the writing class allows students to use a variety of modes to create content to be shared with others. Through this process, students become participants in the creation and flow of knowledge instead of being merely recipients of it (Rodriguez, 2011). For example, students in my class created the points of interest that they wanted to focus on in our class discussion of boyd's chapter. Similarly, students in Professor Amicucci's class contributed to the course materials through sharing relevant materials that they found interesting and worth sharing and discussing. According to Leah Donlan (2012), participation and students' "sense of control" (p. 4) are basic keys to the success of using social media in academic discourses. Therefore, using social media can create a paradigm shift in student learning in the writing class. But how do the examples from my and Ann Amicucci's classes represent or fail to represent other writing teachers' use of social media in their classes?

My goal in this chapter is to answer this question by discussing the findings of a critical study that examined writing teachers' pedagogical uses of three social media platforms: a social network site (Facebook), a microblogging site (Twitter), and a content-sharing community (YouTube) in the first-year composition (FYC) classroom. Findings reveal that social media sites were used to achieve a number of pedagogical purposes, such as helping students understand rhetorical choices and fostering community building and student engagement. However, participants appeared to prefer alphabetic texts to multimodal ones, and to dedicate more class time and attention to analysis rather than production activities on social media sites. These findings mean that while the ways Ann Amicucci and I used social media in our classes may not be unique, they are not necessarily mainstream practices.

SOCIAL MEDIA IN WRITING STUDIES

Writing scholars showed a relatively early interest in studying various social media platforms (e.g., Vie, 2008; Williams, 2008). Ever since, social media has continued to inspire writing scholars to explore its different features and affordances for the writing class. However, the volume of published scholarship on the use of social media in the writing class has not reflected that interest. A number of scholars have reported on the uses of social media in writing classes (Childs, 2013; McWilliams, Hickey, Hines, Conner & Bishop, 2011; Reid, 2011), by college students (Buck, 2012), and by multilingual students (Maranto & Barton, 2010). This body of scholarship was significant for introducing writing teachers, and writing studies in general, to the emerging technologies of social media sites.

In most scholarship published on the use of social media in the writing class, scholars sketched their own experiences with integrating a single social media platform in their respective writing classes. That is, they usually gave readers an idea about one precise activity performed on a solo platform, often with rich description of the outcomes of that activity as evidence that the platform had potentials for teaching writing. While beneficial for their rich detail, accounts of informal research of using social media platforms in teaching writing are limited in their ability to draw a comprehensive picture of the use of social media in the college writing classroom. What is more, informal research does not provide adequate evidence that would prompt writing studies as a field to make any comprehensive conclusions or recommendations about the value of social media in the writing class.

This lack of data-driven research on social media in the writing class can be attributed to two factors. The first factor is the nature of empirical large-scale research, which requires extended time to design a study, collect and analyze data, test hypotheses, and compare findings against previous research to make novel conclusions. This long process conflicts with the very nature of social media development and innovation. Social media platforms develop and change so rapidly that scholars may find it frustrating to design an empirical study that would take months to finish only to realize that the feature they have studied has become obsolete, been discontinued, or been replaced with a more recent and updated feature. The other factor may be the paradigm shift that steered research in writing studies towards more ethnographic and case study research in the past 30 years. However, observations on current research in computers and composition (Mina, 2013) and recent empirical research (see Anson's and Faris' chapters in this volume) confirm that digital media and social media scholars are enriching writing studies steadily with more empirical large-scale studies.

Among the few large-scale studies was Stephanie Vie's (2008), an empirical examination of the personal experiences of 127 instructors and 354 students who used two social networking sites, MySpace and Facebook. Vie's purpose was to examine the digital divide between the new generation of students and the older generation of teachers. The majority of teachers responded to her survey saying that they did not use either site because most of them thought these sites were designed primarily for students, and thus abstained from using them. Based on these findings, Vie concluded that many teachers oppose the use of social networking sites in their classes because they perceive it as a threat to the hierarchy of power and authority in the classroom. Gina Maranto and Matt Barton (2010) supported Vie's conclusion, claiming that teachers believed they compromised their credibility with their students if they were socially connected with them on social media sites.

Vie's (2008) concept of the digital divide between teachers and students is not the only problem that happens when teachers ban social media sites from their arsenal of pedagogical choices. Amber Buck (2012) complicated that divide by arguing that this ban does not allow writing teachers to see social media sites as rhetorical spaces whose affordances could contribute to students' rhetorical maturity. After tracing an undergraduate student's practices on social networking sites for two semesters, Buck found that the student developed "sophisticated rhetorical and literacy skills" (p. 36) during that time. Although Buck's study did not examine teachers' pedagogical choices of social media in the writing class, her findings and conclusions suggested that students' academic and non-academic skills are not separate; on the contrary, they are connected and influence each other. Thus, Buck urged writing teachers to abandon the binary vision that may be the reason behind either the total lack of or the limited integration of social media sites in the writing class.

Similarly, and arguing from a more rhetorical perspective, Maranto and Barton (2010) viewed social networking sites as "vibrant rhetorical spaces" (p. 37) where students make rhetorical choices all the time. Maranto and Barton advocated for using social networking sites as spaces to teach students about identity, social engagement, and community building. They supported their position with two students' experiences of getting engaged in national and international civic movements through Facebook interactions. As Maranto and Barton acknowledged teachers' concerns about privacy and authority, they encouraged teachers to claim a middle ground between completely banning social media and mandating students to "friend" them on social media sites.

Whether or not writing teachers have responded to Maranto and Barton's (2010) or Buck's (2012) suggestions to use social media in the writing class has not been formally examined. In order to narrow this wide gap in writing studies and gain a clearer picture of the position of social media in the FYC classroom, I conducted this study.

METHODOLOGY

Data for this study came from a larger mixed-method study that explored how writing teachers used new media technologies in teaching first-year composition (FYC) classes. A total of 161 participants from a wide range of higher education institutions in the United States completed an online survey that I distributed to subscribers of a number of listservs for writing teachers: Writing Program Administrators List (WPA-L), TechRhet, and Writing Program Administrators–Graduate Organization (WPA-GO). The survey consisted mainly of closed-ended questions and one open-ended question. The first closed-ended question asked participants to check all new media technologies they required their FYC students to use to complete coursework. As the focus of the study was exclusively pedagogical, I did not want teachers to discuss new media technologies used in preparing or managing their work (e.g., creating a video to introduce the course to students); I wanted the focus to be entirely on students and writing in FYC classes. The list included the three most popular social media platforms at that time (early 2013): YouTube, Facebook, and Twitter. However, and in order to capture all possible technologies teachers may have used, I added an "other" option for teachers to report their choice of technologies not included in the list. Although teachers added a number of technologies to that list in their answers, no other social media platforms were added. Thus, the analysis of social media reported in this study is constrained to YouTube, Facebook, and Twitter. In addition to the numerical data yielded from answers to that closed-ended question, I used verbal data from teachers' narrative responses to an open-ended question about purposes, reasons, and activities for using social media in teaching writing.

DATA ANALYSIS

In this study, numerical data came from answers to closed-ended questions. These numbers were used to run descriptive statistical tests of frequency and percentages that were important to identify the commonly used social-media platforms and the frequent uses of each platform in teaching FYC (Gall, Gall & Borg, 2007; Srnka & Koeszegi, 2007).

Verbal data in this study came from answers to the open-ended question on the survey, and I used an inductive approach to analyzing these data. Qualitative content analysis of verbal data helps unpack the thematic patterns in written texts (Creswell, 2014). The goal of the content analysis was to gain a richer understanding of first-year composition teachers' uses of social media platforms in their classes.

DATA CODING AND CATEGORIZATION

According to most authors (Creswell, 2014; Marshal & Rossman, 2011; Stake, 2010), qualitative analysis starts with two fundamental steps: data coding and data categorization. Katherine J. Srnka and Sabine T. Koeszegi (2007) recommended reading all of the data prior to developing codes. For this study, I read teachers' responses to the open-ended question in the survey thoroughly. During that process, I took notes and recorded initial thoughts and possible themes regarding the uses of these technologies. This helped me capture all possible themes and identify iterative ones. Srnka and Koeszegi also recommended the use of *thought units* or units of meaning as the basic unit for data coding. Thought units "comprise one idea communicated, no matter whether it is expressed in a sentence, a verb object sequence, a single word" (Srnka & Koeszegi, 2007, p. 36). This concept was adopted for the analysis of verbal data in this study. Applying this theoretical idea to data, the unit of analysis was a different use of the stated technology within the same participant's response. For example, one participant wrote, "I use Facebook to have students learn how to understand and examine the importance of audience. I also use Facebook to teach the difference between summary and analysis." This response contains two different uses of Facebook. Thus, this participant's response contained two thought units, each of which received its own code.

DATA CODING VALIDATION

To validate data coding, and consequently findings, I asked a research assistant to analyze 10 percent of the data (Creswell, 2002; Srnka & Koeszegi, 2007). Twenty random responses totaling 978 words were selected and copied to two separate files for data coding validation. I shared the coding scheme with the research assistant and we agreed on a method of coding. After three rounds of validation, I calculated the Pearson product-moment correlation coefficient (Pearson's r) to obtain inter-coder reliability (Gall et al., 2007). We reached a high level of inter-coder reliability of $r = 0.779$, which meant the coding scheme was valid to code the complete set of data.

SOCIAL MEDIA USES IN THE FYC CLASSROOM

Numerical analysis of data showed that 98 (59.7%), 27 (16.4%), and 21 (12.8%) participating teachers used YouTube, Facebook, and Twitter, respectively, in their classes. According to one participant, YouTube videos are easily available and accessible to all students. This availability may account for the relatively high percentage of teachers reporting using YouTube videos in their writing classes. As for Facebook, the assumption that Facebook is "used by virtually all students," as one participant put it, may have encouraged participants to design activities that utilize the affordances of Facebook in teaching writing. On the other side, and in accord with other research findings (e.g., Lin, Hoffman & Borengasser, 2013), Twitter seems to be less favorable compared to other social media sites. The fact that Twitter is a more public platform with less user control over content sharing and more concerns about privacy may have contributed to making Twitter the least used social media site among participants in this study.

After inductive analysis of verbal data, there were two approaches to thematically group and present findings: by social media platform or by the pedagogical uses of the various platforms. After contemplating both options, I chose the second approach because the goal of this study was to gain insight into writing teachers' current practices pertaining to the use of social media in teaching writing. Therefore, I decided to categorize findings by the pedagogical purpose

269

of using various social media platforms in the writing class because I wanted to privilege pedagogy over technologies.

Although Facebook and Twitter are generally known for their heavy use of multimedia, they were used more as text-rich technologies, or technologies that are used to produce alphabetical text in digital spaces. Not surprisingly, YouTube was mainly used as a media-rich technology, technology that requires the incorporation of different modes of expression (e.g., images and sound). The three sites were reportedly used to achieve the following pedagogical purposes: helping students understand rhetorical choices, enhancing learners' analytical and reflective thinking skills, developing student writing skills, and building communities and student engagement. In the coming sections, I zoom in on these themes in order to unpack participants' use of the three social media sites in teaching FYC classes.

HELPING STUDENTS UNDERSTAND RHETORICAL CHOICES

Participants described how they used social media as a form of visual rhetoric and multimodality in order to help students develop a better understanding of rhetorical choices across modalities. Among the activities participants reported was one of creating a profile page on Facebook "that represented their intellectual and scholarly identity." The teacher asked students to create that page using images, videos, links to articles, and music and songs that enabled them to represent their identity as students and their scholarly activities. Such an activity is expected to encourage students to consider the variety of rhetorical choices available in order to best represent themselves professionally in the virtual space of a social networking site.

Interwoven with the important purpose of considering rhetorical choices is the need to understand audience awareness, the sensitivity the writer develops for real and possible readers of their writing. Lisa Ede and Andrea Lunsford (1984) referred to these as invoked and addressed audiences, respectively. When using the term audience, I mean to suggest a group of readers that is not limited to teachers and students, but also includes the many unseen readers addressed when multimodal texts are circulated widely via social media sites. One participating teacher asked students to design an advocacy film on a given civic or political issue. The teacher told students "that the film should attempt to persuade a specific audience and have a specific purpose." Although that teacher did not provide further details about that project, it can be assumed that the purpose of creating advocacy videos was for students to learn how to make informed rhetorical choices with the aim of persuading their target audience. In an earlier study, Abby Dubisar and Jason Palmeri (2010) concluded that political remix videos enable students to employ their own thoughts and beliefs to reach larger audiences. This conclusion can be extended to advocacy films students created and distributed through their social media accounts.

This multimodal approach to enhancing students' understanding of rhetorical choices seems to tap into students' everyday use of multimedia to achieve this crucial goal in the writing class where social media platforms were also used to build critical thinking skills as well.

ENHANCING LEARNERS ANALYTICAL AND REFLECTIVE THINKING SKILLS

The desire to develop students' skills in argument, analysis, and critique predominates in writing classes. One can hardly read a scholarly work or engage in an academic discussion without building critical thinking and rhetorical skills, a core purpose that teachers strive to develop and strengthen. The writing teachers who participated in this study displayed great loyalty and commitment to achieving these essential goals. They mainly referred to the various activities they designed for social media platforms.

One participant asked students to read and analyze comments on a YouTube video. The teacher chose a video that triggered a myriad of comments and asked students to read through the comments and categorize them thematically. I consider this an exciting, authentic analysis of information on the web. This activity corresponds to Alexander Fedorov's (2010) recommendation that students should become critically aware of the information delivered through media. Engaging in the informal practice of reading comments on YouTube videos is an example of how social media sites can be convenient spaces to "blend formal and informal learning experiences" (Donlan, 2012, p. 3). This blend can develop students' analytical and research skills because categorizing findings around themes is an essential skill in inquiry-based writing courses.

Participants also showed a preference for integrating videos into a variety of analytical activities. One teacher, for example, chose YouTube videos and asked students to analyze the arguments in the videos. Another teacher seemed to have extended this activity to include a production component. In their response, this teacher communicated that they started the semester by asking students to analyze traditional typographical texts before they were required to use visual rhetoric as an alternative way to construct the same argument in videos near the end of the semester. Erik Ellis (2013) proposed that composition teachers should teach students the basics of visual analysis before teaching them to compose a multimodal text. Ellis' suggestion parallels the traditional approach to textual analysis in our classes in which teachers usually start by teaching students to analyze written texts before asking them to compose one. That participant's reported activity is an effective application of Ellis' approach and an extension of traditional analysis and production activities in the writing class into the new territories of multimodality utilizing a social media platform such as YouTube.

Many of the reflective thinking activities reported by participating teachers concentrated on behaviors and practices related to the use of social media platforms. In other words, the class activities that teachers created to facilitate and promote critical thinking focused more on students and their social-media-related behavior, particularly on the social networking site Facebook. These activities, which I discuss below, appear to build on students' everyday practices and their uses of social media as a means of situating their media experience "within an academic context centering on rhetorical activities" (Journet, 2007, p. 116).

In the first activity, one participant said they used Facebook writing practices as a springboard to let students see their social media behavior as writing, and to reflect on this type of writing rhetorically. The teacher's rationale for that activity was to demonstrate to students how writing is part and parcel of their lives even if they do not recognize social media as a platform for writing or their activities on those platforms as writing. This activity seems to aim at developing critical literacy as Stuart Selber (2004) defined it. Selber argued that critical literacy starts with understanding one's current beliefs and practices before attempting to critique and challenge them. This is what that teacher seemed to have accomplished through the Facebook writing analysis activity.

A second activity comes from another participant who utilized Twitter to teach students about networked learning. The teacher tried to situate students' writing on Twitter within a larger discourse of crowdsourcing. The teacher noted that they wanted students to see "how knowledge is crowd-sourced amongst open networks of individuals who are trying to share ideas." Jennifer A. Hudson (2007) contended that the main purpose for using technologies is to promote dialogic thinking. This participant apparently wanted students to engage in dialogic thinking by expanding their conversation beyond their individual tweets and to the larger picture of dialogue among individuals who share ideas and engage in a reciprocal thinking process.

These multimedia-rich activities (as few as they actually are), the rationale behind them, and their perceived value to the development of reflective and critical thinking magnify the role of widespread and available social media sites in teaching critical thinking skills to undergraduate students. These teachers' reports indicate how multimodal work on social media platforms can be geared towards achieving sophisticated rhetorical purposes by drawing students' attention to the affordances of other media and to their choices in various rhetorical situations. Moreover, social media sites may also be used to improve students' traditional writing skills.

Developing Students' Writing Skills

Because this study examined the uses of three social media platforms in FYC classes, it was not surprising to find that text production was a major goal among participating teachers. The texts teachers described in their answers included primarily alphabetic texts (i.e., texts that are solely print texts even if produced and disseminated in a digital space).

Twitter was used for enhancing students' academic writing skills. Twitter's restriction of limiting text to 140 characters per tweet seems to have encouraged teachers to use the site to develop "more focused writing skills," as one teacher claimed. According to several participants, these skills included "writing with brevity and clarity" and "writing tightly and concisely." With the goal of improving students' writing skills in mind, three participating teachers designed an activity around summarizing class readings they asked students to complete via Twitter. One participant claimed that when students have to fit their summary of reading within Twitter's 140-character limit, they learn to write succinctly.

This finding ties neatly with Jenna McWilliams, Daniel Hickey, Mary Beth Hines, Jennifer Conner, and Stephen C. Bishop's (2011) assertion that Twitter can be a viable platform for developing students' literacy skills beyond simple reading and writing. Alec R. Hosterman (2012) also advocated using the platform to enhance students' linguistic abilities due to the character restraint built into Twitter's design.

However, even among participants who used Twitter in their writing classes, privacy issues were cited as the biggest reservation. In order to overcome this concern, Meng-Fen Grace Lin, Ellen S. Hoffman, and Claire Borengasser (2013) suggested creating a class hashtag to filter course-related tweets without the need for professors or students to follow each other, which I believe could protect the privacy of both professors and students while using Twitter in class. This is why I created a unique course hashtag for my students to use in the activity described at the opening of this chapter. Even though only one participant referred to creating a class hashtag, I strongly recommend using hashtags to facilitate collecting students' tweets without any concerns about teacher or student privacy.

Combining traditional and non-traditional genres, some teachers described assignments that included multimodal texts, such as producing videos to be shared on YouTube. One teacher argued that students who work with images to create an assigned video "gain a better understanding of Creative Commons and copyright for the twenty-first century." This attention to using Creative Commons is likely to enhance students' ability to integrate sources fairly and effectively in their texts in both print and multimodal texts, a traditionally challenging task for many writing teachers.

In addition to using social media sites to develop the aforementioned skills, and similar to the Social Media 4880 Facebook page description cited earlier, participants seem to have leveraged the social nature of these sites to build communities of interaction and communication in the writing class.

COMMUNITY BUILDING AND STUDENT ENGAGEMENT

Building a community of teachers and students that extends beyond classroom walls was a common purpose of using social media sites among participants in this study. Student engagement was the ultimate goal of building a community of students who communicate and interact in and out of class through different social media platforms. Before explaining how social media promotes student engagement, it is important to establish a consensus on what I mean by engagement. I chose Ronald A. Yaros' (2012) definition of engagement as a "situational interest in a particular environment such as a social network" (p. 60). Yaros' definition matches the context of this study because he contended that students are actually engaged when they have sustained interest not only in the content being presented but also in the media used in presenting that content. As students demonstrate interest in social media sites, they become engaged in the content presented on these sites.

In this study, social media sites were perceived by participating teachers as platforms for potentially extending and sustaining class discussions. Facebook, for instance, was mostly used as a means of communication between teachers and students. A number of participants cited using Facebook groups as an alternative to email communication with students. Other participants reported using Facebook private groups for communication and out-of-class discussion. Having a course Facebook page for communication and interaction between the teacher and students was recommended by one student in Amicucci's (2014) study in which she explored students' non-academic practices on social media. As Facebook becomes more ubiquitous in students' lives (Elavsky, 2012), the walls of Facebook private groups may replace discussion boards very soon.

Moving to Twitter, teachers reported that Twitter was mainly used as an immediate and additional channel of communication among students (see also Faris' findings about Twitter for communication among students in his chapter in this volume). However, some teachers mentioned that they used Twitter to keep the conversation going between class sessions. One teacher elaborated, saying that they encouraged students "to tweet during class to our class hashtag and outside of class to engage with the material outside of our meeting session." Even though Twitter was used or suggested for similar purposes in other disciplines

(Grosseck & Holotescu, 2008; Hosterman, 2012; Lin, Hoffman & Borengasser, 2013; Miners, 2010; Stevens, 2008), these participating teachers' self-reports about using Twitter for extending class discussions are the first data from writing teachers.

Student engagement can be seen in their participation in discussions as a form of communication requiring a great deal of interaction between teacher and students, enhancing meaning making, and developing a better command of writing concepts. This style of communication takes place on social media sites where much interaction and engagement occurs. Hence, Lily Zeng, Holly Hall, and Mary Jackson Pitts (2012) strongly recommended using social media for community building and sharing information. Yaros (2012) also emphasized that engagement facilitates knowledge and learning transfer, and thus he concluded that the appropriate use of social media in class can provide numerous opportunities for sharing beyond the brick and mortar of the classroom.

DISCUSSION

This study explored the integration of three social media platforms in teaching FYC in U.S. higher education institutions to understand the position of social media in teaching writing. Findings show that participants displayed a preference for alphabetic texts as compared to multimodal texts and for analytical activities as opposed to production-based ones.

ALPHABETIC VS. MULTIMODAL TEXTS

It is obvious that writing teachers who participated in this study wanted their FYC students to produce texts in a variety of forms and modalities. However, participants seemed to pay considerably more attention to the production of alphabetic texts than multimodal ones. This unbalanced attention to alphabetic over multimodal texts may be due to the traditional inclination toward verbal literacy and alphabetic texts at the expense of other modalities of text in writing studies (Selfe, 2009; Shipka, 2013). Writing teachers seem to have what Heather Urbanski (2010) described as persistent nostalgia for print texts. Most of the activities teachers designed for social media in this study focused primarily on alphabetic text, even on YouTube, a video-sharing platform, or Facebook, known as a platform for multimodal composing (Eisenlauer, 2014). People communicate on Facebook using various modes: They upload and share images and videos, share links to favorite articles and websites, and/or use virtual stickers and emotions to express their opinions and feelings about a given post. Briefly put, communication on Facebook is multimodal. Thus, the findings of the study indicate that social media is being stripped of its non-alphabetic (multimodal and multimedia) meaning-making affordances.

Akiko Hemmi, Sian Bayne, and Ray Land (2009) provided a plausible interpretation of faculty's approach toward alphabetic versus multimodal texts; they argued that academia is characterized by slow adoption of new approaches while embracing an inherent preference for traditional models or the methodological status quo. This interpretation can be validated by reflecting on how participants in this study seemed to preserve the supremacy of alphabetic texts in almost all the activities they designed for social media platforms. Another possible interpretation of the use of social media for production of primarily alphabetic text could be the technical challenges faced by teachers and students in creating multimodal texts, or the fact that composing multimodal texts is time consuming (McNaught, Lam, Kwok & Ho, 2011). This obstacle seems to have persisted since Vie's (2008) study. Many teachers in Vie's study claimed to have too little time to spend on learning or using technology and this made them reluctant to incorporate technology into their writing classes. Similarly, participants in this study may not be willing to invest more time or effort in learning and teaching students about creating multimodal content to be circulated through social media platforms. Urbanski (2010) offered some other reasons for writing teachers' avoidance of social media in their classes. Reasons included "the lack of guiding/orientation documents," the pressure that "we 'have' to use it," and fears of security and privacy breaches (p. 241). Availability and easy access to resources and technical support at institutions may facilitate more incorporation of multimodal composing by teachers who use social media platforms.

According to Yaros (2012), one reason behind the popularity of social media networks, particularly Facebook, is the ability to personalize content using multimodal and textual elements. When writing teachers restrict content development on social media to textual elements, they in fact deprive students from fully expressing themselves in a way that mimics their non-academic use of social media (see Anson's chapter in this volume). Writing studies scholars have argued similarly. Cynthia L. Selfe (2009) described composing as a "multimodal rhetorical activity" (p. 616) and she criticized the exclusion of multimodality in the writing class because she saw this as denying students "valuable" meaning-making methods. She patently opposed the supremacy of print text and the perception of the linguistic mode of communication as more elite than other modes. To Selfe, this dichotomy is unfair for students who need all modes to comprehend their multimodal lives and establish their identity in an increasingly multimodal world.

Frank Serafini (2014) also contended that the "exclusion" of multimodality from the writing classes is problematic because of "the multimodal nature of modern communication" (p. 17). Serafini viewed multimodality as a means to enrich students' literacies because it is what students consume and produce in their lives. He added that teachers should learn about the media students use in order to be able to engage them in class work.

Along the same lines of thought, Urbanski (2010) warned against alienation in the writing class that may occur when students believe a teacher does not appreciate their life experiences. This understanding may directly and indirectly reflect on students' performance in the writing classes. When teachers insist on ignoring and degrading the texts students deal with outside the writing class, students may lose interest in the texts teachers insist on using and producing, no matter how important. As a result, students may experience a different form of digital divide pertaining to the discrepancy in uses of social media in and outside of the writing class. According to Urbanski, this new digital divide means that teachers "run the risk of alienating our students" (p. 248). Thus, the divide is not between students and their teachers' perception of social media sites, as Vie (2008) concluded a few years ago; the divide is now between students' everyday practices on social media and their academic practices.

Writing teachers should thus embrace Gunther Kress and Theo van Leeuwen's (2001) understanding of how multimodality has changed writing from being a "recording" of thoughts to "an originating medium" (p. 92) to be distributed, or shared using social media terms. This fundamental understanding resonates with Jason Ranker's (2008) and Kress' (1999) arguments that as students move between images, text, and sound, they transform and transfer their learning across modes. Furthermore, teachers should be more willing to acknowledge that using social media in the writing class embraces students' craving for spaces where they can experience novel methods of doing academic work, spaces that resemble and build on the "digital media environments in which they work and play" (Andrews, 2010, p. 254).

ANALYSIS VS. PRODUCTION ACTIVITIES

The second conclusion to be garnered from this study is teachers' preference for analysis over production activities. As discussed in the previous section, most participants reported asking students to analyze either the content of social media sites or their own behavior and writing on these sites. A feasible explanation of this phenomenon is the considerable ease of locating content and choosing existing behaviors to analyze versus the time-intensive process of designing and implementing production activities. Although analytical activities are crucial for developing students' critical thinking skills, as I argued earlier, an important aspect of social media is the possibility of creating content easily (Rodriguez,

2011), which contradicts what most teachers reported in this study. Rodriguez cited Hoffman's conclusion from his case study research that using social media in teaching increases student engagement, collaborative learning, and sense of ownership. Engagement and the sense of ownership cannot be guaranteed without students becoming actively involved in creating their own content.

Describing her experience working with students to design and produce a multimodal website, Jennifer Sheppard (2009) related the production of multimodal texts to the "traditional print-based literacies and rhetorical practices" valued by most writing teachers (p. 122). She emphasized that producing multimodal texts has additional rhetorical and literacy value beyond that of traditional texts. She particularly discussed the value of students' attention to media choices and the affordances of different technologies students had to use to address the fundamental rhetorical concerns: audience, purpose, and context. Sheppard's conclusions about the complexity of skills students acquire through the production of multimodal text support Kress and van Leeuwen's (2001) argument that multimodal texts incorporate different semiotics and therefore function as a replacement of verbal texts to represent and express oneself. The findings of this study confirm these arguments even though most participants did not incorporate many multimodal production activities in their writing classes.

Extending the conversation to students' future lives and careers, Matt Levinson (2010) strongly warned that lack of participation may become a new aspect of the digital divide. Levinson argued that unless teachers provide students with access to experiences and skills required in the increasingly participatory culture of work, students are not adequately prepared to play their "future roles as 21st-century citizens and workers" (p. ix). Moreover, Peter Duffy and Axel Bruns (2006) suggested that faculty should provide students with opportunities to experience the skills they will need outside the classroom and in their future careers in order to develop the competencies they will need after graduation. Students will most likely be required to produce text in different modalities in their workplaces, so overlooking production activities and multimodal composing in their writing class may negatively affect students' careers.

IMPLICATIONS AND RECOMMENDATIONS

The 2013 National Survey of Student Engagement (NSSE) annual report stated that "technology has become interwoven into the college experience" (p. 23), including social networking sites. The report concluded that student use of technology "was positively related to student engagement" (p. 23). Although the NSSE report is not limited to writing classes, it gives college educators and administrators an insight into the direction of trends in higher education institutions. Students are increasingly engaging with their course work through the use of social media sites. This significant finding from the NSSE report supports the findings of this study relating to student engagement in and out of class when required to use different forms of new media technologies, specifically social media platforms. Apparently, the use of social media is proliferating across disciplines in higher education, a situation that should alert teachers of FYC classes to the paradigm shift that higher education is experiencing.

Amicucci (2014) recommended that teachers should build on the skills and expertise that students have developed over years of using social media in non-academic contexts. Writing teachers need to acknowledge and offer varied means of expression, particularly when integrating social media platforms in their classes. Based on students' suggestions in Amicucci's study, she recommended creating activities and assignments that merge writing practices from both academic and non-academic contexts. Amicucci's recommendations respond to Urbanski's (2010) fear that "we betray our students when we expect them to think like us, to value what we value, and to devalue what we reject or degrade simply because we tell them to do so" (p. 247).

Applying the results of the NSSE report to composition classes implies more than just acknowledging the changes sweeping higher education classes. It means promoting the informed and critical use of social media in writing classes so that students do not experience a digital divide between these classes and classes in their respective disciplines on one hand, and between the supremacy of print literacy in writing classes and the set of varied literacies they develop outside these classes.

REFERENCES

Amicucci, A. N. (2014). "How they really talk": Two students' perspectives on digital literacies in the writing classroom. *Journal of Adolescent & Adult Literacy, 57*(6), 483–491.

Andrews, A. (2010). Making Dorothy Parker my MySpace friend: A classroom application for social networks. In H. Urbanski (Ed.), *Essays on new media rhetoric: Writing and the digital generation* (pp. 252–254). Jefferson, NC: McFarland & Company

boyd, d. (2014). *It's complicated: The social lives of networked teens*. New Haven, CT: Yale University Press.

Buck, A. (2012). Examining digital literacy practices on social network sites. *Research in the Teaching of English, 47*(1), 9–37.

Childs, E. (2013). Using Facebook as a teaching tool. *Kairos: A Journal of Rhetoric, Technology, and Pedagogy*. Retrieved from http://praxis.technorhetoric.net/index.php /Using_Facebook_as_a_Teaching_Tool.

Creswell, J. W. (2014). *Research design: Qualitative, quantitative, and mixed methods approaches* (4th ed.). Thousand Oaks, CA: SAGE.

Donlan, L. (2012). Exploring the views of students on the use of Facebook in university teaching and learning. *Journal of Further and Higher Education, 1*(17), 1–17.

Dubisar, A. M. & Palmeri, J. (2010). Palin/pathos/Peter Griffin: Political video remix and composition pedagogy. *Computers and Composition, 27*(2), 77–93.

Duffy, P. D. & Bruns, A. (2006, September 26). *The use of blogs, wikis and RSS in education: A conversation of possibilities.* Paper presented at the Online Learning and Teaching Conference, Brisbane, Australia.

Ede, L. & Lunsford, A. (1984). Audience addressed/audience invoked: The role of audience in composition theory and pedagogy. *College Composition and Communication, 35*(2), 155–171.

Eisenlauer, V. (2014). Facebook: A multimodal discourse analysis of (semi)-automated communication mode. In S. Norris & C. D. Maier (Eds.), *Interactions, images and texts: A reader in multimodality* (pp. 311–321). Berlin, Germany: Walter de Gruyter.

Elavsky, C. M. (2012). You can't go back now: Incorporating "disruptive" technologies in the large lecture hall. In H. S. N. Al-Deen & J. A. Hendricks (Eds.), *Social media: Usage and impact* (pp. 75–91). Lanham, MD: Lexington Books.

Ellis, E. (2013). Back to the future? The pedagogical promise of the (multimedia) essay. In T. Bowen & C. Whithaus (Eds.), *Multimodal literacies and emerging genres* (pp. 37–72). Pittsburgh, PA: University of Pittsburgh Press.

Fedorov, A. (2010). Media educational practices in teacher training. *Acta Didactica Napocensia, 3*(3), 57–70.

Gall, M. D., Gall, J. P. & Borg, W. R. (2007). *Education research: An introduction* (8th ed.). Boston, MA: Pearson.

Grosseck, G. & Holotescu, C. (2008, April 17–18). *Can we use Twitter for educational activities?* Paper presented at the 4th International Scientific Conference on eLearning and Software for Education, Bucharest, Romania.

Hemmi, A., Bayne, S. & Land, R. (2009). The appropriation and repurposing of social technologies in higher education. *Journal of Computer Assisted Learning, 25*(1), 19–30.

Hosterman, A. R. (2012). Tweeting 101: Twitter and the college classroom. In H. S. N. Al-Deen & J. A. Hendricks (Eds.), *Social media: Usage and impact* (pp. 93–110). Lanham, MD: Lexington Books.

Hudson, J. A. (2007). Writing, technology and writing technologies: Developing multiple literacies in first-year college composition students. *International Journal of Learning, 13*(12), 93–100.

Journet, D. (2007). Inventing myself in multimodality: Encouraging senior faculty to use digital media. *Computers and Composition, 24*(2), 107–120.

Kress, G. R. (1999). "English" at the crossroads: Rethinking curricula of communication in the context of the turn to the visual. In G. E. Hawisher & C. L. Selfe (Eds.), *Passions, pedagogies, and 21st century technologies* (pp. 66–88). Logan, UT: Utah State University Press.

Kress, G. R. & van Leeuwen, T. (2001). *Multimodal discourse: The modes and media of contemporary communication*. New York, NY: Bloomsbury Academics.

Levinson, M. (2010). *From fear to Facebook: One school's journey*. Washington, DC: International Society for Technology in Education.

Lin, M. F. G., Hoffman, E. S. & Borengasser, C. (2013). Is social media too social for class? A case study of Twitter use. *TechTrends, 57*(2), 39–45.

Maranto, G. & Barton, M. (2010). Paradox and promise: Myspace, Facebook, and the sociopolitics of social networking in the writing classroom. *Computers and Composition, 27*(1), 36–47.

Marshal, C. & Rossman, G.B. (2011). *Designing qualitative research* (5th ed.). Thousand Oaks, CA: SAGE.

McNaught, C., Lam, P., Kwok, M. & Ho, E. C. L. (2011). Building institutional capacity for the use of social media. In B. White, I. King & P. Tsang (Eds.), *Social media tools and platforms in learning environments* (pp. 137–152). New York, NY: Springer.

McWilliams, J., Hickey, D. T., Hines, M. B., Conner, J. M. & Bishop, S. C. (2011). Using collaborative writing tools for literary analysis: Twitter, fan fiction and The Crucible in the secondary English classroom. *Journal of Media Literacy Education, 2*(3), 238–245.

Mina, L. (2013). On the digital rhetorics of fans and fan communities. *Computers and Writing Conference Review*. Retrieved from http://www.digitalrhetoriccollaborative.org/2013/08/02/on-the-digital-rhetorics-of-fans-and-fan-communities-session-k1/.

Miners, Z. (2010). Twitter goes to college: Students and profs use "tweets" to communicate in and outside of class. Retrieved from http://www.usnews.com/education/articles/2010/08/16/twitter-goes-to-college-.

National Survey of Student Engagement (2013). NSSE annual results 2013: A fresh look at student engagement. Retrieved from http://nsse.iub.edu/NSSE_2013_Results/index.cfm.

Ranker, J. (2008). Making meaning on the screen: Digital video production about the Dominican Republic. *International Reading Association, 51*(1), 410–422.

Reid, J. (2011). "We don't Twitter, we Facebook": An alternative pedagogical space that enables critical practices in relation to writing. *English Teaching: Practice and Critique, 10*(1), 58–80.

Rodriguez, J. E. (2011). Social media use in higher education: Key areas to consider for educators. *MERLOT Journal of Online Learning and Teaching, 7*(4), 539–550.

Selber, S. A. (2004). *Multiliteracies for a digital age*. Carbondale, IL: Southern Illinois University Press.

Selfe, C. L. (2009). The movement of air, the breath of meaning: Aurality and multimodal composing. *College Composition and Communication, 60*(4), 616–663.

Serafini, F. (2014). *Reading the visual: An introduction to teaching multimodal literacy*. New York, NY: Teachers College Press, Columbia University.

Sheppard, J. (2009). The rhetorical work of multimedia production practices: It's more than just technical skill. *Computers and Composition, 26*(2), 122–131.

Shipka, J. (2013). Including, but not limited to, the digital: Composing multimodal texts. In T. Bowen & C. Whithaus (Eds.), *Multimodal literacies and emerging genres* (pp. 73–89). Pittsburgh, PA: University of Pittsburgh Press.

Social Media 4880. (2015). About. Retrieved from https://www.facebook.com /Rhetoric4880/info?tab=page_info.

Srnka, K. J. & Koeszegi, S. T. (2007). From words to numbers: How to transform qualitative data into meaningful quantitative results. *Schmalenbach Business Review, 59*(1), 29–57.

Stake, R.E. (2010). *Qualitative research: Studying how things work.* New York, NY: Guilford.

Stevens, V. (2008). Trial by Twitter: The rise and slide of the year's most viral microblogging platform. *TESL-EJ, 12*(1). Retrieved from http://www.tesl-ej.org/ej45/int .html.

Urbanski, H. (2010). Meeting the digital generation in the classroom: A reflection on the obstacles. In H. Urbanski (Ed.), *Essays on new media rhetoric: Writing and the digital generation* (pp. 239–251). Jefferson, NC: McFarland.

Vie, S. (2008). Digital divide 2.0: "Generation M" and online social networking sites in the composition classroom. *Computers and Composition, 25*(1), 9–23.

Williams, B. (2008). "What South Park character are you?": Popular culture, literacy, and online performances of identity. *Computers and Composition, 25*(1), 24–39.

Yaros, R. A. (2012). Social media in education: Effects of personalization and interactivity on engagement and collaboration. In H. S. N. Al-Deen & J. A. Hendricks (Eds.), *Social media: Usage and impact* (pp. 57–74). Lanham, MD: Lexington Books.

Zeng, L., Hall, H. & Pitts, M. J. (2012). Cultivating a community of learners: The potential challenges of social media in higher education. In H. S. N. Al-Deen & J. A. Hendricks (Eds.), *Social media: Usage and impact* (pp. 111–126). Lanham, MD: Lexington Books.

CHAPTER 15

CONTEXTUALIZING STUDENTS' MEDIA IDEOLOGIES AND PRACTICES: AN EMPIRICAL STUDY OF SOCIAL MEDIA USE IN A WRITING CLASS

Michael J. Faris

Texas Tech University

Writing scholars have increasingly encouraged teachers to incorporate social media in writing courses, situating social media as important sites of rhetorical action and literacy (Buck, 2012; Daer & Potts, 2014; Maranto & Barton, 2010; Vie, 2008). While calls for using social media in writing classes have become numerous, there have been relatively few empirical studies of actual practices in writing classes, and most scholarship has been anecdotal (as Lilian W. Mina also observes elsewhere in this collection). How do students engage with social media? What understandings do they bring to writing classes? How do their educational practices with social media mesh and conflict with their personal practices with these sites? How do students understand and engage with social media in pedagogical settings? This chapter explores these questions by sharing the results of an IRB-approved empirical study of students' literacy practices and understandings of those practices (Gershon, 2010) in a 2013 upper-division class on social media at the University of Wisconsin–Eau Claire.[1]

I want to start by suggesting that we know very little about our students' actual practices and understandings of social media, despite growing bodies of scholarship that explore teenagers' and young adults' social media practices in rich detail (see, for example, boyd, 2014; Buck, 2012; Gershon, 2010; Ito et al., 2010; Pigg et al., 2014; Mina, this volume). A reason for this gap in understanding is the overgeneralizations many teachers and scholars make about "our students" (and, of course, students make these generalizations as well). These generalizations ignore the specific and situated practices and understandings of new media that students bring to pedagogical settings.

1 This study was approved by the Institutional Review Board at the University of Wisconsin–Eau Claire, protocol #FARISMJ13232013. Students' names in this chapter are pseudonyms.

Popular narratives about young adults and new media do little to contextualize student practices. For instance, the "digital natives" narrative, popularized by Marc Prensky (2001), held that young adults are "all 'native speakers' of the digital language of computers, video games and the Internet" (p. 1). This narrative has been critiqued as one unsupported by empirical research that lumps together a whole generation while ignoring differences among youth, especially socioeconomic class, race, and access to technologies (Hargittai, 2010; Jones, 2011). Additionally, students' potential comfort with social media does not necessarily translate into critical engagement with those sites (Daer & Potts, 2014; Vie, 2008). We still have little understanding of students' practices and understandings of new media sites in particular contexts and situations. Teachers often rely on narratives about an entire generation, which can occlude the actual practices and understandings of social media by students at particular institutions and in specific classes.

These generational narratives are frequently reproduced in the halls of our buildings and in conversations among teachers. For example, in 2013, various news services reported on Daniel Miller's ethnographic research in a village north of London, generalizing from his research to claim that young adults were fleeing Facebook because adults (especially parents) were joining the site, which was deemed "dead and buried" (see for example Tate, 2013). The media coverage of his research prompted Miller (2013) to respond in a blog post, stressing that his research was applicable only to his ethnographic site in Britain. Other findings by the Pew Research Internet Center that teenagers "have waning enthusiasm" for Facebook and more teens were using Twitter (Madden et al., 2013) gained similar traction in mass media, leading lead researcher Mary Madden (2013) to later clarify that they didn't find that teens were leaving Facebook, but were rather diversifying their social media usage. But mass media didn't report on Madden's or Miller's clarifications, and continued to report sensationally rather than with nuance. In the halls of my institution at the time (and elsewhere I'm sure), casual conversations among teachers revolved around how students were leaving Facebook because it was uncool and flocking to Twitter.

Narratives that draw on the "digital natives" trope or claims that youth are fleeing Facebook for Twitter can lead teachers to make unwarranted assumptions about our own students' literacy practices and ideologies. It is important, I contend, for writing teachers to attend to the situated practices and understandings of social media that our students are bringing to writing classes. Because the goal of writing teachers is to help students make choices as writers and rhetors, writing teachers are well positioned to address questions about social media literacies and to teach new literacy practices in emerging digital environments (Wysocki,

2004). As literacy scholars have long argued, literacy is not a matter of mastering a single set of skills; rather, literacy activities are social, multiple, and situated in particular contexts (Street, 1995). I follow Cynthia L. Selfe (1999) and others in the field in understanding literacies as "a complex set of socially and culturally situated values, practices, and skills involved in operating linguistically within the context of electronic environments, including reading, writing, and communicating" (p. 11; see also Lankshear & Knobel, 2008; Selber, 2004). The ecological turn in rhetoric and writing studies has encouraged us to attend to not just how individuals create texts, but how people engage in media ecologies—especially technologically rich environments (Brooke, 2009; Buck, 2012; Dobrin & Weisser, 2002). In *Lingua Fracta*, Collin Gifford Brooke (2009) argued that scholars and teachers should attend to interfaces, exploring "ecologies of practice" rather than the production of stabilized texts (p. 6). However, digital interfaces are not the same for everybody, as they are dynamic and constantly changing. As Brooke argued, because of the dynamics of new media (like frequent updates on blog posts, dynamic and constantly updating Twitter streams and Facebook newsfeeds, and continuously updated wikis), there is an "absence of shared experience" in new media environments (p. 11). Further, users bring different experiences to interfaces, and thus, Brooke advocated a perspective of looking from, attending to how users approach interfaces differently at different moments, influenced by their experiences, familiarity, purposes—a perspective that encourages us to attend to the dynamic relationships between actors and changing interfaces (pp. 133, 140). Or, as Sidney Dobrin and Christian Weisser (2002) explained, "writers enter into particular environments with a certain ideological code and then contend with their environments as best these codes allow" (p. 576).

While literacy and writing scholars are accustomed to discussing differing literacy practices and ideologies, I draw from communication scholar Ilana Gershon's (2010) discussion of media ideologies and idioms of practice to assist in understanding how students in my study brought with them differing understandings of social media environments and differing understandings of practices. These analytic concepts, I suggest, are useful for writing teachers and literacy scholars to explore how students approach, use, and understand new media. In her discussion of how young adults end relationships via technology, Gershon (2010) defined media ideologies as "a set of beliefs about communicative technologies with which users and designers explain perceived media structures and meaning" (p. 3). In other words, beliefs about a medium influence and shape how people use that medium, and those beliefs are shaped by how they understand other media that they view as similar or different. Gershon explained that idioms of practice are those shared practices that users of media develop over time through shared experiences and conversations (p. 6). These concepts are helpful in understanding why people approach new media with different expectations and engage in different practices. Because social media are new and changing, users develop a variety of media ideologies and idioms of practice for particular sites, often leading to conflicting understandings and practices in those sites. Gershon's discussion of defriending others on Facebook is instructive here. Because of differing idioms of practice, Facebook users have different notions of what it means to defriend someone on Facebook. Some of her participants saw this action as casual, going through "regular bouts of defriending," while others saw this action as "an excessive act of hostility" (p. 42). Because our idioms of practice are developed over time, through shared experiences and discussions about new media, they lead to different under-standings and practices on new media sites. These practices are informed by media ideologies—what media we compare new media to and how casual or formal we see the media.

If we are to effectively teach social media literacies, we need to understand our particular students' media ideologies and idioms of practice—that is, what social media practices they are bringing to class, how those practices were shaped and formed, and how they understand social media as sites of social activity. I am not advocating that we understand these practices and ideologies in order to correct them: The goal of teaching social media literacies is not mastery of a set of skills, but gaining practice in a variety literacy activities and perspective on those practices (Daer & Potts, 2014).

This chapter argues, in part, that writing teachers need to attend to the par-ticular media ideologies and idioms of practice of their students. With this study, I provide an example of an approach to understanding students' practices and ideologies. Before explaining the study in depth, I first start with a discussion of privacy ethics relating to teaching with social media and researching student lit-eracy practices on social media. I then explain the context of the course and this study's methods in the following sections. In the discussion section, I explore themes that arose from the study relating to the issue of students' prior social media activities before the class, their understanding of new sites through these prior experiences, their perceptions of interacting with classmates and teachers online, and challenges of integrating school-based social media practices into their work habits and privacy practices. I close this chapter with implications related to these interrelated themes for understanding students' practices with social media and their own perceptions of those practices in localized contexts. I present these implications in the forms of questions that teachers need to ask in relation to students' idioms of practice and media ideologies.

DIGITAL PRIVACY: A FEW NOTES ON TEACHING AND RESEARCH ETHICS

Before turning to a discussion of this study specifically, a note on ethics regarding privacy is warranted. As writing teachers require students to use social media sites, and as teacher-researchers explore student literacies in these sites, we must confront the changing landscape of privacy in digital environments. I cannot do justice to every aspect of privacy and ethics in this chapter, but I do want to raise a few issues regarding student privacy, first regarding how I introduced issues of privacy in the course I am discussing, and then regarding research ethics. Writing for the Web has numerous affordances, including increased permanence and access—two affordances that we need to take into account as teachers and researchers.

At the start of the term, before students set up accounts on social media sites, I have conversations with them about issues of privacy and access. These conversations revolve around informational privacy, accessibility privacy, and expressive privacy (DeCew, 1997). We discuss how privacy is a matter of managing access to information and access to the self, as well as having spaces in which to express oneself and develop an identity. Importantly, privacy concerns are social (related to their social relationships with others), economic (related to companies having access to information), and legal (related to educational laws like the Federal Rights and Privacy Act [FERPA]). Students and I have conversations around a variety of related issues: whether to use their name or be pseudonymous on a site, whether to create a dummy email account to manage their required social media accounts, whether to use already existing accounts for coursework or whether to create new accounts, whether to use a profile picture with their likeness or not, and more. Each of these questions has multiple implications. Some students are not that concerned. Others want to separate their social activity on a site like Twitter from their educational activity. Some students do not want information posted under their name, which will then be accessible later after college when they are searching for jobs. I also want to respect their expressive privacy, and so do not follow them on Twitter, but rather ask that they use a course hashtag if they want their classmates and me to see their tweets. I also provide a brief statement on my syllabus:

> Because we will be using non-university services (Yammer, Diigo, Twitter, and possibly others), you will need to create accounts for these sites. You may use already created accounts (if you have them), but you are also welcome to create new accounts. I encourage you to consider creating pseudonymous

usernames for some of these accounts in order to explore them with less risk (and perhaps even using a dummy email account). I legally cannot (and ethically will not) require you to use your real name, with the exception of Yammer, which is a private network and requires your UWEC email address.

This last statement is important: While interpretations of FERPA vary from institution to institution, it is generally understood that teachers cannot reveal records about students. My interpretation of FERPA is that teachers can require students to share their work online, but should not require students to publicly attach their name to a course. Thus, I often require students to engage in publicly shared work (e-portfolios, blogs, tweets, and so forth), but I do not require them to use their real name if that work is attached to a course. In the case of using Diigo in this class, for instance, students belonged to a publicly accessible group, where others could see membership. Thinking through—and discussing with students—the social and legal implications of their profiles and activities is crucial not only for students' safety and legal protection, but also to help our students make informed decisions about their online presences.

Another aspect of privacy is that information companies are collecting more and more data about users, and using that information, through aggregation, to analyze populations. (Estee Beck's chapter in this collection explores the use of individual, prosumer labor to create massive amounts of data that is then used to surveil users.) Indeed, Google's and Facebook's ad revenue relies on this information. While responses to this development over the last few decades have ranged from the libertarian (let Google do what it wants!) to the paranoid (Google is Big Brother!), I think it's important to present information to students and help them make decisions. For example, are they concerned, and should they log off of Google, Twitter, or Facebook when they're not using it? Also, as teachers, we should be concerned about requiring accounts not affiliated with our institutions—we are, in effect, compelling students to provide data to private corporations. And our institutional software—like learning management systems—is designed to protect student information. Because of this dynamic, I believe we need to have thoroughly developed pedagogical rationales for requiring accounts on services. What opportunities for practicing and exploring literacies do they provide that wouldn't be provided by using institutional software? (If a sole goal is to have a threaded discussion, then why not use Blackboard, even with its less-than-ideal interface, rather than require students to use Facebook?)

Further, there are privacy implications for teacher-researchers as well. Twitter keeps archives of users' tweets, and even though Twitter makes it difficult to find older tweets through its interface, Google's search algorithm makes it easy to find tweets through searching for quotations. Changes in accessibility and permanence made possible by the Web affect the ethics of how we name and quote research participants (McIntire-Stasburg, 2007; McKee & Porter, 2009). Quoting or referencing text from the Web can draw attention to that text, and though texts (like students' tweets) may be publicly accessible in one way, writers may view them as private, or contextually private—that is, public in that it's accessible, but understood in context as private communication (Nissenbaum, 2010). For these reasons, while I quote from my students' video logs, and occasionally from other materials that are not accessible online, I do not quote students' tweets so as to protect their anonymity. While my students certainly understood their tweets as public, they also understood Twitter "as a place where people gather to share conversations" rather than a space of published material (McKee & Porter, 2009, p. 81).

PROJECT BACKGROUND: THE CONTEXT OF THE COURSE

In spring 2013, I designed a "Topics in Popular Culture" course as "Social Media and Society" to explore changing literacy practices in social media environments. Twenty-four students initially enrolled in the course, twenty of whom participated in this research study. Students came from a variety of liberal arts disciplines and included eleven white women, eight white men, and one African American man, all traditionally college-aged (between ages 18 and 24).

The goals of the course included gaining practice with social media, recognizing the affordances of digital media, articulating theories and arguments about digital literacy, and analyzing arguments and practices about and in social media environments. In addition to readings, course assignments included reading responses; video logs reflecting on their experiences using social media; a print or multimedia literacy narrative exploring experiences writing with digital media; a presentation introducing a social media site to the class; a final project that built off a literature review and took the format of a variety of deliverables; and, of course, engagement in social media for the class.

As I designed this course and study, I wanted to select social media environments for the class that would introduce students to a wide array of practices and experiences and would provide opportunities to discuss differences in site architecture, user experiences, and practices. I required that students use three social media sites:

1. *Twitter*, a micro-blogging platform in which users send missives of 140 characters or less, and can follow and respond to other users. Students used a course hashtag (#engl372) to follow each other's tweets. I selected Twitter because, after Facebook, it is probably the most well-known social

media site, and thus students could draw on their own familiarity of the site (either first-hand, second-hand, or from cultural narratives and mass media). As Stephanie Vie (2008) has suggested, writing teachers should incorporate social media sites that students likely have some familiarity with, but probably do not use or think through critically. Additionally, because Twitter is by default public, and because its user base is so large, it provides ample opportunities to witness it in use for many different (and at times conflicting) purposes. As a public forum, Twitter also served as useful terrain for exploring conflicting notions of the public/private distinction and different conventions for practicing privacy and publicity.

2. *Yammer*, a social networking site limited to those within a network (a business or school). I created a private group within our university's Yammer network for students to share resources and hold online conversations. Yammer provided a different type of environment to explore digital sociality and literacy than Twitter: Akin to Facebook, only limited to other members of the university network, Yammer allowed students to explore how conversations in one medium (a site like Facebook or Yammer) are different than one like Twitter. In this way, I viewed Yammer as a site that could help explore some of the implications of Facebook and similar social networking sites.

3. *Diigo*, a social bookmarking site that allows users to save and share bookmarks online. Students saved resources to our shared group and tagged those bookmarks with relevant labels. Diigo serves a different purpose than Yammer or Twitter, both of which are focused more on the immediate present. Diigo, as a curation and bookmarking site, focuses on creating searchable archives, and thus has a more "past-based" focus (what have I read in the past, rather than what I am reading and sharing now). In using Diigo and asking students to share resources with each other, my intent was, in part, to draw on the affordances of new media to explore notions of collaboration, curation, and folksonomies (Rice, 2008) with students.

Students and I collaborated on an assignment sheet to develop minimum requirements during an eight-week period in the term, including having profiles (that did not have to include one's likeness or identifying characteristics), saving relevant resources to Diigo, contributing to conversations weekly on Yammer, and tweeting regularly. Some tweets were responses to required prompts, and other tweets were up to students to decide how they wanted to contribute. Students were to experiment and explore a variety of styles of tweets, and we explored the implications of divergent and diverse practices as a class. My aim was that students would develop an assortment of uses for these sites, and ultimately see and recognize a wide array of practices.

METHOD

I designed a mixed-methods research study of students' activities and perceptions in order to employ a "rhetorical methodology" (Sullivan & Porter, 1997, p. 9) that triangulates data and methods through multiple sources (DePew, 2007). To provide a robust picture of students' idioms of practice and media ideologies, I gathered data through several methods: 1) an automated archive of tweets using the course hashtag; 2) analysis of students' Yammer posts; 3) students' reflective video logs; 4) an initial survey about students' practices; 5) students' writing projects; and 6) my own observations and notes about the class.[1]

While this study draws on all of these data points, I draw from their video logs most frequently in this chapter. Students posted three- to six-minute videos to our class' private YouTube account five times throughout the term, responding to a series of questions about their perceptions and experiences with social media. Questions asked students to explain and reflect on their experiences using social media, what they learned, what challenges they encountered, what their practices were like, and how they understood the sites we were using. These video logs were downloaded and transcribed, and the transcripts were coded.

DISCUSSION: FOUR THEMES

This discussion explores four themes relevant to social media and writing pedagogy: 1) students' understanding of social media sites through the lenses of their prior experiences; 2) students' perceptions of encountering and interacting with teachers on social media; 3) students' practices and perceptions of interacting with each other in social media environments; and 4) issues related to integrating school-based and self-sponsored social media literacies, including issues of work habits and privacy. Before discussing these themes, I first describe the prior literacy activities of students in this study. Throughout the discussion of these themes, I highlight how students' decisions on social media sites and their understandings of those sites and their decisions are informed and shaped by their media ideologies and idioms of practice.

---

1   Tweets were archived using Martin Hawksey's Twitter Archiving Google Spreadsheet (TAGS), available at http://mashe.hawksey.info/2013/02/twitter-archive-tagsv5/. Because Twitter's search application programming interface (API) is not fully reliable, the archive does not represent all tweets from students.

STUDENTS' PRIOR LITERACY PRACTICES USING SOCIAL MEDIA

Students' use of social media can vary widely, from limited use of only one site (or none at all) to heavy engagement on many sites for a variety of purposes. On one end of the spectrum was Don, who used only Facebook and no other sites, and explained that social media was "not much for me. I prefer face-to-face interaction." On the other end of the spectrum were Angela and Katherine, whom I discuss more below. While every student in the study mentioned using Facebook, other sites were used less: Eight had Twitter accounts, seven used Instagram, and five had used Tumblr. A few students had used other services, like SnapChat, Google+, Pinterest, Reddit, and Foursquare. But numbers don't give a complete picture: Users turn to these sites for a variety of purposes and in a variety of ways. Russell, for instance, had a Twitter account before class, but had never tweeted and used it mainly to follow news and celebrities. Or Tricia, who had a Pinterest account but didn't consider it social media, because she doesn't engage with other users or "pin" things. She explained, "I just look at all the pictures and waste time." And sometimes students test out a site and realize it is not for them. For example, Justin reported that while he had a Tumblr account, he had posted on it only once.

I draw on Mizuki Ito and her research team's (2010) taxonomy of "genres of participation" to categorize students' prior social media practices. They categorized practices into either friendship-driven practices ("hanging out") or interest-driven practices, those practices where "the interests come first, and [those interests] structure the peer network and friendship" (p. 16). They further categorize interest-driven activities as either "messing around"—activities that mark "the beginning of a more intense engagement with new media" (p. 54)—or "geeking out," "intense commitment or engagement with media or technology" (p. 65). After discussing students' out-of-school practices, I briefly describe their experiences with social media in school.

Hanging out. The most frequently cited reason for using a social media site was keeping in contact with friends and family, especially those who students could not see face-to-face often. Many students were busy and sites like Facebook were effective ways for them to stay in touch with friends they couldn't see often or family members back home. Stacy, for instance, explained that she didn't have time for long phone conversations and Facebook allowed her to chat quickly with her mother and see photos of cousins she couldn't see often.

Messing around. A small group of students also expressed that they used social media for messing around: keeping up with news, following celebrities or sports figures on Twitter, and finding and saving strong examples of sports news stories (for a few of the journalism students). For a few students, networks of affiliation on Tumblr and LiveJournal were important for interest-driven activities. Anica, for example, shared her reviews of books on Goodreads and followed the blogs of authors like Neil Gaiman on the site.

Geeking out. Two students in this study engaged in what Ito et al. (2010) called geeking out. As Ito et al. explained, geeking out doesn't have to be related to interests that are considered "geeky" or to a "geek" identity; instead, it's about expertise, credibility, and intensity in a community of shared interests (p. 66). Angela had been highly active live-tweeting at professional conferences, where she saw how powerful it could be for networking and having a backchannel for presentations; she was disappointed by her journalism classes where Twitter was used sparingly and had numerous accounts she had started and abandoned. Katherine was the most engaged in interest-driven activities. She explained, "You name it, I've probably tried it." Describing herself as "a little scene kid," Katherine was on Twitter in its early years to interact with her favorite bands, and before that was on MySpace to engage with the music industry. Katherine was the only student in the class to explicitly discuss meeting strangers online through sites like LiveJournal, and she shared her fan-fiction on the website Mibba, where she reported having 516 readers and 57 recommenders.

In sum, students' self-sponsored social media use prior to this course mirrored the activities described by Ito et al. (2010): Hanging out with friends and family was the most frequently cited activity, some students dabbled in messing around, and a few explored the intensity of geeking out.

Compared to their personal lives, their educational experiences involved little engagement with social media. Only four students mentioned using social media in a course before. Angela and Joel had been in a journalism course that required live-tweeting a lecture to practice that style of reporting, but had only done so for one lecture, a requirement of three tweets. Angela also expressed frustration that her teachers who required blogging didn't understand the blogging software, how to assess students' blogs, and how to integrate blogging into the classroom. My students' experiences confirm other educational research: Social media is not thoroughly integrated across the curriculum. A 2013 survey by Pearson Learning Solutions found that while more professors are using social media in their teaching than in the past (41 percent of their respondents), most of those professors are using blogs and wikis and no other social media. Very few seem to be using sites like Twitter, Facebook, and LinkedIn, and consuming social media (like podcasts) is much more common than creating it or commenting on it (Seaman & Tinti-Kane, 2013).

Students' self-sponsored learning activities on social media seemed to be more valuable experiences than teacher-sponsored activities. For example, when they took a series of courses together, the English education students in this class created a Facebook group to support each other. Tricia and Russell both described how the group was more convenient than texting or emailing friends because of the wider network of support and the quicker responses to questions in the group. The Facebook group provided a way to "clear things up" for Russell and provided "instant answers to your questions" for Tricia. Other students expressed that social media was useful for working on projects with classmates because it helped with managing busy and conflicting schedules when meeting face-to-face was difficult. They had found ways to incorporate social media informally into their educational experiences in ways that helped them successfully manage coursework. In contrast, Joel expressed that "there really wasn't much of an educational use" to live-tweeting a lecture without any follow-up discussion.

THEME 1: COMPARISONS TO PRIOR MEDIA

Students' histories and prior experiences with social media mattered as they used social media in this course in ways that both assisted in and interfered with their understandings and uses of these sites. As a social networking site for educational and work environments, Yammer incorporates features that are similar to Facebook, and students quickly intuited that they should understand Yammer like they do Facebook. For example, Anica understood Yammer as "just an academic Facebook." Students' media ideologies helped students to understand the site's general architecture, as students drew upon useful similarities: profiles, posts that are either available to an entire network or within a private group, threaded comments on posts, and so on.

But these comparisons also led to difficulties during the first few weeks using Yammer. Everyone in the network (school or organization) can view a post on Yammer, in contrast to most users' experiences on Facebook, where a post is shared with only one's friends (unless a user sets their privacy settings more broadly than friends-only). I had created a private Yammer group for the course so that content shared within the group was only accessible to the class. However, the distinction between network and group was difficult for some students to grasp in practice. Early in the term, students often unintentionally shared their posts with the entire network instead of within the course group. For instance, Katherine "wasn't familiar with the interface, so like when I shared my [literacy narrative], I only posted it to my wall and I guess I didn't realize that it was that much like Facebook, and I needed to put it in the group, and that it was possible to share to all of the Eau Claire community. That was a little daunting." Stacy did the same and struggled to figure out how to delete her original post. Some students, like Anica, did not appreciate their profiles being accessible to the entire university network: "If I wanted to be everybody's friend who goes to our school, I would friend everybody on Facebook." Anica chose to make her profile picture one of her cat to protect her privacy.

After I alerted students to the accessibility of their posts, they often took these posts down and reposted them within the private group. However, this happened often enough that a learning technology specialist on campus noticed and emailed me. She encouraged, perhaps even admonished, me to have students post course-related content to the class group, because posts irrelevant to the whole network could harm the development of the larger community. Additionally, she noted that if students were posting to the entire network, they should have a professional profile picture (in contrast to Anica, who preferred not to).

As Dànielle Nicole DeVoss, Ellen Cushman, and Jeffrey T. Grabill (2005) have argued, institutional infrastructures provide both support and disruptions for digital writing in classes. "Writing within digital spaces," they wrote, "occurs within a matrix of local and more global policies, standards, and practices. These variables often emerge as visible and at times invisible statements about what types of work are possible and valuable" (p. 16). We can see here an instantiation of these variables at play: The values and policies (implicit and explicit) of network administrators were at odds with the values of some of my students (Anica's value of privacy, for instance). Further, a network administrator saw this as an opportunity to "correct" student behavior and to professionalize students who were not ideal users. Indeed, the "when [of infrastructure] is acutely felt when students are seen as potential threats to the networks as opposed to its users" (p. 30). I had a goal different from "correcting" behavior, and used this email conversation as an opportunity to discuss with students differences between policies and practices, and the different conventions of various sites based on discourse communities and purposes. As DeVoss, Cushman, and Grabill noted, policies—shaped by and shapers of ideology—help to define digital writing and shape "who gets to learn it, where, and how" (p. 17).

While this discussion is related to institutional issues around Yammer's network structure and students' comparisons of Yammer to Facebook, it raises issues about social media in general: Students will approach new media through lenses of media that are familiar to them—drawing on their ideologies about media and their prior practices—leading to mistakes, breaches in their own privacy ethics, and perhaps practices that are at odds with the values of other stakeholders (like network administrators). Explaining the architecture of a new site is not sufficient to prevent these issues (though I question whether prevention of mistakes is a primary goal): I had explained how Yammer works numerous times during class.

Transference of media ideologies played out in other sites in the class as well, for better or worse. Students compared and contrasted Twitter to various print and digital media, including Facebook, Tumblr, newspapers, passing notes and holding side conversations in class, letters to the editor, living room conversations, texting, and search engines. These comparisons helped to highlight affordances of Twitter, including filtering news, finding more perspectives on events than the mainstream media provides, sharing one's perspective with a public, and having a backchannel during class. But these comparisons also led to confusion: Tricia, for example, compared favoriting tweets to "liking" Facebook posts, and wasn't sure what the implications for favoriting were; retweeting further confused her, as she wasn't sure what that meant for representing her own persona.

One upshot of students' struggles with understanding a site's architecture is the importance of using social media in writing classes that allow for students to make mistakes and to learn about the differences in sites. For students who are often afraid of making mistakes, this can lead to anxiety. Tricia, for example, was very concerned about "messing up" on Twitter, worrying that she would "sound like a guy" when she retweeted a funny tweet about a guy discussing his girlfriend, and wondering how others would interpret her favoriting these tweets. If a writing class is a space to experiment, to take risks and make mistakes, and even to make failure a meaningful and worthwhile experience, then it is important to allow space for making mistakes, to encourage taking risks and trying out new things, and to incorporate risk-taking into assessment (Carr, 2013; Reilly & Atkins, 2013).

Additionally, these experiences speak to the importance of teachers having some familiarity with a social media site before assigning it, as Vie (2008) has argued. But it also speaks to the necessity of teaching functional literacies that involve the ability to navigate new spaces and learn how to troubleshoot problems (Selber, 2004). As Stuart Selber (2004) has argued, functional literacies are thoroughly social; for example, part of being functionally literate involves learning the language others use to describe problems and the conventions that communities share on a site. While I thoroughly agree with Vie (2008) that it is important for teachers be familiar with social media, I also believe that it can be useful pedagogically to learn about social media sites along with students and to model problem-solving strategies when new issues arise in class. This practice can make a teachers' own assumptions about a site (and their own expectations drawing from their own media ideologies and idioms of practice) visible, and assist in students' critical reflection on their own assumptions, comparisons between sites, and practices they carry with them.

THEME 2: STUDENTS' INTERACTIONS WITH TEACHERS ON SOCIAL MEDIA

Teachers are often concerned about how their social media profiles and activities will be interpreted by students. Teachers may also be concerned about "invading" spaces that students feel are "theirs" by requiring students to use social media environments popular with youth (Maranto & Barton, 2010). Because of the shifting nature of professional, public, and private boundaries on social media, teachers need to ask questions about their own presence on these sites and how students will interpret and interact with them online. As a teacher, should I use a social media account that is solely for the class, or should I use an already existing account that also has other social purposes? What sort of ethos should I present on a site? If a site is being used for a class, should I friend or follow current students?

Students' discussions of interacting with teachers online suggest that care, media ideologies, and context are important aspects of those interactions. Generally, students in this study expressed amicability about finding their teachers on Facebook in their video logs. Anica's views of seeing content from teachers on Facebook are representative of many of her classmates: "If anything, it makes me more aware that they have an outside life that they have too, aside from teaching, which is kind of nice." Those who had friended former teachers expressed interest in experiencing their teachers as real people, and didn't see those teachers' presence on Facebook as ethos-harming. And generally, these students' teachers (both high school and college) had developed policies of only friending students after they had completed high school or the college class.

The only two negative responses came from Justin and Don, and they spoke to appropriate professional behavior and the sort of genres that Facebook recalls. Justin shared his experience seeing a professor's post on Facebook:

> Last semester she actually had a couple Facebook posts that were kind of questionable about her criticizing a student. . . . They were kind of mean and—I don't know—it just didn't seem like something that should come from a professor, and eventually a couple weeks after that post, she put out an apology on Facebook, and I think she took a little break from [Facebook] for a while.

While Justin noted a case of a teacher acting questionably on Facebook, Don drew on his media ideologies about Facebook and his experiences in high school to imagine a potential interaction with a teacher online:

> For some reason, it's just strange and—it's like in high school, if you saw your high school teacher at the grocery store or something. It's, you know, it was the weirdest thing ever. Like, they shouldn't have a life outside of high school.

Students' interpretations and willingness to interact with a teacher on social media will depend, in part, on their media ideologies about those particular sites and their idioms of practice they bring to those sites.

Maranto and Barton's (2010) warning that using Facebook in a class might seem like an invasion of a space away from adults is now likely an outdated perspective to many of our students, who are friends with older relatives and former teachers already. And some students benefit from networking with teachers online: The English education students in this course stressed the usefulness of being friends with teachers, because it provided mentorship, and students like Russell expressed how useful it was to set up meetings with me through Twitter or get updates about the course without checking his email. Ultimately, teachers need to think in terms of access and care when deciding how to present themselves on social media, when deciding whether to assign certain sites to students, and when discussing those interactions during metadiscursive conversations with students.

By care here, I mean a sort of situated respect for others and concern for the welfare of others (Porter, 1998, pp. 92–94, 154). One might think that it's important for a teacher to have a professional, scholarly identity presentation on a social networking site so that students would interpret the teacher's ethos as credible and professional. However, I would like to suggest that how one interacts and develops a situated ethics of care is more important than an "appropriate" scholarly ethos. In a study of student perceptions of teachers based on their Twitter stream, Kirsten A. Johnson (2011) found that students were more likely to find a teacher credible if their Twitter account was comprised of "very personal" or "very conversational" tweets compared to a Twitter stream solely composed of scholarly tweets (pp. 33–34). She speculated that perhaps care was a more important indicator of credibility for students on social media than scholarly competence. While Johnson's study was an experiment decontextualized from actual classroom practices, it does point to how a teacher disclosing personal information on social media can actually be helpful in building trust— as does the experiences of some of my students in this study. And the converse, not showing care, as in the case of Justin's teacher, harms that trust building.

Access, too, is important to think through, and here is where particular groups of students' media ideologies play a role in determining what sites teachers should inhabit along with students. As we saw above, students differ in how they understand a teacher's presence on a site. While many of the students in my study were comfortable with friending former teachers on Facebook, Don compared Facebook to a public space (the grocery store) that he saw as a realm distinct from the space of a school. We might consider social media sites as spaces that students have media ideologies about, understanding them differently in terms of access to the self and away from parents, teachers, and other authorities. Students in this study often referenced high school when discussing Facebook—understandable, given how Facebook remediates many high school genres, like yearbooks, "cruising" car culture, and hang-out spots like arcades (Bogost, 2010; Maranto & Barton, 2010). For other social media spaces, how do students understand them? What media ideologies do they draw upon to understand the site and access to the site? Given that much social media is used for self-expression and identity development away from authority figures—what Judith Wagner DeCew (1997) called "expressive privacy"—even if the space is publicly accessible (boyd, 2014), we need to consider students' media ideologies about specific sites in specific times and spaces.

THEME 3: STUDENTS' INTERACTIONS WITH EACH OTHER IN SOCIAL MEDIA ENVIRONMENTS

Overwhelmingly, students reported that using Twitter and Yammer helped to create a classroom community and helped them get to know their classmates more personally. Tricia's and Nolan's comments are representative of their classmates' claims. Tricia explained, "In class, it's more student-to-teacher, like I'm answering your questions, and then on social media, I'm actually talking and responding, tweeting back to classmates directly, which is pretty nice. I like that aspect of it." Nolan claimed, "It is definitely leading to relationships with people in the class who I wouldn't have spoken to otherwise."

The archives of students' Twitter and Yammer activity both confirm and challenge these claims. Figures 15.1 and 15.2 visualize students' engagement with each other on Twitter and Yammer, respectively. Arrows represent the direction of a response; the thicker an edge (the line connecting two students), the more replies that user sent to another user. A node's size represents a student's replies to classmates: The larger the node, the more responses they wrote.

Some, like Russell, interacted with numerous classmates: He replied to 11 classmates on Twitter and to 13 on Yammer. Others were less interactive, including Alex, who didn't reply to any tweets or Yammer posts all term, in part because he didn't post much on Yammer or Twitter all term. And interactivity is not captured solely through replies and comments: Alicia, for example, tweeted about classmates' presentations without mentioning their username, and retweeted classmates (which don't show up as replies in Figure 15.2). Many students claimed that social media seemed to provide a place for quieter students to "talk," and this played out in the data. For instance, April was quiet in class and explained in a video log how she felt that everyone thinks too fast in class and she was always behind during class conversations. She was a frequent tweeter and responded to nearly half of her classmates throughout the term.

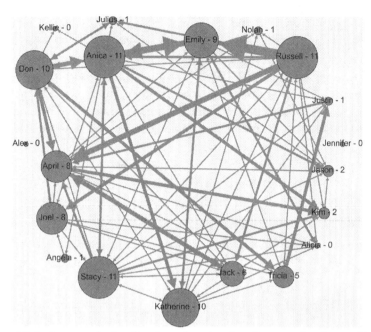

Figure 15.1. A network visualization of students' replies to each other on Twitter.

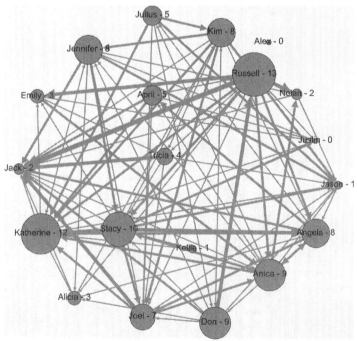

Figure 15.2. A network visualization of students' responses to each other on Yammer.

But we should be skeptical of some claims about increased engagement online: The students who replied to tweets the most—Russell, Anica, Emily, Stacy, and Don—were some of the most talkative during class. And Nolan, who claimed to be creating new relationships, only responded to one tweet (from Jason, though he did retweet classmates occasionally), and only responded to Yammer posts by Jack and Jason. Nolan was much more active in responding to his classmates' comments during class. He provided an interesting anecdote, though: "One time I commented on Jason's post, and then I saw him outside of class, and he like waved to me and laughed, and for some reason I just knew that that's what he was laughing about."

Nolan's claim about himself and his anecdote give me pause: Teachers should be cautious about measuring engagement through visible metrics like replies and comments. Though replies and comments are important for a variety of pedagogical reasons—practicing those activities, contributing to conversations, challenging ideas, developing a voice in a particular medium—they are not the sole measurement for engagement. Social media works through a logic of visibility, as does assessment (we can only assess what we see), but we can't rely solely on literacy activities that are visible in these environments. (And further, such metrics can be means of teacher control; see Losh, 2014.) We need to value listening and reading as well. Kim, for example, showed to me that she was quite aware of her classmates' various "perspectives on the readings and videos that we watch" on Twitter, though she only responded to two classmates' tweets throughout the term. Thus, regarding assessment of social media practices in writing classes, it may be more useful to evaluate reflections, which can show metacognitive understanding of students' practices and allow for risk taking rather than perfection (Daer & Potts, 2014; McKee & DeVoss, 2013; Reilly & Atkins, 2013).

THEME 4: INTEGRATING SCHOOL-BASED AND SELF-SPONSORED SOCIAL MEDIA LITERACIES: WORK HABITS, CONTEXTUAL PRIVACY, AND CONVERGENT AUDIENCES

Tensions between school-based literacies and out-of-school literacies come to the forefront when writing teachers ask students to use social media, as social media use for class may clash or conflict with students' self-sponsored social media literacies. (Though self-sponsored literacies can also be very supportive of academic literacies; see Chris M. Anson's chapter in this collection.) In this section, I discuss two issues that arose for my students out of tensions between school-based use and personal use of social media: work habits and contextual privacy.

Students in this course tended to conceptually organize their school-based literacies separately from their out-of-school literacies, leading to difficulties in managing their work habits and integrating social media into their school-based writing. This does not mean that students separated schoolwork and social media in space and time. Emily is a good example of this: Before this class, she had used Twitter to manage her desire to talk with friends while working on a paper. Knowing that co-present friends would be a distraction for finishing a paper, Emily used Twitter to manage conversations so that she could both work effectively and maintain social contact. (See Patricia Portanova's chapter in this collection on how students develop metacognitive strategies for managing multiple media while composing.)

Again and again, students expressed that the biggest challenge was remembering to check in on these sites, read each other's posts, and post themselves. Students are trained in print literacies for education, and might not see much of their digital activity as involving required schoolwork. (Even most digital educational activities model print activities, like downloading PDF readings from a learning management system or writing essays in Microsoft Word.) The conceptual schemas that students had developed over time—their idioms of practice—allowed them to check social media frequently for personal reasons, but to forget to do so for class. Stacy, though she was trying to cut back on her Facebook use, explained, "When I open my computer's web browser, I almost always immediately start typing in 'Facebook' without even thinking about it, even if I don't want to go to that site!" She explained that while she has habits of checking social media, she didn't remember to use the course-based social media sites unless she wrote it down. Jack said that he tweeted a lot for personal reasons, but often forgot to do so for class. Nolan expressed that he's developed habits of social media "for fun" and hadn't yet developed a habit of it being required. Tricia expressed that her poor memory for checking social media often meant she missed out on responding in a timely manner to her classmates' tweets and comments to her. And even though some students kept the default settings for daily email notifications from Yammer and Diigo, many, like Kim, "kind of ignored those emails."

Clearly, integrating social media into work habits was a challenge for many of these students, but I view it as a productive challenge, and one writing teachers must face as we move from courses that teach traditional print essays to courses that teach for a variety of literacies.

Another tension that students faced was their contextual privacy (Nissenbaum, 2010), or managing what danah boyd (2014, p. 31) called "collapsed contexts," while integrating their social and school-based literacies. Students already have developed strategies for managing privacy using social media. Emily's example of using Twitter to manage contact with friends is one example, and Nolan provided another: In high school, to have privacy from parents, he contacted friends through social media instead of a landline phone (see boyd, 2014, for more on this type of privacy management). Students who already had Twitter accounts prior to this class especially had to manage privacy tensions. Angela, for instance, decided to create a second account for the class, but quickly found that she struggled to remember which account she was logged into when tweeting for class or for personal reasons; midway through the term she reverted to using just a single account. Kim created a new account as well, concerned that she would lose followers if she tweeted for class a lot. Russell explained that he had friends who were excited to see him finally start tweeting but then expressed disappointment that all his tweets were for class. Jack, who used his personal account for class, had friends who were annoyed that he was filling up their Twitter feeds with class tweets, and fielded tweets from friends telling him to stop.

These are just a few of the instances when students had to manage collapsed contexts on Twitter and decide how they wanted to integrate, or attempt to make separate, their personal social media use and school-based use. Again, as with work habits, these tensions provide opportunities to explore conflicting practices and media ideologies with social media. While students often struggled through managing new work habits and contending with collapsed contexts, they were largely successful (as is evidenced by over 200 Yammer posts and over 800 tweets by students throughout the term).

CONCLUSION: QUESTIONS TO CONSIDER ABOUT STUDENTS' MEDIA IDEOLOGIES AND IDIOMS OF PRACTICE

This study adds to research and scholarship exploring the complexities of integrating social media into writing classes. Students in this study showed that experiences with social media can vary widely; that students use their experiences with some sites in order to understand new environments; that, depending on their media ideologies, they are comfortable interacting with teachers on some sites; and that they can struggle to integrate social media into their work habits. I close with some questions to consider when incorporating social media in writing classes:

Before teaching, where and how is social media being taught across the curriculum at your institution? What practices are valued and being taught elsewhere at the university?

What idioms of practice and media ideologies are your students bringing to the class? How do these idioms of practice challenge or conform to popular narratives about young adults and digital media?

What sort of activities do you want students to gain practice and perspective in? How do their prior experiences align with or challenge some of those practices? What social media platforms are useful for these practices?

What examples can you provide for students of a variety of practices in these environments to help them explore implications they might not recognize because of their own media ideologies?

What are the implications of using your already existing accounts as a teacher? Will you use your personal Twitter, Facebook, or other account, or create a new one specifically for working with students? How might students interpret your account based on their media ideologies and your persona presented on the site? Similarly, what are the implications of students using already existing accounts?

How will students assess their own practices? How will you assess their practices? What media ideologies are they carrying forward to see certain practices as successes or failures? What media ideologies are you drawing upon to see successes, struggles, and failures? How can these online spaces be used to allow for making mistakes?

How will you assist students in managing and integrating social media into their work habits?

How will you assist students in managing collapsed contexts and managing their social privacy in online environments?

What technologies are students bringing to class, and how do they use them for social media? Are there technology resources on your campus, such as devices students can borrow?

Young adults are not a monolithic group of digital natives ready to excel in social media literacies in our writing classes. The idioms of practice and media ideologies they bring into class will vary and lead to mistakes, struggles, and conflicting understandings of sites and practices. How, ultimately, can we develop our own awareness of students' practices and beliefs in order to provide a learning environment where they can experiment and practice? Overall, our goal should be to assist in developing our students' rhetorical faculties, or "the degree to which a student interprets a problem, recognizes how their learning can inform a solution, and then produces a context-appropriate solution" (Daer & Potts, 2014, pp. 26–27). In order to assist in this rhetorical development, I believe, we need to attend to—and help our students be reflective about—our students' particular media ideologies and idioms of practice that shape and influence their literacy practices.

REFERENCES

Bogost, I. (2010). Ian became a fan of Marshall McLuhan on Facebook and suggested you become a fan too. In D. E. Wittkower (ed.), *Facebook and philosophy: What's on your mind?* Chicago, IL: Open Court.

boyd, d. (2014). *It's complicated: The social lives of networked teens.* New Haven, CT: Yale University Press.

Brooke, C. G. (2009). *Lingua fracta: Towards a rhetoric of new media.* Cresskill, NJ: Hampton.

Buck, A. (2012). Examining social media literacies on social network sites. *Research in the Teaching of English, 47*(1), 9–38.

Carr, A. (2013). In support of failure. *Composition Forum, 27.* Retrieved from http://compositionforum.com/issue/27/failure.php.

Daer, A. R. & Potts, L. (2014). Teaching and learning with social media: Tools, cultures, and best practices. Programmatic Perspectives, 6(2), 21–40.

DeCew, J. W. (1997). *In pursuit of privacy: Law, ethics, and the rise of technology.* Ithaca, NY: Cornell University Press.

DePew, K. E. (2007). Through the eyes of researchers, rhetors, and audiences. In H. A. McKee & D. N. DeVoss (Eds.), *Digital writing research: Technologies, methodologies and ethical issues* (pp. 49–69). Cresskill, NJ: Hampton Press.

DeVoss, D. N., Cushman, E. & Grabill, J. T. (2005). Infrastructure and composing: The *when* of new media writing. *College Composition and Communication, 57*(1), 14–44.

Dobrin, S. I. & Weisser, C. R. (2002). Breaking ground in ecocomposition: Exploring relationships between discourse and environments. *College English, 64*(5), 566–589.

Gershon, I. (2010). *The breakup 2.0: Disconnecting over new media.* Ithaca, NY: Cornell University Press.

Hargittai, E. (2010). Digital na(t)ives? Variations in Internet skills and uses among members of the "net generation." *Sociological Inquiry, 80*(1), 92–113.

Ito, M., et al. (2010). *Hanging out, messing around, and geeking out: Kids living and learning with new media.* Cambridge, MA: The MIT Press.

Johnson, K. A. (2011). The effect of Twitter posts on students' perceptions of instructor credibility. *Learning, Media and Technology, 36*(1), 21–38.

Jones, C. (2011). Students, the net generation, and digital natives: Accounting for educational change. In M. Thomas (Ed.), *Deconstructing digital natives: Young people, technology, and the new literacies* (pp. 30–45). New York, NY: Routledge.

Lankshear, C. & Knobel, M. (Eds). (2008). *Digital literacies: Concepts, policies and practices.* New York, NY: Peter Lang.

Losh, E. (2014). *The war on learning: Gaining ground in the digital university.* Cambridge, MA: The MIT Press.

Madden, M. (2013, August 15). Teens haven't abandoned Facebook (yet). *Pew Research Internet Project.* Retrieved from http://www.pewinternet.org/2013/08/15/teens-havent-abandoned-facebook-yet/.

Madden, M., Lenhart, A., Cortesi, S., Gasser, U., Duggan, M., Smith, A. & Beaton, M. (2013, May 21). Teens, social media, and privacy. *Pew Research Internet Project.* Retrieved from http://www.pewinternet.org/2013/05/21/teens-social-media-and -privacy/.

Maranto, G. & Barton, M. (2010). Paradox and promise: MySpace, Facebook, and the sociopolitics of social networking in the writing classroom. *Computers and Composition, 27*(1), 36–47.

McIntire-Strasburg, J. (2007). Multimedia research: Difficult questions with indefinite answers. In H. A. McKee & D. N. DeVoss (Eds.), *Digital writing research: Technologies, methodologies and ethical issues* (pp. 287–300). Cresskill, NJ: Hampton Press.

McKee, H. A. & DeVoss, D. N. (Eds.). (2013). *Digital writing assessment & evaluation.* Logan, UT: Computers and Composition Digital Press/Utah State University Press. Retrieved from http://ccdigitalpress.org/dwae.

McKee, H. A. & Porter, J. E. (2009). *The ethics of Internet research: A rhetorical case-based approach.* New York, NY: Peter Lang.

Miller, D. (2013, December 30). Scholarship, integrity, and going viral [Blog entry]. Global Social Media Impact Study. Retrieved from http://blogs.ucl.ac.uk/social -networking/2013/12/30/scholarship-integrity-and-going-viral/.

Nissenbaum, H. (2010). *Privacy in context: Technology, policy, and the integrity of social life.* Stanford, CA: Stanford University Press.

Pigg, S., Grabill, J. T., Brunk-Chavez, B., Moore, J. L., Rosinski, P. & Curran, P. G. (2014). Ubiquitous writing, technologies, and the social practice of literacies of coordination. *Written Communication, 31*(1), 91–117.

Prensky, M. (2001). Digital natives, digital immigrants. *On the Horizon, 9*(5), 1–6.

Porter, J. E. (1998). *Rhetorical ethics and internetwork writing.* Greenwich, CT: Ablex.

Reilly, C. A. & Atkins, A. T. (2013). Rewarding risk: Designing aspirational assessment processes for digital writing projects. In H. A. McKee & D. N. DeVoss (Eds.), *Digital writing & evaluation.* Logan, UT: Computers and Composition Digital Press/Utah State University Press. Retrieved from http://ccdigitalpress.org/dwae/04_reilly.html.

Rice, J. (2008). Folksono(me). *JAC, 28*(1–2), 181–208.

Seaman, J. & Tinti-Kane, H. (2013, September). Social media for teaching and learning. Retrieved from http://www.pearsonlearningsolutions.com/higher-education /social-media-survey.php.

Selber, S. A. (2004). *Multiliteracies for a digital age.* Carbondale, IL: Southern Illinois University Press.

Selfe, C. L. (1999). *Technology and literacy in the twenty-first century: The importance of paying attention.* Carbondale, IL: Southern Illinois University Press.

Street, B. V. (1995). *Social literacies: Critical approaches to literacy in development, ethnography and education.* London, England: Longman.

Sullivan, P. & Porter, J. E. (1997). *Opening spaces: Writing technologies and critical research practices.* Westport, CT: Ablex.

Tate, R. (2013, December 27). Facebook is "dead and buried" to teens, and that's just fine for Facebook. *Wired.* Retrieved from http://www.wired.com/2013/12/facebook -teens-2/.

Vie, S. (2008). Digital divide 2.0: "Generation M" and online social networking sites in the composition classroom. *Computers and Composition, 25*(1), 9–23.

Wysocki, A. F. (2004). Opening new media to writing: Openings & justifications. In A. F. Wysocki, J. Johnson-Eilola, C. L. Selfe & G. Sirc, *Writing new media: Theory and applications for expanding the teaching of composition* (pp. 1–41). Logan, UT: Utah State University Press.

CHAPTER 16

INTELLECTUAL, ARGUMENTATIVE, AND INFORMATIONAL AFFORDANCES OF PUBLIC FORUMS: POTENTIAL CONTRIBUTIONS TO ACADEMIC LEARNING

Chris M. Anson

North Carolina State University

In a case study, Amber Buck (2012) described the literacy practices of Ronnie, an undergraduate student at a large midwestern university. Through multiple sources of data, including a time-use diary, interviews, and a profile tour of Ronnie's social network sites, Buck painstakingly documented what Paul Prior and Jody Shipka (2003) called the "chronotopic laminations" of his literate practices—the "dispersed and fluid places, times, people, and artifacts that are tied together in literate action" (p. 181). As Buck (2012) showed, Ronnie's online activity is "intricately woven into the tapestry of his daily literacy practices" and plays a "large role in how he interacts with others in his personal and professional life as well as how he presents himself to different audiences" (pp. 9–10).

Ronnie's practices are by no means unique. They resemble those of students on and off campuses across the United States and around the world. In "Writing in the 21st Century," Yancey (2009) pointed out that because of digital technology

> writers are *everywhere*—on bulletin boards and in chat rooms and in emails and in text messages and on blogs. . . . Such writing is what Deborah Brandt has called self-sponsored writing: a writing that belongs to the writer, not to an institution, with the result that people—students, senior citizens, employees, volunteers, family members, sensible *and* non-sensible people alike—want to compose and do—on the page and on the screen and on the network—to *each other.* (p. 4, emphasis in original)

For Kevin Roozen (2009) and other scholars, these "vernacular literacies" represent "informally learned activities, rooted in everyday experience and serv[ing] everyday purposes" (as cited in Barton & Hamilton, 1998, p. 251).

Yet critics and academics alike continue to level harsh criticisms against students' online interactions, particularly their use of social media, claiming that it strips away imagination and creative uses of language (Pacheco, 2012), "degrades" writing ability (Hansen, 2013), and sends essay skills "down the plug hole" (Henry, 2013). Typical concerns include the fragmentation of attention, the invasion of "text speak" and other linguistic features of Internet-based writing into academic papers, and the effects of fast, brief online writing on students' ability to frame and sustain arguments. Franzen (2013) bemoaned technology's promotion of "intolerably shallow forms of social engagement" and asked what will happen to people who "want to communicate in depth, individual to individual, in the quiet and permanence of the printed word." Similarly, texting is said to be "pillaging our punctuation; savaging our sentences; [and] raping our vocabulary" (Humphrys, 2007). Yet these claims remain unsupported by formal research and are not even based on careful descriptive inquiry into the nature and contexts of the public writing in which students are engaged online.

This chapter argues that self-sponsored, digitally mediated literate activities can provide forms of tacit learning—especially about discourse—that mirror the learning encouraged and expected in school. However, academic and self-sponsored writing are often thought to exist in different worlds. Students don't see many relationships between their online self-sponsored writing and their papers and other academic work (Lenhart, Arafeh, Smith & Macgill, 2008), and teachers are reluctant to bring students' personal use of technology into the classroom (Levin, Arafeh, Lenhart & Rainie, 2002). But keeping these two worlds of literate practices apart may be unwise. As Stephanie Vie (2008) has argued, intentionally and carefully bridging the two domains, both in foundational writing courses and in courses across the curriculum, may strengthen students' learning, foster more conscious rhetorical awareness, teach them skills of reasonable civic participation, and facilitate the transfer of discursive ability across diverse communities of practice.

ACADEMIC AND SELF-SPONSORED WRITING: HOW MUCH?

Unless they liked to keep diaries or write poems and stories, few young people engaged in self-sponsored writing before the advent of the Internet. Thompson (2009) went so far as to claim that "most Americans never wrote anything, ever, that wasn't a school assignment" (para. 5). Kathleen Blake Yancey (2009) explained that before the Internet, the association of writing with hard work and difficulty, with school testing, even with penmanship, pushed all but the most literarily inclined students away from self-sponsored writing. However, almost half of today's parents believe that their teenage children write more than they did at the same age, and another 20 percent say they write at least as much (Pew, 2014).

The importance of schooling for the advancement of written literacy is indisputable. Yet the quantity of writing students produce in school does not appear to have increased significantly over the past decades. Data from the National Assessment of Educational Progress (NAEP) from both 2007 and 2011 show that high school students write little in school. In 2007, between 70 percent and 90 percent of high school seniors wrote common school genres somewhere between never and once a month (National Center for Education Statistics, 2013). The 2011 NAEP data show that 82 percent of seniors wrote between zero and three pages per week in language arts classes; almost 40 percent wrote one page or less (National Center for Education Statistics, 2013). Large course loads, underfunding, lack of teacher development, and the association of writing with standardized testing all militate against assigning and responding thoughtfully to acceptable amounts of purposeful writing in the schools.

Although they may be less extensive, data from higher education point in the same direction. According to the National Survey of Student Engagement, which is administered to over 700 U.S. four-year colleges and universities each year, in 2014 and 2015, 76 percent of first-year students reported writing no papers longer than 10 pages; another 19 percent reported writing one or two such papers during the current year (National Survey of Student Engagement, 2016). Seniors did not fare much better: 41 percent reported writing no papers longer than 11 pages; another 34 percent reported writing one or two such papers (National Survey of Student Engagement, 2016). The median for the number of pages written in the first year is 69 (less than one page a week, assuming a five-course load) and 109 for seniors (not much more than one page a week) (R. M. Gonyea, personal communication, 2015). Fewer than half of all students take a course in which they must write more than 20 pages during the semester (Arum & Roska, 2011). Results from the 2014 Faculty Survey of Student Engagement (FSSE) show that in most lower-division courses, 80 to 90 percent of faculty members assign no papers of more than 10 pages (Indiana University, 2014). The data reporting the number of shorter papers, while more substantial, still leave much to be desired (National Survey of Student Engagement, 2016). Of course, length and amount of writing alone do not always correlate with improved writing experiences (Anderson, Anson, Gonyea & Paine, 2015); much depends on the nature and quality of assignments and how they are used in the course. However, a national study of 2,101 assignments across the curricula of 100 U.S. postsecondary institutions also documents the lack of systematic attention to audiences and purposes beyond the teacher playing the role of an examiner (Melzer, 2014). Problematic assumptions about writing continue to work against its richer and more principled integration into all courses and curricula: it's the responsibility of composition teachers; it intrudes on "coverage" of the material; its grading takes too much time away from research and other responsibilities; or it's not highly relevant to the learning of a content area (math, physics, chemistry, etc.). In spite of the continued development of writing-across-the-curriculum programs (Thaiss & Porter, 2010), no evidence suggests a nationwide increase in student writing in higher education. In addition, research suggests that teachers infrequently incorporate new communication technologies into the classroom (beyond visual display such as PowerPoint or occasional discussion forums), which further limits their exposure to the relationship between writing and other media.

But a lack of purposeful writing is no longer the case in students' personal lives. The amount of writing students are now doing outside of academic settings approaches or exceeds what they do in school. Researchers at Stanford University collected every piece of writing produced by a random sample of 189 students over five years, yielding over 14,000 texts (Keller, 2009). The study showed that students were "deeply engaged" with their self-sponsored writing: "For these students, extracurricular writing is very important, often more important than any of the writing they are doing for classes" (Lunsford, 2007, p. 3). Students were generally less enthusiastic about their academic writing because it lacked purpose and wasn't instrumental. In contrast, their self-sponsored writing often had specific goals such as keeping a group organized or doing something political. Likewise, a recent study of ten undergraduates found fewer instances of audience awareness and fewer writing decisions based on audience concerns when students talked about their academic writing than when they talked about their self-sponsored writing (Rosinski, 2016).

Other research corroborates these findings. In a study at Michigan State University, a group of students was asked to record everything they wrote during a two-week period (blogging, texting, academic papers, etc.), noting time, genre, audience, location, and purpose. In their diaries and in the researchers' interviews, students described their nonacademic and socially driven writing "as more persistent and meaningful to them than their in-class work" (Keller, 2009). Likewise, a recent Pew study (2014) revealed that "the vast majority of teens have eagerly embraced written communication with their peers as they share messages on their social network pages, in emails and instant messages online"; 93 percent of teens surveyed said they frequently write for their own pleasure (Lenhart, Arafeh, Smith & Macgill, 2008, p. i).

Students' engagement in self-sponsored writing clearly emerges from the massive growth of the Internet and the ubiquity of digital devices for participating in every imaginable form of interaction. The Internet has afforded the unprecedented growth of writing across multiple platforms, in hundreds of emerging genres, among hundreds of millions of users worldwide, and in rapidly multiplying communities and activities such as buying, selling, and trading; sharing hobbies or special interests; or discussing issues in dozens of domains such as health, the law, politics, and education. Facebook now has 1.23 billion daily active users and 1.15 billion daily active mobile users; 1.86 billion people use the site at least once a month. Among those aged 12–17, almost three in four (73%) use the site ("Company Info," 2016). People aged 18–24 send and receive an average of 3,853 texts per month, or 128 per day (TextRequest, 2017). Meanwhile, additional forms of chat, such as WhatsApp and BBM, may cut into the number of text messages while simultaneously creating net gains in overall messaging (Crocker, 2013; Kalinchuk, 2013). The Radicati Group reported that there were 4.92 billion email accounts worldwide in 2017, and that number is expected to increase by 7 percent yearly through 2019 (Radicati Group, 2017). Website hosting and interaction is equally robust. On WordPress (just one of hundreds of Web hosting sites), 409 million people currently view over 24.6 billion pages per month, and users write 87.6 million new posts and nearly 44.6 million new comments per month (WordPress, 2017).

SWITCHING LENSES: A SOCIAL PRACTICES VIEW OF LITERATE ACTIVITY

If we view our students' participation in this prodigious textual activity through our usual academic lens, the result sometimes looks like so much digital waste, an effluence of emotion-laden responses, name-calling, and vapid status updates, as suggested in just three (of 9,506,164) YouTube posts responding to a news report about a whale crashing into a South African couple's sailboat because they were pursuing it too closely:

> michael: what the hell who gives the damn about a whale and the boat
>
> gorrilaboy22: lol this whale forgot his life jacket.
>
> Sputnikmedia: why does everybody name their boats intrepid LOL

Such activity looks quite different, however, if we take what the New London Group and other scholars call a "social practices" or "learning ecology" orientation to literacy (Gee, 1996; Street, 1993; see also Hull & Schultz, 2001). Based on sociocultural activity theories and theories of situated discourse, this orientation sees learning not just in terms of the minds of individuals but these individuals' relationship to contexts and to other people. Learning "derives from participation in joint activities, is inextricably tied to social practices, and is mediated by artifacts over time" (Greenhow, 2013, p. 20; see also Greenhow, Robelia & Hughes, 2009). This orientation breaks down traditional hierarchies that place some forms of writing above others. Tweets, truncated and constrained, play multiple rhetorical, informational, and social roles across vast digital landscapes. Responses on forums or blogs, as well as text messages do the same. All writing is equal in the sense that it serves particular social, informational, and rhetorical purposes as a function of a community's needs and interests. But if we look below its surface structure features, it also reflects deeper meta-level processes, such as negotiating face, or making and defending persuasive claims, or extending a community's knowledge.

Most publicly available sites create their own self-defined audiences, some relatively stable and coherent, others wildly fluctuating and fleeting. Among the former are fan sites for sports teams, constantly visited by more enduring and loyal audiences to get updates and to carry on conversations. Among the latter are sites such as YouTube, where audiences flock momentarily and virally to videos, often because links are posted on other sites such as Facebook. Many users may view a single video only once and some will post a comment; the result is a multimedia blend of visual and textual elements.

Consider Purplepride.org, a fan site for the Minnesota Vikings NFL football team. The website includes news, photos, audio and video clips, team and game day information, and links to a series of forums (with archives) on various topics related to football. The most central of these is the "Vikings Fans Forum," which at this writing has almost 500,000 posts and 21,184 threads. Total posts to the site, which has 11,535 members, exceed 1,102,000. While middle or high school students are working hard to learn argumentative strategies in often banal, purposeless assignments, here they might practice those strategies tacitly in their self-sponsored writing. The style and register of the exchanges is clearly nonacademic, with abbreviations, informal lexis, and oral features similar to online chats or text messages. Looking into the "deep structures" of the exchanges, however, we can see evidence of argumentative properties students are expected to use in academic work. Although many discussions resemble what Nancy L. Stein and Christopher A. Miller (1990) called "social argument" (the kind experienced in every household when issues or actions must be debated), participants are still strategically supporting particular positions. In fact, members of this and similar forums often demand support for claims more vehemently than do many teachers. To facilitate dialog and interaction, participants also must learn to concede to opposing views, reason from logic, and share and negotiate information requiring skills of numeracy, historical accuracy, and prediction.

Strictly speaking, such forums are not social networking sites, which are usually defined as

> web-based services that allow individuals to (1) construct a
> public or semi-public profile within a bounded system, (2)
> articulate a list of other users with whom they share a con-
> nection, and (3) view and traverse their list of connections
> and those made by others within the system. (boyd & Ellison,
> 2007)

But to investigate the effects of students' self-sponsored online activities on their academic learning, it's essential to expand and re-theorize the nature of the social beyond such bounded and profile-based systems. First, sites strongly associated with social networking, such as Facebook, realize wide degrees of both "social" and "networking." A user can set up a Facebook page with minimal personal information, friend a lot of people, and then mostly read their posts without sharing information or interacting with them. Some Facebook pages, such as those of restaurants, double as static websites that people visit purely to find information (such as location and hours).

Sites such as YouTube, which are technically not defined as social networking sites, nevertheless promote massive amounts of interaction and engagement. Unlike Facebook, commenters may be unknown to each other and anonymous (although the system allows for links to profiles and personal information). Interaction is typically fleeting (although extended exchanges can occur, especially when posters don't agree with each other). The subject of interaction is usually limited to the content of the posted video, but can also link to other sites and information. Such sites, therefore, allow for significant social interaction among both known and unknown users. In a one-year ethnographic study of YouTube participation, Patricia G. Lange (2007) demonstrated how "YouTube participants used both technical and symbolic mechanisms to attempt to delineate different social networks" (p. 378). The analysis led her to propose

> new categories of nuanced behavior types that are neither
> strictly public nor strictly private . . . [P]arts of social net-
> works, as supported by media circuits, can be examined to

shed light on the dynamics of social network creation, maintenance, and negotiation. (p. 378)

An expanded notion of what counts as social networking allows us to consider the influence of wider contexts and degrees of interaction than what is constrained to Facebook and other bounded systems.

In addition, there is no necessary relationship between the degree of social networking allowed at a site and its intellectual affordances or potential for learning. Interaction on sites like Facebook can be banal and uninformative while exchanges on YouTube can involve significant informational and intellectual work. Judgments of the learning potential of a particular site must account not only for its interactional affordances but the extent to which users can make it a personal learning environment (PLE) and use it for self-regulated learning (see Dabbagh & Kitsantas, 2001, including their review of the literature on PLEs).

WIDENING THE LENS

To mine and analyze the discourse of online social interaction (including interaction that extends beyond the conventional definition of social networking)—what James P. Gee and Elisabeth R. Hayes (2011) called "passionate affinity spaces" (p. 69)—I engaged in a sustained descriptive study of diverse sites, all of which revealed similar rhetorical and linguistic principles and practices, as well as various kinds of reasoning, problem-solving, and idea-sharing, that should be of interest to teachers. This inquiry was primarily interpretive, based on an analysis of the users' posts and exchanges and the kinds of deep-structure cognitive, informational, and rhetorical features beneath these surface forms. However, as I will suggest later, more formal case studies, data-mining, and quantitative descriptive research are needed to extend, refine, or counter the conclusions here.

Sites included two dozen YouTube videos that, like the whale video, generated thousands of comments; several years of posts by school-aged children to forums on National Geographic for Kids; several additional fan sites for NFL football teams; several forums at Reddit.com, especially subreddits devoted to particular areas of interest; and several independent forums on specialized topics. Some sites are heavily moderated to ensure that posts conform to standards of decency and relevance. Others freely tolerate all messages, but sometimes provide a way for users to flag inappropriate posts for removal or vote to like particular posts. Some sites attract tens of thousands of viewers and participants and others are far more limited in membership. Each site, however, decenters the role of authorship, accepts mass participation and "distributed expertise," and creates "valid and rewardable roles for all who pitch in" (Lankshear & Knobel, 2007, p. 227). The sites also typically value inclusion and participation but may do so according to tacit rules of membership or the lack thereof; posters may or may not be ostracized or ridiculed, depending on the cohesiveness of membership and established rhetorical boundaries. At some sites, flaming is common; at others it is rare.

It is also important to realize the sites connect a wide array of individuals across every demographic imaginable, from pre-teens to retirees, lawyers to factory workers, Ph.D.s to high school dropouts. But the diversity of audiences that populate interactive sites can provide powerful resources for students who are otherwise restricted by age and educational environment to interact with often like-minded peers; thus this becomes an issue with important instructional implications. The diversity of perspectives is a far cry from pre-Internet academic peer groups that were often self-reinforcing and driven toward achieving ideological consensus (see Trimbur, 1989).

Two extended examples typical of what appears in these sites will demonstrate the range of rhetorical and intellectual capacities promoted by online social interaction, providing a context to consider how teachers might exploit social networking more fully in academic settings and how they might pursue more formal research on the effect of students' self-sponsored online interactions and their academic learning. The first is a one-minute video posted to YouTube promoting Dove's "self-esteem campaign for girls," which is designed to be "an agent of change to inspire and educate girls and young women about a wider definition of beauty" (Dove, 2011). The video shows in one minute of fast-motion film the transformation of a young woman into a billboard model. First, several kinds of makeup are applied to her face and her hair is coiffed. A still photo of her enhanced appearance is then photo-manipulated in continued fast-motion: Her neck and eyebrows are raised, her face is subtly stretched or shrunk in different places, and her cheekbones are enhanced (see comparison in Figures 16.1 and 16.2). The last few seconds show the finished photo enlarged on a street billboard, beneath which two women are passing by. A final caption reads: "No wonder our perception of beauty is distorted." This fades to: "Take part in the Dove Real Beauty Workshop for Girls" and a URL (Dove Campaign, n.d.). The video won the Grand Prix at the 2007 Cannes International Advertising Festival. Although Dove posted its video on YouTube, several other users reposted it. Together, the various uploaded versions yielded thousands of written responses. By the time of this writing, the video at the link I used had been viewed 5,483,084 times and contained 1,144 comments.

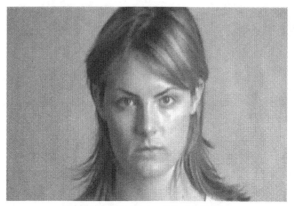

Figure 16.1. Dove Model Before

Figure 16.2. Dove Model After

In addition to the typical banal chatter, the Dove installation has attracted many more sober and thoughtful responses. One poster (Kaylee) expresses outrage: "This absolutely disgusts me. Shame on these people creating a false sense of beauty. This is why the celebrities are going without makeup, to show how they really look and to prove that this is not them." This sentiment is repeated dozens of times in various forms. At first, some of the responses appear to be criticizing the Dove commercial itself, but on closer inspection it's clear that their concerns are directed at the purveyors of photo manipulation and other forms of fake beauty. When responders do mistakenly criticize Dove as the company creating artificial beauty, they are soon corrected by other posters.

Another contributor, Jamie, shifts the burden back to consumers by asking us to consider what's motivating businesses to create such images:

Affordances of Public Forums

> I agree that creating a false sense of beauty has harmed the self
> esteem of countless women, as well as disturbed the perspec-
> tives of both sexes, but don't blame these people. These people
> are doing their jobs—selling a product using methods they've
> found to be most effective among their client base. And who
> is their client base? We are. Truth be told, it is us, the consum-
> ers, who ought to be held most responsible for the disillusion-
> ment we see here.

This post has the effect of reorienting blame and making even those who
are disgusted at least partly culpable, thereby extending the discussion in a new
direction. TemporaryPoet then calls attention to the difference between makeup
and photo manipulation: "To be honest, I'm fine with the make-up—it's supposed to enhance. It's the photoshopping that makes me feel sick." By pulling
the two forms of fake beauty apart, TemporaryPoet asks us to deal with each on
its own terms. Makeup—thousands of years old—appears less problematic than
deliberately altering the physical structure of a person's face.

In the context of mounting consensus against photo manipulation, Ivy27V
offers the perspective of someone working in photography and graphic art—an
intended career goal:

> I clearly understand what this video is trying to say and i
> agree 100% to ignore what the world thinks is beautiful be-
> cause that type of beauty isn't real. . . . But on the other hand
> to state that PHOTOSHOP is the problem now thats where
> u get me. im studying to be a photographer and im learning
> all the fun and exciting things you can do with it people need
> to understand that photography is an art form. you might as
> well say make up is the problem too lol.

As someone learning the craft and science of photography, Ivy27V further
complicates the discussion by focusing on the difference between the technology
as a value-neutral tool and the uses to which it is put. The post displays some of
the characteristics of fast, unedited writing, but Ivy27V's ethos serves to extend
viewers' conceptions of the audience visiting the site.

Further expanding and complicating the issues, EyeLean5280 compares
photography to other human art forms and introduces the idea of artifice:

> There have always been impossible ideals of beauty, but when
> artists made them out of paint or marble, it was clear to
> everyone that they were artificial. In their hearts, most people
> *believe* photographs, even though they know they can be

319

altered. When people see photos, their subconscious accepts them at face value (so to speak). That's why the beauty industry is so destructive these days. To make it worse, the ideal pushed is artistically cheap and intellectually bankrupt. Blech.

In addition to comments on the substance of the commercial, some posters also offer thoughts about its compositional effectiveness. Brittney considers the producers' decision to show two women walking (obliviously) beneath the billboard in the final scene: "i feel this commercial would have had more impact if when it zoomed out to the billboard, a little girl passing by stared at it for a second." Vorpal22 returns to the issue of culpability, adding that the companies may be aware of their ads' negative effects: "If they know that their advertising campaigns are having a psychologically detrimental effect on society at large and they still pursue them, then I'd say that they are at fault." Cutforcuties then wonders why companies don't just use actual models:

Yeah except in the real world, why would they bother spending so much time photoshopping when they could just hire models that are ALREADY considered perfect in the society? this ad is just nothing but a marketing scheme gaining so called empathy from women ourselves thinking buying Dove will let us see the end of this kind of manipulation when they themselves are creating one.

In a post rich with irony, Nathan opens up the possibility that, in spite of their campaign for natural beauty, Dove itself may be part of the problem:

Everyone, please overlook/maintain naivete about the fact that dove is owned by the parent company (Unilever) that owns Axe deodorant. They're playing us consumers on both ends to make a little coin. But please, stay ignorant so they can maximize their money off us.

Along these lines, Brinah writes,

I saw the casting call ad which said specifically that the women must not have any blemishes or tattoos. I thought it was a very contradictory thing to say considering the company is supposed to be promoting self esteem and embracing your flaws. wow.

Brinah appears to be correct—a New York area casting call for print models in Dove's Real Women campaign favored those who had "beautiful arms and legs and face," were "well-groomed and clean" with "natural bodies, nicely fit, not too curvy and not too athletic," and had "flawless skin with no tattoos and scars" (Odell, 2014).

These posts live among hundreds of others that briefly express reactions ("disgusting," "that's crazy," "whoah!," "what has this world come to?"). But in their midst is also considerable direct exchange between and among the posters. The usual brevity of responses masks the underlying processes that viewers who visit the comments are engaged in: reading, thinking, reconsidering, reading more and rethinking, extending knowledge and perspectives, perhaps writing and posting a comment, reading more and then reading responses to what they have written and reacting in turn. A lively high school or college class session designed to analyze the video and provoke critical thinking might look much like what can be found at the site, perhaps without most of the simple, reactive comments. Here, posters are comparing views about beauty and how it's manifested, using irony and other tropes to express positions, occasionally playing with language, and extending and expanding their awareness of broader issues, contradictions, and hypocrisies surrounding definitions of beauty. There is also evidence of "lay expertise" when some posters offer confirmable information that adds complexity to the self-sponsored, collaborative analysis generated by viewers.

The second example is a news item about the killing of pilot whales by residents of the Faroe Islands in what are called "grindadráp" ("whale slaughters"), or "grinds." The sparsely populated Faroe Islands are located in the North Atlantic between Iceland and Norway, and are under the sovereignty of Denmark. When a pod of migrating pilot whales is spotted, men on speedboats and jet skis surround the whales and drive them into a cove, where they're manually killed and hauled to shore with grappling hooks. The event is watched by Faroese onlookers who include children. Populating the Internet are images of the coves during a grind, the sea bright red from the blood. Pilot whales, their bodies slashed open, are stacked up on the shore. Against sharp and extensive worldwide criticism, the Faroese vigorously defend the grinds, which are part of the heritage of the Faroese (the most direct descendants of the Vikings).

Commentary on the grinds can be found across dozens of Internet sites, some sponsored by animal rights and environmental organizations and some including heavily trafficked public forums. The posts I analyzed came from the Digital Journal site, which has over 40,000 content creators in 200 countries and reaches audiences of millions of monthly visitors. Topics include arts, auto, business, crime, entertainment, environment, food, health, lifestyle, politics, religion, science, sports, and travel. Visitors to Digital Journal can easily find other posts on the same or similar topics and visit related stories and pages.

This particular story reports on a grind of 230 pilot whales just days before (Batt, 2012), and includes a five-minute video produced by Hans Peter Roth.

The video shows the gutting, measuring, and marking of dead whales, which are moved with heavy equipment back into the water to be hauled by boat to a main harbor for processing. Children jump around on the dead whales, whose bodies are slashed open at the spinal cord almost to decapitation. One scene shows what appears to be the surreptitious removal of a whale fetus from a dead female and its disposal in a special yellow bin. At the end of the video, against a backdrop of a blood-stained sea, the words "Culture? Tradition? Worthwhile? Feel free to have your own opinion" appear.

In response to this story, Sasha writes,

> I feel sick. I am hurt to see that mankind could be so cruel.
> The manner in which the whales are killed is also so brutal.
> I've never seen a sea of blood before. It is horrific, even babies
> and pregnant females are killed. I hope the animal rights
> agencies are doing something to help these voiceless/helpless
> creatures.

Others echo her sentiments—"disgusting," "cruel," "barbaric," "no one should visit there," "how can they expose their kids to this?" But when some posters push back or raise alternative perspectives, there is again evidence of intellectual engagement of exactly the sort that characterizes a lively, successful discussion in a high school or college classroom. Paula, for example, writes,

> The Faroese ARE saying their whaling is for sustenance.
> They've never claimed otherwise. They take the meat from the
> hunts, and distribute it equally among the community. The
> Faroese have to import pretty much everything except fish,
> mutton, and dairy. One of the reasons they are doing so well
> is because they hunt the pilot whales. It's a cheap source of
> protein, that requires less pollution than beef or other com-
> mercially raised meat. They are living off the land, what's so
> bad about that?

Raven then adds,

> I disagree with the killing of whales, but I have to call people
> who can eat beef from the millions of cattle farmed and killed
> in horrific ways every day in the US alone hypocrites. I'm veg-
> an because I believe in no harm to any creature, cow or whale.

Bobbi mentions the high levels of toxins in the whales, which suggests that larger issues of pollution could end up stopping their consumption anyway—a point variously used both ironically ("just go ahead faroes . . . kill and eat away") and as a comment about global environmental degradation.

In another case of the lay expert or opinion leader role, Phred provide some eye-witness accounts from a visit to Iceland and reflects on global reduction in resources:

> Rotting baleen was tossed hither and yon on all sides of the main gangway from the water up to the processing plant. Human beings have had this idea of Manifest Destiny for a long time, that the resources of the planet are there to be exploited so that we can enrich ourselves. Those resources are going to come up short one day if we keep exploiting them as we do now. We will no doubt have to tighten our belts (and stop killing whales in so-called cultural events) for maybe some generations to come. But humankind will get through these tough times.

Such posts, which express various degrees of authority from experience, occupation, or casual-to-serious inquiry, stand out from the others because they bring some additional knowledge that moves the discussion from pure opinion or knee-jerk reaction to more complex analysis. As mentioned earlier, they may also be written by posters in various age groups—a feature of forums that makes them strikingly different than the typical homogeneous classroom. Here, other participants do the job usually left to the teacher: to deepen consideration of issues from multiple perspectives and to bring personal and historical information into the mix.

For anyone who comes to the information about the grinds either supporting or condemning the continued practice, it is not difficult to see how posts complicate and vex the situation, creating cognitive dissonance and deeper thought. For example, in addition to the information already cited, posters point out

- that the Faroese government strictly controls the grinds;
- that a government-sanctioned, painless way to kill the whales must be used;
- but that the question of pain is in dispute;
- that pilot whales are not endangered;
- but that the destruction of pilot whales by other means (death from boats in shipping lanes and in large-scale net fishing, for example) is diminishing their numbers, calling the grinds into question over the long term;

- that beef cattle, chickens, and hogs live in appalling and inhumane conditions in the United States and are put to death in ways no less cruel than the whales;
- but that the slaughter of these livestock is not often seen publicly;
- that the grinds take place on a relatively small scale (about 800 whales per year) compared with practices in countries like Japan.

Self-correction of false or misleading information also occurs, with corroborating links or cited facts—a practice that Adol Esquivel, Funda Meric-Bernstam, and Elmer V. Bernstam (2006) found in a content analysis of 4,600 postings to a breast cancer support site. Only ten posts were found by medical experts to be false or misleading, seven of which were corrected by other participants within an average of four hours and 33 minutes.

Just as in the Dove commercial (as well as all the forums I analyzed, which are similar to thousands of other sites), comments on the grinds reveal multiple rhetorical, linguistic, conceptual, and information-giving and receiving skills at work, as well as multiple functions of language that scholars such as Michael A. K. Halliday (1975) placed at the center of human interaction and that educators believe should be part of the repertoire of students' literate experiences in school. These interactions are admittedly without a teacher or mediator, raw and undifferentiated, and subject to the usual flaming or name calling (one poster writes in response to a critic of the grinds, "I think you are ignorant and stupid. If you want to eat meat, you have to kill an animal. That's it"). But serious intellectual work is quite common—work that involves and hones skills of problem-solving, argumentation, the negotiation of alternate views, the mediation of ideological clashes, critical examination of related contexts and issues, and the sharing of further material through eyewitness accounts or links to deeper and more extensive background reading. Much of this obviously takes place on the participants' own time, when they might otherwise be unengaged in anything resembling academic learning or the consideration of important subjects.

BRIDGING LITERACIES: NEEDED RESEARCH ON TEACHING AND LEARNING

Critical analysis of the relationship between self-sponsored writing and academic writing must include the question of improved ability. If students are now writing more than any generation in history, shouldn't new, tacitly learned skills flow effortlessly from their interactions at their favorite forums into their causal analysis of the Mexican revolution or their report on gel formation of peptides in food biology? But such is not apparently the case. National Assessment of Educational Progress (NAEP) literacy scores, for example, have remained flat for the decades before and since the advent of the Internet (National Center for Education Statistics, 2014)—a point that alarmist critics of technology have been quick to exploit (e.g., Bauerlein, 2008).

In addition to the lack of academic connections to self-sponsored literacies, considerable new research is revealing the challenges students face when they move across different discursive communities and try to transfer knowledge and ability to them (Anson & Moore, 2016; Yancey, Robertson & Taczak, 2014). No writing scholars believe that students effortlessly transfer knowledge and ability from one discursive domain to a new, unfamiliar one (Brent, 2011). But there is growing consensus that certain educational processes can encourage the kind of rhetorical awareness that facilitates the deployment of existing ability in new settings (Anson & Moore, 2016; Beaufort, 2007; Wardle, 2009; Yancey, Robertson & Taczak, 2014). In light of the considerable overlap we can discern between the discourse of self-sponsored digital interaction and the demands of academic writing tasks, more intentional bridging of the two promises to strengthen students' knowledge *about* writing in addition to their meta-awareness of various rhetorical, stylistic, and genre-based strategies (see Downs & Wardle, 2007).

However, much is still to be learned about the relationship between the two domains of practice. Can we study and document in more than an impressionistic way what deep-structure intellectual, rhetorical, and informational capacities are learned or practiced through self-sponsored online writing? How does that learning compare with the processes students use to gain similar capacities in academic contexts? Does bridging students' self-sponsored online writing activities and their academic work bring tacit experience and learning into consciousness, and with what effect? Does such bridging return to affect the nature and quality of students' self-sponsored writing, not just their academic work?

This and other research can help us not only to understand the underlying intellectual processes fostered by students' self-sponsored digital writing, but to find ways in which we might connect it to their academic study. Clearly, self-sponsored, nonacademic writing will only increase and involve a larger percentage of the population, especially globally. As Andrea Lunsford (2010) pointed out, the changes we are experiencing in communication technologies

> alter the very grounds of literacy as the definition, nature, and
> scope of writing are all shifting away from the consumption
> of discourse to its production across a wide range of genre and
> media, away from individual "authors" and to participatory
> and collaborative partners-in-production; away from a single

static standard of correctness to a situated understanding of audience and context and purpose for writing. (para. 9)

Continuing to keep students' self-sponsored digital literacies at arm's length from their academic work may only isolate and narrow the classroom as a context for literacy development, drive its activities increasingly into obsolescence, and cause us to miss rich opportunities for the development of rhetorical, linguistic, social, and intellectual dimensions of literacy.

REFERENCES

Anderson, P., Anson, C. M., Gonyea, R. M. & Payne, C. (2015). The contributions of writing to learning and development: Results from a large-scale multi-institutional study. *Research in the Teaching of English, 50*(2), 199–235.

Anson, C. M. & Moore, J. L. (2016). *Critical transitions: Writing and the question of transfer.* Fort Collins, CO: The WAC Clearinghouse and University Press of Colorado. Retrieved from https://wac.colostate.edu/books/ansonmoore/.

Arum, R. & Roska, J. (2011). *Academically adrift: Limited learning on college campuses.* Chicago, IL: University of Chicago Press.

Barton, D. & Hamilton, E. (1998). *Local literacies: Reading and writing in one community.* London, England: Routledge.

Batt, E. (2012, August 9). Over 230 pilot whales killed in Faroe Islands in last two days. Retrieved from http://www.digitaljournal.com/article/330455.

Bauerlein, M. (2008). *The dumbest generation: How the digital age stupefies young Americans and jeopardizes our future (or, don't trust anyone under 30).* New York, NY: Penguin.

Beaufort, A. (2007). *College writing and beyond: A new framework for university writing instruction.* Logan, UT: Utah State University Press.

boyd, d. m. & Ellison, N. B. (2007). Social network sites: Definition, history, and scholarship. *Journal of Computer-Mediated Communication, 13*(1), 210–230.

Brandt, D. (1998). Sponsors of literacy. *College Composition and Communication, 49*(2), 165–185.

Brent, D. (2011). Transfer, transformation, and rhetorical knowledge: Insights from transfer theory. *Journal of Business and Technical Communication, 25*(4), 396–420.

Brinah. (n.d.). Dove: Evolution commercial [YouTube comment]. Retrieved from https://www.youtube.com/watch?v=iYhCn0jf46U.

Brittney. (n.d.). Dove: Evolution commercial [YouTube comment]. Retrieved from https://www.youtube.com/watch?v=iYhCn0jf46U.

Buck, A. (2012). Examining digital literacy practices on social network sites. *Research in the Teaching of English, 47*(1), 9–38.

Facebook. (2017). Company Info. *Facebook.* Retrieved from http://newsroom.fb.com /company-info/.

Crocker, P. (2013, January 15). Converged-mobile-messaging analysis and forecasts [PDF file]. Retrieved from http://www.tyntec.com/resources/whitepapers /converged-mobile-messaging.

Cutforcuties. (n.d.). Dove: Evolution commercial [YouTube comment]. Retrieved from https://www.youtube.com/watch?v=iYhCn0jf46U.

Dabbagh, N. & Kitsantas, A. (2012). Personal learning environments, social media, and self-regulated learning: A natural formula for connecting formal and informal learning. *The Internet and Higher Education, 15*(1), 3–8.

Dove. (n.d.). The Dove® campaign for real beauty. Retrieved from http://www.dove.us /Social-Mission/campaign-for-real-beauty.aspx.

Dove. (2011, May 2). Dove: Evolution [Video file]. Welcome to the Dove channel. Retrieved from https://www.youtube.com/watch?v=O600kDpBNj4.

Downs, D. & Wardle, E. (2007). Teaching about writing, righting misconceptions: (Re)envisioning "first-year composition" as "introduction to writing studies." *College Composition and Communication, 58*(4), 552–585.

Esquivel, A., Funda Meric-Bernstam, F. & Bernstam, E. V. (2006). Accuracy and self-correction of information received from an Internet breast cancer list: Content analysis. *BMJ, 332*(7547), 939–942. Retrieved from http://www.ncbi.nlm.nih.gov /pmc/articles/PMC1444809/.

Experian Marketing Services. (2013). The 2013 digital marketer report and webinar series. Retrieved from http://www.experian.com/marketing-services/2013-digital -marketer-report.html?WT.srch=PR_EMS_DMReport_020813_DMReport%22.

EyeLean5220. (n.d.). Dove: Evolution commercial [YouTube comment]. Retrieved from https://www.youtube.com/watch?v=iYhCn0jf46U

Franzen, J. (2013, September 14). While we are busy tweeting, texting and spending, the world is drifting towards disaster. Retrieved from http://www.alternet.org /culture/jonathan-franzen-while-we-are-busy-tweeting-texting-and-spending-world -drifting-towards.

Gee, J. P. (1996). *Social linguistics and literacies: Ideology in discourses* (2nd ed.). London, England: Falmer Press.

Gee, J. P. (2004). *Situated language and learning: A critique of traditional schooling.* New York, NY: Routledge.

Gee, J. P. & Hayes, E. R. (2011). Language and learning in the digital age. New York, NY: Routledge.

Greenhow, C., Robelia, B. & Hughes, J. E. (2009). Learning, teaching, and scholarship in a digital age. *Educational Researcher, 38*(4), 246–259.

Halliday, M. A. K. (1975). *Learning how to mean.* London, England: Edward Arnold.

Hansen, L. (2013, June 10). Six things social media is ruining. Retrieved from http:// theweek.com/article/index/245370/6-things-social-media-is-ruining#axzz34 6EDb4tP.

Henry, J. (2013, January 20). Art of essay-writing damaged by Twitter and Facebook, Cambridge don warns. *The Telegraph.* Retrieved from http://www.telegraph.co.uk /technology/social-media/9813109/Art-of-essay-writing-damaged-by-Twitter-and -Facebook-Cambridge-don-warns.html.

Hull, G. & Schultz, K. (2001). Literacy and learning out of school: A review of theory and research. *Review of Educational Research, 71*(4), 575–611.

Humphrys, J. (2007, September 24). I h8 txt msgs: How texting is wrecking our language. *Daily Mail.* Retrieved from http://www.dailymail.co.uk/news/article-483511/I-h8-txt-msgs-How-texting-wrecking-language.html.

Indiana University. (2014). FSSE 2014 Aggregate Frequencies. *National Survey of Student Engagement.* Retrieved from http://fsse.iub.edu/html/overall_results.cfm.

Ivy27V. (n.d.). Dove: Evolution commercial [YouTube comment]. Retrieved from https://www.youtube.com/watch?v=iYhCn0jf46U.

Jamie. (n.d.). Dove: Evolution commercial [YouTube comment]. Retrieved from https://www.youtube.com/watch?v=iYhCn0jf46U.

Kalinchuk, A. (2013). Chat apps to double SMS text messaging by end of 2013. Retrieved from http://www.digitaltrends.com/mobile/chat-apps-to-double-sms-traffic-by-cnd-of-2013.

Kaylee. (n.d.). Dove: Evolution commercial [YouTube comment]. Retrieved from https://www.youtube.com/watch?v=iYhCn0jf46U.

Keller, J. (2009, June 11). Studies explore whether the Internet makes students better writers. *The Chronicle of Higher Education.* Retrieved from http://chronicle.com/article/Studies-Explore-Whether-the/44476/.

Lange, P. G. (2007). Publicly private and privately public: Social networking on YouTube. *Journal of Computer-Mediated Communication, 13*(1), 361–380.

Lankshear, C. & Knobel, M. (2007). Researching new literacies: Web 2.0 practices and insider perspectives. *E–Learning, 4*(3). Retrieved from http://ldm.sagepub.com/content/4/3.toc.

Lenhart, A., Arafeh, S. Smith, A. & Macgill, A. (2008, April 25). Writing, technology, and teens. *Pew Internet and American Life Project.* Retrieved from http://www.pewinternet.org/2008/04/24/writing-technology-and-teens/.

Levin, D., Arafeh, S., Lenhart, A. & Rainie, L. (2002, August 14). The digital disconnect: The widening gap between Internet-savvy students and their schools. *Pew Internet and American Life Project.* Retrieved from http://www.pewinternet.org/2002/08/14/the-digital-disconnect-the-widening-gap-between-internet-savvy-students-and-their-schools/.

Lunsford, A. (2007, February). *The Stanford Study of Writing* [PDF file]. Report to the Senate, Stanford University. Retrieved from https://ssw.stanford.edu/sites/default/files/Senate_report_February_2007.pdf .

Melzer, D. (2014). *Assignments across the curriculum: A national study of college writing.* Logan, UT: Utah State University Press.

Nathan. (n.d.). Dove: Evolution commercial [YouTube comment]. Retrieved from https://www.youtube.com/watch?v=iYhCn0jf46U.

National Center for Education Statistics (2013, June). *The nation's report card: Trends in academic progress 2012.* Retrieved from http://nces.ed.gov/nationsreportcard/pubs/main2012/2013456.aspx.

National Survey of Student Engagement (2016). *NSSE Report Builder.* Retrieved from http://nsse.indiana.edu/html/summary_tables.cfm.

Odell, A. (2010, June 28). Dove seeks women with "flawless skin" and "no scars" for its next Real Beauty Campaign. Retrieved from http://nymag.com/thecut/2010/06/dove_seeks_women_with_flawless.html.

Pacheco, W. (2012, July 18). Professor says teens' social-media lingo hurts academic writing. *Orlando Sentinel.* Retrieved from http://articles.orlandosentinel.com/2012-07-18/features/os-ucf-social-media-writing-camp-20120716_1_social-media-text-messages-zombie.

Pew Research Internet Project (2014). Mobile technology fact sheet. Retrieved from http://www.pewinternet.org/fact-sheets/mobile-technology-fact-sheet/.

Prior, P. & Shipka, J. (2003). Chronotopic lamination: Tracing the contours of literate activity. In C. Bazerman & D. Russell (Eds.), *Writing selves/writing societies: Research from activity perspectives* (pp. 180–238) Fort Collins, CO: The WAC Clearinghouse. Retrieved from https://wac.colostate.edu/books/selves_societies/.

PurplePride.org. (2014). Minnesota Vikings message boards. Retrieved from http://www.purplepride.org/.

Radicati, S. (2016). *Email statistics report, 2015–2019* (PDF). Retrieved from http://www.radicati.com/wp/wp-content/uploads/2015/02/Email-Statistics-Report-2015-2019-Executive-Summary.pdf.

Roozen, K. (2009). "Fan fic-ing" English studies: A case study exploring the interplay of vernacular literacies and disciplinary engagement. *Research in the Teaching of English, 44*(2), 136–169.

Rosinski, P. (2016). Students' perceptions of the transfer of rhetorical knowledge between digital self-sponsored writing & academic writing: The importance of authentic contexts and reflection. In C. M. Anson & J. L. Moore (Eds.), *Critical transitions: Writing and the question of transfer* (pp. 247–270). Fort Collins, CO: The WAC Clearinghouse and University Press of Colorado. Retrieved from https://wac.colostate.edu/books/ansonmoore/.

Stein, N. L. & Miller, C. A. (1990). I win—you lose: The development of argumentative thinking. In B. Dorval (Ed.), *Conversational organization and its development* (pp. 265–309). Norwood, NJ: Ablex.

Street, B. V. (1993). The new literacy studies. *Journal of Research in Reading, 16*(2), 81–97.

TemporaryPoet. (n.d.). Dove: Evolution commercial [YouTube comment]. Retrieved from https://www.youtube.com/watch?v=iYhCn0jf46U.

TextRequest.com. (n.d.) Retrieved from https://www.textrequest.com/blog/many-texts-people-send-per-day/ .

Thaiss, C. & Porter, T. (2010). The state of WAC/WID in 2010: Methods and results of the U.S. survey of the international WAC/WID mapping project. *College Composition and Communication, 61*(3), 524–70.

Thompson, C. (2009, August 24). Clive Thompson on the new literacy. *Wired.* Retrieved from http://www.wired.com/2009/08/st-thompson-7/.

Trimbur, J. (1989). Consensus and difference in collaborative learning. *College English, 51*(6), 602–616.

Vie, S. (2008). Digital divide 2.0: "Generation M" and online social networking sites in the composition classroom. *Computers and Composition, 25*(1), 9–23.

Vorpal22. (n.d.). Dove: Evolution commercial [YouTube comment]. Retrieved from https://www.youtube.com/watch?v=iYhCn0jf46U.

Wardle, E. (2009). "Mutt genres" and the goal of FYC: Can we help students write the genres of the university? *College Composition and Communication, 60*, 765–789.

WordPress.com (2017). About Us. Retrieved from http://en.wordpress.com/about/.

Yancey, K. B. (2009). *Writing in the 21st century: A report from the national council of teachers of English.* Urbana, IL: National Council of Teachers of English.

Yancey, K. B., Robertson, L. & Taczak, K. (2014). *Writing across contexts: Transfer, composition, and sites of writing.* Logan, UT: Utah State University Press.

CONTRIBUTORS

Tabetha Adkins is Dean of the University College and Associate Professor of Literature & Languages at Texas A&M University-Commerce. Her research focuses on literacy and social justice, and her work has appeared in various venues including *Literacy in Composition Studies, Community Literacy Journal,* and *Composition Studies.*

Kara Poe Alexander is Associate Professor of English and Director of the University Writing Center at Baylor University, where she has previously served as the coordinator of Professional Writing and Rhetoric. She teaches courses in literacy studies, multimodal composition, research methods, and composition pedagogy. Her research explores literacy, identity, and pedagogy within composition and digital writing settings. Her work has appeared in *College Composition and Communication; Composition Forum; Composition Studies; Computers and Composition; Journal of Business and Technical Writing; Kairos: A Journal of Rhetoric, Technology, and Pedagogy; Rhetoric Review; Technical Communication Quarterly;* and several edited collections.

Chris M. Anson is Distinguished University Professor, Professor of English, and Director of the Campus Writing and Speaking Program at North Carolina State University, where he teaches graduate and undergraduate courses in language, composition, and literacy and works with faculty across the curriculum to improve undergraduate education in the areas of writing, speaking, and digital literacies. Before moving to NCSU in 1999, he spent fifteen years at the University of Minnesota, where he directed the Program in Composition from 1988–1996 and was Professor of English and Morse-Alumni Distinguished Teaching Professor. He has published many books and articles on writing studies and related areas and has spoken widely across the United States and in 29 other countries. He is past Chair of the Conference on College Composition and Communication and past President of the Council of Writing Program Administrators. His full CV can be found at www.ansonica.net.

Kristin L. Arola is Associate Professor of Rhetoric, Composition & Technology at Washington State University where she also serves as Director of Graduate Studies for the Department of English. Her research focuses on the intersections between indigenous rhetoric and multimodal pedagogy. Along with numerous articles and book chapters, she is co-author of *Writer/Designer: Making Multimodal Projects,* and co-editor of both *Cross Talk in Comp Theory* and *Composing (Media) = Composing (Embodiment).*

Estee Beck is Assistant Professor of Professional and Technical Writing/ Digital Humanities in the Department of English at The University of Texas at Arlington. She holds a Ph.D. in English with a specialization in rhetoric and writing from Bowling Green State University. Her research engagements span computers and writing, rhetoric and composition, digital rhetoric, surveillance and privacy, professional and technical communication, and digital humanities. She has published in *Kairos: A Journal of Rhetoric, Technology, and Pedagogy; Computers & Composition: An International Journal; Computers & Composition Online*; and *Hybrid Pedagogy*.

Crystal Broch Colombini is Assistant Professor of English at the University of Texas at San Antonio and researches in a range of topics related to rhetoric and economics. She is particularly interested in how citizens use rhetoric to navigate financial crisis and hardship.

Amber Buck is Assistant Professor of English at the University of Alabama, where she teaches undergraduate courses in multimodal composition and graduate courses in the Composition, Rhetoric, and English Studies graduate program. Specializing in social media and digital literacies, her current project consists of longitudinal studies of social media users. Her work has been published in *Research in the Teaching of English, Computers and Composition*, and the edited collections *Literacy in Practice* and *Stories That Speak to Us: Exhibits from the Digital Archive of Literacy Narratives*.

Cory Bullinger is a graduate of the M.A. English, Technical Communication program at the University of Central Florida. She is currently employed as a Technical Writer at FIS in Orlando. Her professional interests include editing, end-user documentation for dynamic environments, and the changing role of the technical writer in the digital era.

Caroline Dadas is Associate Professor at Montclair State University, where her areas of specialty include queer online rhetorics, public sphere theories, civic rhetorics, digital writing, and research methods. Her primary research agenda involves studying the intersections of civic participation and digital environments. Her work has also appeared in the journals *College Composition and Communication, Computers and Writing, New Media and Society, Composition Forum*, and *Computers and Composition Online*. She is currently co-editing a collection on queer methodological approaches entitled *Re/Orienting Writing Studies: Queer Methods, Queer Projects*. Professor Dadas' teaching interests reach across professional writing, rhetorical theory, composition, and digital writing.

Michael J. Faris is Assistant Professor of English at Texas Tech University, where he teaches and researches in the Technical Communication and Rhetoric program. His research interests include digital rhetoric and literacies and queer and sexuality studies. He has published on digital literacy practices and pedagogies in the *Journal of Business and Technical Communication, Communication Design Quarterly, College Composition and Communication*, and *Composition Forum*.

Lindsey Hall is a recent graduate of the M.A. in English program at the University of Texas at San Antonio. Her research interests include writing in social media and first-year composition.

Leslie A. Hahner is Associate Professor of Communication at Baylor University. Her work focuses on the constitutive function of visual and spatial rhetorics on public culture. Her work has appeared in *Communication and Critical/Cultural Studies, Critical Studies in Media Communication, Feminist Formations*, the *Quarterly Journal of Speech, Rhetoric & Public Affairs*, and numerous other outlets. She can be reached at Leslie_Hahner@baylor.edu.

William Hart-Davidson is Associate Professor in the Department of Writing, Rhetoric & American Cultures and Associate Dean of Graduate Education in the College of Arts & Letters at Michigan State University. A senior researcher in the Writing, Information, and Digital Experience (WIDE) research center, his research lies at the intersection of rhetoric theory and user experience, with an emphasis on developing software to visualize and provide feedback for learners in both informal and formal environments. His recent work focuses on computational rhetoric and its applications in a variety of domains including informal learning, public policy, and health care. Bill is also co-inventor of Eli Review and co-founder of an MSU spinoff company, Drawbridge Inc., that provides Eli along with other learning and research services.

Les Hutchinson is a soon-to-be doctoral candidate in Rhetoric and Writing at Michigan State University. Her research focuses on the intersections of intellectual property and privacy in social media, and how those intersections impact users' rights to their personal data, particularly those of children. She teaches first-year writing, technical writing, and digital and visual rhetoric. In her free time, she enjoys chasing her two children around in her backyard (weather permitting) and cuddling with her three cats. You can find her playing with identity representation and professionalism in Twitter, Instagram, and Facebook under her myriad of digital selves.

Lilian W. Mina is Assistant Professor of English at Auburn University at Montgomery where she teaches graduate courses in the Master of Teaching Writing program and upper-division writing courses in the Department of English and Philosophy. She researches digital rhetoric with focus on multimodal composing, the integration of social media platforms in teaching writing, and identity construction in online writing spaces. Her research on multilingual composition is centered around empowering multilingual writers through the use of digital technologies, incorporating translingual practices, and examining students' prior (digital) writing experiences. She is also interested in professional development of writing teachers, professionalization of graduate students, empirical research methods, and undergraduate research.

Patricia Portanova is Associate Professor of English at Northern Essex Community College where she teaches writing and communication. She is co-chair of the Conference on College Composition and Communication Cognition and Writing SIG and has served as chair of the Northeast Writing Across the Curriculum Consortium (NEWACC). Her research focuses on writing with distractions, working with multilingual student writers, and writing with the community. She has led workshops and presented at several regional colleges and national conferences including CCCC, NCTE, IWCA, and NCPTW. She holds a doctorate in Composition Studies from the University of New Hampshire and has taught at several colleges in Massachusetts.

Liza Potts is Associate Professor in the Department of Writing, Rhetoric, and American Cultures at Michigan State University where she is the Director of WIDE Research and the founder of the Experience Architecture program. Her research interests include digital rhetoric, Internet studies, participatory culture, and social user experience. Her work has been published in *Technical Communication Quarterly*, *Journal of Business and Technical Communication*, and *Technical Communication*.

Stephanie Vie is Associate Professor and Department Chair of Writing and Rhetoric at the University of Central Florida in Orlando. Her work has been published in numerous edited collections and journals including *Computers and Composition; Computers and Composition Online; Kairos: A Journal of Rhetoric, Technology, and Pedagogy; First Monday*; and *Technoculture*. She's currently at work on a manuscript titled *Literate Acts in Social Media* that studies faculty and former students' use of social media over the course of a decade. She tweets at @digirhet.

Douglas M. Walls is Assistant Professor of English at North Carolina State University where he teaches in the Masters of Science in Technical Communication program. His research is in digital rhetoric, especially in the user experiences of traditionally marginalized or underrepresented groups. His work has appeared in both traditional and new media forms in *Computers and Composition; An International Journal; Kairos: A Journal of Rhetoric, Technology, and Pedagogy*; and *The Journal of Business and Technical Communication*.

Bronwyn T. Williams is Professor of English and Director of the University Writing Center at the University of Louisville. He writes and teaches on issues of literacy, identity, digital media, and popular culture. His books include *Shimmering Literacies: Popular Culture and Reading and Writing Online*, *New Media Literacies and Participatory Popular Culture Across Borders* (with Amy Zenger), and *Identity Papers: Literacy and Power in Higher Education*. His current project is the forthcoming book, *Literacy Practices and Perceptions of Agency: Composing Identities* (Routledge), to be published in 2018.